Rl

JUL 1 0 1997

NO LONGER PROPERTY OF
SEATTLE PUBLIC LIBRARY

REC'D DOUGLASS-TRUTH LIBRARY

JUL 1 0 1997

THE OXFORD

Frederick Douglass Reader

THE OXFORD

Frederick Douglass Reader

❖

Edited with an Introduction

by

William L. Andrews

New York   Oxford
OXFORD UNIVERSITY PRESS
1996

OXFORD UNIVERSITY PRESS

Oxford   New York
Athens   Auckland   Bangkok   Bombay
Calcutta   Cape Town   Dar es Salaam   Delhi
Florence   Hong Kong   Istanbul   Karachi
Kuala Lumpur   Madras   Madrid   Melbourne
Mexico City   Nairobi   Paris   Singapore
Taipei   Tokyo   Toronto

and associated companies in
Berlin   Ibadan

Copyright © 1996 by Oxford University Press, Inc.

Published by Oxford University Press, Inc.,
198 Madison Avenue, New York, New York 10016

Oxford is a registered trademark of Oxford University Press

All rights reserved. No part of this publication may be reproduced,
stored in a retrieval system, or transmitted, in any form or by any means,
electronic, mechanical, photocopying, recording, or otherwise,
without the prior permission of Oxford University Press.

Library of Congress Cataloging-in-Publication Data
Douglass, Frederick, 1817?–1895.
[Prose works. Selections]
The Oxford Frederick Douglass reader / edited with an introduction
by William L. Andrews.
p.   cm.
Includes bibliographical references.
ISBN 0-19-509118-3
1. Douglass, Frederick, 1817?–1895.
2. Abolitionists—United States—Biography.
3. Afro-American abolitionists—Biography.
4. Slaves—United States—Biography.
5. Antislavery movements—United States—History—19th century.
I. Andrews, William L., 1946–   .   II. Title.
E449.D749   1996
973.8' 092—dc20
[B]   95–10369

1 3 5 7 9 8 6 4 2

Printed in the United States of America
on acid-free paper

Acknowledgments

❖

This volume was prepared during my fellowship year at the Center for Advanced Study in the Behavioral Sciences. I am grateful for financial support provided by the Andrew W. Mellon Foundation. I am also grateful for the library and editing assistance of Lisa Photos, Mark Hodin, and Leslie Reynard.

Contents

❖

Contents

Note on the Text

❖

Unless otherwise stated, the source of each text included in this edition is the first printed edition of that text. Exceptions are "Letter to His Old Master," which is reprinted from the version appended to *My Bondage and My Freedom* (1855); "What To the Slave Is the Fourth of July?," which is reprinted from the version of this speech that appeared in 1852 in a Rochester, New York, pamphlet; and the chapters selected from the second part of *Life and Times of Frederick Douglass* (first published in 1881), which are reprinted from the 1892 revised and expanded edition of that text. In these three cases I have reprinted what I believe to be the final published version of these texts over which Douglass had editorial control. Bibliographical information on each text in this *Reader* is provided in the headnotes.

No attempt has been made to regularize spellings, capitalizations, italicizing, or punctuation among the texts included in this volume. Both uncapitalized and capitalized variants of the word "Negro" appear in Douglass's corpus, for instance. Although the term is not capitalized in *The Heroic Slave* (1853), in *Life and Times* (1881, 1892) "Negro" appears, though not to the exclusion of "negro." For the sake of consistency within texts, I have corrected aberrant spellings, capitalizations, and punctuation practices when they appear to be the result of a printing error. In a few instances, I have supplied a missing word or word ending, evidently omitted through a printing error, in brackets. My guiding editorial principle, however, has been to reproduce faithfully the texts themselves as they were originally published.

Chronology

❖

1818   Frederick Augustus Washington Bailey born in February at Holme Hill Farm, in Talbot County on the Eastern Shore of Maryland, the son of Harriet Bailey, a slave, and an unknown white man.

1825   Death of Harriet Bailey.

1826   Sent to live with Hugh and Sophia Auld in Baltimore. Receives initial reading lessons from Sophia Auld. Works as family servant and errand boy.

1833   Returned to his master, Thomas Auld, in St. Michaels, Talbot County, Maryland.

1834   Hired for a year to Edward Covey, a local farmer known for his skill in "breaking" recalcitrant slaves. In August reaches a turning-point in his slave career after successfully resisting a Covey beating.

1836   Returned to Baltimore to learn the caulking trade.

1838   Escapes slavery on September 3 with the aid of borrowed American merchantman seaman's papers and money from his fiancée, Anna Murray, a free black woman of Baltimore. Marries Anna on September 15 in New York. Moves to New Bedford, Massachusetts, changes his name to Frederick Douglass, and finds work as a general laborer.

1839   Licensed to preach by the New Bedford African Methodist Episcopal Zion church.

1841   Becomes a salaried lecturer for the Massachusetts Anti-Slavery Society. Travels throughout New England recounting his experiences as a slave. Staunchly advocates William Lloyd Garrison's brand of nonviolent, nonpolitical agitation against slavery.

1845   *Narrative of the Life of Frederick Douglass, an American Slave, Written by Himself* published by the Anti-Slavery office in Boston. Douglass goes on extended speaking tour of Great Britain.

1847 Freedom purchased by British friends. Returns to the United States, moves to Rochester, New York, and launches his own antislavery weekly, *The North Star*.

1848 Attends Seneca Falls Woman's Rights convention. Publishes "To My Old Master, Thomas Auld" in *The North Star*.

1851 Breaks with Garrison over antislavery strategy. Starts *Frederick Douglass' Paper* with financial support of Gerrit Smith, a New York abolitionist.

1852 Delivers famous address, "What To the Slave Is the Fourth of July?" in Rochester; later published as a pamphlet.

1853 *The Heroic Slave* published in *Autographs for Freedom*, edited by Douglass's friend and advisor, Julia Griffiths.

1855 *My Bondage and My Freedom* published by Miller, Orton, and Mulligan in New York.

1859 Begins *Douglass' Monthly*. Discusses with John Brown the latter's plan to arm a guerrilla army at Harper's Ferry to help Virginia slaves escape. Opposes the plan. Flees to Canada after warrant is issued for his arrest as an accomplice in Brown's raid on the arsenal at Harper's Ferry, Virginia.

1860 Death of daughter Annie. Supports Abraham Lincoln for president of the United States.

1861 Welcomes the outbreak of the Civil War. Lobbies Lincoln to allow black men to enter the Union Army.

1863 Becomes recruiting agent for the 54th Massachusetts Infantry regiment, in which sons Charles Remond Douglass and Lewis Henry Douglass serve. Stops publishing *Douglass' Monthly*.

1864 Works for Lincoln's re-election and for prosecution of the war until slavery is extirpated.

1866 Criticizes Reconstruction policies of President Andrew Johnson; advocates black suffrage in the South. Begins career as a lyceum lecturer on a variety of topics, the most widely requested of which is "Self-Made Men."

1868 Attacked by friends in the feminist movement for placing a higher priority on black manhood suffrage than on women's suffrage.

1870 Moves to Washington, D.C. to become editor-in-chief of *The New National Era*, a reformist weekly.

1871   Appointed by President Ulysses S. Grant to serve as assistant secretary to a commission considering possible annexation of the Dominican Republic. Recommends annexation in *New National Era*.

1872   Campaigns for Grant. House in Rochester destroyed by fire.

1874   Named president of the Freedmen's Savings and Trust Company; bank fails within a few months. Loses substantial investments in the collapse of the Freedmen's bank and in the closing of *The New National Era*.

1877   Appointed U.S. Marshal for District of Columbia by President Rutherford B. Hayes. Returns to St. Michaels to visit relatives and former master, Hugh Auld.

1878   Moves to Cedar Hill estate in Anacostia, District of Columbia.

1879   Criticized because of his public censure of the Exoduster migration from the South to Kansas.

1881   Appointed Recorder of Deeds for the District of Columbia. *Life and Times of Frederick Douglass* published by the Park publishing company of Hartford, Connecticut.

1882   Death of Anna Murray Douglass.

1883   Increasingly disenchanted with national government's failure to protect African American civil rights in the South.

1884   Marries Helen Pitts, a white woman active in women's rights work. Condemned by many blacks and whites alike for interracial marriage.

1886–87   Tours Europe and Egypt with Helen Douglass.

1889   Appointed Minister and Consul General to Haiti by President Benjamin Harrison.

1891   Resigns as Minister to Haiti after breakdown of negotiations for leasing of the port at Môle St. Nicolas.

1892   Expanded edition of *Life and Times of Frederick Douglass* published by De Wolfe, Fiske, and Company of Boston.

1893   Introduces Ida B. Wells's pamphlet *The Reason Why the Colored American Is Not in the World Columbian Exposition* in Chicago.

1894   *The Lessons of the Hour*, a denunciation of lynching, published as a pamphlet in Baltimore, Maryland.

1895   Dies at Cedar Hill on February 20 after addressing the National Council of Women. Buried February 26 in Rochester's Mount Hope Cemetery.

The Oxford

Frederick Douglass Reader

Introduction

❖

In the introduction to Frederick Douglass's second autobiography, *My Bondage and My Freedom* (1855), James McCune Smith, a black physician and abolitionist from New York, hailed Douglass as "a Representative American man—a type of his countrymen" (173).[1] In his struggle from obscurity in slavery to antislavery luminary, Douglass had "passed through every gradation of rank comprised in our national make-up, and bears upon his person and upon his soul every thing that is American" (174). Douglass's record of "self-elevation" thus marked him as a "noble example" on which all Americans, white as well as black, might pattern themselves. Smith went on to recommend Douglass's autobiography because it was "an American book, for Americans, in the fullest sense of the idea" (178). Having transcended racial difference, Douglass's "noble example" qualified him for heroic status according to national standards of Americanism that, officially at least, recognized no artificial distinctions among men, valuing the individual instead according to egalitarian, achievement-oriented, and democratic standards promulgated in the founding documents of the American Revolution. Douglass's prominence in the international human rights arena gave Smith an opportunity that black civil rights activists had long awaited: the chance to recreate a national myth in their own image, or rather in the image of Frederick Douglass, the self-elevated black American as true exemplar and representative of all that was admirable in the American experiment.

Although nationalistic rhetoric pervades Smith's introduction, he did not fail to point out that Frederick Douglass was more than an American hero. He was also a *black* American hero, whose achievements bore equally compelling witness, in Smith's view, to Douglass's racial heritage as well as to his affiliation with all that was good about America. Smith called attention to what *My Bondage and My Freedom* revealed about the industry and ingenuity of Douglass's grandmother and the intellectual ambition of his mother, who learned to read despite the oppressive conditions of her enslavement. To the maternal side of Douglass's family, the Baileys, whose roots lay in Africa, Smith attributed much of Douglass's distinction as an abolitionist orator, a journalist and editor, and a best-selling author. "For his energy, perse-

3

verance, eloquence, invective, sagacity, and wide sympathy," Smith deduced, "he [Douglass] is indebted to his negro blood" (177). The "grafting of the Anglo-Saxon on good, original, negro stock" had yielded an American of unusual "versatility of talent" in Frederick Douglass (177). From this Smith drew a deliberately controversial conclusion: that the most "American" thing about Douglass was the blending of black and white in the man, for "the Americans," Smith asserted, are actually "a *mixed race*" (178).

James McCune Smith's challenge in introducing the author of *My Bondage and My Freedom* in a brief space gives pause to any editor, especially one like myself, who tries to introduce the breadth and variety of Douglass's career as a speaker and writer. Yet there is good reason to follow Smith's line of reflection on Douglass as a man whose life, literary career, and sociopolitical significance centered on the negotiation of his multiple identities as an American, a Negro, and a mix of the two. It is neither inaccurate nor unfair, though it may seem simplistic, to suggest that the fundamental theme of Douglass's greatest writing was his own evolving sense of selfhood. What drove Douglass to become a writer in 1845, in spite of the risks he knew he was taking, was a personal need and a political obligation to define himself publicly. In the words of the famous title of his first book, he was determined to be known as Frederick Douglass, "an American slave, written by himself." The defining elements of the identity he formulated in his classic 1845 fugitive slave narrative—Frederick Douglass the American, the one-time slave, the writer by and for himself, the subject of his own text, not the object of someone else's—would be recast and reevaluated throughout Douglass' long writing career. But the terms by which he accounted for himself from the outset would remain his literary stock in trade, creating both opportunities for and obstacles to the change and growth that characterize Douglass's lifelong literary experiments in self and social analysis.

The recent combined publication of Douglass's autobiographies in the prestigious Library of America series attests to the enormous respect that Douglass's personal writing now receives from the academic world and from an even larger general readership.[2] The two collections of essays on Douglass's writing that have appeared since 1990 underline what has become the accepted critical estimate of him—that he was a major figure in the development of the American I-narrative tradition.[3] Through first-person writing Douglass gave form and significance to a self-consciousness that in its engagement with issues of personal autonomy and social authority evokes comparison with that of Benjamin Franklin, Margaret Fuller, Henry David Thoreau, and Booker T. Washington, each an indispensable American autobiographical writer.[4] Yet as he wrote the texts on which his considerable literary reputation now rests, Douglass was sensitive to the charge often leveled at those who record their own lives for public consumption, particularly in a democracy, namely, that such work betrays egotism, vanity, and self-aggrandizement. In a letter that prefaces *My Bondage and My Freedom*, Douglass denied that his purpose had been "to illustrate any heroic achievements of a man." Rather, he was out to "vindicate a just and beneficent principle" on behalf of "the whole human family," that is, the principle of freedom (166). In the conclusion of *Life and Times of Frederick Douglass* (1881), the memoirist reiterated his contention that his forays into personal history had an altruistic purpose. "I have written out my experience here, not in order to exhibit my wounds and bruises and to awaken and attract sympathy to myself personally, but as a part of the history of a profoundly interesting period in American life and progress" (309).

Still, no matter how much he embraced universal humanistic ideals as the motive of his writing or portrayed his memoirs as chapters in the great chronicle of American history, the man who had been born a chattel could not ignore the fact that in the public eye he was first and always a Negro, a representative of black America. This public role as black America's chief witness in a half-century of debate over "what is called the negro problem" (316) Douglass accepted and often relished. He knew this role had given him fame; through it, and sometimes in spite of it, he had made his mark. Thus in his last autobiography, he observed, "I do not wish it to be imagined by any that I am insensible to the singularity of my career, or to the peculiar relation I sustain to the history of my time and country" (318). But exactly what to make of that "singularity"—was it owing to himself alone irrespective of race, or to his racial heritage (and if so, to which side of his family? or to the mix of both?), or to the fact that he was an American who had lived and in his later years preached the creed of the "self-made man"? In an era in which notions of individual identity, race, and nationhood were crudely and often invidiously contrived, a writer of Douglass's intellectual acuity and integrity was hard to put to devise clear-cut, conclusive answers.

I have often been bluntly and sometimes very rudely asked, of what color my mother was, and of what color was my father? In what proportion does the blood of the various races mingle in my veins, especially how much white blood and how much black blood entered into my composition? Whether I was not part Indian as well as African and Caucasian? Whether I considered myself more African than Caucasian, or the reverse? Whether I derived my intelligence from my father, or from my mother, from my white, or from my black blood? Whether persons of mixed blood are as strong and healthy as persons of either of the races whose blood they inherit? Whether persons of mixed blood do permanently remain of the mixed complexion or finally take on the complexion of one or the other of the two or more races of which they may be composed? Whether they live as long and raise as large families as other people? Whether they inherit only evil from both parents and good from neither? Whether evil dispositions are more transmissible than good? Why did I marry a person of my father's complexion instead of marrying one of my mother's complexion?[5] How is the race problem to be solved in this country? Will the negro go back to Africa or remain here? (317)

In the last edition of his *Life and Times* (1892), Douglass noted that "under this shower of purely American questions, more or less personal, I have endeavored to possess my soul in patience and get as much good out of life as was possible with so much to occupy my time; and though often perplexed, seldom losing my temper, or abating heart or hope for the future of my people" (317). Douglass took pride in the fact that a measure of his "peculiar relation" to the time and his country had been his decision, since his early days in the antislavery movement, "to stand for the freedom of people of all colors" (318). Yet at the end of a life of agitation for freedom and equality regardless of color, the paradox of Frederick Douglass the public figure—both "representative American man" and American pleading for representation in the councils of power in his own country—proved as inescapable as the endless unanswerable questions the private Frederick Douglass had to endure concerning his personal, racial, and national sense of identity.

The man who became internationally famous as Frederick Douglass was born in the backcountry of Maryland's Eastern Shore, the son of Harriet Bailey, a slave, and an unknown white man. By naming her child Frederick Augustus Washington Bailey, which evoked the commanding examples of European, classical, and American national patriarchs, Harriet Bailey tried to endow her son with a dignity and sense of destiny that would belie his status as a fatherless slave. What she was not able to give him was the knowledge of his own birthday. Throughout his adult life Douglass tried futilely to uncover this simple but profoundly meaningful reference to his own origins as an individual, a self. Recent biographers have had the good fortune to locate the property book of Douglass's first master, Aaron Anthony, in which the birth of Frederick Bailey is recorded as February 1818.[6] But as a slave boy Frederick could get nowhere when he inquired into his beginnings. In his first autobiography, *Narrative of the Life of Frederick Douglass* (1845), Douglass cites his master's resistance to these inquiries as the source of his earliest resentment of his enslaved condition. It was the desire for this knowledge that individualized Frederick in his master's eyes, earning him a reputation as "a restless spirit" even in childhood (31). Ironically, slavery's attempt to deny Frederick a sense of himself only spurred him on toward increasingly self-assertive behavior.

Before he was old enough to be put into the fields to work, Frederick was selected to go to Baltimore in 1826 to become a servant in the home of Sophia and Hugh Auld. Like her sister-in-law Lucretia Anthony Auld, who had befriended Frederick on the Eastern Shore plantation where he spent his early childhood, Sophia Auld treated her obviously talented new servant with unusual kindness. She went so far as to begin reading lessons with Frederick, until her husband angrily closed the books on further efforts to brighten the mental outlook of their slave. Refusing to accept Hugh Auld's dictates, Frederick took his first covertly rebellious steps toward freedom by teaching himself to read and write. In his later autobiographies, Douglass portrayed his acquisition of the tools of literacy as crucial to the expansion of his mental outlook and ultimately to the unfolding of new dimensions of individual potential within himself.

In 1833 a quarrel between Hugh Auld and his brother Thomas, Frederick's legal owner, resulted in the latter's return to his boyhood home in St. Michaels, Maryland. Tensions between the recalcitrant black youth and his master convinced Thomas Auld to hire Frederick out as a farm worker under the supervision of Edward Covey, a local slave-breaker. After six months of unstinting labor, repeated humiliations, and merciless whippings, the desperate sixteen-year-old slave fought back, resisting one of Covey's attempted beatings and intimidating his tormentor sufficiently to prevent future attacks. Douglass's dramatic account of his struggle with Covey would become the heroic turning-point of each of his future autobiographies, one of the most celebrated scenes in nineteenth-century American literature.

In the spring of 1836 Frederick went back to Baltimore to learn the caulking trade in the city's shipyards. What Hugh Auld did not take from his earnings the youth invested in a scheme to seize his freedom. With the financial aid of his future spouse, Anna Murray, a self-supporting free black domestic worker, and masquerading as a free merchant sailor, Frederick Bailey took a northbound train out of Baltimore on September 3, 1838 and arrived in New York City the next day. Before a month had passed he and Anna were reunited, married, and living in New Bedford, Connecticut as Mr. and Mrs. Frederick Douglass, the new last name recommended by a friend in New Bedford's thriving African American community. Less than three years later Douglass joined the abolitionist movement as a full-time lecturer for the Massachusetts Anti-Slavery Society, under the leadership of William Lloyd Garrison. Appearing on the antislavery lecture circuit throughout New England and as far west as Indiana, Douglass spoke daily, and as often as three times a day, to audiences that frequently were suspicious if not downright hostile to his hard-hitting attacks on slavery and northern racism. His intellectual brilliance, imposing physique, and rhetorical skill soon brought him national notoriety as a platform orator.[7]

Rumors that a man of such accomplished address could never have been a slave fueled Douglass's decision to put his life's story into print for the first time in 1845. He was by no means the first fugitive slave to create a personal narrative of his experience in bondage.[8] But he was among the first to realize that by authoring his own account, rather than simply dictating his story to another (as most previous fugitive slave narrators had done), he could strike at a root justification of slavery, the assumption that black people lacked the mental capacity and awareness of self that found its fullest human expression in writing. Published by the Massachusetts Anti-Slavery Society, the *Narrative of the Life of Frederick Douglass, An American Slave, Written by Himself* sold more than 30,000 copies in the first five years of its existence. An international bestseller, its contemporary readership far outstripped that of such classic white American autobiographies as Thoreau's *Walden* (1854). William Lloyd Garrison introduced Douglass's *Narrative* by stressing for the first time in print the representativeness of Douglass, at least insofar as his experience of slavery had been. "The experience of FREDERICK DOUGLASS, as a slave, was not a peculiar one; . . . his case may be regarded as a very fair specimen of the treatment of slaves in Maryland" (26). But there was something extraordinary and highly individualized about Douglass too, which his friend and abolitionist sponsor pointed to when he remarked on the memorable style of Douglass's literary self-presentation. The *Narrative* contained "many passages of great eloquence and power," epitomized in an incident in which Douglass portrayed himself "soliloquizing respecting his fate" as he stood on the banks of the Chesapeake Bay and poured out his longing to be free (26–27). The image of Douglass delivering his impassioned apostrophe to the white-sailed ships of the Chesapeake, symbols of an elusive liberty to a despondent slave, forecast the ultimate triumph of Douglass the fugitive at the end of his autobiography, when he mounts the abolitionist platform for the first time to tell the world who he is. The climactic moment of self-liberation in the *Narrative* shifts the import of Douglass's heroism from the realm of the physical (the successful bout with Covey the slave-breaker) to the sphere of the psyche. Douglass's greatest conquest, in a sense, is over himself, or at least over the slavish part of himself that, until the dramatic breakthrough scene at the end of the *Narrative*, felt that a black man must remain anonymous, that he must not speak his mind before whites, that he has nothing worthwhile to say. Integrated intellectually and psychologically by this empowering act of speech, and integrated socially and politically into the antislavery movement as a consequence of giving the speech, Douglass stands at the end of his *Narrative* secure in himself and in his vocation as an important voice of the antislavery movement.

Fearing that publication of his *Narrative* would make him an easy target for slavecatchers, Douglass went on a lecture tour in England immediately after the *Narrative* was published. When he returned triumphantly to the United States two years later in the spring of 1847, he had resolved, against the advice of many of his Garrisonian associates, to become an editor and a journalist as well as a lecturer. On December 3, 1847, Douglass launched the second phase of his literary career, publishing the first issue of his antislavery weekly, *The North Star*, from his Rochester, New York press room. Douglass knew that many abolitionists thought he was spreading his talents too thin and that he could do more good by concentrating on his antislavery speaking. Douglass replied that it was incumbent on African Americans to play an equal role on all fronts of the antislavery campaign.

> It is evident we [black Americans] must be our own representatives and advocates, not exclusively, but peculiarly—not distinct from, but in connection with our white friends. In the grand struggle for liberty and equality now waging, it is meet, right and essential that there should arise in our ranks authors and editors, as well as orators, for it is in these capacities that the most permanent good can be rendered to our cause.[9]

In "To Our Oppressed Countrymen," a statement of purpose that introduced *The North Star* to its readers, Douglass announced: "While our paper shall be mainly Anti-Slavery, its columns shall be freely opened to the candid and decorous discussion of all measures and topics of a moral and humane character, which may serve to enlighten, improve, and elevate mankind. Temperance, Peace, Capital Punishment, Education,—all subjects claiming the attention of the public mind may be freely and fully discussed here."[10] Although Douglass did not mention women's rights in this initial list of reforms to be espoused by his newspaper, *The North Star* endorsed the pioneering movement for equality for women, as part of the paper's front-page slogan, "Right is of no sex," plainly testified.[11] The only male to make a substantive contribution to the historic feminist convention at Seneca Falls, New York in July 1848, Douglass wrote a highly supportive review of the convention's Declaration of Sentiments in *The North Star*. During the post-Civil War debates over the Fifteenth Amendment to the Constitution, some suffragists attacked Douglass for refusing to link the claims of women to what he argued was a life-and-death political necessity for black men, especially in the South, to secure the right to vote. When the Fifteenth Amendment was ratified, however, Douglass immediately dedicated the last of the newspapers with which he was associated, *The New National Era*, to agitation for full voting rights for women.[12]

Under a succession of titles, from *The North Star* (1847–1851) to

Frederick Douglass' Paper (1851–1860) and finally *Douglass' Monthly* (1859–1863), Douglass kept his newspaper going longer than any previous African American journalistic enterprise, authoring most of the articles and editorials himself. One of the literary highlights of his newspaper was the novella, *The Heroic Slave*, which Douglass first unveiled in March 1853. Although he did not advance the claim, Douglass's novella is generally considered the first African American work of fiction. The hero of the story, Madison Washington, had been celebrated in antislavery circles for having led a successful mutiny aboard the slave ship *Creole* in November 1841. After the takeover Washington and his cohorts changed the ship's destination to Nassau, where the rebellious slaves were given asylum and set free. Douglass contributed to the Washington myth by reconstructing the slave mutineer into a model of black militancy, aggressive in pursuit of his rights, but self-controlled in his use of violence—in sum, a hero who exemplified an uncompromising commitment to justice balanced by a disposition toward mercy. By stressing at the start of *The Heroic Slave* that his Virginia protagonist "loved liberty as well as did Patrick Henry," "deserved it as much as Thomas Jefferson," and "fought for it with a valor" as strong as George Washington himself (132), Douglass placed the African American freedom struggle squarely in the American Revolutionary tradition. As if in response to Harriet Beecher Stowe's romanticized image of her slave hero, Uncle Tom, pacific, forgiving, and ultimately victimized, Madison Washington was endowed with a pride in blackness and a devotion to the national ideal of liberty that rendered him both an African and an American paragon. Glorifying Washington's principled use of violence in the service of a political end, the editor of *The North Star* showed how much the events of the 1850s were pushing him away from those, like Garrison, who preached that slavery could only be overcome by a war of words that eschewed politics in favor of moral appeal.

On July 5, 1852, Douglass delivered his most electrifying antislavery speech, "What To the Slave Is the Fourth of July?", in which he articulated for his mostly white audience at Rochester's Corinthian Hall the bitter sense of alienation that many African Americans felt in the wake of the passage of the Fugitive Slave Law of 1850. At the height of his powers as an antislavery speaker and writer, Douglass professed little satisfaction in his personal success story or his representative status, hammering home instead his sense of "the disparity" rather than the affinity between himself and white Americans. "Fellow-citizens, pardon me," he asked in mock innocence, "why am I called upon to speak here to-day? What have I, or those I represent, to do with your national independence? Are the great principles of political freedom and of natural justice, embodied in that Declaration of Independence, extended to us?" Douglass answered his own rhetorical question by observing, "I am not included within the pale of this glorious anniversary!" (115–116). Hadn't recent events in Washington, particularly the passage of the Fugitive Slave Law, proven that there was really no difference between free states and slave states for African Americans? If a slavecatcher could come to Rochester and drag a black man or woman away to the South just by convincing a federal magistrate that he owned that man or woman, then in Douglass's words, "New York has become as Virginia." Now that the southern slaveocracy was dictating to the northern democracy, Douglass dismissed those who wanted to go on singing the empty national chorus about "independence" and the "inalienable rights of man." The time had come for a new discourse devoted to "fire," to "thunder," to "blasting reproach" and "stern rebuke" (118).

Douglass's scornful condemnation of the consensus evoked by traditional Independence Day speeches in the United States was not just a rhetorical device for the occasion. Personal as well as political developments in the 1850s caused him to feel more alienated, more embattled, and more uncertain about his own future and that of the antislavery movement and the nation than he had ever felt before. During the early 1850s the once close relationship between Douglass and William Lloyd Garrison ruptured in a split that forced the black man to reassess his philosophy and goals as a reformer. Out of this time of soul-searching came Douglass's second autobiography, *My Bondage and My Freedom* (1855).[13]

In this remarkable re-evaluation of his life from the standpoint of almost fifteen years of freedom, Douglass melded his experience in the South and the North into a pattern of repeated initiations that revealed unsettling parallels between his struggle for freedom in Maryland and his search for dignity in Massachusetts. The last chapters of *My Bondage and My Freedom* significantly revise the 1845 *Narrative*'s overwhelmingly optimistic image of life for Frederick Douglass in the so-called free North. In the *Narrative* Douglass portrays the North as steadily shedding its racist prejudices in favor of the ideology of individualist egalitarianism. Fred Bailey rises by dint of his own efforts and ambitions from fugitive slave to independent dock worker to salaried orator in a progressive, biracial social movement. But in *My Bondage and My Freedom* Douglass no longer soft-pedals what he had long known first-hand about the North's pervasive racism, social discrimination, and hypocrisy. He clinches his attack on the North as false to its own ideology of individualism in the final chapter of *My Bondage and My Freedom*, where he reviews his rise and fall as a standard-bearer among the Garrisonians.

The 1845 *Narrative* concludes with Douglass comfortably integrated into the abolitionist fold as a platform lecturer. Implicit in this ending is the impression that the only thing that stood between Douglass's finding his voice and speaking freely in the North was his individual, or personal, sense of unworthiness. In *My Bondage and My Freedom*, however, the greatest restrictions on Douglass's self-expression in the antislavery movement emerge not from his initial underdeveloped sense of himself *as* an individual but from the abolitionists' inability to allow him to *be* an individual. "Tell your story, Frederick," Douglass recalls his mentor, Garrison, urging him on the speaker's platform. But the white abolitionists also remind the ex-slave that *they* "will take care of the philosophy" (213). In other words, the ex-slave should feel free to narrate the facts of his life, but his white sponsors will provide the proper interpretation of those facts.

Douglass argues in *My Bondage and My Freedom* that he eventually had to break with Garrison and his followers because he was too dedicated to his own individuality to allow men like Garrison to dictate to him what or how he should speak. In one sense *My Bondage and My Freedom* celebrates Douglass as a true intellectual individualist whose dedication to the ideology of genuine equality outweighs his gratitude to the likes of Garrison or his fear of being read out of the antislavery movement for refusing to play his assigned role. Just as clearly *My Bondage and My Freedom* reveals that there were social and political forces within America that proclaimed the gospel of freedom and held up the individual conscience as the highest moral law while also demanding that the individual conscience of a man like Douglass be conformed to the moral law as *those* forces defined it. This insight into the repressive character of the ideology of American individualism constitutes one of Douglass's most powerful analyses of a dominant sociopolitical myth in nineteenth-century United States. Insisting on his moral and social right to express his own individuality, Douglass closed his second autobiography with an acknowledgment of his need for an anchor in the northern African American community if he was ever to achieve a fully liberated sense of self.

Frederick Douglass welcomed the Civil War. Disgusted by efforts in Washington in the late 1850s to appease the South, he was convinced that slavery would never be destroyed through political compromise or solely peaceful means. Thus when the war began, Douglass lobbied President Lincoln on two fronts: to abolish slavery and to let African Americans join in the fight for what Douglass persisted in calling a war to end slavery.[14] When Lincoln signed the Emancipation Proclamation on January 1, 1863, Douglass was overjoyed, despite an awareness of its limitations. A month later *Douglass' Monthly* published "Men of Color, To Arms!", Douglass's rallying cry for African American enlistment into the Union Army. In this speech Douglass portrayed the war as a "golden opportunity" for black men to demonstrate manly self-respect, pride in race, and love of country, a set of interlocking identifications that sustained Douglass's version of the American Dream, though sorely tested, through the crises of the 1850s and 1860s. In the heat of the moment Douglass prophesied that the black soldiers who stormed the bastions of slavery in the South would "forever wipe out the dark reproaches unsparingly hurled against us by our enemies," allowing African Americans to "rise in one bound from social degradation to the plane of common equality with all other varieties of men" (225). The black man's willingness to make the supreme sacrifice, death in the service of a united free America, would finally and forever integrate him into social and political equality, if not fraternity, with the white man.

Although the African American soldier's formidable contribution to the Union cause did not bring about the sweeping and fundamental social changes that Douglass envisioned, the collapse of the slave power that marked the end of the Civil War did bring him a deep sense of fulfillment. For a while the man who embodied the antislavery movement to so many was not sure what to do in the aftermath of slavery. Soon, however, he decided to capitalize on his popularity as an orator by pursuing a career as a lecturer. Welcoming opportunities to agitate from the platform for the civil rights of African Americans, Douglass enjoyed greater success, especially among whites, for his lecture, "Self-Made Men," which he wrote in the late 1850s and became his mainstay during the post-emancipation years when he remained in popular demand as a speaker.[15] Douglass's identification with the American myth of success is one reason why Howard Carroll included Douglass's story in *Twelve Americans* (1883), a collection of biographies of public men who rose from "primitive surroundings" to exemplify "the astonishing social and material development of the Republic."[16]

Douglass approached his third autobiography, *Life and Times of Frederick Douglass* (1881),[17] with a sense of justifiable pride in what he had accomplished as a civil servant, a Republican party insider, an advisor to presidents, and a spokesman for freedmen and freedwomen throughout the nation. As he surveyed his life from his desk at Cedar Hill, the fifteen-acre estate overlooking Washington, D.C. that he purchased in 1878, Douglass, like many successful memoirists of his era, did not feel immodest about structuring the later years of his *Life and Times* around a succession of "firsts" that he, as a black man, actuated or helped to bring into effect. The list of these signal attainments, summed up in a chapter entitled "Weighed in the Balance," mixes the substantial with the symbolic. Appointments to the presidency of the Freedmen's bank in 1874 and to the office of federal marshal of the District of Columbia in 1876 are ranked with selection for official participation in the 1875 state funeral of Henry Wilson, "the first time in history that a colored man had been made a pall-bearer at the funeral . . . of a Vice-President of the United States" (286). Readers today may wonder whether such appointments constituted more than tokens of political preferment all too easily granted to and accepted by a single prominent individual, while millions of black people in the South had their political future bartered away, often by the same politicians who rewarded Douglass for services rendered. The author of *Life and Times* was not insensitive to such criticism, but he preferred to see his successes as opening a door, hitherto closed, to opportunity for African Americans who would follow him. From this perspective, an individual of color had both a right and an obligation to pursue and publicize success as an inspiration to his or her people and as a refutation of those who still regarded colored people as not fully capable of competing and winning in the demanding laissez-faire socioeconomic environment of post-Civil War America.

Life and Times frankly acknowledges several occasions when Douglass's standing as the spokesman of black America had been challenged and his ideas on particular issues rejected by a significant segment of his own people. "I never found myself more widely and painfully at variance with leading colored men of the country than when I opposed the effort to set in motion a wholesale exodus of colored people of the South to the northern states," Douglass observed of the so-called Exoduster migrations of the late 1870s.[18] He was especially stung by accusations of having betrayed the most inspiring theme of his own life when he censured ex-slaves for seeking freedom and a chance to build a better life outside the South. Yet Douglass's rejoinder, which he went to great lengths in *Life and Times* to expound, offered African Americans in the post-Reconstruction South little more than a history lesson in the steady improvements in the South's racial situation, capped by some distinctly ahistorical advice: "the negro of the South may wisely bide his time. The situation at the moment is exceptional and transient. The permanent powers of the government are all on his side" (296). "Every indication favors the position that the wrongs and hardships which [southern black people] suffer are soon to be redressed" (297).

Douglass's optimism about the amelioration of racial injustice in the South, as well as his conviction that the federal government was committed to enforcing the Fourteenth and Fifteenth Amendments, allowed him to counsel forebearance and patience in the late 1870s in a manner uncharacteristic of his response to racial injustices in earlier years. More unfortunately, his criticism of the Exoduster movement was couched in language that made him sound patronizing and insensitive to the harsh realities that the African American rank-and-file, especially in the post-Reconstruction South, were facing. To the self-made man secure in his position atop Cedar Hill, "this exodus" seemed at best a misguided "attempt to climb up some other way" (297). A defensive class consciousness led Douglass in the Conclusion of the 1881 *Life and Times* to address his white middle-class reader in the deferential manner of a slightly embarrassed emissary just returned from a backward province. "I have aimed to assure them [African Americans] that knowledge can be obtained under difficulties; that poverty may give place to competency; that obscurity is not an absolute bar to distinction, and that a way is open to welfare and happiness to all who will resolutely and wisely pursue that way" (310). "I have urged upon them self-reliance, self-respect, industry, perseverance, and economy" (310). Unfortunately, Douglass regretfully acknowledges, "my views at this point receive but limited endorsement among my people." As if to underline the distance between his own brand of rugged individualistic independence and the tendencies of black people in the opposite direction, Douglass adds ruefully: "they, for the most part, think they have means of procuring special favor and help from the Almighty; and, as their 'faith is the substance of things hoped for and the evidence of things not seen,' they find much in this expression which is true to faith, but utterly false to fact" (311).

The apologetic stance with regard to African American shortcomings that Douglass took at the end of the 1881 *Life and Times* calls attention to a widening gap between the relatively advantaged African American middle class in the urban North and the exploited black working class in the rural South in the late nineteenth century.[19] More than any previous autobiography of his, *Life and Times* argues that the recording of Douglass's individual successes is a social and political act designed to benefit a struggling black community. But more than any previous autobiography, the 1881 *Life and Times* struggles to demonstrate how the personal code and social career of a nineteenth-century African American individualist could be applicable to a southern black community entering an era in which collective survival, not individual success, would become paramount.

On some matters of individual conscience Douglass refused ever to get in step with the mainstream of black American thinking in the late nineteenth century. After being reproached by prominent African American clergymen for his "covert infidelity,"[20] Douglass learned to keep his religious liberalism mostly to himself. Only to a select few and then only in carefully chosen language, such as is reflected in his 1886 letter to the Rev. Theophilus Gould Steward of the African Methodist Episcopal Church, would Douglass hint at his distance from the evangelical orthodoxy of the large majority of his black contemporaries. His marriage to Helen Pitts in 1884, seventeen months after the death of his first wife, Anna Murray Douglass, brought expressions of outraged betrayal from many sectors of the African American community. Douglass calmly dismissed any contention that in marrying a white woman he had failed to exemplify pride in his own race. On one fundamental social and political issue, however, Douglass in the last decade of his life demonstrated renewed and invigorated solidarity with black people irrespective of differences over class or education or religious persuasion. Witnessing the incontrovertible rise of white supremacy in the South, crystallized in what Ida B. Wells called the "red record" of lynching,[21] Douglass felt impelled once more to step forward as the heroic spokesman of his people both on the lecture platform and in autobiography.

Despite the poor sales of the 1881 *Life and Times*, Douglass contracted a decade later to publish a new version of his autobiography that would carry the story of his life up to the early 1890s. The 1892 edition of *Life and Times* preserved and updated its author's image as racial trailblazer, but, in the self-celebrating chapter "Recorder of Deeds," Douglass tallied with unusual candor the costs of such success, particularly to his reputation in the African American community. He also commented on the furor over his marriage to Helen Pitts and the complaints from "my Afro-American critics" about his willingness to remain in the Recorder of Deeds position even after Grover Cleveland, a Democrat, had been elected president in 1885. This last edition of his *Life and Times* acknowledges more openly than ever before the challenges Douglass faced from thoughtful African Americans who felt he had been coopted by affluence, self-interest, political debts, and an undue regard for white acceptance. Yet Douglass clung to his traditional role as the spokesman for black America. His parting message as both personal historian and national chronicler no longer required that blacks elevate themselves to a higher American standard. Instead Douglass denounced America in 1892 for "national deterioration," a moral, social, and political declension that defied the very notion of mutual progress for whites and blacks that Douglass had himself invoked in the Conclusion of the 1881 version of his autobiography.

The Supreme Court decision of 1883, which declared unconstitutional the landmark Civil Rights Law of 1875, had ratified the reversion of America to "the old spirit of slavery and nothing else" (338). "Naked and defenseless against the action of a malignant, vulgar, and pitiless prejudice from which the Constitution plainly intended to shield them" (332), black Americans, Douglass maintained, needed an advocate more in the 1890s than at any time since "before they were set free" (316). Inspired by Wells's fearless example, Douglass enlisted in 1892 in her campaign to combat lynching, seizing lecture opportunities in 1893 and 1894 in Detroit, Chicago, Washington, D.C., and Boston to deliver his last great speech for social justice, *The Lessons of the Hour*. In a blistering attack on the South for its "blood chilling horrors and fiendish excesses perpetrated against the colored people" (341), Douglass excoriated not only the mob rule epidemic in the South in the 1890s but also the false contention, accepted throughout the United States, that lynching was an understandable, if not always justifiable, reaction to assaults on white women by the legendary "black brute." Douglass countered with the charge that lynching was simply the latest in a series of efforts by white supremacists to discredit, disempower, and, in the 1890s, to disfranchise black Americans, especially in the South where their numbers gave them real political potential. Where these reactionary tendencies ultimately led Douglass could not foresee. "But the favor with which this cowardly proposition of disfranchisement has been received by public men, white and black, by Republicans as well as Democrats, has shaken my faith in the nobility of the nation" (356).

Published as a handsome pamphlet in 1894, *The Lessons of the Hour* was Douglass's last major literary work. As his biographer William S. McFeely says, *The Lessons of the Hour* had no appreciable effect on the worsening conditions of African American sociopolitical existence in the South, or any other part of the United States where equal opportunity and equal protection under the law were under challenge from white supremacy. Nevertheless, no one should underestimate the import of Douglass's refusal in the last chapters of the 1892 *Life and Times* and in *The Lessons of the Hour* to countenance tamely the rampant violations of his ideal of America. Despite his profound distress over the downward trend of events, Douglass in the 1890s, as in the dispiriting 1850s, persisted in his belief that "the man who is right is a majority" (174). Since right (and rights) gained nothing from a silent majority, Douglass's speaking and writing never swerved from his conviction that the moral individual had an absolute responsibility in a democracy to articulate his or her view of the truth until such time as the rest of the people could discern it. Frederick Douglass's basic idea of his own individuality, his own quintessential identity, lay not in his racial affiliations or his American allegiances but in his sense of himself as a person with a moral mission. As he affirmed in 1892, his lifelong mission was "to stand for the freedom of people of all colors, until in our land the last yoke was broken and the last bondsman was set free" (318). Grappling with the meaning and measurement of freedom in the multiple and often conflicting cultural, social, economic, and political arenas of nineteenth-century America, Douglass previewed for readers of today many of the problems we face in realizing that mission of liberty for all. The strain of balancing a representative self-image and a redeeming social vision inevitably showed in Douglass's life and work, particularly in the autobiographies. Yet through it all Douglass stood, not just for freedom, but for intellectual and moral integrity in the articulation and pursuit of freedom. He stands today memorialized, as the modern poet Robert Hayden reminds us,[22] "not with statues' rhetoric . . . but with the lives grown out of his life, the lives / fleshing his dream of the beautiful needful thing." Freedom.

Notes

1. All quotations from Douglass's autobiographies cited in this introduction refer to this text.

2. See Frederick Douglass, *Autobiographies* (New York: Library of America, 1994). The textual note that appends this edition, provided by Henry Louis Gates, Jr., has been of particular use in the editing of the the *Oxford Frederick Douglass Reader*.

3. See Eric J. Sundquist, ed., *Frederick Douglass: New Literary and Historical Essays* (Cambridge: Cambridge U P, 1990), and William L. Andrews, ed., *Critical Essays on Frederick Douglass* (Boston: G. K. Hall, 1991).

4. See for example, William L. Andrews, "*My Bondage and My Freedom* and the American Literary Renaissance of the 1850s," in Andrews, ed., *Critical Essays on Frederick Douglass*, pp. 133–147; James Olney, "The Founding Fathers: Frederick Douglass and Booker T. Washington," in Deborah E. McDowell and Arnold Rampersad, eds., *Slavery in the Literary Imagination* (Baltimore: Johns Hopkins U P, 1989), pp. 1–24; and Rafia Zafar, "Franklinian Douglass: The Afro-American as Representative Man," in Sundquist, ed., *Frederick Douglass: New Literary and Historical Essays*, pp. 99–117.

5. In defense of his marriage to Helen Pitts in January 1884, seventeen months after the death of his first wife, Anna Murray Douglass, whom he married two weeks after his successful escape to freedom in September 1838, Douglass remarked that his first marriage was to a woman of his mother's race and his second to a woman of his father's. See Philip S. Foner, ed., *Life and Writings of Frederick Douglass*, vol. 4 (New York: International, 1955), p. 116.

6. In *Young Frederick Douglass: The Maryland Years* (Baltimore: Johns Hopkins U P, 1980), Dickson J. Preston revealed the existence of Aaron Anthony's property book, with its inscription of the month and year of Frederick Bailey's birth. The two major biographies of Douglass are: Benjamin Quarles, *Frederick Douglass* (1948; rpt. New York: Atheneum, 1968), and William S. McFeely, *Frederick Douglass* (New York: W. W. Norton, 1991).

7. For more information on Douglass's style of oratory and on his reception in the press, see John W. Blassingame, ed., *The Frederick Douglass Papers*, Series One: Speeches, Debates, and Interviews, 5 vols. (New Haven: Yale U P, 1979–).

8. For treatments of the fugitive slave narrative and Douglass's contribution to it, see William L. Andrews, *To Tell a Free Story: The First Century of Afro-American Autobiography, 1760–1865* (Urbana: U of Illinois P, 1986), and Frances Smith Foster, *Witnessing Slavery*, 2d ed. (Madison: U of Wisconsin P, 1993).

9. Douglass, "Our Paper and Its Prospects," in Philip S. Foner, ed., *Life and Writings of Frederick Douglass*, vol. 1 (New York: International, 1950), p. 281.

10. "To Our Oppressed Countrymen," in Foner, ibid., p. 283.

11. The full motto of *The North Star* reads: "Right is of no Sex—Truth is of no Color—God is the Father of us all, and we are all Brethren."

12. For a thorough discussion of Douglass's view of the relationship between women's and African American civil rights, see Philip S. Foner, ed., *Frederick Douglass on Women's Rights* (Westport, Conn.: Greenwood, 1976).

13. *My Bondage and My Freedom* (Auburn, N.Y.: Miller, Orton, and Mulligan, 1855).

14. The most complete study of Douglass's role in the Civil War is in David W. Blight, *Frederick Douglass' Civil War* (Baton Rouge: Louisiana State U P, 1989).

15. See "The Trials and Triumphs of Self-Made Men" in Blassingame, ed. *The Frederick Douglass Papers,* Series One, Vol. 3, pp. 289–300, and "Self-Made Men: An Address Delivered in Carlisle, Pennsylvania, in March 1893," in *The Frederick Douglass Papers,* Series One, Vol. 5, pp. 545–75. The best analysis of this speech and its significance is in Waldo Martin, *The Mind of Frederick Douglass* (Chapel Hill: U of North Carolina P, 1984), pp. 254–65.

16. Howard Carroll, *Twelve Americans* (New York: Harper & Brothers, 1883), p. vii.

17. *Life and Times of Frederick Douglass* (Hartford, Conn.: Park, 1881).

18. The standard study of the Exoduster movement is by Nell Irvin Painter, *Exodusters* (New York: Knopf, 1976).

19. Douglass's *Life and Times* was not the only autobiography by a member of the African American "Talented Tenth" to disclose this class consciousness. See also Elizabeth Keckley, *Behind the Scenes* (New York: G. W. Carleton, 1868); William Wells Brown, *My Southern Home* (Boston: A. G. Brown, 1880); and John Mercer Langston, *From the Virginia Plantation to the National Capitol* (Hartford, Conn.: American Publishing, 1894). For more on class consciousness in late nineteenth-century black America, see Willard B. Gatewood, *Aristocrats of Color* (Bloomington: Indiana U P, 1990), and Janette Thomas Greenwood, *Bittersweet Legacy: The Black and White "Better Classes" in Charlotte, 1850–1910* (Chapel Hill: U of North Carolina P, 1994).

20. See the controversy over Douglass's refusal in 1870 to thank God more than human activists for the blessing of emancipation, in Martin, *The Mind of Frederick Douglass,* pp. 178–80.

21. Ida B. Wells, *A Red Record: Tabulated Statistics and Alleged Causes of Lynchings in the United States, 1892–1893–1894* (Chicago: Donohue & Henneberry, 1895).

22. Robert Hayden, "Frederick Douglass," in *Selected Poems* (New York: October House, 1966).

CHAPTER 1

Narrative of the Life of Frederick Douglass, An American Slave, Written by Himself (1845)

D ouglass's *Narrative*, published in May 1845 by his Boston friends in the American Anti-Slavery Society, is probably the most influential literary work, except for *Uncle Tom's Cabin* (1853), generated by the American antislavery movement. Without the example Douglass set in the *Narrative*, Harriet Beecher Stowe's novel would have looked very different, since her fugitive slave firebrand, George Harris, is based directly on the image Stowe had of Douglass. Since the 1960s the *Narrative of the Life of Frederick Douglass* has grown in critical acclaim to the point where it is now treated less as a document that influenced other literary works than as a major work of mid-nineteenth century literature itself.

Priced at fifty cents a copy, the *Narrative*'s first printing of 5000 copies sold out in four months. To satisfy demand, four additional reprintings of 2000 copies each were brought out within a year. By 1850 approximately 30,000 copies of the *Narrative* had been sold in the United States and Great Britain. In 1846 a Dutch translation and in 1848 a French translation of the *Narrative* helped spread Douglass's fame on the European continent. Sales were helped greatly by positive reviews, such as the one Margaret Fuller, American transcendentalist and feminist author, wrote for the *New York Tribune* on June 10, 1845. Fuller congratulated Douglass for infusing into his writing "the thoughts, the feelings and the adventures that have been so affecting through the living voice." She went on to say that she had never read a narrative "more simple, true, coherent, and warm with genuine feeling." Other reviewers observed similarities between Douglass's style and that of John Bunyan or Daniel Defoe. By 1849 a reviewer of several prominent slave narratives, including Douglass's, stated that "the immense circulation" of these narratives had permeated the North, with the result that more people were being abolitionized by reading ex-slave autobiographies than by "all the theoretical arguments" against slavery mounted on the platform or in the press. In addition to what it did to change the mind of the North about the injustice of slavery, Douglass's *Narrative* also had a profoundly stimulative effect on the intellectual aspirations of black America, inspiring a number of major early African American writers, including William Wells Brown and Harriet Jacobs, to undertake literary careers of their own.

The collapse of slavery dampened public interest in Douglass's *Narrative*. For almost a century it remained out of print and largely forgotten, except among scholars, until it was revived in the 1960s as a prototypical expression of an emerging black consciousness making the transition from slavery to freedom. In recent years the *Narrative* has been applauded as the epitome of the antebellum fugitive slave narrative tradition, a classic narrative of ascent in the African American literary canon, and a lasting contribution to the portrait of the romantic individualist in nineteenth-century American literature.

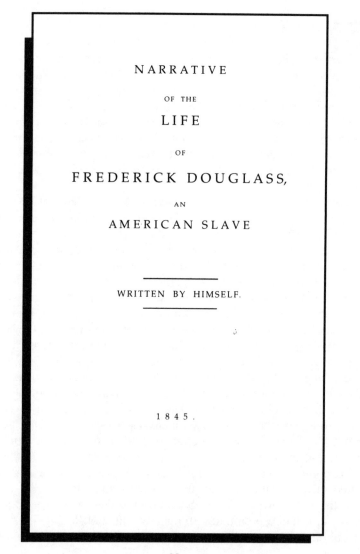

NARRATIVE

OF THE

LIFE

OF

FREDERICK DOUGLASS,

AN

AMERICAN SLAVE

WRITTEN BY HIMSELF.

1 8 4 5 .

PREFACE

In the month of August, 1841, I attended an anti-slavery convention in Nantucket, at which it was my happiness to become acquainted with FREDERICK DOUGLASS, the writer of the following Narrative. He was a stranger to nearly every member of that body; but, having recently made his escape from the southern prison-house of bondage, and feeling his curiosity excited to ascertain the principles and measures of the abolitionists,—of whom he had heard a somewhat vague description while he was a slave,—he was induced to give his attendance, on the occasion alluded to, though at that time a resident of New Bedford.

Fortunate, most fortunate occurrence!—fortunate for the millions of his manacled brethren, yet panting for deliverance from their awful thraldom!—fortunate for the cause of negro emancipation, and of universal liberty!—fortunate for the land of his birth, which he has already done so much to save and bless!—fortunate for a large circle of friends and acquaintances, whose sympathy and affection he has strongly secured by the many sufferings he has endured, by his virtuous traits of character, by his ever-abiding remembrance of those who are in bonds, as being bound with them!—fortunate for the multitudes, in various parts of our republic, whose minds he has enlightened on the subject of slavery, and who have been melted to tears by his pathos, or roused to virtuous indignation by his stirring eloquence against the enslavers of men!—fortunate for himself, as it at once brought him into the field of public usefulness, "gave the world assurance of a MAN," quickened the slumbering energies of his soul, and consecrated him to the great work of breaking the rod of the oppressor, and letting the oppressed go free!

I shall never forget his first speech at the convention—the extraordinary emotion it excited in my own mind—the powerful impression it created upon a crowded auditory, completely taken by surprise—the applause which followed from the beginning to the end of his felicitous remarks. I think I never hated slavery so intensely as at that moment; certainly, my perception of the enormous outrage which is inflicted by it, on the godlike nature of its victims, was rendered far more clear than ever. There stood one, in physical proportion and stature commanding and exact—in intellect richly endowed—in natural eloquence a prodigy—in soul manifestly "created but a little lower than the angels"—yet a slave, ay, a fugitive slave,—trembling for his safety, hardly daring to believe that on the American soil, a single white person could be found who would befriend him at all hazards, for the love of God and humanity! Capable of high attainments as an intellectual and moral being—needing nothing but a comparatively small amount of cultivation to make him an ornament to society and a blessing to his race—by the law of the land, by the voice of the people, by the terms of the slave code, he was only a piece of property, a beast of burden, a chattel personal, nevertheless!

A beloved friend from New Bedford prevailed on Mr. DOUGLASS to address the convention. He came forward to the platform with a hesitancy and embarrassment, necessarily the attendants of a sensitive mind in such a novel position. After apologizing for his ignorance, and reminding the audience that slavery was a poor school for the human intellect and heart, he proceeded to narrate some of the facts in his own history as a slave, and in the course of his speech gave utterance to many noble thoughts and thrilling reflections. As soon as he had taken his seat, filled with hope and admiration, I rose, and declared that PATRICK HENRY, of revolutionary fame, never made a speech more eloquent in the cause of liberty, than the one we had just listened to from the lips of that hunted fugitive. So I believed at that time—such is my belief now. I reminded the audience of the peril which surrounded this self-emancipated young man at the North,—even in Massachusetts, on the soil of the Pilgrim Fathers, among the descendants of revolutionary sires; and I appealed to them, whether they would ever allow him to be carried back into slavery,— law or no law, constitution or no constitution. The response was unanimous and in thunder-tones—"NO!" "Will you succor and protect him as a brother-man—a resident of the old Bay State?" "YES!" shouted the whole mass, with an energy so startling, that the ruthless tyrants south of Mason and Dixon's line might almost have heard the mighty burst of feeling, and recognized it as the pledge of an invincible determination, on the part of those who gave it, never to betray him that wanders, but to hide the outcast, and firmly to abide the consequences.

It was at once deeply impressed upon my mind, that, if Mr. DOUGLASS could be persuaded to consecrate his time and talents to the promotion of the anti-slavery enterprise, a powerful impetus would be given to it, and a stunning blow at the same time inflicted on northern prejudice against a colored complexion. I therefore endeavored to instil hope and courage into his mind, in order that he might dare to engage in a vocation so anomalous and responsible for a person in his situation; and I was seconded in this effort by warm-hearted friends, especially by the late General Agent of the Massachusetts Anti-Slavery Society, Mr. JOHN A. COLLINS, whose judgment in this instance entirely coincided with my own. At first, he could give no encouragement; with unfeigned diffidence, he expressed his conviction that he was not adequate to the performance of so great a task; the path marked out was wholly an untrodden one; he was sincerely apprehensive that he should do more harm than good. After much deliberation, however, he consented to make a trial; and ever since that period, he has acted as a lecturing agent, under the auspices either of the American or the Massachusetts Anti-Slavery Society. In labors he has been most abundant; and his success in combating prejudice, in gaining proselytes, in agitating the public mind, has far surpassed the most sanguine expectations that were raised at the commencement of his brilliant career. He has borne himself with gentleness and meekness, yet with true manliness of character. As a public speaker, he excels in pathos, wit, comparison, imitation, strength of reasoning, and fluency of language. There is in him that union of head and heart, which is indispensable to an enlightenment of the heads and a winning of the hearts of others. May his strength continue to be equal to his day! May he continue to "grow in grace, and in the knowledge of God," that he may be increasingly serviceable in the cause of bleeding humanity, whether at home or abroad!

It is certainly a very remarkable fact, that one of the most efficient advocates of the slave population, now before the public, is a fugitive slave, in the person of FREDERICK DOUGLASS; and that the free colored population of the United States are as ably represented by one of their own number, in the person of CHARLES LENOX REDMOND, whose eloquent appeals have extorted the highest applause of multitudes on both sides of the Atlantic. Let the calumniators of the colored race despise themselves for their baseness and illiberality of spirit, and henceforth cease to talk of the natural inferiority of those who require nothing but time and opportunity to attain to the highest point of human excellence.

It may, perhaps, be fairly questioned, whether any other portion of the population of the earth could have endured the privations, sufferings and horrors of slavery, without having become more degraded in the scale of humanity than the slaves of African descent. Nothing has been left undone to cripple their intellects, darken their minds, debase their moral nature, obliterate all traces of their relationship to mankind; and yet how wonderfully they have sustained the might load of a most frightful bondage, under which they have been groaning for centuries! To illustrate the effect of slavery on the white man,—to show that he has no powers of endurance, in such a condition, superior to those of his black brother,—DANIEL O'CONNELL, the distinguished advocate of universal emancipation, and the mightiest champion of prostrate but not conquered Ireland, relates the following anecdote in a speech delivered by him in the Conciliation Hall, Dublin, before the Loyal National Repeal Association, March 31, 1845. "No matter," said Mr. O'CONNELL, "under what specious term it may disguise itself, slavery is still hideous. *It has a natural, an inevitable tendency to brutalize every noble faculty of man.* An American sailor, who was cast away on the shore of Africa, where he was kept in slavery for three years, was, at the expiration of that period, found to be imbruted and stultified— he had lost all reasoning power; and having forgotten his native language, could only utter some savage gibberish between Arabic and English, which nobody could understand, and which even he himself found difficulty in pronouncing. So much for the humanizing influence of THE DOMESTIC INSTITUTION!" Admitting this to have been an extraordinary case of mental deterioration, it proves at least that the white slave can sink as low in the scale of humanity as the black one.

Mr. DOUGLASS has very properly chosen to write his own Narrative, in his own style, and according to the best of his ability, rather than to employ some one else. It is, therefore, entirely his own production; and, considering how long and dark was the career he had to run as a slave,—how few have been his opportunities to improve his mind since he broke his iron fetters,—it is, in my judgment, highly creditable to his head and heart. He who can peruse it without a tearful eye, a heaving breast, an afflicted spirit,—without being filled with an unutterable abhorrence of slavery and all its abettors, and animated with a determination to seek the immediate overthrow of that execrable system,—without trembling for the fate of this country in the hands of a righteous God, who is ever on the side of the oppressed, and whose arm is not shortened that it cannot save,—must have a flinty heart, and be qualified to act the part of a trafficker "in slaves and the souls of men." I am confident that it is essentially true in all its statements; that nothing has been set down in malice, nothing exaggerated, nothing drawn from the imagination; that it comes short of the reality, rather than overstates a single fact in regard to SLAVERY AS IT IS. The experience of FREDERICK DOUGLASS, as a slave, was not a peculiar one; his lot was not especially a hard one; his case may be regarded as a very fair specimen of the treatment of slaves in Maryland, in which State it is conceded that they are better fed and less cruelly treated than in Georgia, Alabama, or Louisiana. Many have suffered incomparably more, while very few on the plantations have suffered less, than himself. Yet how deplorable was his situation! what terrible chastisements were inflicted upon his person! what still more shocking outrages were perpetrated upon his mind! with all his noble powers and sublime aspirations, how like a brute was he treated, even by those professing to have the same mind in them that was in Christ Jesus! to what dreadful liabilities was he continually subjected! how destitute of friendly counsel and aid, even in his greatest extremities! how heavy was the midnight of woe which shrouded in blackness the last ray of hope, and filled the future with terror and gloom! what longings after freedom took possession of his breast, and how his misery augmented, in proportion as he grew reflective and intelligent,—thus demonstrating that a happy slave is an extinct man! how he thought, reasoned, felt, under the lash of the driver, with the chains upon his limbs! what perils he encountered in his endeavors to escape from his horrible doom! and how signal have been his deliverance and preservation in the midst of a nation of pitiless enemies!

This Narrative contains many affecting incidents, many passages of great eloquence and power; but I think the most thrilling one of them all is the description DOUGLASS gives of his feelings, as he stood soliloquizing respecting his fate, and the chances of his one day being a freeman, on the banks of the Chesapeake Bay—viewing the receding vessels as they flew with their white wings before the breeze, and apostrophizing them as animated by the living spirit of freedom. Who can read that passage, and be insensible to its pathos and sublimity? Compressed into it is a whole Alexandrian library of thought, feeling, and sentiment—all that can, all that need be urged, in the form of expostulation, entreaty, rebuke, against that crime of crimes,—making man the property of his fellow-man! O, how accursed is that system, which entombs the godlike mind of man, defaces the divine image, reduces those who by creation were crowned with glory and honor to a level with four-footed beasts, and exalts the dealer in human flesh above all that is called God! Why should its existence be prolonged one hour? Is it not evil, only evil, and that continually? What does its presence imply but the absence of all fear of God, all regard for man, on the part of the people of the United States? Heaven speed is eternal overthrow!

So profoundly ignorant of the nature of slavery are many persons, that they are stubbornly incredulous whenever they read or listen to any recital of the cruelties which are daily inflicted on its victims. They do not deny that the slaves are held as property; but that terrible fact seems to convey to their minds no idea of injustice, exposure to outrage, or savage barbarity. Tell them of cruel scourgings, of mutilations and brandings, of scenes of pollution and blood, of the banishment of all light and knowledge, and they affect to be greatly indignant at such enormous exaggerations, such wholesale misstatements, such abominable libels on the character of the southern planters! As if all these direful outrages were not the natural results of slavery! As if it were less cruel to reduce a human being to the condition of a thing, than to give him a severe flagellation, or to deprive him of necessary food and clothing! As if whips, chains, thumb-screws, paddles, bloodhounds, overseers, drivers, patrols, were not all indispensable to keep the slaves down, and to give protection to their ruthless oppressors! As if, when the marriage institution is abolished, concubinage, adultery, and incest, must not necessarily abound; when all the rights of humanity are annihilated, any barrier remains to protect the victim from the fury of the spoiler; when absolute power is assumed over life and liberty, it will not be wielded with destructive sway! Skeptics of this character abound in society. In some few instances, their incredulity arises from a want of reflection; but, generally, it indicates a hatred of the light, a desire to shield slavery from the assaults of its foes, a contempt of the colored race, whether bond or free. Such will try to discredit the shocking tales of slaveholding cruelty which are recorded in this truthful Narrative; but they will labor in vain. Mr. DOUGLASS has frankly disclosed the place of his birth, the names of those who claimed owner-ship in his body and soul, and the names also of those who committed the crimes which he has alleged against them. His statements, there-fore, may easily be disproved, if they are untrue.

In the course of his Narrative, he relates two instances of murder-ous cruelty,—in one of which a planter deliberately shot a slave be-longing to a neighboring plantation, who had unintentionally gotten within his lordly domain in quest of fish; and in the other, an overseer blew out the brains of a slave who had fled to a stream of water to escape a bloody scourging. Mr. DOUGLASS states that in neither of these instances was any thing done by way of legal arrest or judicial investi-gation. The Baltimore American, of March 17, 1845, relates a similar case of atrocity, perpetrated with similar impunity—as follows:— "*Shooting a Slave.*—We learn, upon the authority of a letter from Charles country, Maryland, received by a gentleman of this city, that a young man, named Matthews, a nephew of General Matthews, and whose father, it is believed, holds an office at Washington, killed one of the slaves upon his father's farm by shooting him. The letter states that young Matthews had been left in charge of the farm; that he gave an order to the servant, which was disobeyed, when he proceeded to the house, *obtained a gun, and, returning, shot the servant.* He immedi-ately, the letter continues, fled to his father's residence, where he still remains unmolested."—Let it never be forgotten, that no slaveholder or overseer can be convicted of any outrage perpetrated on the person of a slave, however diabolical it may be, on the testimony of colored witnesses, whether bond or free. By the slave code, they are adjudged to be as incompetent to testify against a white man, as though they were indeed a part of the brute creation. Hence, there is no legal pro-tection in fact, whatever there may be in form, for the slave population; and any amount of cruelty may be inflicted on them with impunity. Is it possible for the human mind to conceive of a more horrible state of society?

The effect of a religious profession on the conduct of southern mas-ters is vividly described in the following Narrative, and shown to be any thing but salutary. In the nature of the case, it must be in the highest degree pernicious. The testimony of Mr. DOUGLASS, on this point, is sustained by a could of witnesses, whose veracity is unim-peachable. "A slaveholder's profession of Christianity is a palpable im-posture. He is a felon of the highest grade. He is a man-stealer. It is of no importance what you put in the other scale."

Reader! are you with the man-stealers in sympathy and purpose, or on the side of their down-trodden victims? If with the former, then are you the foe of God and man. If with the latter, what are you pre-pared to do and dare in their behalf? Be faithful, be vigilant, be untir-ing in your efforts to break every yoke, and let the oppressed go free. Come what may—cost what it may—inscribe on the banner which you

unfurl to the breeze, as your religious and political motto—"No Compromise with Slavery! No Union with Slaveholders!"

WM. LLOYD GARRISON

Boston, *May* 1, 1845

LETTER
FROM WENDELL PHILLIPS, ESQ.

Boston, *April* 22, 1845

My Dear Friend:

You remember the old fable of "The Man and the Lion," where the
lion complained that he should not be so misrepresented "when the
lions wrote history."

I am glad the time has come when the "lions write history." We
have been left long enough to gather the character of slavery from the
involuntary evidence of the masters. One might, indeed, rest sufficiently satisfied with what, it is evident, must be, in general, the results
of such a relation, without seeking farther to find whether they have
followed in every instance. Indeed, those who stare at the half-peck of
corn a week, and love to count the lashes on the slave's back, are seldom the "stuff" out of which reformers and abolitionists are to be
made. I remember that, in 1838, many were waiting for the results of
the West India experiment, before they could come into our ranks.
Those "results" have come long ago; but, alas! few of that number have
come with them, as converts. A man must be disposed to judge of
emancipation by other tests than whether it has increased the produce
of sugar,—and to hate slavery for other reasons than because it starves
men and whips women,—before he is ready to lay the first stone of
his anti-slavery life.

I was glad to learn, in your story, how early the most neglected of
God's children waken to a sense of their rights, and of the injustice
done them. Experience is a keen teacher; and long before you had mastered your A B C, or knew where the "white sails" of the Chesapeake
were bound, you began, I see, to gauge the wretchedness of the slave,
not by his hunger and want, not by his lashes and toil, but by the cruel
and blighting death which gathers over his soul.

In connection with this, there is one circumstance which makes
your recollections peculiarly valuable, and renders your early insight
the more remarkable. You come from that part of the country where
we are told slavery appears with its fairest features. Let us hear, then,
what it is at its best estate—gaze on its bright side, if it has one; and
then imagination may task her powers to add dark lines to the picture,
as she travels southward to that (for the colored man) Valley of the
Shadow of Death, where the Mississippi sweeps along.

Again, we have known you long, and can put the most entire con-

29

fidence in your truth, candor, and sincerity. Every one who has heard you speak has felt, and, I am confident, every one who reads your book will feel, persuaded that you give them a fair specimen of the whole truth. No one-sided portrait,—no wholesale complaints,—but strict justice done, whenever individual kindliness has neutralized, for a moment, the deadly system with which it was strangely allied. You have been with us, too, some years, and can fairly compare the twilight of rights, which your race enjoy at the North with that "noon of night" under which they labor south of Mason and Dixon's line. Tell us whether, after all, the half-free colored man of Massachusetts is worse off than the pampered slave of the rice swamps!

In reading your life, no one can say that we have unfairly picked out some rare specimens of cruelty. We know that the bitter drops, which even you have drained from the cup, are no incidental aggravations, no individual ills, but such as must mingle always and necessarily in the lot of every slave. They are the essential ingredients, not the occasional results, of the system.

After all, I shall read your book with trembling for you. Some years ago, when you were beginning to tell me your real name and birthplace, you may remember I stopped you, and preferred to remain ignorant of all. With the exception of a vague description, so I continued, till the other day, when you read me your memoirs. I hardly knew, at the time, whether to thank you or not for the sight of them, when I reflected that it was still dangerous, in Massachusetts, for honest men to tell their names! They say the fathers, in 1776, signed the Declaration of Independence with the halter about their necks. You, too, publish your declaration of freedom with danger compassing you around. In all the broad lands which the Constitution of the United States overshadows, there is no single spot,—however narrow or desolate,— where a fugitive slave can plant himself and say, "I am safe." The whole armory of Northern Law has no shield for you. I am free to say that, in your place, I should throw the MS. into the fire.

You, perhaps, may tell your story in safety, endeared as you are to so many warm hearts by rare gifts, and a still rarer devotion of them to the service of others. But it will be owing only to your labor, and the fearless efforts of those who, trampling the laws and Constitution of the country under their feet, are determined that they will "hide the outcast," and that their hearths shall be, spite of the law, an asylum for the oppressed, if, some time or other, the humblest may stand in our streets, and bear witness in safety against the cruelties of which he has been the victim.

Yet it is sad to think, that these very throbbing hearts which welcome your story, and from your best safeguard in telling it, are all beating contrary to the "statute in such case made and provided." Go on, my dear friend, till you, and those who, like you, have been saved, so as by fire, from the dark prison-house, shall stereotype these free, illegal pulses into statutes; and New England, cutting loose from a blood-stained Union, shall glory in being the house of refuge for the oppressed;—till we no longer merely *"hide* the outcast," or make a merit of standing idly by while he is hunted in our midst; but, consecrating anew the soil of the Pilgrims as an asylum for the oppressed, proclaim our *welcome* to the slave so loudly, that the tones shall reach every hut in the Carolinas, and make the broken-hearted bondman leap up at the thought of old Massachusetts.

God speed the day!

Till then, and ever,

Yours truly,

WENDELL PHILLIPS.

FREDERICK DOUGLASS.

CHAPTER I

I was born in Tuckahoe, near Hillsborough, and about twelve miles from Easton, in Talbot county, Maryland. I have no accurate knowledge of my age, never having seen any authentic record containing it. By far the larger part of the slaves know as little of their ages as horses know of theirs, and it is the wish of most masters within my knowledge to keep their slaves thus ignorant. I do not remember to have ever met a slave who could tell of his birthday. They seldom come nearer to it than planting-time, harvest-time, cherry-time, spring-time, or fall-time. A want of information concerning my own was a source of unhappiness to me even during childhood. The white children could tell their ages. I could not tell why I ought to be deprived of the same privilege. I was not allowed to make any inquiries of my master concerning it. He deemed all such inquiries on the part of a slave improper and impertinent, and evidence of a restless spirit. The nearest estimate I can give makes me now between twenty-seven and twenty-eight years of age. I come to this, from hearing my master say, some time during 1835, I was about seventeen years old.

My mother was named Harriet Bailey. She was the daughter of Isaac and Betsey Bailey, both colored, and quite dark. My mother was of a darker complexion than either my grandmother or grandfather.

My father was a white man. He was admitted to be such by all I ever heard speak of my parentage. The opinion was also whispered that my master was my father; but of the correctness of this opinion, I know nothing; the means of knowing was withheld from me. My mother and I were separated when I was but an infant—before I knew her as my mother. It is a common custom, in the part of Maryland from which I ran away, to part children from their mothers at a very early age. Frequently, before the child has reached its twelfth month, its mother is taken from it, and hired out on some farm a considerable distance off, and the child is placed under the care of an old woman, too old for field labor. For what this separation is done, I do not know, unless it be to hinder the development of the child's affection toward its mother, and to blunt and destroy the natural affection of the mother for the child. This is the inevitable result.

I never saw my mother, to know her as such, more than four or five times in my life; and each of these times was very short in duration, and at night. She was hired by a Mr. Stewart, who lived about twelve miles from my home. She made her journeys to see me in the night, travelling the whole distance on foot, after the performance of her day's work. She was a field hand, and a whipping is the penalty of not being in the field at sunrise, unless a slave has special permission from his or her master to the contrary—a permission which they seldom get, and one that gives to him that gives it the proud name of being a kind master. I do not recollect of ever seeing my mother by the light of day. She was with me in the night. She would lie down with me, and get me to sleep, but long before I waked she was gone. Very little communication ever took place between us. Death soon ended what little we could have while she lived, and with it her hardships and suffering. She died when I was about seven years old, on one of my master's farms, near Lee's Mill. I was not allowed to be present during her illness, at her death, or burial. She was gone long before I knew any thing about it. Never having enjoyed, to any considerable extent, her soothing presence, her tender and watchful care, I received the tidings of her death with much the same emotions I should have probably felt at the death of a stranger.

Called thus suddenly away, she left me without the slightest intimation of who my father was. The whisper that my master was my father, may or may not be true; and, true or false, it is of but little consequence to my purpose whilst the face remains, in all its glaring odiousness, that slaveholders have ordained, and by law established, that the children of slave women shall in all cases follow the condition of their mothers; and this is done too obviously to administer to their own lusts, and make gratification of their wicked desires profitable as well as pleasurable; for by this cunning arrangement, the slaveholder, in cases not a few, sustains to his slaves the double relation of master and father.

I know of such cases; and it is worthy of remark that such slaves invariably suffer greater hardships, and have more to contend with, than others. They are, in the first place, a constant offence to their mistress. She is ever disposed to find fault with them; they can seldom do any thing to please her; she is never better pleased than when she sees them under the lash, especially when she suspects her husband of showing to his mulatto children favors which he withholds from his black slaves. The master is frequently compelled to sell this class of his slaves, out of deference to the feelings of his white wife; and, cruel as the deed may strike any one to be, for a man to sell his own children to human flesh-mongers, it is often the dictate of humanity for him to do so; for, unless he does this, he must not only whip them himself, but must stand by and see one white son tie up his brother, of but few shades darker complexion than himself, and ply the gory lash to his naked back; and if he lisp one word of disapproval, it is set down to his parental partiality, and only makes a bad matter worse, both for himself and the slave whom he would protect and defend.

Every year brings with it multitudes of this class of slaves. It was doubtless in consequence of a knowledge of this fact, that one great statesman of the south predicted the downfall of slavery by the inevitable laws of population. Whether this prophecy is ever fulfilled or not, it is nevertheless plain that a very different-looking class of people are springing up at the south, and are now held in slavery, from those originally brought to this country from Africa; and if their increase will do no other good, it will do away the force of the argument, that God cursed Ham, and therefore American slavery is right. If the lineal descendants of Ham are alone to be scripturally enslaved, it is certain that slavery at the south must soon become unscriptural; for thousands are ushered into the world, annually, who, like myself, owe their existence to white fathers, and those fathers most frequently their own masters.

I have had two masters. My first master's name was Anthony. I do not remember his first name. He was generally called Captain Anthony—a title which, I presume, he acquired by sailing a craft on the Chesapeake Bay. He was not considered a rich slaveholder. He owned two or three farms, and about thirty slaves. His farms and slaves were under the care of an overseer. The overseer's name was Plummer. Mr. Plummer was a miserable drunkard, a profane swearer, and a savage monster. He always went armed with a cowskin and a heavy cudgel. I have known him to cut and slash the women's heads so horribly, that even master would be enraged at his cruelty, and would threaten to whip him if he did not mind himself. Master, however, was not a humane slaveholder. It required extraordinary barbarity on the part of an overseer to affect him. He was a cruel man, hardened by a long life of slaveholding. He would at times seem to take great pleasure in whipping a slave. I have often been awakened at the dawn of day by the most heart-rending shrieks of an own aunt of mine, whom he used to tie up to a joist, and whip upon her naked back till she was literally covered with blood. No words, no tears, no prayers, from his gory victim, seemed to move his iron heart from its bloody purpose. The louder she screamed, the harder he whipped; and where the blood ran fastest, there he whipped longest. He would whip her to make her scream, and whip her to make her hush; and not until overcome by fatigue, would he cease to swing the blood-clotted cowskin. I remember the first time I ever witnessed this horrible exhibition. I was quite a child, but I well remember it. I never shall forget it whilst I remember any thing. It was the first of a long series of such outrages, of which I was doomed to be a witness and a participant. It struck me with awful force. It was the blood-stained gate, the entrance to the hell of slavery, through which I was about to pass. It was a most terrible spectacle. I wish I could commit to paper the feelings with which I beheld it.

This occurrence took place very soon after I went to live with my old master, and under the following circumstances. Aunt Hester went out one night,—where or for what I do not know,—and happened to be absent when my master desired her presence. He had ordered her not to go out evenings, and warned her that she must never let him catch her in company with a young man, who was paying attention to her, belonging to Colonel Lloyd. The young man's name was Ned Roberts, generally called Lloyd's Ned. Why master was so careful of her, may be safely left to conjecture. She was a woman of noble form, and of graceful proportions, having very few equals, and fewer superiors, in personal appearance, among the colored or white women of our neighborhood.

Aunt Hester had not only disobeyed his orders in going out, but had been found in company with Lloyd's Ned; which circumstance, I found, from what he said while whipping her, was the chief offence. Had he been a man of pure morals himself, he might have been thought interested in protecting the innocence of my aunt; but those who knew him will not suspect him of any such virtue. Before he commenced whipping Aunt Hester, he took her into the kitchen, and stripped her from neck to waist, leaving her neck, shoulders, and back, entirely naked. He then told her to cross her hands, calling her at the same time a d——d b——h. After crossing her hands, he tied them with a strong rope, and led her to a stool under a large hook in the joist, put in for the purpose. He made her get upon the stool, and tied her hands to the hook. She now stood fair for his infernal purpose. Her arms were stretched up at their full length, so that she stood upon the ends of her toes. He then said to her, "Now, you d——d b——h, I'll learn you how to disobey my orders!" and after rolling up his sleeves, he commenced to lay on the heavy cowskin, and soon the warm, red blood (amid heart-rending shrieks from her, and horrid oaths from him) came dripping to the floor. I was so terrified and horror-stricken at the sight, that I hid myself in a closet, and dared not venture out till long after the bloody transaction was over. I expected it would be my turn next. It was all new to me. I had never seen any thing like it before. I had always lived with my grandmother on the outskirts of the plantation, where she was put to raise the children of the younger women. I had therefore been, until now, out of the way of the bloody scenes that often occurred on the plantation.

CHAPTER II

My master's family consisted of two sons, Andrew and Richard; one daughter, Lucretia, and her husband, Captain Thomas Auld. They lived in one house, upon the home plantation of Colonel Edward Lloyd. My master was Colonel Lloyd's clerk and superintendent. He was what might be called the overseers of the overseers. I spent two years of childhood on this plantation in my old master's family. It was here that I witnessed the bloody transaction recorded in the first chapter; and as I received my first impressions of slavery on this plantation, I will give some description of it, and of slavery as it there existed. The plantation is about twelve miles north of Easton, in Talbot county, and is situated on the border of Miles River. The principal products raised upon it were tobacco, corn, and wheat. These were raised in great abundance; so that, with the products of this and the other farms belonging to him, he was able to keep in almost constant employment a large sloop, in carrying them to market at Baltimore. This sloop was named Sally Lloyd, in honor of one of the colonel's daughters. My master's son-in-law, Captain Auld, was master of the vessel; she was otherwise manned by the colonel's own slaves. Their names were Peter, Isaac, Rich, and Jake. These were esteemed very highly by the other slaves, and looked upon as the privileged ones of the plantation; for it was no small affair, in the eyes of the slaves, to be allowed to see Baltimore.

Colonel Lloyd kept from three to four hundred slaves on his home plantation, and owned a large number more on the neighboring farms belonging to him. The names of the farms nearest to the home plantation were Wye Town and New Design. "Wye Town" was under the overseership of a man named Noah Willis. New Design was under the overseership of a Mr. Townsend. The overseers of these, and all the rest of the farms, numbering over twenty, received advice and direction from the managers of the home plantation. This was the great business place. It was the seat of government for the whole twenty farms. All disputes among the overseers were settled here. If a slave was convicted of any high misdemeanor, became unmanageable, or evinced a determination to run away, he was brought immediately here, severely whipped, put on board the sloop, carried to Baltimore, and sold to Austin Woolfolk or some other slave-trader, as a warning to the slaves remaining.

Here, too, the slaves of all the other farms received their monthly allowance of food, and their yearly clothing. The men and women slaves received, as their monthly allowance of food, eight pounds of pork, or its equivalent in fish, and one bushel of corn meal. Their yearly clothing consisted of two coarse linen shirts, one pair of linen trousers, like the shirts, one jacket, one pair of trousers for winter, made of coarse negro cloth, one pair of stockings, and one pair of shoes; the whole of which could not have cost more than seven dollars. The allowance of the slave children was given to their mothers, or the old women having the care of them. The children unable to work in the field had neither shoes, stockings, jackets, nor trousers, given to them; their clothing consisted of two coarse linen shirts per year. When these failed them, they went naked until the next allowance-day. Children from seven to ten years old, of both sexes, almost naked, might be seen at all seasons of the year.

There were no beds given the slaves, unless one coarse blanket be considered such, and none but the men and women had these. This, however, is not considered a very great privation. They find less difficulty from the want of beds, than from the want of time to sleep; for when their day's work in the field is done, the most of them having their washing, mending, and cooking to do, and having few or none of the ordinary facilities for doing either of these, very many of their sleeping hours are consumed in preparing for the field the coming day; and when this is done, old and young, male and female, married and single, drop down side by side, on one common bed,—the cold, damp floor,—each covering himself or herself with their miserable blankets; and here they sleep till they are summoned to the field by the driver's horn. At the sound of this, all must rise, and be off to the field. There must be no halting; every one must be at his or her post; and woe betides them who hear not this morning summons to the field; for if they are not awakened by the sense of hearing, they are by the sense of feeling; no age nor sex finds any favor. Mr. Severe, the overseer, used to stand by the door of the quarter, armed with a large hickory stick and heavy cowskin, ready to whip any one who was so unfortunate as not to hear, or, from any other cause, was prevented from being ready to start for the field at the sound of the horn.

Mr. Severe was rightly named: he was a cruel man. I have seen him whip a woman, causing the blood to run half an hour at the time; and this, too, in the midst of her crying children, pleading for their mother's release. He seemed to take pleasure in manifesting his fiendish barbarity. Added to his cruelty, he was a profane swearer. It was enough to chill the blood and stiffen the hair of an ordinary man to hear him talk. Scarce a sentence escaped him but that was commenced or concluded by some horrid oath. The field was the place to witness his cruelty and profanity. His presence made it both the field of blood and of blasphemy. From the rising till the going down of the sun, he was cursing, raving, cutting, and slashing among the slaves of the field, in the most frightful manner. His career was short. He died very soon after I went to Colonel Lloyd's; and he died as he lived, uttering, with his dying groans, bitter curses and horrid oaths. His death was regarded by the slaves as the result of a merciful providence.

Mr. Severe's place was filled by a Mr. Hopkins. He was a very different man. He was less cruel, less profane, and made less noise, than Mr. Severe. His course was characterized by no extraordinary demonstrations of cruelty. He whipped, but seemed to take no pleasure in it. He was called by the slaves a good overseer.

The home plantation of Colonel Lloyd wore the appearance of a country village. All the mechanical operations for all the farms were performed here. The shoemaking and mending, the blacksmithing, cartwrighting, coopering, weaving, and grain-grinding, were all performed by the slaves on the home plantation. The whole place wore a business-like aspect very unlike the neighboring farms. The number of houses, too, conspired to give it advantage over the neighboring farms. It was called by the slaves the *Great House Farm*. Few privileges were esteemed higher, by the slaves of the out-farms, than that of being selected to do errands at the Great House Farm. It was associated in their minds with greatness. A representative could not be prouder of his election to a seat in the American Congress, than a slave on one of the out-farms would be of his election to do errands at the Great House Farm. They regarded it as evidence of great confidence reposed in them by their overseers; and it was on this account, as well as a constant desire to be out of the field from under the driver's lash, that they esteemed it a high privilege, one worth careful living for. He was called the smartest and most trusty fellow, who had this honor conferred upon him the most frequently. The competitors for this office sought as diligently to please their overseers, as the office-seekers in the political parties seek to please and deceive the people. The same traits of character might be seen in Colonel Lloyd's slaves, as are seen in the slaves of the political parties.

The slaves selected to go to the Great House Farm, for the monthly allowance for themselves and their fellow-slaves, were peculiarly enthusiastic. While on their way, they would make the dense old woods, for miles around, reverberate with their wild songs, revealing at once the highest joy and the deepest sadness. They would compose and sing as they went along, consulting neither time nor tune. The thought that came up, came out—if not in the word, in the sound;—and as frequently in the one as in the other. They would sometimes sing the most pathetic sentiment in the most rapturous tone, and the most rapturous sentiment in the most pathetic tone. Into all of their songs they would manage to weave something of the Great House Farm. Especially would they do this, when leaving home. They would then sing most exultingly the following words:—

"I am going away to the Great House Farm!
O, yea! O, yea! O!"

This they would sing, as a chorus, to words which to many would seem unmeaning jargon, but which, nevertheless, were full of meaning to themselves. I have sometimes thought that the mere hearing of those songs would do more to impress some minds with the horrible character of slavery, than the reading of whole volumes of philosophy on the subject could do.

I did not, when a slave, understand the deep meaning of those rude and apparently incoherent songs. I was myself within the circle; so that I neither saw nor heard as those without might see and hear. They told a tale of woe which was then altogether beyond my feeble comprehension; they were tones loud, long, and deep; they breathed the prayer and complaint of souls boiling over with the bitterest anguish. Every tone was a testimony against slavery, and a prayer to God for deliverance from chains. The hearing of those wild notes always depressed my spirit, and filled me with ineffable sadness. I have frequently found myself in tears while hearing them. The mere recurrence to those songs, even now, afflicts me; and while I am writing these lines, an expression of feeling has already found its way down my cheek. To those songs I trace my first glimmering conception of the dehumanizing character of slavery. I can never get rid of that conception. Those songs still follow me, to deepen my hatred of slavery, and quicken my sympathies for my brethren in bonds. If any one wishes to be impressed with the soul-killing effects of slavery, let him go to Colonel Lloyd's plantation, and, on allowance-day, place himself in the deep pine woods, and there let him, in silence, analyze the sounds that shall pass through the chambers of his soul,—and if he is not thus impressed, it will only be because "there is no flesh in his obdurate heart."

I have often been utterly astonished, since I came to the north, to find persons who could speak of the singing, among slaves, as evidence of their contentment and happiness. It is impossible to conceive of a greater mistake. Slaves sing most when they are most unhappy. The songs of the slave represent the sorrows of his heart; and he is relieved by them, only as an aching heart is relieved by its tears. At least, such is my experience. I have often sung to drown my sorrow, but seldom to express my happiness. Crying for joy, and singing for joy, were alike uncommon to me while in the jaws of slavery. The singing of a man cast away upon a desolate island might be as appropriately considered as evidence of contentment and happiness, as the singing of a slave; the songs of the one and of the other are prompted by the same emotion.

CHAPTER III

Colonel Lloyd kept a large and finely cultivated garden, which afforded almost constant employment for four men, besides the chief gardener, (Mr. M'Durmond.) This garden was probably the greatest attraction of the place. During the summer months, people came from far and near—from Baltimore, Easton, and Annapolis—to see it. It abounded in fruits of almost every description, from the hardy apple of the north to the delicate orange of the south. This garden was not the least source of trouble on the plantation. Its excellent fruit was quite a temptation to the hungry swarms of boys, as well as the older slaves, belonging to the colonel, few of whom had the virtue or the vice to resist it. Scarcely a day passed, during the summer, but that some slave had to take the lash for stealing fruit. The colonel had to resort to all kinds of stratagems to keep his slaves out of the garden. The last and most successful one was that of tarring his fence all around; after which, if a slave was caught with any tar upon his person, it was deemed sufficient proof that he had either been into the garden, or had tried to get in. In either case, he was severely whipped by the chief gardener. This plan worked well; the slaves became as fearful of tar as of the lash. They seemed to realize the impossibility of touching *tar* without being defiled.

The colonel also kept a splendid riding equipage. His stable and carriage-house presented the appearance of some of our large city livery establishments. His horses were of the finest form and noblest blood. His carriage-house contained three splendid coaches, three or four gigs, besides dearborns and barouches of the most fashionable style.

This establishment was under the care of two slaves—old Barney and young Barney—father and son. To attend to this establishment was their sole work. But it was by no means an easy employment; for in nothing was Colonel Lloyd more particular than in the management of his horses. The slightest inattention to these was unpardonable, and was visited upon those, under whose care they were placed, with the severest punishment; no excuse could shield them, if the colonel only suspected any want of attention to his horses—a supposition which he frequently indulged, and one which, of course, made the office of old and young Barney a very trying one. They never knew when they were safe from punishment. They were frequently whipped when least deserving, and escaped whipping when most deserving it. Every thing depended upon the looks of the horses, and the state of Colonel Lloyd's own mind when his horses were brought to him for use. If a horse did not move fast enough, or hold his head high enough, it was owing to some fault of his keepers. It was painful to stand near the stable-door, and hear the various complaints against the keepers when a horse was taken out for use. "This horse has not had proper attention. He has not been sufficiently rubbed and curried, or he has not been properly fed; his food was too wet or too dry; he got it too soon or too late; he was too hot or too cold; he had too much hay, and not enough of grain; or he had too much grain, and not enough of hay; instead of old Barney's attending to the horse, he had very improperly left it to his son." To all these complaints, no matter how unjust, the slave must answer never a word. Colonel Lloyd could not brook any contradiction from a slave. When he spoke, a slave must stand, listen, and tremble; and such was literally the case. I have seen Colonel Lloyd make old Barney, a man between fifty and sixty years of age, uncover his bald head, kneel down upon the cold, damp ground, and receive upon his naked and toil-worn shoulders more than thirty lashes at the time. Colonel Lloyd had three sons—Edward, Murray, and Daniel,—and three sons-in-law, Mr. Winder, Mr. Nicholson, and Mr. Lowndes. All of these lived at the Great House Farm, and enjoyed the luxury of whipping the servants when they pleased, from old Barney down to William Wilkes, the coach-driver. I have seen Winder make one of the house-servants stand off from him a suitable distance to be touched with the end of his whip, and at every stroke raise great ridges upon his back.

To describe the wealth of Colonel Lloyd would be almost equal to describing the riches of Job. He kept from ten to fifteen house-servants. He was said to own a thousand slaves, and I think this estimate quite within the truth. Colonel Lloyd owned so many that he did not know them when he saw them; nor did all the slaves of the out-farms know him. It is reported of him, that, while riding along the road one day, he met a colored man, and addressed him in the usual manner of speaking to colored people on the public highways of the south: "Well, boy, whom do you belong to?" "To Colonel Lloyd," replied the slave. "Well, does the colonel treat you well?" "No, sir," was the ready reply. "What, does he work you too hard?" "Yes, sir." "Well, don't he give you enough to eat?" "Yes, sir, he gives me enough, such as it is."

The colonel, after ascertaining where the slave belonged, rode on; the man also went on about his business, not dreaming that he had been conversing with his master. He thought, said, and heard nothing more of the matter, until two or three weeks afterwards. The poor man was then informed by his overseer that, for having found fault with his master, he was now to be sold to a Georgia trader. He was immediately chained and handcuffed; and thus, without a moment's warning, he was snatched away, and forever sundered, from his family and friends, by a hand more unrelenting than death. This is the penalty of telling the truth, of telling the simple truth, in answer to a series of plain questions.

It is partly in consequence of such facts, that slaves when inquired of as to their condition and the character of their masters, almost universally say they are contented, and that their masters are kind. The slaveholders have been known to send in spies among their slaves, to ascertain their views and feelings in regard to their condition. The frequency of this has had the effect to establish among the slaves the maxim, that a still tongue makes a wise head. They suppress the truth rather than take the consequences of telling it, and in so doing prove themselves a part of the human family. If they have any thing to say of their masters, it is generally in their masters' favor, especially when speaking to an untried man. I have been frequently asked, when a slave, if I had a kind master, and do not remember ever to have given a negative answer; nor did I, in pursuing this course, consider myself as uttering what was absolutely false; for I always measured the kindness of my master by the standard of kindness set up among slaveholders around us. Moreover, slaves are like other people, and imbibe prejudices quite common to others. They think their own better than that of others. Many, under the influence of this prejudice, think their own masters are better than the masters of other slaves; and this, too, in some cases, when the very reverse is true. Indeed, it is not uncommon for slaves even to fall out and quarrel among themselves about the relative goodness of their masters, each contending for the superior goodness of his own over that of the others. At the very same time, they mutually execrate their masters when viewed separately. It was so on our plantation. When Colonel Lloyd's slaves met the slaves of Jacob Jepson, they seldom parted without a quarrel about their masters; Colonel Lloyd's slaves contending that he was the richest, and Mr. Jepson's slaves that he was the smartest, and most of a man. Colonel Lloyd's slaves would boast his ability to buy and sell Jacob Jepson. Mr. Jepson's slaves would boast his ability to whip Colonel Lloyd. These quarrels would almost always end in a fight between the parties, and those that whipped were supposed to have gained the point at issue. They seemed to think that the greatness of their masters was transferable to themselves. It was considered as being bad enough to be a slave; but to be a poor man's slave was deemed a disgrace indeed!

CHAPTER IV

Mr. Hopkins remained but a short time in the office of overseer. Why his career was so short, I do not know, but suppose he lacked the necessary severity to suit Colonel Lloyd. Mr. Hopkins was succeeded by Mr. Austin Gore, a man possessing, in an eminent degree, all those traits of character indispensable to what is called a first-rate overseer. Mr. Gore had served Colonel Lloyd, in the capacity of overseer, upon one of the out-farms, and had shown himself worthy of the high station of overseer upon the home or Great House Farm.

Mr. Gore was proud, ambitious, and persevering. He was artful, cruel, and obdurate. He was just the man for such a place, and it was just the place for such a man. It afforded scope for the full exercise of all his powers, and he seemed to be perfectly at home in it. He was one of those who could torture the slightest look, word, or gesture, on the part of the slave, into impudence, and would treat it accordingly. There must be no answering back to him; no explanation was allowed a slave, showing himself to have been wrongfully accused. Mr. Gore acted fully up to the maxim laid down by slaveholders,—"It is better that a dozen slaves suffer under the lash, than that the overseer should be convicted, in the presence of the slaves, of having been at fault." No matter how innocent a slave might be—it availed him nothing, when accused by Mr. Gore of any misdemeanor. To be accused was to be convicted, and to be convicted was to be punished; the one always following the other with immutable certainty. To escape punishment was to escape accusation; and few slaves had the fortune to do either, under the overseership of Mr. Gore. He was just proud enough to demand the most debasing homage of the slave, and quite servile enough to crouch, himself, at the feet of the master. He was ambitious enough to be contented with nothing short of the highest rank of overseers, and persevering enough to reach the height of his ambition. He was cruel enough to inflict the severest punishment, artful enough to descend to the lowest trickery, and obdurate enough to be insensible to the voice of a reproving conscience. He was, of all the overseers, the most dreaded by the slaves. His presence was painful; his eye flashed confusion; and seldom was his sharp, shrill voice heard, without producing horror and trembling in their ranks.

Mr. Gore was a grave man, and, though a young man, he indulged in no jokes, said no funny words, seldom smiled. His words were in perfect keeping with his looks, and his looks were in perfect keeping with his words. Overseers will sometimes indulge in a witty word, even with the slaves; not so with Mr. Gore. He spoke but to command, and commanded but to be obeyed; he dealt sparingly with his words, and bountifully with his whip, never using the former where the latter would answer as well. When he whipped, he seemed to do so from a sense of duty, and feared no consequences. He did nothing reluctantly, no matter how disagreeable; always at his post, never inconsistent. He never promised but to fulfil. He was, in a word, a man of the most inflexible firmness and stone-like coolness.

His savage barbarity was equalled only by the consummate coolness with which he committed the grossest and most savage deeds upon the slaves under his charge. Mr. Gore once undertook to whip one of Colonel Lloyd's slaves, by the name of Demby. He had given Demby but few stripes, when, to get rid of the scourging, he ran and plunged himself into a creek, and stood there at the depth of his shoulders, refusing to come out. Mr. Gore told him that he would give him three calls, and that, if he did not come out at the third call, he would shoot him. The first call was given. Demby made no response, but stood his ground. The second and third calls were given with the same result. Mr. Gore then, without consultation or deliberation with any one, not even giving Demby an additional call, raised his musket to his face, taking deadly aim at his standing victim, and in an instant poor Demby was no more. His mangled body sank out of sight, and blood and brains marked the water where he had stood.

A thrill of horror flashed through every soul upon the plantation, excepting Mr. Gore. He alone seemed cool and collected. He was asked by Colonel Lloyd and my old master, why he resorted to this extraordinary expedient. His reply was, (as well as I can remember,) that Demby had become unmanageable. He was setting a dangerous example to the other slaves,—one which, if suffered to pass without some such demonstration on his part, would finally lead to the total subversion of all rule and order upon the plantation. He argued that if one slave refused to be corrected, and escaped with his life, the other slaves would soon copy the example; the result of which would be, the freedom of the slaves, and the enslavement of the whites. Mr. Gore's defence was satisfactory. He was continued in his station as overseer upon the home plantation. His fame as an overseer went abroad. His horrid crime was not even submitted to judicial investigation. It was committed in the presence of slaves, and they of course could neither institute a suit, nor testify against him; and thus the guilty perpetrator of one of the bloodiest and most foul murders goes unwhipped of justice, and uncensured by the community in which he lives. Mr. Gore lived in St. Michael's, Talbot country, Maryland, when I left there; and if he is still alive, he very probably lives there now; and if so, he is now, as he was then, as highly esteemed and as much respected as though his guilty soul had not been stained with his brother's blood.

I speak advisedly when I say this,—that killing a slave, or any colored person, in Talbot country, Maryland, is not treated as a crime, either by the courts or the community. Mr. Thomas Lanman, of St. Michael's, killed two slaves, one of whom he killed with a hatchet, by knocking his brains out. He used to boast of the commission of the awful and bloody deed. I have heard him do so laughingly, saying, among other things, that he was the only benefactor of his country in the company, and that when others would do as much as he had done, we should be relieved of "the d———d niggers."

The wife of Mr. Giles Hick, living but a short distance from where I used to live, murdered my wife's cousin, a young girl between fifteen and sixteen years of age, mangling her person in the most horrible manner, breaking her nose and breastbone with a stick, so that the poor girl expired in a few hours afterward. She was immediately buried, but had not been in her untimely grave but a few hours before she was taken up and examined by the coroner, who decided that she had come to her death by severe beating. The offence for which this girl was thus murdered was this:—She had been set that night to mind Mrs. Hick's baby, and during the night she fell asleep, and the baby cried. She, having lost her rest for several nights previous, did not hear the crying. They were both in the room with Mrs. Hicks. Mrs. Hicks, finding the girl slow to move, jumped from her bed, seized an oak stick of wood by the fireplace, and with it broke the girl's nose and breastbone, and thus ended her life. I will not say that this most horrid murder produced no sensation in the community. It did produce sensation, but not enough to bring the murderess to punishment. There was a warrant issued for her arrest, but it was never served. Thus she escaped not only punishment, but even the pain of being arraigned before a court for her horrid crime.

Whilst I am detailing bloody deeds which took place during my stay on Colonel Lloyd's plantation, I will briefly narrate another, which occurred about the same time as the murder of Demby by Mr. Gore.

Colonel Lloyd's slaves were in the habit of spending a part of their nights and Sundays in fishing for oysters, and in this way made up the deficiency of their scanty allowance. An old man belonging to Colonel Lloyd, while thus engaged, happened to get beyond the limits of Colonel Lloyd's, and on the premises of Mr. Beal Bondly. At this trespass, Mr. Bondly took offence, and with his musket came down to the shore, and blew its deadly contents into the poor old man.

Mr. Bondly came over to see Colonel Lloyd the next day, whether to pay him for his property, or to justify himself in what he had done, I know not. At any rate, this whole fiendish transaction was soon hushed up. There was very little said about it at all, and nothing done. It was a common saying, even among little white boys, that it was worth a half-cent to kill a "nigger," and a half-cent to bury one.

CHAPTER V

As to my own treatment while I lived on Colonel Lloyd's plantation, it was very similar to that of the other slave children. I was not old enough to work in the field, and there being little else than field work to do, I had a great deal of leisure time. The most I had to do was to drive up the cows at evening, keep the fowls out of the garden, keep the front yard clean, and run of errands for my old master's daughter, Mrs. Lucretia Auld. The most of my leisure time I spent in helping Master Daniel Lloyd in finding his birds, after he had shot them. My connection with Master Daniel was of some advantage to me. He became quite attached to me, and was a sort of protector of me. He would not allow the older boys to impose upon me, and would divide his cakes with me.

I was seldom whipped by my old master, and suffered little from any thing else than hunger and cold. In hottest summer and coldest winter, I was kept almost naked—no shoes, no stockings, no jacket, no trousers, nothing on but a coarse tow linen shirt, reaching only to my knees. I had no bed. I must have perished with cold, but that, the coldest nights, I used to steal a bag which was used for carrying corn to the mill. I would crawl into this bag, and there sleep on the cold, damp, clay floor, with my head in and feet out. My feet have been so cracked with the frost, that the pen with which I am writing might be laid in the gashes.

We were not regularly allowanced. Our food was coarse corn meal boiled. This was called *mush*. It was put into a large wooden tray or trough, and set down upon the ground. The children were then called, like so many pigs, and like so many pigs they would come and devour the mush; some with oyster-shells, others with pieces of shingle, some with naked hands, and none with spoons. He that ate fastest got most; he that was strongest secured the best place; and few left the trough satisfied.

I was probably between seven and eight years old when I left Colonel Lloyd's plantation. I left it with joy. I shall never forget the ecstasy with which I received the intelligence that my old master (Anthony) had determined to let me go to Baltimore, to live with Mr. Hugh Auld, brother to my old master's son-in-law, Captain Thomas Auld. I received this information about three days before my departure. They were three of the happiest days I ever enjoyed. I spent the most part of all these three days in the creek, washing off the plantation scurf, and preparing myself for my departure.

The pride of appearance which this would indicate was not my own. I spent the time in washing, not so much because I wished to, but because Mrs. Lucretia had told me I must get all the dead skin off my feet and knees before I could go to Baltimore; for the people in Baltimore were very cleanly, and would laugh at me if I looked dirty. Besides, she was going to give me a pair of trousers, which I should not put on unless I got all the dirt off me. The thought of owning a pair of trousers was great indeed! It was almost a sufficient motive, not only to make me take off what would be called by pig-drovers the mange, but the skin itself. I went at it in good earnest, working for the first time with the hope of reward.

The ties that ordinarily bind children to their homes were all suspended in my case. I found no severe trial in my departure. My home was charmless; it was not home to me; on parting from it, I could not feel that I was leaving any thing which I could have enjoyed by staying. My mother was dead, my grandmother lived far off, so that I seldom saw her. I had two sisters and one brother, that lived in the same house with me; but the early separation of us from our mother had well nigh blotted the fact of our relationship from our memories. I looked for home elsewhere, and was confident of finding none which I should relish less than the one which I was leaving. If, however, I found in my new home hardship, hunger, whipping, and nakedness, I had the consolation that I should not have escaped any one of them by staying. Having already had more than a taste of them in the house of my old master, and having endured them there, I very naturally inferred my ability to endure them elsewhere, and especially at Baltimore; for I had something of the feeling about Baltimore that is expressed in the proverb, that "being hanged in England is preferable to dying a natural death in Ireland." I had the strongest desire to see Baltimore. Cousin Tom, though not fluent in speech, had inspired me with that desire by his eloquent description of the place. I could never point out any thing at the Great House, no matter how beautiful or powerful, but that he had seen something at Baltimore far exceeding, both in beauty and strength, the object which I pointed out to him. Even the Great House itself, with all its pictures, was far inferior to many buildings in Baltimore. So strong was my desire, that I thought a gratification of it would fully compensate for whatever loss of comforts I should sustain by the exchange. I left without a regret, and with the highest hopes of future happiness.

We sailed out of Miles River for Baltimore on a Saturday morning. I remember only the day of the week, for at that time I had no knowledge of the days of the month, nor the months of the year. On setting sail, I walked aft, and gave to Colonel Lloyd's plantation what I hoped would be the last look. I then placed myself in the bows of the sloop, and there spent the remainder of the day in looking ahead, interesting myself in what was in the distance rather than in things near by or behind.

In the afternoon of that day, we reached Annapolis, the capital of the State. We stopped but a few moments, so that I had no time to go on shore. It was the first large town that I had ever seen, and though it would look small compared with some of our New England factory villages, I thought it a wonderful place for its size—more imposing even than the Great House Farm!

We arrived at Baltimore early on Sunday morning, landing at Smith's Wharf, not far from Bowley's Wharf. We had on board the sloop a large flock of sheep; and after aiding in driving them to the slaughter-house of Mr. Curtis on Louden Slater's Hill, I was conducted by Rich, one of the hands belonging on board of the sloop, to my new home in Alliciana Street, near Mr. Gardner's ship-yard, on Fells Point.

Mr. and Mrs. Auld were both at home, and met me at the door with their little son Thomas, to take care of whom I had been given. And here I saw what I had never seen before; it was a white face beaming with the most kindly emotions; it was the face of my new mistress, Sophia Auld. I wish I could describe the rapture that flashed through my soul as I beheld it. It was a new and strange sight to me, brightening up my pathway with the light of happiness. Little Thomas was told, there was his Freddy,— and I was told to take care of little Thomas; and thus I entered upon the duties of my new home with the most cheering prospect ahead.

I look upon my departure from Colonel Lloyd's plantation as one of the most interesting events of my life. It is possible, and even quite probable, that but for the mere circumstance of being removed from that plantation to Baltimore, I should have to-day, instead of being here seated by my own table, in the enjoyment of freedom and the happiness of home, writing this Narrative, been confined in the galling chains of slavery. Going to live at Baltimore laid the foundation, and opened the gateway, to all my subsequent prosperity. I have ever regarded it as the first plain manifestation of that kind providence which has ever since attended me, and marked my life with so many favors. I regarded the selection of myself as being somewhat remarkable. There were a number of slave children that might have been sent from the plantation to Baltimore. There were those younger, those older, and those of the same age. I was chosen from among them all, and was the first, last, and only choice.

I may be deemed superstitious, and even egotistical, in regarding this event as a special interposition of divine Providence in my favor. But I should be false to the earliest sentiments of my soul, if I suppressed the opinion. I prefer to be true to myself, even at the hazard of incurring the ridicule of others, rather than to be false, and incur my own abhorrence. From my earliest recollection, I date the entertainment of a deep conviction that slavery would not always be able to hold me within its foul embrace; and in the darkest hours of my career in slavery, this living word of faith and spirit of hope departed not from me, but remained like ministering angels to cheer me through the gloom. This good spirit was from God, and to him I offer thanksgiving and praise.

CHAPTER VI

My new mistress proved to be all she appeared when I first met her at the door,—a woman of the kindest heart and finest feelings. She had never had a slave under her control previously to myself, and prior to her marriage she had been dependent upon her own industry for a living. She was by trade a weaver; and by constant application to her business, she had been in a good degree preserved from the blighting and dehumanizing effects of slavery. I was utterly astonished at her goodness. I scarcely knew how to behave towards her. She was entirely unlike any other white woman I had ever seen. I could not approach her as I was accustomed to approach other white ladies. My early instruction was all out of place. The crouching servility, usually so acceptable a quality in a slave, did not answer when manifested toward her. Her favor was not gained by it; she seemed to be disturbed by it. She did not deem it impudent or unmannerly for a slave to look her in the face. The meanest slave was put fully at ease in her presence, and none left without feeling better for having seen her. Her face was made of heavenly smiles, and her voice of tranquil music.

But, alas! this kind heart had but a short time to remain such. The fatal poison of irresponsible power was already in her hands, and soon commenced its infernal work. That cheerful eye, under the influence of slavery, soon became red with rage; that voice, made all of sweet accord, changed to one of harsh and horrid discord; and that angelic face gave place to that of a demon.

Very soon after I went to live with Mr. and Mrs. Auld, she very kindly commenced to teach me the A, B, C. After I had learned this, she assisted me in learning to spell words of three or four letters. Just at this point of my progress, Mr. Auld found out what was going on, and at once forbade Mrs. Auld to instruct me further, telling her, among other things, that it was unlawful, as well as unsafe, to teach a slave to read. To use his own words, further, he said, "If you give a nigger an inch, he will take an ell. A nigger should know nothing but to obey his mater—to do as he is told to do. Learning would *spoil* the best nigger in the world. Now," said he, "if you teach that nigger (speaking of myself) how to read, there would be no keeping him. It would forever unfit him to be a slave. He would at once become unmanageable, and of no value to his master. As to himself, it could do him no good, but a great deal of harm. It would make him discontented and unhappy." These words sank deep into my heart, stirred up sentiments within that lay slumbering, and called into existence an entirely new train of thought. It was a new and special revelation, explaining dark and mysterious things, with which my youthful understanding had struggled, but struggled in vain. I now understood what had been to me a most perplexing difficulty—to wit, the white man's power to enslave the black man. It was a grand achievement, and I prized it highly. From that moment, I understood the pathway from slavery to freedom. It was just what I wanted, and I got it at a time when I the least expected it. Whilst I was saddened by the thought of losing the aid of my kind mistress, I was gladdened by the invaluable instruction which, by the merest accident, I had gained from my master. Though conscious of the difficulty of learning without a teacher, I set out with high hope, and a fixed purpose, at whatever cost of trouble, to learn how to read. The very decided manner with which he spoke, and strove to impress his wife with the evil consequences of giving me instruction, served to convince me that he was deeply sensible of the truths he was uttering. It gave me the best assurance that I might rely with the utmost confidence on the results which, he said, would flow from teaching me to read. What he most dreaded, that I most desired. What he most loved, that I most hated. That which to him was a great evil, to be carefully shunned, was to me a great good, to be diligently sought; and the argument which he so warmly urged, against my learning to read, only served to inspire me with a desire and determination to learn. In learning to read, I owe almost as much to the bitter opposition of my master, as to the kindly aid of my mistress. I acknowledge the benefit of both.

I had resided but a short time in Baltimore before I observed a marked difference, in the treatment of slaves, from that which I had witnessed in the country. A city slave is almost a freeman, compared with a slave on the plantation. He is much better fed and clothed, and enjoys privileges altogether unknown to the slave on the plantation. There is a vestige of decency, a sense of shame, that does much to curb and check those outbreaks of atrocious cruelty so commonly enacted upon the plantation. He is a desperate slaveholder, who will shock the humanity of his non-slaveholding neighbors with the cries of his lacerated slave. Few are willing to incur the odium attaching to the reputation of being a cruel master; and above all things, they would not be known as not giving a slave enough to eat. Every city slaveholder is anxious to have it known of him, that he feeds his slaves well; and it is due to them to say, that most of them do give their slaves enough to eat. There are, however, some painful exceptions to this rule. Directly opposite to us, on Philpot Street, lived Mr. Thomas Hamilton. He owned two slaves. Their names were Henrietta and Mary. Henrietta was about twenty-two years of age, Mary was about fourteen; and of all the mangled and emaciated creatures I ever looked upon, these two were the most so. His heart must be harder than stone, that could look upon these unmoved. The head, neck, and shoulders of Mary were literally cut to pieces. I have frequently felt her head, and found it nearly covered with festering sores, caused by the lash of her cruel mistress. I do not know that her master ever whipped her, but I have been an eye-witness to the cruelty of Mrs. Hamilton. I used to be in Mr. Hamilton's house nearly every day. Mrs. Hamilton used to sit in a large chair in the middle of the room, with a heavy cowskin always by her side, and scarce an hour passed during the day but was marked by the blood of one of these slaves. The girls seldom passed her without her saying, "Move faster, you *black gip!*" at the same time giving them a blow with the cowskin over the head or shoulders, often drawing the blood. She would then say, "Take that, you *black gip!*"—continuing, "If you don't move faster, I'll move you!" Added to the cruel lashings to which these slaves were subjected, they were kept nearly half-starved. They seldom knew what it was to eat a full meal. I have seen Mary contending with the pigs for the offal thrown into the street. So much was Mary kicked and cut to pieces, that she was oftener called *"pecked"* than by her name.

CHAPTER VII

I lived in Master Hugh's family about seven years. During this time, I succeeded in learning to read and write. In accomplishing this, I was compelled to resort to various stratagems. I had no regular teacher. My mistress, who had kindly commenced to instruct me, had, in compliance with the advice and direction of her husband, not only ceased to instruct, but had set her face against my being instructed by any one else. It is due, however, to my mistress to say of her, that she did not adopt this course of treatment immediately. She at first lacked the depravity indispensable to shutting me up in mental darkness. It was at least necessary for her to have some training in the exercise of irresponsible power, to make her equal to the task of treating me as though I were a brute.

My mistress was, as I have said, a kind and tender-hearted woman; and in the simplicity of her soul she commenced, when I first went to live with her, to treat me as she supposed one human being ought to treat another. In entering upon the duties of a slaveholder, she did not seem to perceive that I sustained to her the relation of a mere chattel, and that for her to treat me as a human being was not only wrong, but dangerously so. Slavery proved as injurious to her as it did to me. When I went there, she was a pious, warm, and tender-hearted woman. There was no sorrow or suffering for which she had not a tear. She had bread for the hungry, clothes for the naked, and comfort for every mourner that came within her reach. Slavery soon proved its ability to divest her of these heavenly qualities. Under its influence, the tender heart became stone, and the lamblike disposition gave way to one of tiger-like fierceness. The first step in her downward course was in her ceasing to instruct me. She now commenced to prac-tise her husband's precepts. She finally became even more violent in her opposition than her husband himself. She was not satisfied with simply doing as well as he had commanded; she seemed anxious to do better. Nothing seemed to make her more angry than to see me with a newspaper. She seemed to think that here lay the danger. I have had her rush at me with a face made all up of fury, and snatch from me a newspaper, in a manner that fully revealed her apprehension. She was an apt woman; and a little experience soon demonstrated, to her satis-faction, that education and slavery were incompatible with each other.

From this time I was most narrowly watched. If I was in a separate room any considerable length of time, I was sure to be suspected of having a book, and was at once called to give an account of myself. All this, however, was too late. The first step had been taken. Mistress, in teaching me the alphabet, had given me the *inch*, and no precaution could prevent me from taking the *ell*.

The plan which I adopted, and the one by which I was most suc-cessful, was that of making friends of all the little white boys whom I met in the street. As many of these as I could, I converted into teach-ers. With their kindly aid, obtained at different times and in different places, I finally succeeded in learning to read. When I was sent of er-rands, I always took my book with me, and by going one part of my errand quickly, I found time to get a lesson before my return. I used also to carry bread with me, enough of which was always in the house, and to which I was always welcome; for I was much better off in this regard than many of the poor white children in our neighborhood. This bread I used to bestow upon the hungry little urchins, who, in return, would give me that more valuable bread of knowledge. I am strongly tempted to give the names of two or three of those little boys, as a testimonial of the gratitude and affection I bear them; but prudence forbids;—not that it would injure me, but it might embarrass them; for it is almost an unpardonable offence to teach slaves to read in this Christian country. It is enough to say of the dear little fellows, that they lived on Philpot Street, very near Durgin and Bailey's shipyard. I used to talk this matter of slavery over with them. I would sometimes say to them, I wished I could be as free as they would be when they got to be men. "You will be free as soon as you are twenty-one, *but I am a slave for life!* Have not I as good a right to be free as you have?" These words used to trouble them; they would express for me the liveliest sympathy, and console me with the hope that something would occur by which I might be free.

I was now about twelve years old, and the thought of being *a slave for life* began to bear heavily upon my heart. Just about this time, I got hold of a book entitled "The Columbian orator." Every opportunity I got, I used to read this book. Among much of other interesting matter, I found in it a dialogue between a master and his slave. The slave was represented as having run away from his master three times. The dialogue represented the conversation which took place between them, when the slave was retaken the third time. In this dialogue, the whole argument in behalf of slavery was brought forward by the master, all of which was disposed of by the slave. The slave was made to say some very smart as well as impressive things in reply to his master— things which had the desired though unexpected effect; for the conversation resulted in the voluntary emancipation of the slave on the part of the master.

In the same book, I met with one of Sheridan's mighty speeches on and in behalf of Catholic emancipation. These were choice documents to me. I read them over and over again with unabated interest. They gave tongue to interesting thoughts of my own soul, which had frequently flashed through my mind, and died away for want of utterance. The moral which I gained from the dialogue was the power of truth over the conscience of even a slaveholder. What I got from Sheridan was a bold denunciation of slavery, and a powerful vindication of human rights. The reading of these documents enabled me to utter my thoughts, and to meet the arguments brought forward to sustain slavery; but while they relieved me of one difficulty, they brought on another even more painful than the one of which I was relieved. The more I read, the more I was led to abhor and detest my enslavers. I could regard them in no other light than a band of successful robbers, who had left their homes, and gone to Africa, and stolen us from our homes, and in a strange land reduced us to slavery. I loathed them as being the meanest as well as the most wicked of men. As I read and contemplated the subject, behold! that very discontentment which Master Hugh had predicted would follow my learning to read had already come, to torment and sting my soul to unutterable anguish. As I writhed under it, I would at times feel that learning to read had been a curse rather than a blessing. It had given me a view of my wretched condition, without the remedy. I opened my eyes to the horrible pit, but to no ladder upon which to get out. In moments of agony, I envied my fellow-slaves for their stupidity. I have often wished myself a beast. I preferred the condition of the meanest reptile to my own. Any thing, no matter what, to get rid of thinking! It was this everlasting thinking of my condition that tormented me. There was no getting rid of it. It was pressed upon me by every object within sight or hearing, animate or inanimate. The silver trump of freedom had roused my soul to eternal wakefulness. Freedom now appeared, to disappear no more forever. It was heard in every sound, and seen in every thing. It was ever present to torment me with a sense of my wretched condition. I saw nothing without seeing it, I heard nothing without hearing it, and felt nothing without feeling it. It looked from every star, it smiled in every calm, breathed in every wind, and moved in every storm.

I often found myself regretting my own existence, and wishing myself dead; and but for the hope of being free, I have no doubt but that I should have killed myself, or done something for which I should have been killed. While in this state of mind, I was eager to hear any one speak of slavery. I was a ready listener. Every little while, I could hear something about the abolitionists. It was some time before I found what the word meant. It was always used in such connections as to make it an interesting word to me. If a slave ran away and succeeded in getting clear, or if a slave killed his master, set fire to a barn, or did any thing very wrong in the mind of a slaveholder, it was spoken of as the fruit of *abolition*. Hearing the word in this connection very often, I set about learning what it meant. The dictionary afforded me little or no help. I found it was "the act of abolishing;" but then I did not know what was to be abolished. Here I was perplexed. I did not dare to ask any one about its meaning, for I was satisfied that it was something they wanted me to know very little about. After a patient waiting, I got one of our city papers, containing an account of the number of petitions from the north, praying for the abolition of slavery in the District of Columbia, and of the slave trade between the States. From this time I understood the words *abolition* and *abolitionist*, and always drew near when that word was spoken, expecting to hear something of importance to myself and fellow-slaves. The light broke in upon me by degrees. I went one day down on the wharf of Mr. Waters; and seeing two Irishmen unloading a scow of stone, I went, unasked, and helped them. When we had finished, one of them came to me and asked me if I were a slave. I told him I was. He asked, "Are ye a slave for life?" I told him that I was. The good Irishman seemed to be deeply affected by the statement. He said to the other that it was a pity so fine a little fellow as myself should be a slave for life. He said it was a shame to hold me. They both advised me to run away to the north; that I should find friends there, and that I should be free. I pretended not to be interested in what they said, and treated them as if I did not understand them; for I feared they might be treacherous. White men have been known to encourage slaves to escape, and then, to get the reward, catch them and return them to their masters. I was afraid that these seemingly good men might use me so; but I nevertheless remembered their advice, and from that time I resolved to run away. I looked forward to a time at which it would be safe for me to escape. I was too young to think of doing so immediately; besides, I wished to learn how to write, as I might have occasion to write my own pass. I consoled myself with the hope that I should one day find a good chance. Meanwhile, I would learn to write.

The idea as to how I might learn to write was suggested to me by being in Durgin and Bailey's ship-yard, and frequently seeing the ship carpenters, after hewing, and getting a piece of timber ready for use, write on the timber the name of that part of the ship for which it was intended. When a piece of timber was intended for the larboard side, it would be marked thus—"L." When a piece was for the starboard side, it would be marked thus—"S." A piece for the larboard side forward, would be marked thus—"L. F." When a piece was for starboard side forward, it would be marked thus—"S. F." For larboard aft, it would be marked thus—"L. A." For starboard aft, it would be marked thus—"S. A." I soon learned the names of these letters, and for what they were intended when placed upon a piece of timber in the ship-yard. I immediately commenced copying them, and in a short time was able to make the four letters named. After that, when I met with any boy who I knew could write, I would tell him I could write as well as he. The next word would be, "I don't believe you. Let me see you try it." I would then make the letters which I had been so fortunate as to learn, and ask him to beat that. In this way I got a good many lessons in writing, which it is quite possible I should never have gotten in any other way. During this time, my copy-book was the board fence, brick wall, and pavement; my pen and ink was a lump of chalk. With these, I learned mainly how to write. I then commenced and continued copying the Italics in Webster's Spelling Book, until I could make them all without looking at the book. By this time, my little Master Thomas had gone to school, and learned how to write, and had written over a number of copy-books. These had been brought home, and shown to some of our near neighbors, and then laid aside. My mistress used to go to class meeting at the Wilk Street meeting-house every Monday afternoon, and leave me to take care of the house. When left thus, I used to spend the time in writing in the spaces left in Master Thomas's copy-book, copying what he had written. I continued to do this until I could write a hand very similar to that of Master Thomas. Thus, after a long, tedious effort for years, I finally succeeded in learning how to write.

CHAPTER VIII

In a very short time after I went to live at Baltimore, my old master's youngest son Richard died; and in about three years and six months after his death, my old master, Captain Anthony, died, leaving only his son, Andrew, and daughter, Lucretia, to share his estate. He died while on a visit to see his daughter at Hillsborough. Cut off thus unexpectedly, he left no will as to the disposal of his property. It was therefore necessary to have a valuation of the property, that it might be equally divided between Mrs. Lucretia and Master Andrew. I was immediately sent for, to be valued with the other property. Here again my feelings rose up in detestation of slavery. I had now a new conception of my degraded condition. Prior to this, I had become, if not insensible to my lot, at least partly so. I left Baltimore with a young heart overborne with sadness, and a soul full of apprehension. I took passage with Captain Rowe, in the schooner Wild Cat, and, after a sail of about twenty-four hours, I found myself near the place of my birth. I had now been absent from it almost, if not quite, five years. I, however, remembered the place very well. I was only about five years old when I left it, to go and live with my old master on Colonel Lloyd's plantation; so that I was now between ten and eleven years old.

We were all ranked together at the valuation. Men and women, old and young, married and single, were ranked with horses, sheep, and swine. There were horses and men, cattle and women, pigs and children, all holding the same rank in the scale of being, and were all subjected to the same narrow examination. Silvery-headed age and sprightly youth, maids and matrons, had to undergo the same indelicate inspection. At this moment, I saw more clearly than ever the brutalizing effects of slavery upon both slave and slaveholder.

After the valuation, then came the division. I have no language to express the high excitement and deep anxiety which were felt among us poor slaves during this time. Our fate for life was now to be decided. We had no more voice in that decision than the brutes among whom we were ranked. A single word from the white men was enough—against all our wishes, prayers, and entreaties—to sunder forever the dearest friends, dearest kindred, and strongest ties known to human beings. In addition to the pain of separation, there was the horrid dread of falling into the hands of Master Andrew. He was known to us all as being a most cruel wretch,—a common drunkard, who had, by his reckless mismanagement and profligate dissipation, already wasted a large portion of his father's property. We all felt that we might as well be sold at once to the Georgia traders, as to pass into his hands; for we knew that that would be our inevitable condition,— a condition held by us all in the utmost horror and dread.

I suffered more anxiety than most of my fellow-slaves. I had known what it was to be kindly treated; they had known nothing of the kind. They had seen little or nothing of the world. They were in very deed men and women of sorrow, and acquainted with grief. Their backs had been made familiar with the bloody lash, so that they had become callous; mine was yet tender; for while at Baltimore I got few whippings, and few slaves could boast of a kinder master and mistress than myself; and the thought of passing out of their hands into those of Master Andrew—a man who, but a few days before, to give me a sample of his bloody disposition, took my little brother by the throat, threw him on the ground, and with the heel of his boot stamped upon his head till the blood gushed from his nose and ears—was well calculated to make me anxious as to my fate. After he had committed this savage outrage upon my brother, he turned to me, and said that was the way he meant to serve me one of these days,—meaning, I suppose, when I came into his possession.

Thanks to a kind Providence, I fell to the portion of Mrs. Lucretia, and was sent immediately back to Baltimore, to live again in the family of Master Hugh. Their joy at my return equalled their sorrow at my departure. It was a glad day to me. I had escaped a [fate] worse than lion's jaws. I was absent from Baltimore, for the purpose of valuation and division, just about one month, and it seemed to have been six.

Very soon after my return to Baltimore, my mistress, Lucretia, died, leaving her husband and one child, Amanda; and in a very short time after her death, Master Andrew died. Now all the property of my old master, slaves included, was in the hands of strangers,—strangers who had had nothing to do with accumulating it. Not a slave was left free. All remained slaves, from the youngest to the oldest. If any one thing in my experience, more than another, served to deepen my conviction of the infernal character of slavery, and to fill me with unutterable loathing of slaveholders, it was their base ingratitude to my poor old grandmother. She had served my old master faithfully from youth to old age. She had been the source of all his wealth; she had peopled his plantation with slaves; she had become a great grandmother in his service. She had rocked him in infancy, attended him in childhood, served him through life, and at his death wiped from his icy brow the cold death-sweat, and closed his eyes forever. She was nevertheless left a slave—a slave for life—a slave in the hands of strangers; and in their hands she saw her children, her grandchildren, and her great-grandchildren, divided, like so many sheep, without being gratified with the small privilege of a single word, as to their or her own des-

tiny. And, to cap the climax of their base ingratitude and fiendish barbarity, my grandmother, who was now very old, having outlived my
old master and all his children, having seen the beginning and end of
all of them, and her present owners finding she was of but little value,
her frame already racked with the pains of old age, and complete helplessness fast stealing over her once active limbs, they took her to the
woods, built her a little hut, put up a little mud-chimney, and then
made her welcome to the privilege of supporting herself there in perfect loneliness; thus virtually turning her out to die! If my poor old
grandmother now lives, she lives to suffer in utter loneliness; she lives
to remember and mourn over the loss of children, the loss of grandchildren, and the loss of great-grandchildren. They are, in the language of
the slave's poet, Whittier,—

> "Gone, gone, sold and gone
> To the rice swamp dank and lone,
> Where the slave-whip ceaseless swings,
> Where the noisome insect stings,
> Where the fever-demon strews
> Poison with the falling dews,
> Where the sickly sunbeams glare
> Through the hot and misty air:—
>   Gone, gone, sold and gone
>   To the rice swamp dank and lone,
>   From Virginia hills and waters—
>   Woe is me, my stolen daughters!"

The hearth is desolate. The children, the unconscious children,
who once sang and danced in her presence, are gone. She gropes her
way, in the darkness of age, for a drink of water. Instead of the voices
of her children, she hears by day the moans of the dove, and by night
the screams of the hideous owl. All is gloom. The grave is at the door.
And now, when weighed down by the pains and aches of old age,
when the head inclines to the feet, when the beginning and ending of
human existence meet, and helpless infancy and painful old age combine together—at this time, this most needful time, the time for the
exercise of that tenderness and affection which children only can exercise towards a declining parent—my poor old grandmother, the devoted mother of twelve children, is left all alone, in yonder little hut,
before a few dim embers. She stands—she sits—she staggers—she
falls—she groans—she dies—and there are none of her children or
grandchildren present, to wipe from her wrinkled brow the cold sweat
of death, or to place beneath the sod her fallen remains. Will not a
righteous God visit for these things?

In about two years after the death of Mrs. Lucretia, Master Thomas married his second wife. Her name was Rowena Hamilton. She was the eldest daughter of Mr. William Hamilton. Master now lived in St. Michael's. Not long after his marriage, a misunderstanding took place between himself and Master Hugh; and as a means of punishing his brother, he took me from him to live with himself at St. Michael's. Here I underwent another most painful separation. It, however, was not so severe as the one I dreaded at the division of property; for, during this interval, a great change had taken place in Master Hugh and his once kind and affectionate wife. The influence of brandy upon him, and of slavery upon her, had effected a disastrous change in the characters of both; so that, as far as they were concerned, I thought I had little to lose by the change. But it was not to them that I was attached. It was to those little Baltimore boys that I felt the strongest attachment. I had received many good lessons from them, and was still receiving them, and the thought of leaving them was painful indeed. I was leaving, too, without the hope of ever being allowed to return. Master Thomas had said he would never let me return again. The barrier betwixt himself and brother he considered impassable.

I then had to regret that I did not at least make the attempt to carry out my resolution to run away; for the chances of success are tenfold greater from the city than from the country.

I sailed from Baltimore for St. Michael's in the sloop Amanda, Captain Edward Dodson. On my passage, I paid particular attention to the direction which the steamboats took to go to Philadelphia. I found, instead of going down, on reaching North Point they went up the bay, in a north-easterly direction. I deemed this knowledge of the utmost importance. My determination to run away was again revived. I resolved to wait only so long as the offering of a favorable opportunity. When that came, I was determined to be off.

CHAPTER IX

I have now reached a period of my life when I can give dates. I left Baltimore, and went to live with Master Thomas Auld, at St. Michael's, in March, 1832. It was now more than seven years since I lived with him in the family of my old master, on Colonel Lloyd's plantation. We of course were now almost entire strangers to each other. He was to me a new master, and I to him a new slave. I was ignorant of his temper and disposition; he was equally so of mine. A very short time, however, brought us into full acquaintance with each other. I was made acquainted with his wife not less than with himself. They were well matched, being equally mean and cruel. I was now, for the first time during a space of more than seven years, made to feel the painful gnawings of hunger—a something which I had not experienced before since I left Colonel Lloyd's plantation. It went hard enough with me then, when I could look back to no period at which I had enjoyed a sufficiency. It was tenfold harder after living in Master Hugh's family, where I had always had enough to eat, and of that which was good. I have said Master Thomas was a mean man. He was so. Not to give a slave enough to eat, is regarded as the most aggravated development of meanness even among slaveholders. The rule is, no matter how coarse the food, only let there be enough of it. This is the theory; and in the part of Maryland from which I came, it is the general practice,—though there are many exceptions. Master Thomas gave us enough of neither coarse nor fine food. There were four slaves of us in the kitchen—my sister Eliza, my aunt Priscilla, Henny, and myself; and we were allowed less than a half bushel of corn-meal per week, and very little else, either in the shape of meat or vegetables. It was not enough for us to subsist upon. We were therefore reduced to the wretched necessity of living at the expense of our neighbors. This we did by begging and stealing, whichever came handy in the time of need, the one being considered as legitimate as the other. A great many times have we poor creatures been nearly perishing with hunger, when food in abundance lay mouldering in the safe and smoke-house, and our pious mistress was aware of the fact; and yet that mistress and her husband would kneel every morning, and pray that God would bless them in basket and store!

Bad as all slaveholders are, we seldom meet one destitute of every element of character commanding respect. My master was one of this rare sort. I do not know of one single noble act ever performed by him. The leading trait in his character was meanness; and if there were any other element in his nature, it was made subject to this. He was mean; and, like most other mean men, he lacked the ability to conceal his meanness. Captain Auld was not born a slaveholder. He had been a poor man, master only of a Bay craft. He came into possession of all his slaves by marriage; and of all men, adopted slaveholders are the worse. He was cruel, but cowardly. He commanded without firmness. In the enforcement of his rules, he was at times rigid, and at times lax. At times, he spoke to his slaves with the firmness of Napoleon and the fury of a demon; at other times, he might well be mistaken for an inquirer who had lost his way. He did nothing of himself. He might have passed for a lion, but for his ears. In all things noble which he attempted, his own meanness shone most conspicuous. His airs, words, and actions, were the airs, words, and actions of born slave-holders, and, being assumed, were awkward enough. He was not even a good imitator. He possessed all the disposition to deceive, but wanted the power. Having no resources within himself, he was compelled to be the copyist of many, and being such, he was forever the victim of inconsistency; and of consequence he was an object of contempt, and was held as such even by his slaves. The luxury of having slaves of his own to wait upon him was something new and unprepared for. He was a slaveholder without the ability to hold slaves. He found himself incapable of managing his slaves either by force, fear, or fraud. We seldom called him "master," we generally called him "Captain Auld," and were hardly disposed to title him at all. I doubt not that our conduct had much to do with making him appear awkward, and of consequence fretful. Our want of reverence for him must have perplexed him greatly. He wished to have us call him master, but lacked the firmness necessary to command us to do so. His wife used to insist upon our calling him so, but to no purpose. In August, 1832, my master attended a Methodist camp-meeting held in the Bay-side, Talbot county, and there experienced religion. I indulged a faint hope that his conversion would lead him to emancipate his slaves, and that, if he did not do this, it would, at any rate, make him more kind and humane. I was disappointed in both these respects. It neither made him to be humane to his slaves, nor to emancipate them. If it had any effect on his character, it made him more cruel and hateful in all his ways; for I believe him to have been a much worse man after his conversion than before. Prior to his conversion, he relied upon his own depravity to shield and sustain him in his savage barbarity; but after his conversion, he found religious sanction and support for his slave-holding cruelty. He made the greatest pretensions to piety. His house was the house of prayer. He prayed morning, noon, and night. He very soon distinguished himself among his brethren, and was soon made a class-leader and exhorter. His activity in revivals was great, and he proved himself an instrument in the hands of the church in converting many souls. His house was the preachers' home. They used to take great pleasure in coming there to put up; for while he starved us, he stuffed them. We have had three or four preachers there at a time. The names of those who used to come most frequently while I lived there, were Mr. Storks, Mr. Ewery, Mr. Humphry, and Mr. Hickey. I have also seen Mr. George Cookman at our house. We slaves loved Mr. Cookman. We believed him to be a good man. We thought him instrumental in getting Mr. Samuel Harrison, a very rich slave-holder, to emancipate his slaves; and by some means got the impression that he was laboring to effect the emancipation of all the slaves. When he was at our house, we were sure to be called in to prayers. When the other were there, we were sometimes called in and sometimes not. Mr. Cookman took more notice of us than either of the other ministers. He could not come among us without betraying his sympathy for us, and, stupid as we were, we had the sagacity to see it.

While I lived with my master in St. Michael's, there was a white young man, a Mr. Wilson, who proposed to keep a Sabbath school for the instruction of such slaves as might be disposed to learn to read the New Testament. We met but three times, when Mr. West and Mr. Fairbanks, both class-leaders, with many others, came upon us with sticks and other missiles, drove us off, and forbade us to meet again.

Thus ended our little Sabbath school in the pious town of St. Michael's.

I have said my master found religious sanction for his cruelty. As an example, I will state one of the many facts going to prove the charge. I have seen him tie up a lame young woman, and whip her with a heavy cowskin upon her naked shoulders, causing the warm red blood to drip; and, in justification of the bloody deed, he would quote this passage of Scripture—"He that knoweth his master's will, and doeth it not, shall be beaten with many stripes."

Master would keep this lacerated young woman tied up in this horrid situation four or five hours at a time. I have known him to tie her up early in the morning, and whip her before breakfast; leave her, go to his store, return at dinner, and whip her again, cutting her in the places already made raw with his cruel lash. The secret of master's cruelty toward "Henny" is found in the act of her being almost helpless. When quite a child, she fell into the fire, and burned herself horribly. Her hands were so burnt that she never got the use of them. She could do very little but bear heavy burdens. She was to master a bill of expense; and as he was a mean man, she was a constant offence to him. He seemed desirous of getting the poor girl out of existence. He gave her away once to his sister; but, being a poor gift, she was not disposed to keep her. Finally, my benevolent master, to use his own words, "set her adrift to take care of herself." Here was a recently-converted man, holding on upon the mother, and at the same time turning out her helpless child, to starve and die! Master Thomas was one of the many pious slaveholders who hold slaves for the very charitable purpose of taking care of them.

My master and myself had quite a number of differences. He found me unsuitable to his purpose. My city life, he said, had had a very pernicious effect upon me. It had almost ruined me for every good purpose, and fitted me for every thing which was bad. One of my greatest faults was that of letting his horse run away, and go down to his father-in-law's farm, which was about five miles from St. Michael's. I would then have to go after it. My reason for this kind of carelessness, or carefulness, was, that I could always get something to eat when I went there. Master William Hamilton, my master's father-in-law, always gave his slaves enough to eat. I never left there hungry, no matter how great the need of my speedy return. Master Thomas at length said he would stand it no longer. I had lived with him nine months, during which time he had given me a number of severe whippings, all to no good purpose. He resolved to put me out, as he said, to be broken; and, for this purpose, he let me for one year to a man named Edward Covey. Mr. Covey was a poor man, a farm-renter. He rented the place upon which he lived, as also the hands with which he tilled it. Mr. Covey had acquired a very high reputation for breaking young slaves, and this reputation was of immense value to him. It enabled him to get his farm tilled with much less expense to himself than he could have had it done without such a reputation. Some slave-holders thought it not much loss to allow Mr. Covey to have their slaves one year, for the sake of the training to which they were subjected, without any other compensation. He could hire young help with great ease, in consequence of this reputation. Added to the natural good qualities of Mr. Covey, he was a professor of religion—a pious soul—a member and class-leader in the Methodist church. All of this added weight to his reputation as a "nigger-breaker." I was aware of all the facts, having been made acquainted with them by a young man who had lived there. I nevertheless made the change gladly; for I was sure of getting enough to eat, which is not the smallest consideration to a hungry man.

CHAPTER X

I left Master Thomas's house, and went to live with Mr. Covey, on the 1st of January, 1833. I was now, for the first time in my life, a field hand. In my new employment, I found myself even more awkward than a country boy appeared to be in a large city. I had been at my new home but one week before Mr. Covey gave me a very severe whipping, cutting my back, causing the blood to run, and raising ridges on my flesh as large as my little finger. The details of this affair are as follows: Mr. Covey sent me, very early in the morning of one of our coldest days in the month of January, to the woods, to get a load of wood. He gave me a team of unbroken oxen. He told me which was the in-hand ox, and which the off-hand one. He then tied the end of a large rope around the horns of the in-hand ox, and gave me the other end of it, and told me, if the oxen started to run, that I must hold on upon the rope. I had never driven oxen before, and of course I was very awkward. I, however, succeeded in getting to the edge of the woods with little difficulty; but I had got a very few rods into the woods, when the oxen took fright, and started full tilt, carrying the cart against trees, and over stumps, in the most frightful manner. I expected every moment that my brains would be dashed out against the trees. After running thus for a considerable distance, they finally upset the cart, dashing it with great force against a tree, and threw themselves into a dense thicket. How I escaped death, I do not know. There I was, entirely alone, in a thick wood, in a place new to me. My cart was upset and shattered, my oxen were entangled among the young trees, and there was none to help me. After a long spell of effort, I succeeded in getting my cart righted, my oxen disentangled, and again yoked to the cart. I now proceeded with my team to the place where I had, the day before, been chopping wood, and loaded my cart pretty heavily, thinking in this way to tame my oxen. I then proceeded on my way home. I had now consumed one half of the day.

I got out of the woods safely, and now felt out of danger. I stopped my oxen to open the woods gate; and just as I did so, before I could get hold of my ox-rope, the oxen again started, rushed through the gate, catching it between the wheel and the body of the cart, tearing it to pieces, and coming within a few inches of crushing me against the gate-post. Thus twice, in one short day, I escaped death by the merest chance. On my return, I told Mr. Covey what had happened, and how it happened. He ordered me to return to the woods again immediately. I did so, and he followed on after me. Just as I got into the woods, he came up and told me to stop my cart, and that he would teach me how to trifle away my time, and break gates. He then went to a large gum-tree, and with his axe cut three large switches, and, after trimming them up neatly with his pocket-knife, he ordered me to take off my clothes. I made him no answer, but stood with my clothes on. He repeated his order. I still made him no answer, nor did I move to strip myself. Upon this he rushed at me with the fierceness of a tiger, tore off my clothes, and lashed me till he had worn out his switches, cutting me so savagely as to leave the marks visible for a long time after. This whipping was the first of a number just like it, and for similar offences.

I lived with Mr. Covey one year. During the first six months, of that year, scarce a week passed without his whipping me. I was seldom free from a sore back. My awkwardness was almost always his excuse for whipping me. We were worked fully up to the point of endurance. Long before day we were up, our horses fed, and by the first approach of day we were off to the field with our hoes and ploughing teams. Mr. Covey gave us enough to eat, but scarce time to eat it. We were often less than five minutes taking our meals. We were often in the field from the first approach of day till its last lingering ray had left us; and at saving-fodder time, midnight often caught us in the field binding blades.

Covey would be out with us. The way he used to stand it, was this. He would spend the most of his afternoons in bed. He would then come out fresh in the evening, ready to urge us on with his words, example, and frequently with the whip. Mr. Covey was one of the few slaveholders who could and did work with his hands. He was a hard-working man. He knew by himself just what a man or a boy could do. There was no deceiving him. His work went on in his absence almost as well as in his presence; and he had the faculty of making us feel that he was ever present with us. This he did by surprising us. He seldom approached the spot where we were at work openly, if he could do it secretly. He always aimed at taking us by surprise. Such was his cunning, that we used to call him, among ourselves, "the snake." When we were at work in the cornfield, he would sometimes crawl on his hands and knees to avoid detection, and all at once he would rise nearly in our midst, and scream out, "Ha, ha! Come, come!

Dash on, dash on!" This being his mode of attack, it was never safe to stop a single minute. His comings were like a thief in the night. He appeared to us as being ever at hand. He was under every tree, behind every stump, in every bush, and at every window, on the plantation. He would sometimes mount his horse, as if bound to St. Michael's, a distance of seven miles, and in half an hour afterwards you would see him coiled up in the corner of the wood-fence, watching every motion of the slaves. He would, for this purpose, leave his horse tied up in the woods. Again, he would sometimes walk up to us, and give us orders as though he was upon the point of starting on a long journey, turn his back upon us, and make as though he was going to the house to get ready; and, before he would get half way thither, he would turn short and crawl into a fence-corner, or behind some tree, and there watch us till the going down of the sun.

Mr. Covey's *forte* consisted in his power to deceive. His life was devoted to planning and perpetrating the grossest deceptions. Every thing he possessed in the shape of learning or religion, he made conform to his disposition to deceive. He seemed to think himself equal to deceiving the Almighty. He would make a short prayer in the morning, and a long prayer at night; and, strange as it may seem, few men would at times appear more devotional than he. The exercises of his family devotions were always commenced with singing; and, as he was a very poor singer himself, the duty of raising the hymn generally came upon me. He would read his hymn, and nod at me to commence. I would at times do so; at others, I would not. My non-compliance would almost always produce much confusion. To show himself independent of me, he would start and stagger through with his hymn in the most discordant manner. In this state of mind, he prayed with more than ordinary spirit. Poor man! such was his disposition, and success at deceiving, I do verily believe that he sometimes deceived himself into the solemn belief, that he was a sincere worshipper of the most high God; and this, too, at a time when he may be said to have been guilty of compelling his woman slave to commit the sin of adultery. The facts in the case are these: Mr. Covey was a poor man; he was just commencing in life; he was only able to buy one slave; and, shocking as is the fact, he bought her, as he said, for *a breeder*. This woman was named Caroline. Mr. Covey bought her from Mr. Thomas Lowe, about six miles from St. Michael's. She was a large, able-bodied woman, about twenty years old. She had already given birth to one child, which proved her to be just what he wanted. After buying her, he hired a married man of Mr. Samuel Harrison, to live with him one year; and him he used to fasten up with her every night! The result was, that, at the end of the year, the miserable woman gave birth to twins. At this result Mr. Covey seemed to be highly pleased, both with the man and the wretched woman. Such was his joy, and that of his wife, that nothing they could do for Caroline during her confinement was too good, or too hard, to be done. The children were regarded as being quite an addition to his wealth.

If at any one time of my life more than another, I was made to drink the bitterest dregs of slavery, that time was during the first six months of my stay with Mr. Covey. We were worked in all weathers. It was never too hot or too cold; it could never rain, blow, hail, or snow, too hard for us to work in the field. Work, work, work, was scarcely more the order of the day than of the night. The longest days were too short for him, and the shortest nights too long for him. I was somewhat unmanageable when I first went there, but a few months of this discipline tamed me. Mr. Covey succeeded in breaking me. I was broken in body, soul, and spirit. My natural elasticity was crushed, my intellect languished, the disposition to read departed, the cheerful spark that lingered about my eye died; the dark night of slavery closed in upon me; and behold a man transformed into a brute!

Sunday was my only leisure time. I spent this in a sort of beast-like stupor, between sleep and wake, under some large tree. At times I would rise up, a flash of energetic freedom would dart through my soul, accompanied with a faint beam of hope, that flickered for a moment, and then vanished. I sank down again, mourning over my wretched condition. I was sometimes prompted to take my life, and that of Covey, but was prevented by a combination of hope and fear. My sufferings on this plantation seem now like a dream rather than a stern reality.

Our house stood within a few rods of the Chesapeake Bay, whose broad bosom was ever white with sails from every quarter of the habitable globe. Those beautiful vessels, robed in purest white, so delightful to the eye of freemen, were to me so many shrouded ghosts, to terrify and torment me with thoughts of my wretched condition. I have often, in the deep stillness of a summer's Sabbath, stood all alone upon the lofty banks of that noble bay, and traced, with saddened heart and tearful eye, the countless number of sails moving off to the mighty ocean. The sight of these always affected me powerfully. My thoughts would compel utterance; and there, with no audience but the Almighty, I would pour out my soul's complaint, in my rude way, with an apostrophe to the moving multitude of ships:—

"You are loosed from your moorings, and are free; I am fast in my chains, and am a slave! You move merrily before the gentle gale, and I sadly before the bloody whip! You are freedom's swift-winged angels, that fly round the world; I am confined in bands of iron! O that I were free! O, that I were on one of your gallant decks, and under your protecting wing! Alas! betwixt me and you, the turbid waters roll. Go on, go on. O, that I could also go! Could I but swim! If I could fly! O, why was I born a man, of whom to make a brute! The glad ship is gone; she hides in the dim distance. I am left in the hottest hell of unending slavery. O God, save me! God, deliver me! Let me be free! Is there any

God! Why am I a slave? I will run away. I will not stand it. Get caught, or get clear, I'll try it. I had as well die with ague as the fever. I have only one life to lose. I had as well be killed running as die standing. Only think of it; one hundred miles straight north, and I am free! Try it? Yes! God helping me, I will. It cannot be that I shall live and die a slave. I will take to the water. This very bay shall yet bear me into freedom. The steamboats steered in a north-east course from North Point. I will do the same; and when I get to the head of the bay, I will turn my canoe adrift, and walk straight through Delaware into Pennsylvania. When I get there, I shall not be required to have a pass; I can travel without being disturbed. Let but the first opportunity offer, and, come what will, I am off. Meanwhile, I will try to bear up under the yoke. I am not the only slave in the world. Why should I fret? I can bear as much as any of them. Besides, I am but a boy, and all boys are bound to some one. It may be that my misery in slavery will only increase my happiness when I get free. There is a better day coming."

Thus I used to think, and thus I used to speak to myself; goaded almost to madness at one moment, and at the next reconciling myself to my wretched lot.

I have already intimated that my condition was much worse, during the first six months of my stay at Mr. Covey's, than in the last six. The circumstances leading to the change in Mr. Covey's course toward me form an epoch in my humble history. You have seen how a man was made a slave; you shall see how a slave was made a man. On one of the hottest days of the month of August, 1833, Bill Smith, William Hughes, a slave named Eli, and myself, were engaged in fanning wheat. Hughes was clearing the fanned wheat from before the fan, Eli was turning, Smith was feeding, and I was carrying wheat to the fan. The work was simple, requiring strength rather than intellect; yet, to one entirely unused to such work, it came very hard. About three o'clock of that day, I broke down; my strength failed me; I was seized with a violent aching of the head, attended with extreme dizziness; I trembled in every limb. Finding what was coming, I nerved myself up, feeling it would never do to stop work. I stood as long as I could stagger to the hopper with grain. When I could stand no longer, I fell, and felt as if held down by an immense weight. The fan of course stopped; every one had his own work to do; and no one could do the work of the other, and have his own go on at the same time.

Mr. Covey was at the house, about one hundred yards from the treading-yard where we were fanning. On hearing the fan stop, he left immediately, and came to the spot where we were. He hastily inquired what the matter was. Bill answered that I was sick, and there was no one to bring wheat to the fan. I had by this time crawled away under the side of the post and rail-fence by which the yard was enclosed, hoping to find relief by getting out of the sun. He then asked where I was. He was told by one of the hands. He came to the spot, and, after looking at me awhile, asked me what was the matter. I told him as well as I could, for I scarce had strength to speak. He then gave me a savage kick in the side, and told me to get up. I tried to do so, but fell back in the attempt. He gave me another kick, and again told me to rise. I again tried, and succeeded in gaining my feet; but, stooping to get the tub with which I was feeding the fan, I again staggered and fell. While down in this situation, Mr. Covey took up the hickory slat with which Hughes had been striking off the half-bushel measure, and with it gave me a heavy blow upon the head, making a large wound, and the blood ran freely; and with this again told me to get up. I made no effort to comply, having now made up my mind to let him do his worst. In a short time after receiving this blow, my head grew better. Mr. Covey had now left me to my fate. At this moment I resolved, for the first time, to go to my master, enter a complaint, and ask his protection. In order to [do] this, I must that afternoon walk seven miles; and this, under the circumstances, was truly a severe undertaking. I was exceedingly feeble; made so as much by the kicks and blows which I received, as by the severe fit of sickness to which I had been subjected. I, however, watched my chance, while Covey was looking in an opposite direction, and started for St. Michael's. I succeeded in getting a considerable distance on my way to the woods, when Covey discovered me, and called after me to come back, threatening what he would do if I did not come. I disregarded both his calls and his threats, and made my way to the woods as fast as my feeble state would allow; and thinking I might be overhauled by him if I kept the road, I walked through the woods, keeping far enough from the road to avoid detection, and near enough to prevent losing my way. I had not gone far before my little strength again failed me. I could go no farther. I fell down, and lay for a considerable time. The blood was yet oozing from the wound on my head. For a time I thought I should bleed to death; and think now that I should have done so, but that the blood so matted my hair as to stop the wound. After lying there about three quarters of an hour, I nerved myself up again, and started on my way, through bogs and briers, barefooted and bareheaded, tearing my feet sometimes at nearly every step; and after a journey of about seven miles, occupying some five hours to perform it, I arrived at master's store. I then presented an appearance enough to affect any but a heart of iron. From the crown of my head to my feet, I was covered with blood. My hair was all clotted with dust and blood; my shirt was stiff with blood. My legs and feet were torn in sundry places with briers and thorns, and were also covered with blood. I suppose I looked like a man who had escaped a den of wild beasts, and barely escaped them. In this state I appeared before my master, humbly entreating him to interpose his authority for my protection. I told him all the circumstances as well as I could, and it seemed, as I spoke, at times to affect him. He would then walk the floor, and seek to justify Covey by saying he expected I deserved it. He asked me what I wanted. I told him, to let me get a new home; that as sure as I lived with Mr. Covey again, I should live with but to die with him; that Covey would surely kill me; he was in a fair way for it. Master Thomas ridiculed the idea that there was any danger of Mr. Covey's killing me, and said that he knew Mr. Covey; that he was a good man, and that he could not think of taking me from him; that, should he do so, he would lose the whole year's wages; that I belonged to Mr. Covey for one year, and that I must go back to him, come what might; and that I must not trouble him with any more stories, or that he would himself *get hold of me*. After threatening me thus, he gave me a very large dose of salts, telling me that I might remain in St. Michael's that night, (it being quite late,) but that I must be off back to Mr. Covey's early in the morning; and that if I did not, he would *get hold of me*, which meant that he would whip me. I remained all night, and, according to his orders, I started off to Covey's in the morning, (Saturday morning,) wearied in body and broken in spirit. I got no supper that night, or breakfast that morning. I reached Covey's about nine o'clock; and just as I was getting over the fence that divided Mrs. Kemp's fields from ours, out ran Covey with his cowskin, to give me another whipping. Before he could reach me, I succeeded in getting to the cornfield; and as the corn was very high, it afforded me the means of hiding. He seemed very angry, and searched for me a long time. My behavior was altogether unaccountable. He finally gave up the chase, thinking, I suppose, that I must come home for something to eat; he would give himself no further trouble in looking for me. I spent that day mostly in the woods, having the alternative before me,—to go home and be whipped to death, or stay in the woods and be starved to death. That night, I fell in with Sandy Jenkins, a slave with whom I was somewhat acquainted. Sandy had a free wife, who lived about four miles from Mr. Covey's; and it being Saturday, he was on his way to see her. I told him my circumstances, and he very kindly invited me to go home with him. I went home with him, and talked this whole matter over, and got his advice as to what course it was best for me to pursue. I found Sandy an old adviser. He told me, with great solemnity, I must go back to Covey; but that before I went, I must go with him into another part of the woods, where there was a certain *root*, which, if I would take some of it with me, carrying it *always on my right side*, would render it impossible for Mr. Covey, or any other white man, to whip me. He said he had carried it for years; and since he had done so, he had never received a blow, and never expected to while he carried it. I at first rejected the idea, that the simple carrying of a root in my pocket would have any such effect as he had said, and was not disposed to take it; but Sandy impressed the necessity with much earnestness, telling me it could do no harm, if it did no good. To please him, I at length took the root, and, according to his direction, carried it upon my right side. This was Sunday morning. I immediately started for home; and upon entering the yard gate, out came Mr. Covey on his way to meeting. He spoke to me very kindly, bade me drive the pigs from a lot near by, and passed on towards the church. Now, this singular conduct of Mr. Covey really made me begin to think that there was something in the *root* which Sandy had given me; and had it been on any other day than Sunday, I could have attributed the conduct to no other cause than the influence of that root; and as it was, I was half inclined to think the *root* to be something more than I at first had taken it to be. All went well till Monday morning. On this morning, the virtue of the *root* was fully tested. Long before daylight, I was called to go and rub, curry, and feed, the horses. I obeyed, and was glad to obey. But whilst thus engaged, whilst in the act of throwing down some blades from the loft, Mr. Covey entered the stable with a long rope; and just as I was half out of the loft, he caught hold of my legs, and was about tying me. As soon as I found what he was up to, I gave a sudden spring, and as I did so, he holding to my legs, I was brought sprawling on the stable floor. Mr. Covey seemed now to think he had me, and could do what he pleased; but at this moment—from whence came the spirit I don't know—I resolved to fight; and, suiting my action to the resolution, I seized Covey hard by the throat; and as I did so, I rose. He held on to me, and I to him. My resistance was so entirely unexpected, that Covey seemed taken all aback. He trembled like a leaf. This gave me assurance, and I held him uneasy, causing the blood to run where I touched him with the ends of my fingers. Mr. Covey soon called out to Hughes for help. Hughes came, and, while Covey held me, attempted to tie my right hand. While he was in the act of doing so, I watched my chance, and gave him a heavy kick close under the ribs. This kick fairly sickened Hughes, so that he left me in the hands of Mr. Covey. This kick had the effect of not only weakening Hughes, but Covey also. When he saw Hughes bending over with pain, his courage quailed. He asked me if I meant to persist in my resistance. I told him I did, come what might; that he had used me like a brute for six months, and that I was determined to be used so no longer. With that, he strove to drag me to a stick that was lying just out of the stable door. He meant to knock me down. But just as he was leaning over to get the stick, I seized him with both hands by his collar, and brought him by a sudden snatch to the ground. By this time, Bill came. Covey called upon him for assistance. Bill wanted to know what he could do. Covey said, "Take hold of him, take hold of him!" Bill said his master hired him out to work, and not to help to whip me; so he left Covey and myself to fight out own battle out. We were at it for nearly two hours. Covey at length let me go, puffing and blowing at a great rate, saying that if I had not resisted, he would not have whipped me half so much. The truth was, that he had not whipped me at all. I considered him as getting entirely the worst end of the bargain; for he had drawn no blood from me, but

I had from him. The whole six months afterwards, that I spent with Mr. Covey, he never laid the weight of his finger upon me in anger. He would occasionally say, he didn't want to get hold of me again. "No," thought I, "you need not; for you will come off worse than you did before."

This battle with Mr. Covey was the turning-point in my career as a slave. It rekindled the few expiring embers of freedom, and revived within me a sense of my own manhood. It recalled the departed self-confidence, and inspired me again with a determination to be free. The gratification afforded by the triumph was a full compensation for whatever else might follow, even death itself. He only can understand the deep satisfaction which I experience, who has himself repelled by force the bloody arm of slavery. I felt as I never felt before. It was a glorious resurrection, for the tomb of slavery, to the heaven of freedom. My long-crushed spirit rose, cowardice departed, bold defiance took its place; and I now resolved that, however long I might remain a slave in form, the day has passed forever when I could be a slave in fact. I did not hesitate to let it be known of me, that the white man who expected to succeed in whipping, must also succeed in killing me.

From this time I was never again what might be called fairly whipped, though I remained a slave four years afterwards. I had several fights, but was never whipped.

It was for a long time a matter of surprise to me why Mr. Covey did not immediately have me taken by the constable to the whipping-post, and there regularly whipped for the crime of raising my hand against a white man in defence of myself. And the only explanation I can now think of does not entirely satisfy me; but such as it is, I will give it. Mr. Covey enjoyed the most unbounded reputation for being a first-rate overseer and negro-breaker. It was of considerable importance to him. That reputation was at stake; and had he sent me—a boy about sixteen years old—to the public whipping-post, his reputation would have been lost; so, to save his reputation, he suffered me to go unpunished.

My term of actual service to Mr. Edward Covey ended on Christmas day, 1833. The days between Christmas and New Year's day are allowed as holidays; and, accordingly, we were not required to perform any labor, more than to feed and take care of the stock. This time we regarded as our own, by the grace of our masters; and we therefore used or abused it nearly as we pleased. Those of us who had families at a distance, were generally allowed to spend the whole six days in their society. This time, however, was spent in various ways. The staid, sober, thinking and industrious ones of our number would employ themselves in making corn-brooms, mats, horse-collars, and baskets; and another class of us would spend the time in hunting opossums, hares, and coons. But by far the larger part engaged in such sports and merriments as playing ball, wrestling, running foot-races, fiddling, dancing, and drinking whiskey; and this latter mode of spending the time was by far the most agreeable to the feelings of our masters. A slave who would work during the holidays was considered by our masters as scarcely deserving them. He was regarded as one who rejected the favor of his master. It was deemed a disgrace not to get drunk at Christmas; and he was regarded as lazy indeed, who had not provided himself with the necessary means, during the year, to get whisky enough to last him through Christmas.

From what I know of the effect of these holidays upon the slave, I believe them to be among the most effective means in the hands of the slaveholder in keeping down the spirit of insurrection. Were the slaveholders at once to abandon this practice, I have not the slightest doubt it would lead to an immediate insurrection among the slaves. These holidays serve as conductors, or safety-valves, to carry off the rebellious spirit of enslaved humanity. But for these, the slave would be forced up to the wildest desperation; and woe betide the slave-holder, the day he ventures to remove or hinder the operation of those conductors! I warn him that, in such an event, a spirit will go forth in their midst, more to be dreaded than the most appalling earthquake.

The holidays are part and parcel of the gross fraud, wrong, and inhumanity of slavery. They are professedly a custom established by the benevolence of the slaveholders; but I undertake to say, it is the result of selfishness, and one of the grossest frauds committed upon the down-trodden slave. They do not give the slaves this time because they would not like to have their work during its continuance, but because they know it would be unsafe to deprive them of it. This will be seen by the fact, that the slaveholders like to have their slaves spend those days just in such a manner as to make them as glad of their ending as of their beginning. Their object seems to be, to disgust their slaves with freedom, by plunging them into the lowest depths of dissipation. For instance, the slaveholders not only like to see the slave drink of his own accord, but will adopt various plans to make him drunk. One plan is, to make bets on their slaves, as to who can drink the most whiskey without getting drunk; and in this way they succeed in getting whole multitudes to drink to excess. Thus, when the slave asks for virtuous freedom, the cunning slaveholder, knowing his ignorance, cheats him with a dose of vicious dissipation, artfully labelled with the name of liberty. The most of us used to drink it down, and the result was just what might be supposed: many of us were led to think that there was little to choose between liberty and slavery. We felt, and very properly too, that we had almost as well be slaves to man as to rum. So, when the holidays ended, we staggered up from the filth of our wallowing, took a long breath, and marched to the field,—feeling, upon the whole, rather glad to go, from what our master had deceived us into a belief was freedom, back to the arms of slavery.

I have said that this mode of treatment is a part of the whole system of fraud and inhumanity of slavery. It is so. The mode here adopted to disgust the slave with freedom, by allowing him to see only the abuse of it, is carried out in other things. For instance, a slave loves molasses; he steals some. His master, in many cases, goes off to town, and buys a large quantity; he returns, takes his whip, and commands the slave to eat the molasses, until the poor fellow is made sick at the very mention of it. The same mode is sometimes adopted to make the slaves refrain from asking for more food than their regular allowance. A slave runs through his allowance, and applies for more. His master is enraged at him; but, not willing to send him off without food, gives him more than is necessary, and compels him to eat it within a given time. Then, if he complains that he cannot eat it, he is said to be satisfied neither full nor fasting, and is whipped for being hard to please! I have an abundance of such illustrations of the same principle, drawn from my own observation, but think the cases I have cited sufficient. The practice is a very common one.

On the first of January, 1834, I left Mr. Covey, and went to live with Mr. William Freeland, who lived about three miles from St. Michael's. I soon found Mr. Freeland a very different man from Mr. Covey. Though not rich, he was what would be called an educated southern gentleman. Mr. Covey, as I have shown, was a well-trained negro-breaker and slave-driver. The former (slaveholder though he was) seemed to possess some regard for honor, some reverence for justice, and some respect for humanity. The latter seemed totally insensible to all such sentiments. Mr. Freeland had many of the faults peculiar to slaveholders, such as being very passionate and fretful; but I must do him the justice to say, that he was exceedingly free from those degrading vices to which Mr. Covey was constantly addicted. The one was open and frank, and we always knew where to find him. The other was a most artful deceiver, and could be understood only by such as were skilful enough to detect his cunningly-devised frauds. Another advantage I gained in my new master was, he made no pretensions to, or profession of, religion; and this, in my opinion, was truly a great advantage. I assert most unhesitatingly, that the religion of the south is a mere covering for the most horrid crimes,—a justifier of the most appalling barbarity,—a sanctifier of the most hateful frauds,—and a dark shelter under, which the darkest, foulest, grossest, and most infernal deeds of slaveholders find the strongest protection. Were I to be again reduced to the chains of slavery, next to that enslavement, I should regard being the slave of a religious master the greatest calamity that could befall me. For of all slaveholders with whom I have ever met, religious slaveholders are the worst. I have ever found them the meanest and basest, and most cruel and cowardly, of all others. It was my unhappy lot not only to belong to a religious slaveholder, but to live in a community of such religionists.

71

Very near Mr. Freeland lived the Rev. Daniel Weeden, and in the same neighborhood lived the Rev. Rigby Hopkins. These were members and ministers in the Reformed Methodist Church. Mr. Weeden owned, among others, a woman slave, whose name I have forgotten. This woman's back, for weeks, was kept literally raw, made so by the lash of this merciless, *religious* wretch. He used to hire hands. His maxim was, Behave well or behave ill, it is the duty of a master occasionally to whip a slave, to remind him of his master's authority. Such was his theory, and such his practice.

Mr. Hopkins was even worse than Mr. Weeden. His chief boast was his ability to manage slaves. The peculiar feature of his government was that of whipping slaves in advance of deserving it. He always managed to have one or more of his slaves to whip every Monday morning. He did this to alarm their fears, and strike terror into those who escaped. His plan was to whip for the smallest offences, to prevent the commission of large ones. Mr. Hopkins could always find some excuse for whipping a slave. It would astonish one, unaccustomed to a slaveholding life, to see with what wonderful ease a slaveholder can find things, of which to make occasion to whip a slave. A mere look, word, or motion,—a mistake, accident, or want of power,—are all matters for which a slave may be whipped at any time. Does a slave look dissatisfied? It is said, he has the devil in him, and it must be whipped out. Does he speak loudly when spoken to by his master? Then he is getting high-minded, and should be taken down a button-hole lower. Does he forget to pull off his hat at the approach of a white person? Then he is wanting in reverence, and should be whipped for it. Does he ever venture to vindicate his conduct, when censured for it? Then he is guilty of impudence,—one of the greatest crimes of which a slave can be guilty. Does he ever venture to suggest a different mode of doing things from that pointed out by his master? He is indeed presumptuous, and getting above himself; and nothing less than a flogging will do for him. Does he, while ploughing, break a plough,—or, while hoeing, break a hoe? It is owning to his carelessness, and for it a slave must always be whipped. Mr. Hopkins could always find something of this sort to justify the use of the lash, and he seldom failed to embrace such opportunities. There was not a man in the whole county, with whom the slaves who had the getting their own home, would not prefer to live, rather than with this Rev. Mr. Hopkins. And yet there was not a man any where round, who made higher professions of religion, or was more active in revivals,—more attentive to the class, love-feast, prayer and preaching meetings, or more devotional in his family,—that prayed earlier, later, louder, and longer,—than this same reverend slave-driver, Rigby Hopkins.

But to return to Mr. Freeland, and to my experience while in his employment. He, like Mr. Covey, gave us enough to eat; but, unlike Mr. Covey, he also gave us sufficient time to take our meals. He worked us hard, but always between sunrise and sunset. He required a good deal of work to be done, but gave us good tools with which to work. His farm was large, but he employed hands enough to work it, and with ease, compared with many of his neighbors. My treatment, while in his employment, was heavenly, compared with what I experienced at the hands of Mr. Edward Covey.

Mr. Freeland was himself the owner of but two slaves. Their names were Henry Harris and John Harris. The rest of his hands he hired. These consisted of myself, Sandy Jenkins,* and Handy Caldwell. Henry and John were quite intelligent, and in a very little while after I went there, I succeeded in creating in them a strong desire to learn how to read. This desire soon sprang up in the others also. They very soon mustered up some old spelling-books, and nothing would do but that I must keep a Sabbath school. I agreed to do so, and accordingly devoted my Sundays to teaching these my loved fellow-slaves how to read. Neither of them knew his letters when I went there. Some of the slaves of the neighboring farms found what was going on, and also availed themselves of this little opportunity to learn to read. It was understood, among all who came, that there must be as little display about it as possible. It was necessary to keep our religious masters at St. Michael's unacquainted with the fact, that, instead of spending the Sabbath in wrestling, boxing, and drinking whisky, we were trying to learn how to read the will of God; for they had much rather see us engaged in those degrading sports, than to see us behaving like intellectual, moral, and accountable beings. My blood boils as I think of the bloody manner in which Messrs. Wright Fairbanks and Garrison West, both class-leaders, in connection with many others, rushed in upon us with sticks and stones, and broke up our virtuous little Sabbath school, at St. Michael's—all calling themselves Christians! humble followers of the Lord Jesus Christ! But I am again digressing.

I held my Sabbath school at the house of a free colored man, whose name I deem it imprudent to mention; for should it be known, it might embarrass him greatly, though the crime of holding the school was committed ten years ago. I had at one time over forty scholars, and those of the right sort, ardently desiring to learn. They were of all ages, though mostly men and women. I look back to those Sundays with an amount of pleasure not to be expressed. They were great days to my soul. The work of instructing my dear fellow-slaves was the sweetest engagement with which I was ever blessed. We loved each other, and to leave them at the close of the Sabbath was a severe cross indeed. When I think that these precious souls are to-day shut up in the prison-

---

*This is the same man who gave me the roots to prevent my being whipped by Mr. Covey. He was "a clever soul." We used frequently to talk about the fight with Covey, and as often as we did so, he would claim my success as the result of the roots which he gave me. This superstition is very common among the more ignorant slaves. A slave seldom dies but this his death is attributed to trickery.

house of slavery, my feelings overcome me, and I am almost ready to ask, "Does a righteous God govern the universe? and for what does he hold the thunders in his right hand, if not to smite the oppressor, and deliver the spoiled out of the hand of the spoiler?" These dear souls came not to Sabbath school because it was popular to do so, nor did I teach them because it was reputable to be thus engaged. Every moment they spent in that school, they were liable to be taken up, and given thirty-nine lashes. They came because they wished to learn. Their minds had been starved by their cruel masters. They had been shut up in mental darkness. I taught them, because it was the delight of my soul to be doing something that looked like bettering the condition of my race. I kept up my school nearly the whole year I lived with Mr. Freeland; and, beside my Sabbath school, I devoted three evenings in the week, during the winter, to teaching the slaves at home. And I have the happiness to know, that several of those who came to Sabbath school learned how to read; and that one, at least, is now free through my agency.

The year passed off smoothly. It seemed only about half as long as the year which preceded it. I went through it without receiving a single blow. I will give Mr. Freeland the credit of being the best master I ever had, *till I became my own master*. For the ease with which I passed the year, I was, however, somewhat indebted to the society of my fellow-slaves. They were noble souls; they not only possessed loving hearts, but brave ones. We were linked and interlinked with each other. I loved them with a love stronger than any thing I have experienced since. It is sometimes said that we slaves do not love and confide in each other. In answer to this assertion, I can say, I never loved any or confided in any people more than my fellow-slaves, and especially those with whom I lived at Mr. Freeland's. I believe we would have died for each other. We never undertook to do any thing, of any importance, without a mutual consultation. We never moved separately. We were one; and as much so by our tempers and dispositions, as by the mutual hardships to which we were necessarily subjected by our condition as slaves.

At the close of the year 1834, Mr. Freeland again hired me of my master, for the year 1835. But, by this time, I began to want to live *upon free land* as well as *with Freeland*; and I was no longer content, therefore, to live with him or any other slaveholder. I began, with the commencement of the year, to prepare myself for a final struggle, which should decide my fate one way or the other. My tendency was upward. I was fast approaching manhood, and year after year had passed, and I was still a slave. These thoughts roused me—I must do something. I therefore resolved that 1835 should not pass without witnessing an attempt, on my part, to secure my liberty. But I was not willing to cherish this determination alone. My fellow-slaves were dear to me. I was anxious to have them participate with me in this, my life-giving determination. I therefore, though with great prudence, commenced early to ascertain their views and feelings in regard to their condition, and to imbue their minds with thoughts of freedom. I bent myself to devising ways and means for our escape, and meanwhile strove, on all fitting occasions, to impress them with the gross fraud and inhumanity of slavery. I went first to Henry, next to John, then to the others. I found, in them all, warm hearts and noble spirits. They were ready to hear, and ready to act when a feasible plan should be proposed. This was what I wanted. I talked to them of our want of manhood, if we submitted to our enslavement without at least one noble effort to be free. We met often, and consulted frequently, and told our hopes and fears, recounted the difficulties, real and imagined, which we should be called on to meet. At times we were almost disposed to give up, and try to content ourselves with our wretched lot; at others, we were firm and unbending in our determination to go. Whenever we suggested any plan, there was shrinking—the odds were fearful. Our path was beset with the greatest obstacles; and if we succeeded in gaining the end of it, our right to be free was yet questionable—we were yet liable to be returned to bondage. We could see no spot, this side of the ocean, where we could be free. We knew nothing about Canada. Our knowledge of the north did not extend farther than New York; and to go there, and be forever harassed with the frightful liability of being returned to slavery—with the certainty of being treated tenfold worse than before—the thought was truly a horrible one, and one which it was not easy to overcome. The case sometimes stood thus: At every gate through which we were to pass, we saw a watchman—at every ferry a guard—on every bridge a sentinel—and in every wood a patrol. We were hemmed in upon every side. Here were the difficulties, real or imagined—the good to be sought, and the evil to be shunned. On the one hand, there stood slavery, a stern reality, glaring frightfully upon us,—its robes already crimsoned with the blood of millions, and even now feasting itself greedily upon our own flesh. On the other hand, away back in the dim distance, under the flickering light of the north star, behind some craggy hill or snow-covered mountain, stood a doubtful freedom—half frozen—beckoning us to come and share its hospitality. This in itself was sometimes enough to stagger us; but when we permitted ourselves to survey the road, we were frequently appalled. Upon either side we saw grim death, assuming the most horrid shapes. Now it was starvation, causing us to eat our own flesh;—now we were contending with the waves, and were drowned;—now we were overtaken, and torn to pieces by the fangs of the terrible bloodhound. We were stung by scorpions, chased by wild beasts, bitten by snakes, and finally, after having nearly reached the desired spot,—after swimming rivers, encountering wild beasts, sleeping in the woods, suffering hunger and nakedness,—we were overtaken by our pursuers, and, in our resistance, we were shot dead upon the spot! I say, this picture sometimes appalled us, and made us

> "rather bear those ills we had,
> Than fly to others, that we knew not of."

In coming to a fixed determination to run away, we did more than Patrick Henry, when he resolved upon liberty or death. With us it was a doubtful liberty at most, and almost certain death if we failed. For my part, I should prefer death to hopeless bondage.

Sandy, one of our number, gave up the notion, but still encouraged us. Our company then consisted of Henry Harris, John Harris, Henry Bailey, Charles Roberts, and myself. Henry Bailey was my uncle, and belonged to my master. Charles married my aunt; he belonged to my master's father-in-law, Mr. William Hamilton.

The plan we finally concluded upon was, to get a large canoe belonging to Mr. Hamilton, and upon the Saturday night previous to Easter holidays, paddle directly up the Chesapeake Bay. On our arrival at the head of the bay, a distance of seventy or eighty miles from where we lived, it was our purpose to turn our canoe adrift, and follow the guidance of the north star till we got beyond the limits of Maryland. Our reason for taking the water route was, that we were less liable to be suspected as runaways; we hoped to be regarded as fishermen; whereas, if we should take the land route, we should be subjected to interruptions of almost every kind. Any one having a white face, and being so disposed, could stop us, and subject us to examination.

The week before our intended start, I wrote several protections, one for each of us. As well as I can remember, they were in the following words, to wit:—

> "THIS is to certify that I, the undersigned, have given the bearer, my servant, full liberty to go to Baltimore, and spend the Easter holidays. Written with mine own hand, &c., 1835.
>
> "WILLIAM HAMILTON,
> "Near St. Michael's, in Talbot county, Maryland."

We were not going to Baltimore; but, in going up the bay, we went toward Baltimore, and these protections were only intended to protect us while on the bay.

As the time drew near for our departure, our anxiety became more and more intense. It was truly a matter of life and death with us. The strength of our determination was about to be fully tested. At this time, I was very active in explaining every difficulty, removing every doubt, dispelling every fear, and inspiring all with the firmness indispensable to success in our undertaking; assuring them that half was gained the instant we made the move; we had talked long enough; we were now ready to move; if not now, we never should be; and if we did not intend to move now, we had as well fold our arms, sit down, and acknowledge ourselves fit only to be slaves. This, none of us were prepared to acknowledge. Every man stood firm; and at our last meeting, we pledged ourselves afresh, in the most solemn manner, that, at the time appointed, we would certainly start in pursuit of freedom. This was in the middle of the week, at the end of which we were to be off. We went, as usual, to our several fields of labor, but with bosoms highly agitated with thoughts of our truly hazardous undertaking. We tried to conceal our feelings as much as possible; and I think we succeeded very well.

After a painful waiting, the Saturday morning, whose night was to witness our departure, came. I hailed it with joy, bring what of sadness it might. Friday night was a sleepless one for me. I probably felt more anxious than the rest, because I was, by common consent, at the head of the whole affair. The responsibility of success or failure lay heavily upon me. The glory of the one, and the confusion of the other, were alike mine. The first two hours of that morning were such as I never experienced before, and hope never to again. Early in the morning; we went, as usual, to the field. We were spreading manure; and all at once, while thus engaged, I was overwhelmed with an indescribable feeling, in the fulness of which I turned to Sandy, who was near by, and said, "We are betrayed!" "Well," said he, "that thought has this moment struck me." We said no more. I was never more certain of any thing.

The horn was blown as usual, and we went up from the field to the house for breakfast. I went for the form, more than for want of any thing to eat that morning. Just as I got to the house, in looking out at the lane gate, I saw four white men, with two colored men. The white men were on horseback, and the colored ones were walking behind, as if tied. I watched them a few moments till they got up to our lane gate. Here they halted, and tied the colored men to the gatepost. I was not yet certain as to what the matter was. In a few moments, in rode Mr. Hamilton, with a speed betokening great excitement. He came to the door, and inquired if Master William was in. He was told he was at the barn. Mr. Hamilton, without dismounting, rode up to the barn with extraordinary speed. In a few moments, he and Mr. Freeland returned to the house. By this time, the three constables rode up, and in great haste dismounted, tied their horses, and met Master William and Mr. Hamilton returning from the barn; and after talking awhile, they all walked up to the kitchen door. There was no one in the kitchen but myself and John. Henry and Sandy were up at the barn. Mr. Freeland put his head in at the door, and called me by name, saying, there were some gentlemen at the door who wished to see me. I stepped to the door, and inquired what they wanted. They at once seized me, and, without giving me any satisfaction, tied me—lashing my hands closely together. I insisted upon knowing what the matter was. They at length said, that they had learned I had been in a "scrape," and that I was to be examined before my master; and if their information proved false, I should not be hurt.

In a few moments, they succeeded in tying John. They then turned to Henry, who had by this time returned, and commanded him to cross his hands. "I won't!" said Henry, in a firm tone, indicating his readiness to meet the consequences of his refusal. "Won't you?" said Tom Graham, the constable. "No, I won't!" said Henry, in a still stronger tone. With this, two of the constables pulled out their shining pistols, and swore, by their Creator, that they would make him cross his hands or kill him. Each cocked his pistol, and, with fingers on the trigger, walked up to Henry, saying, at the same time, if he did not cross his hands, they would blow his damned heart out. "Shoot me, shoot me!" said Henry; "you can't kill me but once. Shoot, shoot,— and be damned! *I won't be tied!*" This he said in a tone of loud defiance; and at the same time, with a motion as quick as lightning, he with one single stroke dashed the pistols from the hand of each constable. As he did this, all hands fell upon him, and, after beating him some time, they finally overpowered him, and got him tied.

During the scuffle, I managed, I know not how, to get my pass out, and, without being discovered, put it into the fire. We were all now tied; and just as we were to leave for Easton jail, Betsy Freeland, mother of William Freeland, came to the door with her hands full of biscuits, and divided them between Henry and John. She then delivered herself of a speech, to the following effect:—addressing herself to me, she said, *"You devil! You yellow devil!* it was you that put it into the heads of Henry and John to run away. But for you, you long-legged mulatto devil! Henry nor John would never have thought of such a thing." I made no reply, and was immediately hurried off towards St. Michael's. Just a moment previous to the scuffle with Henry, Mr. Hamilton suggested the propriety of making a search for the protections which he had understood Frederick had written for himself and the rest. But, just at the moment he was about carrying his proposal into effect, his aid was needed in helping to tie Henry; and the excitement attending the scuffle caused them either to forget, or to deem it unsafe, under the circumstances, to search. So we were not yet convicted of the intention to run away.

When we got about half way to St. Michael's, while the constables having us in charge were looking ahead, Henry inquired of me what he should do with his pass. I told him to eat it with his biscuit, and own nothing; and we passed the word around, *"Own nothing;"* and *"Own nothing!"* said we all. Our confidence in each other was unshaken. We were resolved to succeed or fail together, after the calamity had befallen us as much as before. We were now prepared for any thing. We were to be dragged that morning fifteen miles behind horses, and then to be placed in the Easton jail. When we reached St. Michael's, we underwent a sort of examination. We all denied that we ever intended to run away. We did this more to bring out the evidence against us, than from any hope of getting clear of being sold; for, as I have said, we were ready for that. The fact was, we cared but little where we went, so we went together. Our greatest concern was about separation. We dreaded that more than any thing this side of death. We found the evidence against us to be the testimony of one person; our master would not tell who it was; but we came to a unanimous decision among ourselves as to who their informant was. We were sent off to the jail at Easton. When we got there, we were delivered up to the sheriff, Mr. Joseph Graham, and by him placed in jail. Henry, John, and myself, were placed in one room together—Charles, and Henry Bailey, in another. Their object in separating us was to hinder concert.

We had been in jail scarcely twenty minutes, when a swarm of slave traders, and agents for slave traders, flocked into jail to look at us, and to ascertain if we were for sale. Such a set of beings I never saw before! I felt myself surrounded by so many fiends from perdition. A band of pirates never looked more like their father, the devil. They laughed and grinned over us, saying, "Ah, my boys! we have got you, haven't we?" And after taunting us in various ways, they one by one went into an examination of us, with intent to ascertain our value. They would impudently ask us if we would not like to have them for our masters. We would make them no answer, and leave them to find out as best they could. Then they would curse and swear at us, telling us that they could take the devil out of us in a very little while, if we were only in their hands.

While in jail, we found ourselves in much more comfortable quarters than we expected when we went there. We did not get much to eat, nor that which was very good; but we had a good clean room, from the windows of which we could see what was going on in the street, which was very much better than though we had been placed in one of the dark, damp cells. Upon the whole, we got along very well, so far as the jail and its keeper were concerned. Immediately after the holidays were over, contrary to all our expectations, Mr. Hamilton and Mr. Freeland came up to Easton, and took Charles, the two Henrys, and John, out of jail, and carried them home, leaving me alone. I regarded this separation as a final one. It caused me more pain than any thing else in the whole transaction. I was ready for any thing rather than separation. I supposed that they had consulted together, and had decided that, as I was the whole cause of the intention of the others to run away, it was hard to make the innocent suffer with the guilty; and that they had, therefore, concluded to take the others home, and sell me, as a warning to the others that remained. It is due to the noble Henry to say, he seemed almost as reluctant at leaving the prison as at leaving home to come to the prison. But we knew we should, in all probability, be separated, if we were sold; and since he was in their hands, he concluded to go peaceably home.

I was now left to my fate. I was all alone, and within the walls of a stone prison. But a few days before, and I was full of hope. I expected to have been safe in a land of freedom; but now I was covered with gloom, sunk down to the utmost despair. I thought the possibility of freedom was gone. I was kept in this way about one week, at the end of which, Captain Auld, my master, to my surprise and utter astonishment, came up, and took me out, with the intention of sending me, with a gentleman of his acquaintance, into Alabama. But, from some cause or other, he did not send me to Alabama, but concluded to send me back to Baltimore, to live again with his brother Hugh, and to learn a trade.

Thus, after an absence of three years and one month, I was once more permitted to return to my old home at Baltimore. My master sent me away, because there existed against me a very great prejudice in the community, and he feared I might be killed.

In a few weeks after I went to Baltimore, Master Hugh hired me to Mr. William Gardner, an extensive ship-builder, on Fell's Point. I was put there to learn how to calk. It, however, proved a very unfavorable place for the accomplishment of this object. Mr. Gardner was engaged that spring in building two large man-of-war brigs, professedly for the Mexican government. The vessels were to be launched in the July of that year, and in failure thereof, Mr. Gardner was to lose a considerable sum; so that when I entered, all was hurry. There was no time to learn any thing. Every man had to do that which he knew how to do. In entering the ship-yard, my orders from Mr. Gardner were, to do whatever the carpenters commanded me to do. This was placing me at the beck and call of about seventy-five men. I was to regard all these as masters. Their word was to be my law. My situation was a most trying one. At times I needed a dozen pair of hands. I was called a dozen ways in the space of a single minute. Three or four voices would strike my ear at the same moment. It was—"Fred., come help me to cant this timber here."—"Fred., come carry this timber yonder."—"Fred., bring that roller here."—"Fred., go get a fresh can of water."—"Fred., come help saw off the end of this timber."—"Fred., go quick, and get the crowbar."—"Fred., hold on the end of this fall."—"Fred., go to the blacksmith's shop, and get a new punch."—"Hurra, Fred.! run and bring me a cold chisel."—"I say, Fred., bear a hand, and get up a fire as quick as lightning under that steam-box."—"Halloo, nigger! come, turn this grindstone."—"Come, come! move, move! and *bowse* this timber forward."—"I say, darky, blast your eyes, why don't you heat up some pitch?"—"Halloo! halloo! halloo!" (Three voices at the same time.) "Come here!—Go there!—Hold on where you are! Damn you, if you move, I'll knock your brains out!"

This was my school for eight months; and I might have remained there longer, but for a most horrid fight I had with four of the white apprentices, in which my left eye was nearly knocked out, and I was horribly mangled in other respects. The facts in the case were these: Until a very little while after I went there, white and black ship-carpenters worked side by side, and no one seemed to see any impropriety in it. All hands seemed to be very well satisfied. Many of the black carpenters were freemen. Things seemed to be going on very well. All at once, the white carpenters knocked off, and said they would not work with free colored workmen. Their reason for this, as alleged, was, that if free colored carpenters were encouraged, they would soon take the trade into their own hands, and poor white men would be thrown out of employment. They therefore felt called upon at once to put a stop to it. And, taking advantage of Mr. Gardner's necessities, they broke off, swearing they would work no longer, unless he would discharge his black carpenters. Now, though this did not extend to me in form, it did reach me in fact. My fellow-apprentices very soon began to feel it degrading to them to work with me. They began to put on airs, and talk about the "niggers" taking the country, saying we all ought to be killed; and, being encouraged by the journeymen, they commenced making my condition as hard as they could, by hectoring me around, and sometimes striking me. I, of course, kept the vow I made after the fight with Mr. Covey, and struck back again, regardless of consequences; and while I kept them from combining, I succeeded very well; for I could whip the whole of them, taking them separately. They, however, at length combined, and came upon me, armed with sticks, stones, and heavy handspikes. One came in front with a half brick. There was one at each side of me, and one behind me. While I was attending to those in front, and on either side, the one behind ran up with the handspike, and struck me a heavy blow upon the head. It stunned me. I fell, and with this they all ran upon me, and fell to beating me with their fists. I let them lay on for a while, gathering strength. In an instant, I gave a sudden surge, and rose to my hands and knees. Just as I did that, one of their number gave me, with his heavy boot, a powerful kick in the left eye. My eyeball seemed to have burst. When they saw my eye closed, and badly swollen, they left me. With this I seized the handspike, and for a time pursued them. But here the carpenters interfered, and I thought I might as well give it up. It was impossible to stand my hand against so many. All this took place in sight of not less than fifty white ship-carpenters, and not one interposed a friendly word; but some cried, "Kill the damned nigger! Kill him! kill him! He struck a white person." I found my only chance for life was in flight. I succeeded in getting away without an additional blow, and barely so; for to strike a white man is death by

Lynch law,—and that was the law in Mr. Gardner's ship-yard; nor is there much of any other out of Mr. Gardner's ship yard.

I went directly home, and told the story of my wrongs to Master Hugh; and I am happy to say of him, irreligious as he was, his conduct was heavenly, compared with that of his brother Thomas under similar circumstances. He listened attentively to my narration of the circumstances leading to the savage outrage, and gave many proofs of his strong indignation at it. The heart of my once overkind mistress was again melted into pity. My puffed-out eye and blood-covered face moved her to tears. She took a chair by me, washed the blood from my face, and, with a mother's tenderness, bound up my head, covering the wounded eye with a lean piece of fresh beef. It was almost compensation for my suffering to witness, once more, a manifestation of kindness from this, my once affectionate old mistress. Master Hugh was very much enraged. He gave expression to his feelings by pouring out curses upon the heads of those who did the deed. As soon as I got a little the better of my bruises, he took me with him to Esquire Watson's, on Bond Street, to see what could be done about the matter. Mr. Watson inquired who saw the assault committed. Master Hugh told him it was done in Mr. Gardner's ship-yard, at mid-day, where there were a large company of men at work. "As to that," he said, "the deed was done, and there was no question as to who did it." His answer was, he could do nothing in the case, unless some white man would come forward and testify. He could issue no warrant on my word. If I had been killed in the presence of a thousand colored people, their testimony combined would have been insufficient to have arrested one of the murderers. Master Hugh, for once, was compelled to say this state of things was too bad. Of course, it was impossible to get any white man to volunteer his testimony in my behalf, and against the white young men. Even those who may have sympathized with me were not prepared to do this. It required a degree of courage unknown to them to do so; for just at that time, the slightest manifestation of humanity toward a colored person was denounced as abolitionism, and that name subjected its bearer to frightful liabilities. The watchwords of the bloody-minded in that region, and in those days, were, "Damn the abolitionists!" and "Damn the niggers!" There was nothing done, and probably nothing would have been done if I had been killed. Such was, and such remains, the state of things in the Christian city of Baltimore.

Master Hugh, finding he could get no redress, refused to let me go back again to Mr. Gardner. He kept me himself, and his wife dressed my wound till I was again restored to health. He then took me into the ship-yard of which he was foreman, in the employment of Mr. Walter Price. There I was immediately set to calking, and very soon learned the art of using my mallet and irons. In the course of one year from the time I left Mr. Gardner's, I was able to command the highest wages given to the most experienced calkers. I was now of some importance to my master. I was bringing him from six to seven dollars per week. I sometimes brought him nine dollars per week: my wages were a dollar and a half a day. After learning how to calk, I sought my own employment, made my own contracts, and collected the money which I earned. My pathway became much more smooth than before; my condition was now much more comfortable. When I could get no calking to do, I did nothing. During these leisure times, those old notions about freedom would steal over me again. When in Mr. Gardner's employment, I was kept in such a perpetual whirl of excitement, I could think of nothing, scarcely, but my life; and in thinking of my life, I almost forgot my liberty. I have observed this in my experience of slavery,—that whenever my condition was improved, instead of its increasing my contentment, it only increased my desire to be free, and set me to thinking of plans to gain my freedom. I have found that, to make a contented slave, it is necessary to make a thoughtless one. It is necessary to darken his moral and mental vision, and, as far as possible, to annihilate the power of reason. He must be able to detect no inconsistencies in slavery; he must be made to feel that slavery is right; and he can be brought to that only when he ceases to be a man.

I was now getting, as I have said, one dollar and fifty cents per day. I contracted for it; I earned it; it was paid to me; it was rightfully my own; yet, upon each returning Saturday night, I was compelled to deliver every cent of that money to Master Hugh. And why? Not because he earned it,—not because he had any hand in earning it,—not because I owed it to him,—nor because he possessed the slightest shadow of a right to it; but solely because he had the power to compel me to give it up. The right of the grim-visaged pirate upon the high seas is exactly the same.

CHAPTER XI

I now come to that part of my life during which I planned, and finally succeeded in making, my escape from slavery. But before narrating any of the peculiar circumstances, I deem it proper to make known my intention not to state all the facts connected with the transaction. My reasons for pursuing this course may be understood from the following: First, were I to give a minute statement of all the facts, it is not only possible, but quite probable, that others would thereby be involved in the most embarrassing difficulties. Secondly, such a statement would most undoubtedly induce greater vigilance on the part of slaveholders than has existed heretofore among them; which would, of course, be the means of guarding a door whereby some dear brother bondman might escape his galling chains. I deeply regret the necessity that impels me to suppress any thing of importance connected with my experience in slavery. It would afford me great pleasure indeed, as well as materially add to the interest of my narrative, were I at liberty to gratify a curiosity, which I know exists in the minds of many, by an accurate statement of all the facts pertaining to my most fortunate escape. But I must deprive myself of this pleasure, and the curious of the gratification which such a statement would afford. I would allow myself to suffer under the greatest imputations which evil-minded men might suggest, rather than exculpate myself, and thereby run the hazard of closing the slightest avenue by which a brother slave might clear himself of the chains and fetters of slavery.

I have never approved of the very public manner in which some of our western friends have conducted what they call the *underground railroad*, but which, I think, by their open declarations, has been made most emphatically the *upperground railroad*. I honor those good men and women for their noble daring, and applaud them for willingly subjecting themselves to bloody persecution, by openly avowing their participation in the escape of slaves. I, however, can see very little good resulting from such a course, either to themselves or the slaves escaping; while, upon the other hand, I see and feel assured that those open declarations are a positive evil to the slaves remaining, who are seeking to escape. They do nothing towards enlightening the slave, whilst they do much towards enlightening the master. They stimulate him to greater watchfulness, and enhance his power to capture his slave. We owe something to the slaves south of the line as well as to those north of it; and in aiding the latter on their way to freedom, we should be careful to do nothing which would be likely to hinder the former from escaping from slavery. I would keep the merciless slaveholder profoundly ignorant of the means of flight adopted by the slave. I would leave him to imagine himself surrounded by myriads of invisible tormentors, ever ready to snatch from his infernal grasp his trembling prey. Let him be left to feel his way in the dark; let darkness commensurate with his crime hover over him; and let him feel that at every step he takes, in pursuit of the flying bondman, he is running the frightful risk of having his hot brains dashed out by an invisible agency. Let us render the tyrant no aid; let us not hold the light by which he can trace the footprints of our flying brother. But enough of this. I will now proceed to the statement of those facts, connected with my escape, for which I am alone responsible, and for which no one can be made to suffer by myself.

In the early part of the year 1838, I became quite restless. I could see no reason why I should, at the end of each week, pour the reward of my toil into the purse of my master. When I carried to him my weekly wages, he would, after counting the money, look me in the face with a robber-like fierceness, and ask, "Is this all?" He was satisfied with nothing less than the last cent. He would, however, when I made him six dollars, sometimes give me six cents, to encourage me.

It had the opposite effect. I regarded it as a sort of admission of my right to the whole. The fact that he gave me any part of my wages was proof, to my mind, that he believed me entitled to the whole of them. I always felt worse for having received any thing; for I feared that the giving me a few cents would ease his conscience, and make him feel himself to be a pretty honorable sort of robber. My discontent grew upon me. I was ever on the look-out for means of escape; and, finding no direct means, I determined to try to hire my time, with a view of getting money with which to make my escape. In the spring of 1838, when Master Thomas came to Baltimore to purchase his spring goods, I got an opportunity, and applied to him to allow me to hire my time. He unhesitatingly refused my request, and told me this was another stratagem by which to escape. He told me I could go nowhere but that he could get me; and that, in the event of my running away, he should spare no pains in his efforts to catch me. He exhorted me to content myself, and be obedient. He told me, if I would be happy, I must lay out no plans for the future. He said, if I behaved myself properly, he would take care of me. Indeed, he advised me to complete thought-lessness of the future, and taught me to depend solely upon him for happiness. He seemed to see fully the pressing necessity of setting aside my intellectual nature, in order to contentment in slavery. But in spite of him, and even in spite of myself, I continued to think, and to think about the injustice of my enslavement, and the means of escape.

About two months after this, I applied to Master Hugh for the privilege of hiring my time. He was not acquainted with the fact that I had applied to Master Thomas, and had been refused. He too, at first, seemed disposed to refuse; but, after some reflection, he granted me the privilege, and proposed the following terms: I was to be allowed all my time, make all contracts with those for whom I worked, and find my own employment; and, in return for this liberty, I was to pay him three dollars at the end of each week; find myself in calking tools, and in board and clothing. My board was two dollars and a half per week. This, with the wear and tear of clothing and calking tools, made my regular expenses about six dollars per week. This amount I was compelled to make up, or relinquish the privilege of hiring my time. Rain or shine, work or no work, at the end of each week the money must be forthcoming, or I must give up my privilege. This arrange-ment, it will be perceived, was decidedly in my master's favor. It re-lieved him of all need of looking after me. His money was sure. He received all the benefits of slaveholding without its evils; while I en-dured all the evils of a slave, and suffered all the care and anxiety of a freeman. I found it a hard bargain. But, hard as it was, I thought it better than the old mode of getting along. It was a step towards free-dom to be allowed to bear the responsibilities of a freeman, and I was determined to hold on upon it. I bent myself to the work of making money. I was ready to work at night as well as day, and by the most untiring perseverance and industry, I made enough to meet my expenses, and lay up a little money every week. I went on thus from May till August. Master Hugh then refused to allow me to hire my time longer. The ground for his refusal was a failure on my part, one Saturday night, to pay him for my week's time. This failure was occasioned by my attending a camp meeting about ten miles from Baltimore. During the week, I had entered into an engagement with a number of young friends to start from Baltimore to the camp ground early Saturday evening; and being detained by my employer, I was unable to get down to Master Hugh's without disappointing the company. I knew that Master Hugh was in no special need of the money that night. I therefore decided to go to camp meeting, and upon my return pay him the three dollars. I staid at the camp meeting one day longer than I intended when I left. But as soon as I returned, I called upon him to pay him what he considered his due. I found him very angry; he could scarce restrain his wrath. He said he had a great mind to give me a severe whipping. He wished to know how I dared go out of the city without asking his permission. I told him I hired my time, and while I paid him the price which he asked for it, I did not know that I was bound to ask him when and where I should go. This reply troubled him; and, after reflecting a few moments, he turned to me, and said I should hire my time no longer; that the next thing he should know of, I would be running away. Upon the same plea, he told me to bring my tools and clothing home forthwith. I did so; but instead of seeking work, as I had been accustomed to do previously to hiring my time, I spent the whole week without the performance of a single stroke of work. I did this in retaliation. Saturday night, he called upon me as usual for my week's wages. I told him I had no wages; I had done no work that week. Here we were upon the point of coming to blows. He raved, and swore his determination to get hold of me. I did not allow myself a single word; but was resolved, if he laid the weight of his hand upon me, it should be blow for blow. He did not strike me, but told me that he would find me in constant employment in future. I thought the matter over during the next day, Sunday, and finally resolved upon the third day of September, as the day upon which I would make a second attempt to secure my freedom. I now had three weeks during which to prepare for my journey. Early on Monday morning, before Master Hugh had time to make any engagement for me, I went out and got employment of Mr. Butler, at his shipyard near the drawbridge, upon what is called the City Block, thus making it unnecessary for him to seek employment for me. At the end of the week, I brought him between eight and nine dollars. He seemed very well pleased, and asked me why I did not do the same the week before. He little knew what my plans were. My object in working steadily was to remove any suspicion he might entertain of my intent to run away; and in this I succeeded admirably. I suppose he thought

I was never better satisfied with my condition than at the very time during which I was planning my escape. The second week passed, and again I carried him my full wages; and so well pleased was he, that he gave me twenty-five cents, (quite a large sum for a slaveholder to give a slave,) and bade me to make a good use of it. I told him I would.

Things went on without very smoothly indeed, but within there was trouble. It is impossible for me to describe my feelings as the time of my contemplated start drew near. I had a number of warm-hearted friends in Baltimore,—friends that I loved almost as I did my life,—and the thought of being separated from them forever was painful beyond expression. It is my opinion that thousands would escape from slavery, who now remain, but for the strong cords of affection that bind them to their friends. The thought of leaving my friends was decidedly the most painful thought with which I had to contend. The love of them was my tender point, and shook my decision more than all things else. Besides the pain of separation, the dread and apprehension of a failure exceeded what I had experienced at my first attempt. The appalling defeat I then sustained returned to torment me. I felt assured that, if I failed in this attempt, my case would be a hopeless one—it would seal my fate as a slave forever. I could not hope to get off with any thing less than the severest punishment, and being placed beyond the means of escape. It required no very vivid imagination to depict the most frightful scenes through which I should have to pass, in case I failed. The wretchedness of slavery, and the blessedness of freedom, were perpetually before me. It was life and death with me. But I remained firm, and, according to my resolution, on the third day of September, 1838, I left my chains, and succeeded in reaching New York without the slightest interruption of any kind. How I did so,—what means I adopted,—what direction I travelled, and by what mode of convey-ance,—I must leave unexplained, for the reasons before mentioned.

I have been frequently asked how I felt when I found myself in a free State. I have never been able to answer the question with any satisfaction to myself. It was a moment of the highest excitement I ever experienced. I suppose I felt as one may imagine the unarmed mariner to feel when he is rescued by a friendly man-of-war from the pursuit of a pirate. In writing to a dear friend, immediately after my arrival at New York, I said I felt like one who had escaped a den of hungry lions. This state of mind, however, very soon subsided; and I was again seized with a feeling of great insecurity and loneliness. I was yet liable to be taken back, and subjected to all the tortures of slavery. This in itself was enough to damp the ardor of my enthusiasm. But the loneli-ness overcame me. There I was in the midst of thousands, and yet a perfect stranger; without home and without friends, in the midst of thousands of my own brethren—children of a common Father, and yet I dared not to unfold to any one of them my sad condition. I was afraid to speak to any one for fear of speaking to the wrong one, and thereby falling into the hands of money-loving kidnappers, whose business it was to lie in wait for the panting fugitive, as the ferocious beasts of the forest lie in wait for their prey. The motto which I adopted when I started from slavery was this—"Trust no man!" I saw in every white man an enemy, and in almost every colored man cause for distrust. It was a most painful situation; and, to understand it, one must needs experience it, or imagine himself in similar circumstances. Let him be a fugitive slave in a strange land—a land given up to be the hunting-ground for slaveholders—whose inhabitants are legalized kidnappers—where he is every moment subjected to the terrible liability of being seized upon by his fellow-men, as the hideous crocodile seizes upon his prey!—I say, let him place himself in my situation—without home or friends—without money or credit—wanting shelter, and no one to give it—wanting bread, and no money to buy it,—and at the same time let him feel that he is pursued by merciless men-hunters, and in total darkness as to what to do, where to go, or where to stay,— perfectly helpless both as to the means of defence and means of escape,—in the midst of plenty, yet suffering the terrible gnawings of hunger,—in the midst of houses, yet having no home,—among fellow-men, yet feeling as if in the midst of wild beasts, whose greediness to swallow up the trembling and half-famished fugitive is only equalled by that with which the monsters of the deep swallow up the helpless fish upon which they subsist,—I say, let him be placed in this most trying situation,—the situation in which I was placed,—then, and not till then, will he fully appreciate the hardships of, and know how to sympathize with, the toil-worn and whip-scarred fugitive slave.

Thank Heaven, I remained but a short time in this distressed situation. I was relieved from it by the humane hand of Mr. DAVID RUGGLES, whose vigilance, kindness, and perseverance, I shall never forget. I am glad of an opportunity to express, as far as words can, the love and gratitude I bear him. Mr. Ruggles is now afflicted with blindness, and is himself in need of the same kind offices which he was once so forward in the performance of toward others. I had been in New York but a few days, when Mr. Ruggles sought me out, and very kindly took me to his boarding-house at the corner of Church and Lespenard Streets. Mr. Ruggles was then very deeply engaged in the memorable *Darg* case, as well as attending to a number of other fugitive slaves, devising ways and means for their successful escape; and, though watched and hemmed in on almost every side, he seemed to be more than a match for his enemies.

Very soon after I went to Mr. Ruggles, he wished to know of me where I wanted to go; as he deemed it unsafe for me to remain in New York. I told him I was a calker, and should like to go where I could get work. I thought of going to Canada; but he decided against it, and in favor of my going to New Bedford, thinking I should be able to get work there at my trade. At this time, Anna,* my intended wife, came on; for I wrote to her immediately after my arrival at New York, (notwithstanding my homeless, houseless, and helpless condition,) informing her of my successful flight, and wishing her to come on forthwith. In a few days after her arrival, Mr. Ruggles called in the Rev. J. W. C. Pennington, who, in the presence of Mr. Ruggles, Mrs. Michaels, and two or three others, performed the marriage ceremony, and gave us a certificate, of which the following is an exact copy:—

"THIS may certify, that I joined together in holy matrimony Frederick Johnson† and Anna Murray, as man and wife, in the presence of Mr. David Ruggles and Mrs. Michaels.

"JAMES W. C. PENNINGTON.

"New York, Sept. 15, 1838."

Upon receiving this certificate, and a five-dollar bill from Mr. Ruggles, I shouldered one part of our baggage, and Anna took up the other, and we set out forthwith to take passage on board of the steamboat John W. Richmond for Newport, on our way to New Bedford. Mr. Ruggles gave me a letter to a Mr. Shaw in Newport, and told me, in case my money did not serve me to New Bedford, to stop in Newport and obtain further assistance; but upon our arrival at Newport, we were so anxious to get to a place of safety, that, notwithstanding we lacked the necessary money to pay our fare, we decided to take seats in the stage, and promise to pay when we got to New Bedford. We were encouraged to do this by two excellent gentlemen, residents of New Bedford, whose names I afterward ascertained to be Joseph Ricketson and William C. Taber. They seemed at once to understand our circumstances, and gave us such assurance of their friendliness as put us fully at ease in their presence. It was good indeed to meet with such friends, at such a time. Upon reaching New Bedford, we were directed to the house of Mr. Nathan Johnson, by whom we were kindly received, and hospitably provided for. Both Mr. and Mrs. Johnson took a deep and lively interest in our welfare. They proved themselves quite worthy of the name of abolitionists. When the stage-driver found us unable to pay our fare, he held on upon our baggage as security for the debt. I had but to mention the fact to Mr. Johnson, and he forthwith advanced the money.

We now began to feel a degree of safety, and to prepare ourselves for the duties and responsibilities of a life of freedom. On the morning after our arrival at New Bedford, while at the breakfast-table, the question arose as to what name I should be called by. The name given me by my mother was, "Frederick Augustus Washington Bailey." I, however, had dispensed with the two middle names long before I left

---

*She was free.

†I had changed my name from Frederick *Bailey* to that of Johnson.

Maryland, so that I was generally known by the name of "Frederick Bailey." I started from Baltimore bearing the name of "Stanley." When I got to New York, I again changed my name to "Frederick Johnson, " and thought that would be the last change. But when I got to New Bedford, I found it necessary again to change my name. The reason of this necessity was, that there were so many Johnsons in New Bedford, it was already quite difficult to distinguish between them. I gave Mr. Johnson the privilege of choosing me a name, but told him he must not take from me the name of "Frederick." I must hold on to that, to preserve a sense of my identity. Mr. Johnson had just been reading the "Lady of the Lake," and at once suggested that my name be "Douglass." From that time until now I have been called "Frederick Douglass;" and as I am more widely known by that name than by either of the others, I shall continue to use it as my own.

I was quite disappointed at the general appearance of things in New Bedford. The impression which I had received respecting the character and condition of the people of the north, I found to be singularly erroneous. I had very strangely supposed, while in slavery, that few of the comforts, and scarcely any of the luxuries, of life were enjoyed at the north, compared with what were enjoyed by the slaveholders of the south. I probably came to this conclusion from the fact that northern people owned no slaves. I supposed that they were about upon a level with the non-slaveholding population of the south. I knew *they* were exceedingly poor, and I had been accustomed to regard their poverty as the necessary consequence of their being non-slaveholders. I had somehow imbibed the opinion that, in the absence of slaves, there could be no wealth, and very little refinement. And upon coming to the north, I expected to meet with a rough, hard-handed, and uncultivated population, living in the most Spartan-like simplicity, knowing nothing of the ease, luxury, pomp, and grandeur of southern slaveholders. Such being my conjectures, any one acquainted with the appearance of New Bedford may very readily infer how palpably I must have seen my mistake.

In the afternoon of the day when I reached New Bedford, I visited the wharves, to take a view of the shipping. Here I found myself surrounded with the strongest proofs of wealth. Lying at the wharves, and riding in the stream, I saw many ships of the finest models, in the best order, and of the largest size. Upon the right and left, I was walled in by granite warehouses of the widest dimensions, stowed to their utmost capacity with the necessaries and comforts of life. Added to this, almost every body seemed to be at work, but noiselessly so, compared with what I had been accustomed to in Baltimore. There were no loud songs heard from those engaged in loading and unloading ships. I heard no deep oaths or horrid curses on the laborer. I saw no whipping of men; but all seemed to go smoothly on. Every man appeared to understand his work, and went at it with a sober, yet cheerful earnestness, which betokened the deep interest which he felt in what he was doing, as well as a sense of his own dignity as a man. To me this looked exceedingly strange. From the wharves I strolled around and over the town, gazing with wonder and admiration at the splendid churches, beautiful dwellings, and finely-cultivated gardens; evincing an amount of wealth, comfort, taste, and refinement, such as I had never seen in any part of slaveholding Maryland.

Every thing looked clean, new, and beautiful. I saw few or no dilapidated houses, with poverty-stricken inmates; no half-naked children and barefooted women, such as I had been accustomed to see in Hillsborough, Easton, St. Michael's, and Baltimore. The people looked more able, stronger, healthier, and happier, than those of Maryland. I was for once made glad by a view of extreme wealth, without being saddened by seeing extreme poverty. But the most astonishing as well as the most interesting thing to me was the condition of the colored people, a great many of whom, like myself, had escaped thither as a refuge from the hunters of men. I found many, who had not been seven years out of their chains, living in finer houses, and evidently enjoying more of the comforts of life, than the average of slaveholders in Maryland. I will venture to assert that my friend Mr. Nathan Johnson (of whom I can say with a grateful heart, "I was hungry, and he gave me meat; I was thirsty, and he gave me drink; I was a stranger, and he took me in") lived in a neater house; dined at a better table; took, paid for, and read, more newspapers; better understood the moral, religious, and political character of the nation,—than nine tenths of the slaveholders in Talbot county, Maryland. Yet Mr. Johnson was a working man. His hands were hardened by toil, and not his alone, but those also of Mrs. Johnson. I found the colored people much more spirited than I had supposed they would be. I found among them a determination to protect each other from the blood-thirsty kidnapper, at all hazards. Soon after my arrival, I was told of a circumstance which illustrated their spirit. A colored man and a fugitive slave were on unfriendly terms. The former was heard to threaten the latter with informing his master of his whereabouts. Straightway a meeting was called among the colored people, under the stereotyped notice, "Business of importance!" The betrayer was invited to attend. The people came at the appointed hour, and organized the meeting by appointing a very religious old gentleman as president, who, I believe, made a prayer, after which he addressed the meeting as follows: *"Friends, we have got him here, and I would recommend that you young men just take him outside the door, and kill him!"* With this, a number of them bolted at him; but they were intercepted by some more timid than themselves, and the betrayer escaped their vengeance, and has not been seen in New Bedford since. I believe there have been no more such threats, and should there be hereafter, I doubt not that death would be the consequence.

I found employment, the third day after my arrival, in stowing a sloop with a load of oil. It was new, dirty, and hard work for me; but I went at it with a glad heart and a willing hand. I was now my own master. It was a happy moment, the rapture of which can be understood only by those who have been slaves. It was the first work, the reward of which was to be entirely my own. There was no Master Hugh standing ready, the moment I earned the money, to rob me of it. I worked that day with a pleasure I had never before experienced. I was at work for myself and newly-married wife. It was to me the starting-point of a new existence. When I got through with that job, I went in pursuit of a job of calking; but such was the strength of prejudice against color, among the white calkers, that they refused to work with me, and of course I could get no employment.* Finding my trade of no immediate benefit, I threw off my calking habiliments, and prepared myself to do any kind of work I could get to do. Mr. Johnson kindly let me have his wood-horse and saw, and I very soon found myself a plenty of work. There was no work too hard—none too dirty. I was ready to saw wood, shovel coal, carry the hod, sweep the chimney, or roll oil casks,—all of which I did for nearly three years in New Bedford, before I became known to the anti-slavery world.

In about four months after I went to New Bedford, there came a young man to me, and inquired if I did not wish to take the "Liberator." I told him I did; but, just having made my escape from slavery, I remarked that I was unable to pay for it then. I, however, finally became a subscriber to it. The paper came, and I read it from week to week with such feelings as it would be quite idle for me to attempt to describe. The paper became my meat and my drink. My soul was set all on fire. Its sympathy for my brethren in bonds—its scathing denunciations of slaveholders—its faithful exposures of slavery—and its powerful attacks upon the upholders of the institution—sent a thrill of joy through my soul, such as I had never felt before!

I had not long been a reader of the "Liberator," before I got a pretty correct idea of the principles, measures and spirit of the anti-slavery reform. I took right hold of the cause. I could do but little; but what I could, I did with a joyful heart, and never felt happier than when in an anti-slavery meeting. I seldom had much to say at the meetings, because what I wanted to say was said so much better by others. But, while attending an anti-slavery convention at Nantucket, on the 11th of August, 1841, I felt strongly moved to speak, and was at the same time much urged to do so by Mr. William C. Coffin, a gentleman who had heard me speak in the colored people's meeting at New Bedford. It was a severe cross, and I took it up reluctantly. The truth was, I felt myself a slave, and the idea of speaking to white people weighed me down. I spoke but a few moments, when I felt a degree of freedom,

---

*I am told that colored persons can now get employment at calking in New Bedford—a result of anti-slavery effort.

and said what I desired with considerable ease. From that time until now, I have been engaged in pleading the cause of my brethren—with what success, and with what devotion, I leave those acquainted with my labors to decide.

APPENDIX

I find, since reading over the foregoing Narrative, that I have, in several instances, spoken in such a tone and manner, respecting religion, as may possibly lead those unacquainted with my religious views to suppose me an opponent of all religion. To remove the liability of such misapprehension, I deem it proper to append the following brief explanation. What I have said respecting and against religion, I mean strictly to apply to the *slaveholding religion* of this land, and with no possible reference to Christianity proper; for, between the Christianity of this land, and the Christianity of Christ, I recognize the widest possible difference—so wide, that to receive the one as good, pure, and holy, is of necessity to reject the other as bad, corrupt, and wicked. To be the friend of the one, is of necessity to be the enemy of the other. I love the pure, peaceable, and impartial Christianity of Christ: I therefore hate the corrupt, slaveholding, women-whipping, cradle-plundering, partial and hypocritical Christianity of this land. Indeed, I can see no reason, but the most deceitful one, for calling the religion of this land Christianity. I look upon it as the climax of all misnomers, the boldest of all frauds, and the grossest of all libels. Never was there a clearer case of "stealing the livery of the court of heaven to serve the devil in." I am filled with unutterable loathing when I contemplate the religious pomp and show, together with the horrible inconsistencies, which every where surround me. We have men-stealers for ministers, women-whippers for missionaries, and cradle-plunderers for church members. The man who wields the blood-clotted cowskin during the week fills the pulpit on Sunday, and claims to be a minister of the meek and lowly Jesus. The man who robs me of my earnings at the end of each week meets me as a class-leader on Sunday morning, to show me the way of life, and the path of salvation. He who sells my sister, for purposes of prostitution, stands forth as the pious advocate of purity. He who proclaims it a religious duty to read the Bible denies me the right of learning to read the name of the God who made me. He who is the religious advocate of marriage robs whole millions of its sacred influence, and leaves them to the ravages of wholesale pollution. The warm defender of the sacredness of the family relation is the same that scatters whole families,—sundering husbands and wives, parents and children, sisters and brothers,—leaving the hut vacant, and the hearth desolate. We see the thief preaching against theft, and the adulterer against adultery. We have men sold to build churches, women sold to support the gospel, and babes sold to purchase Bibles for the *poor heathen! all for the glory of God and the good of soul!* The slave auctioneer's bell and the church-going bell chime in with each other, and the bitter cries of the heart-broken slave are drowned in the religious shouts of his pious master. Revivals of religion and revivals in the slave-trade go hand in hand together. The slave prison and the church stand near each other. The clanking of fetters and the rattling of chains in the prison, and the pious psalm and solemn prayer in the church, may be heard at the same time. The dealers in the bodies and souls of men erect their stand in the presence of the pulpit, and they mutually help each other. The dealer gives his blood-stained gold to support the pulpit, and the pulpit, in return, covers his infernal business with the garb of Christianity. Here we have religion and robbery the allies of each other—devils dressed in angels' robes, and hell presenting the semblance of paradise.

> "Just God! and these are they,
>   Who minister at thine altar, God of right!
> Men who their hands, with prayer and blessing, lay
>   On Israel's ark of light.
>
> "What! preach, and kidnap men?
>   Give thanks, and rob thy own afflicted poor?
> Talk of thy glorious liberty, and then
>   Bolt hard the captive's door?
>
> "What! servants of thy own
>   Merciful Son, who came to seek and save
> The homeless and the outcast, fettering down
>   The tasked and plundered slave!
>
> "Pilate and Herod friends!
>   Chief priests and rulers, as of old, combine!
> Just God and holy! is that church which lends
>   Strength to the spoiler thine?"

The Christianity of America is a Christianity, of whose votaries it may be as truly said, as it was of the ancient scribes and Pharisees, "They bind heavy burdens, and grievous to be borne, and lay them on men's shoulders, but they themselves will not move them with one of their fingers. All their works they do for to be seen of men.——— They love the uppermost rooms at feasts, and the chief seats in the synagogues, ... and to be called of men, Rabbi, Rabbi.——— But woe unto you, scribes and Pharisees, hypocrites! for ye shut up the kingdom of heaven against men; for ye neither go in yourselves, neither suffer ye them that are entering to go in. Ye devour widows' houses, and for a pretence make long prayers; therefore ye shall receive the greater damnation. Ye compass sea and land to make one proselyte, and when he is made, ye make him twofold more the child of hell than yourselves.————Woe unto you, scribes and Pharisees, hypocrites! for ye pay tithe of mint, and anise, and cumin, and have omitted the weightier matters of the law, judgment, mercy, and faith; these ought ye to have done, and not to leave the other undone. Ye blind guides! which strain at a gnat, and swallow a camel. Woe unto you, scribes and Pharisees, hypocrites! for ye make clean the outside of the cup and of the platter; but within, they are full of extortion and excess.————Woe unto you, scribes and Pharisees, hypocrites! for ye are like unto whited sepulchres, which indeed appear beautiful outward, but are within full of dead men's bones, and of all uncleanness. Even so ye also outwardly appear righteous unto men, but within ye are full of hypocrisy and iniquity."

Dark and terrible as is this picture, I hold it to be strictly true of the overwhelming mass of professed Christians in America. They strain at a gnat, and swallow a camel. Could any thing be more true of our churches? They would be shocked at the proposition of fellowshipping a *sheep*-stealer; and at the same time they hug to their communion a *man*-stealer, and brand me with being an infidel, if I find fault with them for it. They attend with Pharisaical strictness to the outward forms of religion, and at the same time neglect the weightier matters of the law, judgment, mercy, and faith. They are always ready to sacrifice, but seldom to show mercy. They are they who are represented as professing to love God whom they have not seen, whilst they hate their brother whom they have seen. They love the heathen on the other side of the globe. They can pray for him, pay money to have the Bible put into his hand, and missionaries to instruct him; while they despise and totally neglect the heathen at their own doors.

Such is, very briefly, my view of the religion of this land; and to avoid any misunderstanding, growing out of the use of general terms, I mean, by the religion of this land, that which is revealed in the words, deeds, and actions, of those bodies, north and south, calling themselves Christian churches, and yet in union with slaveholders. It is against religion, as presented by these bodies, that I have felt it my duty to testify.

I conclude these remarks by copying the following portrait of the religion of the south, (which is, by communion and fellowship, the religion of the north,) which I soberly affirm is "true to the life," and without caricature or the slightest exaggeration. It is said to have been drawn, several years before the present anti-slavery agitation began, by a northern Methodist preacher, who, while residing at the south, had an opportunity to see slaveholding morals, manners, and piety, with his own eyes. "Shall I not visit for these things? saith the Lord. Shall not my soul be avenged on such a nation as this?"

A PARODY

"Come, saints and sinners, hear me tell
How pious priests whip Jack and Nell,
And women buy and children sell,
And preach all sinners down to hell,
  And sing of heavenly union.

"They'll beat and baa, dona like goats,
Gorge down black sheep, and strain at motes,
Array their backs in fine black coats,
Then seize their negroes by their throats,
  And choke, for heavenly union.

"They'll church you if you sip a dram,
And damn you if you steal a lamb;
Yet rob old Tony, Doll, and Sam,
Of human rights, and bread and ham;
  Kidnapper's heavenly union.

"They'll loudly talk of Christ's reward,
And bind his image with a cord,
And scold, and wing the lash abhorred,
And sell their brother in the Lord
  To handcuffed heavenly union.

"They'll read and sing a sacred song,
And make a prayer both loud and long,
And teach the right and do the wrong,
Hailing the brother, sister throng,
  With words of heavenly union.

"We wonder how such saints can sing,
Or praise the Lord upon the wing,
Who roar, and scold, and whip, and sting,
And to their slaves and mammon cling,
  In guilty conscience union.

"They'll raise tobacco, corn, and rye,
And drive, and thieve, and cheat, and lie,
And lay up treasures in the sky,
By making switch and cowskin fly,
  In hope of heavenly union.

"They'll crack old Tony on the skull,
And preach and roar like Bashan bull,
Or braying ass, of mischief full,
Then seize old Jacob by the wool,
  And pull for heavenly union.

"A roaring, ranting, sleek man-thief,
Who lived on mutton, veal, and beef,
Yet never would afford relief
To needy, sable sons of grief,
  Was big with heavenly union.

" 'Love not the world,' the preacher said,
And winked his eye, and shook his head;
He seized on Tom, and Dick, and Ned,
Cut short their meat, and clothes, and bread,
  Yet still loved heavenly union.

"Another preacher whining spoke
Of One whose heart for sinners broke:
He tied old Nanny to an oak,
And drew the blood at every stroke,
  And prayed for heavenly union.

"Two others oped their iron jaws,
And waved their children-stealing paws;
There sat their children in gewgaws;
By stinting negroes' backs and maws,
  They kept up heavenly union.

"All good from Jack another takes,
And entertains their flirts and rakes,
Who dress as sleek as glossy snakes,
And cram their mouths with sweetened cakes;
  And this goes down for union."

Sincerely and earnestly hoping that this little book may do something toward throwing light on the American slave system, and hastening the glad day of deliverance to the millions of my brethren in bonds—faithfully relying upon the power of truth, love, and justice, for success in my humble efforts—and solemnly pledging myself anew to the sacred cause,—I subscribe myself,

                                        FREDERICK DOUGLASS.

LYNN, *Mass., April 28, 1845.*

CHAPTER 2

"The Rights of Women"

O n July 28, 1848, this brief report on the first United States Woman's Rights convention, held in Seneca Falls, New York on July 19 and 20, 1848, appeared in *The North Star*. The article gave Douglass the opportunity to publicize his unequivocal support of the pioneering American feminist movement. Having attended the convention, he saw clearly what later became a familiar theme in his antislavery speaking and writing: that white supremacy over blacks and male domination of women were often interwoven and dependent on similar prejudices and fears.

As Philip S. Foner has shown in his edition, *Frederick Douglass on Women's Rights* (1976), Douglass and his fledgling newspaper owed much to the support, both emotional and financial, of the antislavery women of Rochester, New York and other northern cities, among them major figures in the women's movement such as Elizabeth Cady Stanton, Susan B. Anthony, Abbey Kelley, and Sarah Remond. In return *The North Star* and later *Frederick Douglass' Paper* gave extensive coverage to women's rights activities and defended the cause editorially on many occasions. This alliance did not preclude Douglass's criticism of white feminists such as Lucy Stone, who received a lecture from the black editor when he learned that she had agreed to speak before a segregated audience in Philadelphia in 1853. Nor did Douglass fail to recognize the special significance of women's rights arguments when applied to the case of slave women. Reviewing the many injustices suffered by white women on account of their sex, he asked,

what are all those wrongs, how trifling, how as the small dust of the balance when compared with the stupendous and ghastly wrongs perpetrated upon the defenseless slave woman? Other women suffer certain wrongs, but the wrongs peculiar to women out of slavery, great and terrible as they are, are endured as well by the slave woman, who has also to bear the ten thousand wrongs of slavery in addition to those common wrongs of woman. (*Douglass' Monthly,* October 1859)

In the turbulent post-Civil War era, when many civil rights activists were faced with a political dilemma—whose claim to the ballot had priority? that of black men or that of women?—Douglass insisted on voting rights for black men first. He had not abandoned his belief in woman's suffrage, he maintained. He had been forced to conclude that, since political exigencies would not allow both black men and women to enter the national house of enfranchisement together, the black man, particularly in the South, needed the protection of the vote more for social survival than the white woman. This stand led to a painful intellectual and political divorce between Douglass and women's rights activists such as Stanton and Anthony. Yet literally to his dying day Douglass continued to speak out in favor of equal rights for women, a fact that caused Stanton to observe in the memorium she wrote at his passing, "He was the only man I ever saw who understood the degradation of the disenfranchisement of women."

❖   ❖   ❖

One of the most interesting events of the past week, was the holding of what is technically styled a Woman's Rights Convention, at Seneca Falls. The speaking, addresses, and resolutions of this extraordinary meeting were almost wholly conducted by women; and although they evidently felt themselves in a novel position, it is but simple justice to say, that their whole proceedings were characterized by marked ability and dignity. No one present, we think, however much he might be disposed to differ from the views advanced by the leading speakers on that occasion, will fail to give them credit for brilliant talents and excellent dispositions. In this meeting, as in other deliberative assemblies, there were frequently differences of opinion and animated discussion; but in no case was there the slightest absence of good feeling and decorum. Several interesting documents, setting forth the rights as well as the grievances of woman, were read. Among these was a declaration of sentiments, to be regarded as the basis of a grand movement for attaining all the civil, social, political and religious rights of woman. As these documents are soon to be published in pamphlet form, under the authority of a Committee of women appointed by that meeting, we will not mar them by attempting any synopsis of their contents. We should not, however, do justice to our own convictions, or to the excellent persons connected with this infant movement, if we did not, in this connection, offer a few remarks on the general subject which the Convention met to consider, and the objects they seek to attain.

In doing so, we are not insensible that the bare mention of this truly important subject in any other than terms of contemptuous ridicule and scornful disfavor, is likely to excite against us the fury of bigotry and the folly of prejudice. A discussion of the rights of animals would be regarded with far more complacency by many of what are called the *wise* and the *good* of our land, than would be a discussion of the rights of woman. It is, in their estimation, to be guilty of evil thoughts, to think that woman is entitled to rights equal with man. Many who have at last made the discovery that negroes have some rights as well as other members of the human family, have yet to be convinced that woman is entitled to any. Eight years ago, a number of persons of this description actually abandoned the anti-slavery cause, lest by giving their influence in that direction, they might possibly be giving countenance to the dangerous heresy that woman, in respect to rights, stands on an equal footing with man. In the judgment of such persons, the American slave system, with all its concomitant horrors, is less to be deplored than this *wicked* idea. It is perhaps needless to say, that we cherish little sympathy for such sentiments, or respect for such prejudices. Standing as we do upon the watch-tower of human freedom, we cannot be deterred from an expression of our approbation of any movement, however humble, to improve, aid and elevate the character and condition of any members of the human family. While it is impossible for us to go into this subject at length, and dispose of the various objections which are often urged against such a doctrine as that of female equality, we are free to say, that in respect to political rights, we hold woman to be justly entitled to all we claim for man. We go farther, and express our conviction that all political rights which it is expedient for man to exercise, it is equally so for woman. All that distinguishes man as an intelligent and accountable being, is equally true of woman; and if that government is only just which governs by the free consent of the governed, there can be no reason in the world for denying to woman the exercise of the elective franchise, or a hand in making and administering the laws of the land. Our doctrine is, that "Right is of no sex." We therefore bid the women engaged in this movement our humble God-speed.

CHAPTER 3

"Letter to His Old Master"

Douglass's open letter to the last man who claimed him as property was published in *The North Star* on September 8, 1848, under the title "To My Old Master, Thomas Auld." The letter was reprinted in the appendix to *My Bondage and My Freedom* (1855), the source for the text reprinted here. In the letter, Thomas Auld is made to represent much more than the individual Douglass knew as a youth. As the former slave warns his former master, "I intend to make use of you as a weapon with which to assail the system of slavery—as a means of concentrating public attention on the system, and deepening the horror of trafficking in the souls and bodies of men." In case Auld did not apprehend the kind of symbol he was to become—in fact, had already become— in Douglass's rhetoric, the letter itself provided an ample case in point. Biographers of Douglass, especially Dickson J. Preston, have pointed out several ways in which the letter is probably not factually accurate, particularly in its indictment of Auld as callously indifferent to Douglass's grandmother, Betsy Bailey, in her last years. During an 1877 reunion with Auld in Maryland, recounted at length in the *Life and Times* (1881), Douglass acknowledged to the dying white man that his 1845 *Narrative* had been wrong in imputing to Auld "ungrateful and cruel treatment of my grandmother" and that he appreciated what Auld had done to "rescue her from destitution." But in 1848, though Douglass knew that Auld was not the villain the *Narrative* made him out to be, the antislavery author chose the propagandistic advantage—and no doubt savored the personal ironies—of finally putting the slaveholder Auld to *his* service. In the process of reinventing Thomas Auld as consummate slaveholding antagonist, Douglass augmented his personal image as heroic defender of his people, particularly those in his own family whom he had left behind in Maryland when he escaped to freedom exactly ten years before he published "To My Old Master, Thomas Auld."

❖ ❖ ❖

To My Old Master, Thomas Auld.*

SIR—The long and intimate, though by no means friendly, relation which unhappily subsisted between you and myself, leads me to hope that you will easily account for the great liberty which I now take in addressing you in this open and public manner. The same fact may possibly remove any disagreeable surprise which you may experience on again finding your name coupled with mine, in any other way than in an advertisement, accurately describing my person, and offering a large sum for my arrest. In thus dragging you again before the public, I am aware that I shall subject myself to no inconsiderable amount of censure. I shall probably be charged with an unwarrantable, if not a wanton and reckless disregard of the rights and proprieties of private life. There are those north as well as south who entertain a much higher respect for rights which are merely conventional, than they do for rights which are personal and essential. Not a few there are in our country, who, while they have no scruples against robbing the laborer of the hard earned results of his patient industry, will be shocked by the extremely indelicate manner of bringing your name before the public. Believing this to be the case, and wishing to meet every reasonable or plausible objection to my conduct, I will frankly state the ground upon which I justify myself in this instance, as well as on former occasions when I have thought proper to mention your name in public. All will agree that a man guilty of theft, robbery, or murder, has forfeited the right to concealment and private life; that the community have a right to subject such persons to the most complete exposure. However much they may desire retirement, and aim to conceal themselves and their movements from the popular gaze, the public have a right to ferret them out, and bring their conduct before the proper tribunals of the country for investigation. Sir, you will undoubtedly make the proper application of these generally admitted principles, and will easily see the light in which you are regarded by me; I will not therefore manifest ill temper, by calling you hard names. I know you to be a man of some intelligence, and can readily determine the precise estimate which I entertain of your character. I may therefore indulge in language which may seem to others indirect and ambiguous, and yet be quite well understood by yourself.

I have selected this day on which to address you, because it is the anniversary of my emancipation; and knowing no better way, I am led to this as the best mode of celebrating that truly important event. Just ten years ago this beautiful September morning, yon bright sun beheld me a slave—a poor degraded chattel—trembling at the sound of your voice, lamenting that I was a man, and wishing myself a brute. The hopes which I had treasured up for weeks of a safe and successful escape from your grasp, were powerfully confronted at this last hour by dark clouds

*It is not often that chattels address their owners. The following letter is unique; and probably the only specimen of the kind extant. It was written while in England.

of doubt and fear, making my person shake and my bosom to heave with the heavy contest between hope and fear. I have no words to describe to you the deep agony of soul which I experienced on that never-to-be-forgotten morning—for I left by daylight. I was making a leap in the dark. The probabilities, so far as I could by reason determine them, were stoutly against the undertaking. The preliminaries and precautions I had adopted previously, all worked badly. I was like one going to war without weapons—ten chances of defeat to one of victory. One in whom I had confided, and one who had promised me assistance, appalled by fear at the trial hour, deserted me, thus leaving the responsibility of success or failure solely with myself. You, sir, can never know my feelings. As I look back to them, I can scarcely realize that I have passed through a scene so trying. Trying, however, as they were, and gloomy as was the prospect, thanks be to the Most High, who is ever the God of the oppressed, at the moment which was to determine my whole earthly career, His grace was sufficient; my mind was made up. I embraced the golden opportunity, took the morning tide at the flood, and a free man, young, active, and strong, is the result.

I have often thought I should like to explain to you the grounds upon which I have justified myself in running away from you. I am almost ashamed to do so now, for by this time you may have discovered them yourself. I will, however, glance at them. When yet but a child about six years old, I imbibed the determination to run away. The very first mental effort that I now remember on my part, was an attempt to solve the mystery—why am I a slave? and with this question my youthful mind was troubled for many days, pressing upon me more heavily at times than others. When I saw the slave-driver whip a slave-woman, cut the blood out of her neck, and heard her piteous cries, I went away into the corner of the fence, wept and pondered over the mystery. I had, through some medium, I know not what, got some idea of God, the Creator of all mankind, the black and the white, and that he had made the blacks to serve the whites as slaves. How he could do this and be *good*, I could not tell. I was not satisfied with this theory, which made God responsible for slavery, for it pained me greatly, and I have wept over it long and often. At one time, your first wife, Mrs. Lucretia, heard me sighing and saw me shedding tears, and asked of me the matter, but I was afraid to tell her. I was puzzled with this question, till one night while sitting in the kitchen, I heard some of the old slaves talking of their parents having been stolen from Africa by white men, and were sold here as slaves. The whole mystery was solved at once. Very soon after this, my Aunt Jinny and Uncle Noah ran away, and the great noise made about it by your father-in-law, made me for the first time acquainted with the fact, that there were free states as well as slave states. From that time, I resolved that I would some day run away. The morality of the act I dispose of as follows: I am myself; you are yourself; we are two distinct persons, equal persons. What you are, I am. You are a man, and so am I. God created both, and made us separate beings. I am not by nature bond to you, or you to me. Nature does not make your existence depend upon me, or mine to depend upon yours. I cannot walk upon your legs, or you upon mine. I cannot breathe for you, or you for me; I must breathe for myself, and you for yourself. We are distinct persons, and are each equally provided with faculties necessary to our individual existence. In leaving you, I took nothing but what belonged to me, and in no way lessened your means for obtaining an *honest* living. Your faculties remained yours, and mine became useful to their rightful owner. I therefore see no wrong in any part of the transaction. It is true, I went off secretly; but that was more your fault than mine. Had I let you into the secret, you would have defeated the enterprise entirely; but for this, I should have been really glad to have made you acquainted with my intentions to leave.

You may perhaps want to know how I like my present condition. I am free to say, I greatly prefer it to that which I occupied in Maryland. I am, however, by no means prejudiced against the state as such. Its geography, climate, fertility, and products, are such as to make it a very desirable abode for any man; and but for the existence of slavery there, it is not impossible that I might again take up my abode in that state. It is not that I love Maryland less, but freedom more. You will be surprised to learn that people at the north labor under the strange delusion that if the slaves were emancipated at the south, they would flock to the north. So far from this being the case, in that event, you would see many old and familiar faces back again to the south. The fact is, there are few here who would not return to the south in the event of emancipation. We want to live in the land of our birth, and to lay our bones by the side of our fathers; and nothing short of an intense love of personal freedom keeps us from the south. For the sake of this, most of us would live on a crust of bread and a cup of cold water.

Since I left you, I have had a rich experience. I have occupied stations which I never dreamed of when a slave. Three out of the ten years since I left you, I spent as a common laborer on the wharves of New Bedford, Massachusetts. It was there I earned my first free dollar. It was mine. I could spend it as I pleased. I could buy hams or herring with it, without asking any odds of anybody. That was a precious dollar to me. You remember when I used to make seven, or eight, or even nine dollars a week in Baltimore, you would take every cent of it from me every Saturday night, saying that I belonged to you, and my earnings also. I never liked this conduct on your part—to say the best, I thought it a little mean. I would not have served you so. But let that pass. I was a little awkward about counting money in New England fashion when I first landed in New Bedford. I came near betraying myself several times. I caught myself saying phip, for fourpence; and at one time a man actually charged me with being a runaway, whereupon I was silly enough to become one by running away from him, for I was greatly afraid he might adopt measures to get me again into slavery, a condition I then dreaded more than death.

I soon learned, however, to count money, as well as to make it, and got on swimmingly. I married soon after leaving you; in fact, I was engaged to be married before I left you; and instead of finding my companion a burden, she was truly a helpmate. She went to live at service, and I to work on the wharf, and though we toiled hard the first winter, we never lived more happily. After remaining in New Bedford for three years, I met with William Lloyd Garrison, a person of whom you have *possibly* heard, as he is pretty generally known among slaveholders. He put it into my head that I might make myself serviceable to the cause of the slave, by devoting a portion of my time to telling my own sorrows, and those of other slaves, which had come under my observation. This was the commencement of a higher state of existence than any to which I had ever aspired. I was thrown into society the more pure, enlightened, and benevolent, that the country affords. Among these I have never forgotten you, but have invariably made you the topic of conversation—thus giving you all the notoriety I could do. I need not tell you that the opinion formed of you in these circles is far from being favorable. They have little respect for your honesty, and less for your religion.

But I was going on to relate to you something of my interesting experience. I had not long enjoyed the excellent society to which I have referred, before the light of its excellence exerted a beneficial influence on my mind and heart. Much of my early dislike of white persons was removed, and their manners, habits, and customs, so entirely unlike what I had been used to in the kitchen-quarters on the plantations of the south, fairly charmed me, and gave me a strong disrelish for the coarse and degrading customs of my former condition. I therefore made an effort so to improve my mind and deportment, as to be somewhat fitted to the station to which I seemed almost providentially called. The transition from degradation to respectability was indeed great, and to get from one to the other without carrying some marks of one's former condition, is truly a difficult matter. I would not have you think that I am now entirely clear of all plantation peculiarities, but my friends here, while they entertained the strongest dislike of them, regard me with that charity to which my past life somewhat entitles me, so that my condition in this respect is exceedingly pleasant. So far as my domestic affairs are concerned, I can boast of as comfortable a dwelling as your own. I have an industrious and neat companion, and four dear children—the oldest a girl of nine years, and three fine boys, the oldest eight, the next six, and the youngest four years old. The three oldest are now going regularly to school—two can read and write, and the other can spell, with tolerable correctness, words of two syllables. Dear fellows! they are all in comfortable beds, and are sound asleep, perfectly secure under my own roof. There are no slaveholders here to rend my heart by snatching them from my arms, or blast a mother's dearest hopes by tearing them from her bosom. These dear children are ours—not to work up into rice, sugar, and tobacco, but to watch over, regard, and protect, and to rear them up in the nurture and admonition of the gospel—to train them up in the paths of wisdom and virtue, and, as far as we can, to make them useful to the world and to themselves. Oh! sir, a slaveholder never appears to me so completely an agent of hell, as when I think of and look upon my dear children. It is then that my feelings rise above my control. I meant to have said more with respect to my own prosperity and happiness, but thoughts and feelings which this recital has quickened, unfits me to proceed further in that direction. The grim horrors of slavery rise in all their ghastly terror before me; the wails of millions pierce my heart and chill my blood. I remember the chain, the gag, the bloody whip; the death-like gloom overshadowing the broken spirit of the fettered bondman; the appalling liability of his being torn away from wife and children, and sold like a beast in the market. Say not that this is a picture of fancy. You well know that I wear stripes on my back, inflicted by your direction; and that you, while we were brothers in the same church, caused this right hand, with which I am now penning this letter, to be closely tied to my left, and my person dragged, at the pistol's mouth, fifteen miles, from the Bay Side to Easton, to be sold like a beast in the market, for the alleged crime of intending to escape from your possession. All this, and more, you remember, and know to be perfectly true, not only of yourself, but of nearly all of the slaveholders around you.

At this moment, you are probably the guilty holder of at least three of my own dear sisters, and my only brother, in bondage. These you regard as your property. They are recorded on your ledger, or perhaps have been sold to human flesh-mongers, with a view to filling your own ever-hungry purse. Sir, I desire to know how and where these dear sisters are. Have you sold them? or are they still in your possession? What has become of them? are they living or dead? And my dear old grandmother, whom you turned out like an old horse to die in the woods—is she still alive? Write and let me know all about them. If my grandmother be still alive, she is of no service to you, for by this time she must be nearly eighty years old—too old to be cared for by one to whom she has ceased to be of service; send her to me at Rochester, or bring her to Philadelphia, and it shall be the crowning happiness of my life to take care of her in her old age. Oh! she was to me a mother and a father, so far as hard toil for my comfort could make her such. Send me my grandmother! that I may watch over and take care of her in her old age. And my sisters—let me know all about them. I would write to them, and learn all I want to know of them, without disturbing you in any way, but that, through your unrighteous conduct, they have been entirely deprived of the power to read and write. You have kept them in utter ignorance, and have therefore robbed them of the sweet enjoyments of writing or receiving letters from absent friends and relatives. Your wickedness and cruelty, committed in this respect on your fellow-creatures, are greater than all the stripes you have laid upon my back or theirs. It is an outrage upon the soul, a war upon the immortal spirit, and one for which you must give account at the bar of our common Father and Creator.

The responsibility which you have assumed in this regard is truly awful, and how you could stagger under it these many years is marvelous. Your mind must have become darkened, your heart hardened, your conscience seared and petrified, or you would have long since thrown off the accursed load, and sought relief at the hands of a sin-forgiving God. How, let me ask, would you look upon me, were I, some dark night, in company with a band of hardened villains, to enter the precincts of your elegant dwelling, and seize the person of your own lovely daughter, Amanda, and carry her off from your family, friends, and all the loved ones of her youth—make her my slave—compel her to work, and I take her wages—place her name on my ledger as property—disregard her personal rights—fetter the powers of her immortal soul by denying her the right and privilege of learning to read and write—feed her coarsely—clothe her scantily, and whip her on the naked back occasionally; more, and still more horrible, leave her unprotected—a degraded victim to the brutal lust of fiendish overseers, who would pollute, blight, and blast her fair soul—rob her of all dignity—destroy her virtue, and annihilate in her person all the graces that adorn the character of virtuous womanhood? I ask, how would you regard me, if such were my conduct? Oh! the vocabulary of the damned would not afford a word sufficiently infernal to express your idea of my God-provoking wickedness. Yet, sir, your treatment of my beloved sisters is in all essential points precisely like the case I have now supposed. Damning as would be such a deed on my part, it would be no more so than that which you have committed against me and my sisters.

I will now bring this letter to a close; you shall hear from me again unless you let me hear from you. I intend to make use of you as a weapon with which to assail the system of slavery—as a means of concentrating public attention on the system, and deepening the horror of trafficking in the souls and bodies of men. I shall make use of you as a means of exposing the character of the American church and clergy—and as a means of bringing this guilty nation, with yourself, to repentance. In doing this, I entertain no malice toward you personally. There is no roof under which you would be more safe than mine, and there is nothing in my house which you might need for your comfort, which I would not readily grant. Indeed, I should esteem it a privilege to set you an example as to how mankind ought to treat each other.

I am your fellow-man, but not your slave.

CHAPTER 4

"What To the Slave Is the Fourth of July?" (1852)

The oration, "What To the Slave Is the Fourth of July?", delivered before a packed house at the Corinthian Hall in Rochester, New York on July 5, 1852, is the most famous antislavery speech Douglass ever gave. Published in pamphlet form under the title *Oration, Delivered in Corinthian Hall, Rochester, July 5th, 1852* (Rochester: Lee & Mann, 1852), the speech has always been a favorite of editors and anthologists because it exhibits so many of Douglass's strengths as a speaker—in particular, his ability to combine incisive social analysis with compelling argumentative skills and an adroit use of rhetoric. One of the most outstanding features of his mature style, showcased in "What To the Slave Is the Fourth of July?", is his self-conscious use of classical figures of speech, such as antithesis, hyperbole, metaphor, irony, and personification.

More than likely Douglass's effective experimentation with these rhetorical figures was what led some of his early listeners to doubt that he had ever been a slave. Douglass tried to answer the skeptics with his 1845 *Narrative,* in which he exploited all his favorite figures of speech while providing extensive details designed to prove that he was who he claimed to be, a self-taught fugitive slave. But after returning from his triumphal British speaking tour in the spring of 1847, Douglass began to see two diverging roles for himself as a speaker in the antislavery movement. On the one hand, he could continue to play the part he was best known for, that of the former slave who spoke autobiographically about the outrages of slavery. On the other hand, he could adopt a new persona who talked less about himself and his former bondage and more about the current condition of African Americans in the North within the context of the larger antislavery struggle. "What To the Slave Is the Fourth of July?", with its measured references to Douglass's personal experience in slavery, its ruthless dissection of the Fugitive Slave Law, and its thorough unmasking of the North's racial hypocrisies, displays Douglass successfully bridging the dual, and by 1852 the increasingly conflicted, roles available to him as an antislavery speaker and social reformer.

The nineteenth-century lecture platform was a stage on which ideas were not merely expounded—they were dramatized through picturesque language, bodily gesture, tone of voice, and pace of delivery. No orator of that era was more at home in this immensely popular arena of public performance than Frederick Douglass. His style and manner of self-presentation on the platform were carefully designed to reinforce the great theme of his speeches: the dignity and humanity of the African American. Douglass's sophistication in marshaling figurative language along with literary allusions and a ready supply of examples from American and European history helped to establish a reputation for oratorical genius that ensured demand for him on the lyceum circuit long after the social cause for which he had first become a speaker—the abolition of slavery—had been won.

❖   ❖   ❖

Mr. President, Friends and Fellow Citizens: He who could address this audience without a quailing sensation, has stronger nerves than I have. I do not remember ever to have appeared as a speaker before any assembly more shrinkingly, nor with greater distrust of my ability, than I do this day. A feeling has crept over me, quite unfavorable to the exercise of my limited powers of speech. The task before me is one which requires much previous thought and study for its proper performance. I know that apologies of this sort are generally considered flat and unmeaning. I trust, however, that mine will not be so considered. Should I seem at ease, my appearance would much misrepresent me. The little experience I have had in addressing public meetings, in country school houses, avails me nothing on the present occasion.

The papers and placards say, that I am to deliver a 4th [of] July oration. This certainly, sounds large, and out of the common way, for me. It is true that I have often had the privilege to speak in this beautiful Hall, and to address many who now honor me with their presence. But neither their familiar faces, nor the perfect gage I think I have of Corinthian Hall, seems to free me from embarrassment.

The fact is, ladies and gentlemen, the distance between this platform and the slave plantation, from which I escaped, is considerable—and the difficulties to be overcome in getting from the latter to the former, are by no means slight. That I am here to-day, is, to me, a matter of astonishment as well as of gratitude. You will not, therefore, be surprised, if in what I have to say, I evince no elaborate preparation, nor grace my speech with any high sounding exordium. With little experience and with less learning, I have been able to throw my thoughts hastily and imperfectly together; and trusting to your patient and generous indulgence, I will proceed to lay them before you.

This, for the purpose of this celebration, is the 4th of July. It is the birthday of your National Independence, and of your political freedom. This, to you, is what the Passover was to the emancipated people of God. It carries your minds back to the day, and to the act of your great deliverance; and to the signs, and to the wonders, associated with that act, and that day. This celebration also marks the beginning of another year of your national life; and reminds you that the Republic of America is now 76 years old. I am glad, fellow-citizens, that your nation is so young. Seventy-six years, though a good old age for a man, is but a mere speck in the life of a nation. Three score years and ten is the allotted time for individual men; but nations number their years by thousands. According to this fact, you are, even now only in the beginning of your national career, still lingering in the period of childhood. I repeat, I am glad this is so. There is hope in the thought, and hope is much needed, under the dark clouds which lower above the horizon. The eye of the reformer is met with angry flashes, portending disastrous times; but his heart may well beat lighter at the thought that America is young, and that she is still in the impressible stage of her existence. May he not hope that high lessons of wisdom, of justice and of truth, will yet give direction to her destiny? Were the nation older, the patriot's heart might be sadder, and the reformer's brow heavier. Its future might be shrouded in gloom, and the hope of its prophets go out in sorrow. There is consolation in the thought, that America is young.—Great streams are not easily turned from channels, worn deep in the course of ages. They may sometimes rise in quiet and stately majesty, and inundate the land, refreshing and fertilizing the earth with their mysterious properties. They may also rise in wrath and fury, and bear away, on their angry waves, the accumulated wealth of years of toil and hardship. They, however, gradually flow back to the same old channel, and flow on as serenely as ever. But, while the river may not be turned aside, it may dry up, and leave nothing behind but the withered branch, and the unsightly rock, to howl in the abyss-sweeping wind, the sad tale of departed glory. As with rivers so with nations.

Fellow-citizens, I shall not presume to dwell at length on the associations that cluster about this day. The simple story of it is, that, 76 years ago, the people of this country were British subjects. The style and title of your "sovereign people" (in which you now glory) was not then born. You were under the British Crown. Your fathers esteemed the English Government as the home government; and England as the fatherland. This home government, you know, although a considerable distance from your home, did, in the exercise of its parental prerogatives, impose upon its colonial children, such restraints, burdens and limitations, as, in its mature judgment, it deemed wise, right and proper.

But, your fathers, who had not adopted the fashionable idea of this day, of the infallibility of government, and the absolute character of its acts, presumed to differ from the home government in respect to the wisdom and the justice of some of those burdens and restraints. They went so far in their excitement as to pronounce the measures of government unjust, unreasonable, and oppressive, and altogether such as ought not to be quietly submitted to. I scarcely need say, fellow-citizens, that my opinion of those measures fully accords with that of your fathers. Such a declaration of agreement on my part, would not be worth much to anybody. It would, certainly, prove nothing, as to what part I might have taken, had I lived during the great controversy of 1776. To say *now* that America was right, and England wrong, is exceedingly easy. Everybody can say it; the dastard, not less than the noble brave, can flippantly discant on the tyranny of England towards the American Colonies. It is fashionable to do so; but there was a time when, to pronounce against England, and in favor of the cause of the colonies, tried men's souls. They who did so were accounted in their day, plotters of mischief, agitators and rebels, dangerous men. To side with the right, against the wrong, with the weak against the strong, and with the oppressed against the oppressor! *here* lies the merit, and the one which, of all others, seems unfashionable in our day. The cause of liberty may be stabbed by the men who glory in the deeds of your fathers. But, to proceed.

Feeling themselves harshly and unjustly treated, by the home government, your fathers, like men of honesty, and men of spirit, earnestly sought redress. They petitioned and remonstrated; they did so in a decorous, respectful, and loyal manner. Their conduct was wholly unexceptionable. This, however, did not answer the purpose. They saw themselves treated with sovereign indifference, coldness and scorn. Yet they persevered. They were not the men to look back.

As the sheet anchor takes a firmer hold, when the ship is tossed by the storm, so did the cause of your fathers grow stronger, as it breasted the chilling blasts of kingly displeasure. The greatest and best of British statesmen admitted its justice, and the loftiest eloquence of the British Senate came to its support. But, with that blindness which seems to be the unvarying characteristic of tyrants, since Pharoah and his hosts were drowned in the Red sea, the British Government persisted in the exactions complained of.

The madness of this course, we believe, is admitted now, even by England; but we fear the lesson is wholly lost on our present rulers.

Oppression makes a wise man mad. Your fathers were wise men, and if they did not go mad, they became restive under this treatment. They felt themselves the victims of grievous wrongs, wholly incurable in their colonial capacity. With brave men there is always a remedy for oppression. Just here, the idea of a total separation of the colonies from the crown was born! It was a startling idea, much more so, than we, at this distance of time, regard it. The timid and the prudent (as has been intimated) of that day, were, of course, shocked and alarmed by it.

111

Such people lived then, had lived before, and will, probably, ever have a place on this planet; and their course, in respect to any great change, (no matter how great the good to be attained, or the wrong to be redressed by it), may be calculated with as much precision as can be the course of the stars. They hate all changes, but silver, gold and copper change! Of this sort of change they are always strongly in favor.

These people were called tories in the days of your fathers; and the appellation, probably, conveyed the same idea that is meant by a more modern, though a somewhat less euphonious term, which we often find in our papers, applied to some of our old politicians.

Their opposition to the then dangerous thought was earnest and powerful; but, amid all their terror and affrighted vociferations against it, the alarming and revolutionary idea moved on, and the country with it.

On the 2d of July, 1776, the old Continental Congress, to the dismay of the lovers of ease, and the worshippers of property, clothed that dreadful idea with all the authority of national sanction. They did so in the form of a resolution; and as we seldom hit upon resolutions, drawn up in our day, whose transparency is at all equal to this, it may refresh your minds and help my story if I read it.

> Resolved, That these united colonies *are*, and of right, ought to be free and Independent States; that they are absolved from all allegiance to the British Crown; and that all political connection between them and the State of Great Britain *is*, and ought to be, dissolved.

Citizens, your fathers made good that resolution. They succeeded; and to-day you reap the fruits of their success. The freedom gained is yours; and you, therefore, may properly celebrate this anniversary. The 4th of July is the first great fact in your nation's history—the very ring-bolt in the chain of your yet undeveloped destiny.

Pride and patriotism, not less than gratitude, prompt you to celebrate and to hold it in perpetual remembrance. I have said that the Declaration of Independence is the RING-BOLT to the chain of your nation's destiny; so, indeed, I regard it. The principles contained in that instrument are saving principles. Stand by those principles, be true to them on all occasions, in all places, against all foes, and at whatever cost.

From the round top of your ship of state, dark and threatening clouds may be seen. Heavy billows, like mountains in the distance, disclose to the leeward huge forms of flinty rocks! That *bolt* drawn, that *chain* broken, and all is lost. *Cling to this day—cling to it,* and to its principles, with the grasp of a storm-tossed mariner to a spar at midnight.

The coming into being of a nation, in any circumstances, is an interesting event. But, besides general considerations, there were peculiar circumstances which make the advent of this republic an event of special attractiveness.

The whole scene, as I look back to it, was simple, dignified and sublime.

The population of the country, at the time, stood at the insignificant number of three millions. The country was poor in the munitions of war. The population was weak and scattered, and the country a wilderness unsubdued. There were then no means of concert and combination, such as exist now. Neither stream nor lightning had then been reduced to order and discipline. From the Potomac to the Delaware was a journey of many days. Under these, and innumerable other disadvantages, your fathers declared for liberty and independence and triumphed.

Fellow Citizens, I am not wanting in respect for the fathers of this republic. The signers of the Declaration of Independence were brave men. They were great men too—great enough to give fame to a great age. It does not often happen to a nation to raise, at one time, such a number of truly great men. The point from which I am compelled to view them is not, certainly, the most favorable; and yet I cannot contemplate their great deeds with less than admiration. They were statesmen, patriots and heroes, and for the good they did, and the principles they contended for, I will unite with you to honor their memory.

They loved their country better than their own private interests; and, though this is not the highest form of human excellence, all will concede that it is a rare virtue, and that when it is exhibited, it ought to command respect. He who will, intelligently, lay down his life for his country, is a man whom it is not in human nature to despise. Your fathers staked their lives, their fortunes, and their sacred honor, on the cause of their country. In their admiration of liberty, they lost sight of all other interests.

They were peace men; but they preferred revolution to peaceful submission to bondage. They were quiet men; but they did not shrink from agitating against oppression. They showed forbearance; but that they knew its limits. They believed in order; but not in the order of tyranny. With them, nothing was "settled" that was not right. With them, justice, liberty and humanity were "final;" not slavery and oppression. You may well cherish the memory of such men. They were great in their day and generation. Their solid manhood stands out the more as we contrast it with these degenerate times.

How circumspect, exact and proportionate were all their movements! How unlike the politicians of an hour! Their statesmanship looked beyond the passing moment, and stretched away in strength into the distant future. They seized upon eternal principles, and set a glorious example in their defence. Mark them!

Fully appreciating the hardship to be encountered, firmly believing the right of their cause, honorably inviting the scrutiny of an on-oking world, reverently appealing to heaven to attest their sincerity, soundly comprehending the solemn responsibility they were about to assume, wisely measuring the terrible odds against them, your fathers, the fathers of this republic, did, most deliberately, under the inspiration of a glorious patriotism, and with a sublime faith in the great principles of justice and freedom, lay deep, the corner-stone of the national superstructure, which has risen and still rises in grandeur around you.

Of this fundamental work, this day is the anniversary. Our eyes are met with demonstrations of joyous enthusiasm. Banners and pennants wave exultingly on the breeze. The din of business, too, is hushed. Even mammon seems to have quitted his grasp on this day. The ear-piercing fife and the stirring drum unite their accents with the ascending peal of a thousand church bells. Prayers are made, hymns are sung, and sermons are preached in honor of this day; while the quick martial tramp of a great and multitudinous nation, echoed back by all the hills, valleys and mountains of a vast continent, bespeak the occasion one of thrilling and universal interest—a nation's jubilee.

Friends and citizens, I need not enter further into the causes which led to this anniversary. Many of you understand them better than I do. You could instruct me in regard to them. That is a branch of knowledge in which you feel, perhaps, a much deeper interest than your speaker. The causes which led to the separation of the colonies from the British crown have never lacked for a tongue. They have all been taught in your common schools, narrated at your firesides, unfolded from your pulpits, and thundered from your legislative halls, and are as familiar to you as household words. They form the staple of your national poetry and eloquence.

I remember, also, that, as a people, Americans are remarkably familiar with all facts which make in their own favor. This is esteemed by some as a national trait—perhaps a national weakness. It is a fact, that whatever makes for the wealth or for the reputation of Americans, and can be had *cheap!* will be found by Americans. I shall not be charged with slandering Americans, if I say I think the American side of any question may be safely left in American hands.

I leave, therefore, the great deeds of your fathers to other gentlemen whose claim to have been regularly descended will be less likely to be disputed than mine!

THE PRESENT

My business, if I have any here to-day, is with the present. The accepted time with God and his cause is the ever-living now.

> "Trust no future, however pleasant,
>   Let the dead past bury its dead;
> Act, act in the living present,
>   Heart within, and God overhead."

We have to do with the past only as we can make it useful to the present and to the future. To all inspiring motives, to noble deeds which can be gained from the past, we are welcome. But now is the time, the important time. Your fathers have lived, died, and have done their work, and have done much of it well. You live and must die, and you must do your work. You have no right to enjoy a child's share in the labor of your fathers, unless your children are to be blest by your labors. You have no right to wear out and waste the hard-earned fame of your fathers to cover your indolence. Sydney Smith tells us that men seldom eulogize the wisdom and virtues of their fathers, but to excuse some folly or wickedness of their own. This truth is not a doubtful one. There are illustrations of it near and remote, ancient and modern. It was fashionable, hundreds of years ago, for the children of Jacob to boast, we have "Abraham to our father," when they had long lost Abraham's faith and spirit. That people contented themselves under the shadow of Abraham's great name, while they repudiated the deeds which made his name great. Need I remind you that a similar thing is being done all over this country to-day? Need I tell you that the Jews are not the only people who built the tombs of the prophets, and garnished the sepulchres of the righteous? Washington could not die till he had broken the chains of his slaves. Yet his monument is built up by the price of human blood, and the traders in the bodies and souls of men, shout—"We have Washington to *our father*." Alas! that it should be so; yet so it is.

> "The evil that men do, lives after them,
> The good is oft' interred with their bones."

Fellow-citizens, pardon me, allow me to ask, why am I called upon to speak here to-day? What have I, or those I represent, to do with your national independence? Are the great principles of political freedom and of natural justice, embodied in that Declaration of Independence, extended to us? and am I, therefore, called upon to bring our humble offering to the national altar, and to confess the benefits and express devout gratitude for the blessings resulting from your independence to us?

Would to God, both for your sakes and ours, that an affirmative answer could be truthfully returned to these questions! Then would my task be light, and my burden easy and delightful. For *who* is there so cold, that a nation's sympathy could not warm him? Who so obdurate and dead to the claims of gratitude, that would not thankfully acknowledge such priceless benefits? Who so stolid and selfish, that would not give his voice to swell the hallelujahs of a nation's jubilee, when the chains of servitude had been torn from his limbs? I am not that man. In a case like that, the dumb might eloquently speak, and the "lame man leap as an hart."

But, such is not the state of the case. I say it with a sad sense of the disparity between us. I am not included within the pale of this glorious anniversary! Your high independence only reveals the immeasurable distance between us. The blessings in which you, this day, rejoice, are not enjoyed in common.—The rich inheritance of justice, liberty, prosperity and independence, bequeathed by your fathers, is shared by you, not by me. The sunlight that brought life and healing to you, has brought stripes and death to me. This Fourth [of] July is *yours*, not *mine. You* may rejoice, *I* must mourn. To drag a man in fetters into the grand illuminated temple of liberty, and call upon him to join you in joyous anthems, were inhuman mockery and sacrilegious irony. Do you mean, citizens, to mock me, by asking me to speak to-day? If so, there is a parallel to your conduct. And let me warn you that it is dangerous to copy the example of a nation whose crimes, towering up to heaven, were thrown down by the breath of the Almighty, burying that nation in irrecoverable ruin! I can to-day take up the plaintive lament of a peeled and woe-smitten people!

"By the rivers of Babylon, there we sat down. Yea! we wept when we remembered Zion. We hanged our harps upon the willows in the midst thereof. For there, they that carried us away captive, required of us a song; and they who wasted us required of us mirth, saying, Sing us one of the songs of Zion. How can we sing the Lord's song in a strange land? If I forget thee, O Jerusalem, let my right hand forget her cunning. If I do not remember thee, let my tongue cleave to the roof of my mouth."

Fellow-citizens; above your national, tumultous joy, I hear the mournful wail of millions! whose chains, heavy and grievous yesterday, are, to-day, rendered more intolerable by the jubilee shouts that reach them. If I do forget, if I do not faithfully remember those bleeding children of sorrow this day, "may my right hand forget her cunning, and may my tongue cleave to the roof of my mouth!" To forget them, to pass lightly over their wrongs, and to chime in with the popular theme, would be treason most scandalous and shocking, and would make me a reproach before God and the world. My subject, then, fellow-citizens, is AMERICAN SLAVERY. I shall see, this day, and its popular characteristics, from the slave's point of view. Standing, there, identified with the American bondman, making his wrongs mine, I do not hesitate to declare, with all my soul, that the character and conduct

116

of this nation never looked blacker to me than on this 4th of July! Whether we turn to the declarations of the past, or to the professions of the present, the conduct of the nation seems equally hideous and revolting. America is false to the past, false to the present, and solemnly binds herself to be false to the future. Standing with God and the crushed and bleeding slave on this occasion, I will, in the name of humanity which is outraged, in the name of liberty which is fettered, in the name of the constitution and the Bible, which are disregarded and trampled upon, dare to call in question and to denounce, with all the emphasis I can command, everything that serves to perpetuate slavery—the great sin and shame of America! "I will not equivocate; I will not excuse;" I will use the severest language I can command; and yet not one word shall escape me that any man, whose judgment is not blinded by prejudice, or who is not at heart a slaveholder, shall not confess to be right and just.

But I fancy I hear some one of my audience say, it is just in this circumstance that you and your brother abolitionists fail to make a favorable impression on the public mind. Would you argue more, and denounce less, would you persuade more, and rebuke less, your cause would be much more likely to succeed. But, I submit, where all is plain there is nothing to be argued. What point in the anti-slavery creed would you have me argue? On what branch of the subject do the people of this country need light? Must I undertake to prove that the slave is a man? That point is conceded already. Nobody doubts it. The slaveholders themselves acknowledge it in the enactment of laws for their government. They acknowledge it when they punish disobedience on the part of the slave. There are seventy-two crimes in the State of Virginia, which, if committed by a black man, (no matter how ignorant he be,) subject him to the punishment of death; while only two of the same crimes will subject a white man to the like punishment.—What is this but the acknowledgement that the slave is a moral, intellectual and responsible being? The manhood of the slave is conceded. It is admitted in the fact that Southern statute books are covered with enactments forbidding, under severe fines and penalties, the teaching of the slave to read or to write.—When you can point to any such laws, in reference to the beasts of the field, then I may consent to argue the manhood of the slave. When the dogs in your streets, when the fowls of the air, when the cattle on your hills, when the fish of the sea, and the reptiles that crawl, shall be unable to distinguish the slave from a brute, *then* will I argue with you that the slave is a man!

For the present, it is enough to affirm the equal manhood of the negro race. Is it not astonishing that, while we are ploughing, planting and reaping, using all kinds of mechanical tools, erecting houses, constructing bridges, building ships, working in metals of brass, iron, copper, silver and gold; that, while we are reading, writing and cyphering, acting as clerks, merchants and secretaries, having among us lawyers, doctors, ministers, poets, authors, editors, orators and teachers; that, while we are engaged in all manner of enterprises common to other men, digging gold in California, capturing the whale in the Pacific, feeding sheep and cattle on the hill-side, living, moving, acting, thinking, planning, living in families as husbands, wives and children, and, above all, confessing and worshipping the Christian's God, and looking hopefully for life and immortality beyond the grave, we are called upon to prove that we are men!

Would you have me argue that man is entitled to liberty? that he is the rightful owner of his own body? You have already declared it. Must I argue the wrongfulness of slavery? Is that a question for Republicans? Is it to be settled by the rules of logic and argumentation, as a matter beset with great difficulty, involving a doubtful application of the principle of justice, hard to be understood? How should I look to-day, in the presence of Americans, dividing, and subdividing a discourse, to show that men have a natural right to freedom? speaking of it relatively, and positively, negatively, and affirmatively. To do so, would be to make myself ridiculous, and to offer an insult to your understanding.—There is not a man beneath the canopy of heaven, that does not know that slavery is wrong *for him.*

What, am I to argue that it is wrong to make men brutes, to rob them of their liberty, to work them without wages, to keep them ignorant of their relations to their fellow men, to beat them with sticks, to flay their flesh with the lash, to load their limbs with irons, to hunt them with dogs, to sell them at auction, to sunder their families, to knock out their teeth, to burn their flesh, to starve them into obedience and submission to their masters? Must I argue that a system thus marked with blood, and stained with pollution, is *wrong?* No! I will not. I have better employments for my time and strength, than such arguments would imply.

What, then, remains to be argued? Is it that slavery is not divine; that God did not establish it; that our doctors of divinity are mistaken? There is blasphemy in the thought. That which is inhuman, cannot be divine! *Who* can reason on such a proposition? They that can, may; I cannot. The time for such argument is past.

At a time like this, scorching irony, not convincing argument, is needed. O! had I the ability, and could I reach the nation's ear, I would, to-day, pour out a fiery stream of biting ridicule, blasting reproach, withering sarcasm, and stern rebuke. For it is not light that is needed, but fire; it is not the gentle shower, but thunder. We need the storm, the whirlwind, and the earthquake. The feeling of the nation must be quickened; the conscience of the nation must be roused; the propriety of the nation must be startled; the hypocrisy of the nation must be exposed; and its crimes against God and man must be proclaimed and denounced.

What, to the American slave, is your 4th of July? I answer; a day that reveals to him, more than all other days in the year, the gross injustice and cruelty to which he is the constant victim. To him, your celebration is a sham; your boasted liberty, an unholy license; your national greatness, swelling vanity; your sounds of rejoicing are empty and heartless; your denunciations of tyrants, brass fronted impudence; your shouts of liberty and equality, hollow mockery; your prayers and hymns, your sermons and thanksgivings, with all your religious parade, and solemnity, are, to him, mere bombast, fraud, deception, impiety, and hypocrisy—a thin veil to cover up crimes which would disgrace a nation of savages. There is not a nation on the earth guilty of practices, more shocking and bloody, than are the people of these United States, at this very hour.

Go where you may, search where you will, roam through all the monarchies and despotisms of the old world, travel through South America, search out every abuse, and when you have found the last, lay your facts by the side of the every day practices of this nation, and you will say with me, that, for revolting barbarity and shameless hypocrisy, America reigns without a rival.

THE INTERNAL SLAVE TRADE

Take the American slave-trade, which, we are told by the papers, is especially prosperous just now. Ex-Senator Benton tells us that the price of men was never higher than now. He mentions the fact to show that slavery is in no danger. This trade is one of the peculiarities of American institutions. It is carried on in all the large towns and cities in one half of this confederacy; and millions are pocketed every year, by dealers in this horrid traffic. In several states, this trade is a chief source of wealth. It is called (in contradistinction to the foreign slave-trade) *"the internal slave-trade."* It is, probably, called so, too, in order to divert from it the horror with which the foreign slave-trade is contemplated. That trade has long since been denounced by this government, as piracy. It has been denounced with burning words, from the high places of the nation, as an execrable traffic. To arrest it, to put an end to it, this nation keeps a squadron, at immense cost, on the coast of Africa. Everywhere, in this country, it is safe to speak of this foreign slave-trade, as a most inhuman traffic, opposed alike to the laws of God and of man. The duty to extirpate and destroy it, is admitted even by our DOCTORS OF DIVINITY. In order to put an end to it, some of these last have consented that their colored brethren (nominally free) should leave this country, and establish themselves on the western coast of Africa! It is, however, a notable fact, that, while so much execration is poured out by Americans, upon those engaged in the foreign slave-trade, the men engaged in the slave-trade between the states pass without condemnation, and their business is deemed honorable.

119

Behold the practical operation of this internal slave-trade, the American slave-trade, sustained by American politics and American religion. Here you will see men and women, reared like swine, for the market. You know what is a swine-drover? I will show you a man-drover. They inhabit all our Southern States. They perambulate the country, and crowd the highways of the nation, with droves of human stock. You will see one of these human flesh jobbers, armed with pistol, whip and bowie-knife, driving a company of a hundred men, women, and children, from the Potomac to the slave market at New Orleans. These wretched people are to be sold singly, or in lots, to suit purchasers. They are food for the cotton-field, and the deadly sugar-mill. Mark the sad procession, as it moves wearily along, and the inhuman wretch who drives them. Hear his savage yells and his blood-chilling oaths, as he hurries on his affrighted captives! There, see the old man, with locks thinned and gray. Cast one glance, if you please, upon that young mother, whose shoulders are bare to the scorching sun, her briny tears falling on the brow of the babe in her arms. See, too, that girl of thirteen, weeping, *yes!* weeping, as she thinks of the mother from whom she has been torn! The drove moves tardily. Heat and sorrow have nearly consumed their strength; suddenly you hear a quick snap, like the discharge of a rifle; the fetters clank, and the chain rattles simultaneously; your ears are saluted with a scream, that seems to have torn its way to the centre of your soul! The crack you heard, was the sound of the slave-whip; the scream you heard, was from the woman you saw with the babe. Her speed had faltered under the weight of her child and her chains! that gash on her shoulder tells her to move on. Follow this drove to New Orleans. Attend the auction; see men examined like horses; see the forms of women rudely and brutally exposed to the shocking gaze of American slave-buyers. See this drove sold and separated for ever; and never forget the deep, sad sobs that arose from that scattered multitude. Tell me citizens, WHERE, under the sun, you can witness a spectacle more fiendish and shocking. Yet this is but a glance at the American slave-trade, as it exists, at this moment, in the ruling part of the United States.

I was born amid such sights and scenes. To me the American slave-trade is a terrible reality. When a child, my soul was often pierced with a sense of its horrors. I lived on Philpot Street, Fell's Point, Baltimore, and have watched from the wharves, the slave ships in the Basin, anchored from the shore, with their cargoes of human flesh, waiting for favorable winds to waft them down the Chesapeake. There was, at that time, a grand slave mart kept at the head of Pratt Street, by Austin Woldfolk. His agents were sent into every town and county in Maryland, announcing their arrival, through the papers, and on flaming *"hand-bills,"* headed CASH FOR NEGROES. These men were generally well dressed men, and very captivating in their manners. Ever ready to drink, to treat, and to gamble. The fate of many a slave has depended upon the turn of a single card; and many a child has been snatched from the arms of its mother, by bargains arranged in a state of brutal drunkenness.

The flesh-mongers gather up their victims by dozens, and drive them, chained, to the general depot at Baltimore. When a sufficient number have been collected here, a ship is chartered, for the purpose of conveying the forlorn crew to Mobile, or to New Orleans. From the slave prison to the ship, they are usually driven in the darkness of night; for since the anti-slavery agitation, a certain caution is observed.

In the deep still darkness of midnight, I have been often aroused by the dead heavy footsteps, and the piteous cries of the chained gangs that passed our door. The anguish of my boyish heart was intense; and I was often consoled, when speaking to my mistress in the morning, to hear her say that the custom was very wicked; that she hated to hear the rattle of the chains, and the heart-rending cries. I was glad to find one who sympathised with me in my horror.

Fellow-citizens, this murderous traffic is, to-day, in active operation in this boasted republic. In the solitude of my spirit, I see clouds of dust raised on the highways of the South; I see the bleeding footsteps; I hear the doleful wail of fettered humanity, on the way to the slave-markets, where the victims are to sold like *horses, sheep,* and *swine,* knocked off to the highest bidder. There I see the tenderest ties ruthlessly broken, to gratify the lust, caprice and rapacity of the buyers and sellers of men. My soul sickens at the sight.

> "Is this the land your Fathers loved,
> The freedom which they toiled to win?
> Is this the earth whereon they moved?
> Are these the graves they slumber in?"

But a still more inhuman, disgraceful, and scandalous state of things remains to be presented.

By an act of the American Congress, not yet two years old, slavery has been nationalized in its most horrible and revolting form. By that act, Mason & Dixon's line has been obliterated; New York has become as Virginia; and the power to hold, hunt, and sell men, women, and children, as slaves remains no longer a mere state institution, but is now an institution of the whole United States. The power is co-extensive with the star-spangled banner, and American Christianity. Where these go, may also go the merciless slave-hunter. Where these are, man is not sacred. He is a bird for the sportsman's gun. By that most foul and fiendish of all human decrees, the liberty and person of every man are put in peril. Your broad republican domain is hunting ground for *men. Not* for thieves and robbers, enemies of society, merely, but for men guilty of no crime. Your law-makers have commanded all good citizens to engage in this hellish sport. Your President, your Secretary of State, your *lords, nobles,* and ecclesiastics, enforce, as a duty you owe to your free and glorious country, and to your God, that you do this accursed thing. Not fewer than forty Americans have, within the past two years, been hunted down, and, without a moment's warning, hurried away in chains, and consigned to slavery, and excruciating torture. Some of these have had wives and children, dependent on them for bread; but of this, no account was made. The right of the hunter to his prey stands superior to the right of marriage, and to *all* rights in this republic, the rights of God included! For black men there are neither law, justice, humanity, nor religion. The Fugitive Slave *Law* makes MERCY TO THEM, A CRIME; and bribes the judge who tries them. An American JUDGE GETS TEN DOLLARS FOR EVERY VICTIM HE CONSIGNS to slavery, and five, when he fails to do so. The oath of any two villains is sufficient, under this hell-black enactment, to send the most pious and exemplary black man into the remorseless jaws of slavery! His own testimony is nothing. He can bring no witnesses for himself. The minister of American justice is bound by the law to hear but *one* side; and *that* side, is the side of the oppressor. Let this damning fact be perpetually told. Let it be thundered around the world, that, in tyrant-killing, king-hating, people-loving, democratic, Christian America, the seats of justice are filled with judges, who hold their offices under an open and palpable *bribe,* and are bound, in deciding in the case of a man's liberty, *to hear only his accusers!*

In glaring violation of justice, in shameless disregard of the forms of administering law, in cunning arrangement to entrap the defenceless, and in diabolical intent, this Fugitive Slave Law stands alone in the annals of tyrannical legislation. I doubt if there be another nation on the globe, having the brass and the baseness to put such a law on the statute-book. If any man in this assembly thinks differently from me in this matter, and feels able to disprove my statements, I will gladly confront him at any suitable time and place he may select.

RELIGIOUS LIBERTY

I take this law to be one of the grossest infringements of Christian Liberty, and, if the churches and ministers of our country were not stupidly blind, or most wickedly indifferent, they, too, would so regard it.

At the very moment that they are thanking God for the enjoyment of civil and religious liberty, and for the right to worship God according to the dictates of their own consciences, they are utterly silent in respect to a law which robs religion of its chief significance, and makes it utterly worthless to a world lying in wickedness. Did this law concern the *"mint, anise* and *cummin"*—abridge the right to sing psalms, to partake of the sacrament, or to engage in any of the ceremonies of religion, it would be smitten by the thunder of a thousand pulpits. A general shout would go up from the church, demanding *repeal, repeal, instant repeal!*—And it would go hard with that politician who presumed to solicit the votes of the people without inscribing this motto on his banner. Further, if this demand were not complied with, another Scotland would be added to the history of religious liberty, and the stern old covenanters would be thrown into the shade. A John Knox would be seen at every church door, and heard from every pulpit, and Fillmore would have no more quarter than was shown by Knox, to the beautiful, but treacherous Queen Mary of Scotland.—The fact that the church of our country, (with fractional exceptions,) does not esteem "the Fugitive Slave Law" as a declaration of war against religious liberty, implies that that church regards religion simply as a form of worship, an empty ceremony, and *not* a vital principle, requiring active benevolence, justice, love and good will towards man. It esteems sacrifice above mercy; psalm-singing above right doing; solemn meetings above practical righteousness. A worship that can be conducted by persons who refuse to give shelter to the houseless, to give bread to the hungry, clothing to the naked, and who enjoin obedience to a law forbidding these acts of mercy, is a curse, not a blessing to mankind. The Bible addresses all such persons as "scribes, pharisees, hypocrites, who pay tithe of *mint, anise,* and *cummin,* and have omitted the weightier matters of the law, judgment, mercy and faith."

THE CHURCH RESPONSIBLE

But the church of this country is not only indifferent to the wrongs of the slave, it actually takes sides with the oppressors. It has made itself the bulwark of American slavery, and the shield of American slave-hunters. Many of its most eloquent Divines, who stand as the very lights of the church, have shamelessly given the sanction of religion, and the Bible, to the whole slave system.—They have taught that man may, properly, be a slave; that the relation of master and slave is ordained of God; that to send back an escaped bondman to his master is clearly the duty of all the followers of the Lord Jesus Christ; and this horrible blasphemy is palmed off upon the world for Christianity.

For my part, I would say, welcome infidelity! welcome atheism! welcome anything! in preference to the gospel, *as preached by those Divines!* They convert the very name of religion into an engine of tyranny, and barbarous cruelty, and serve to confirm more infidels, in this age, than all the infidel writings of Thomas Paine, Voltaire, and Bolingbroke, put together, have done! These ministers make religion a cold and flinty-hearted thing, having neither principles of right action, nor bowels of compassion. They strip the love of God of its beauty, and leave the throne of religion a huge, horrible, repulsive form. It is a religion for oppressors, tyrants, man-stealers, and *thugs*. It is not that *"pure and undefiled religion"* which is from above, and which is *"first pure, then peaceable, easy to be entreated,* full of mercy and good fruits, *without partiality, and without hypocrisy."* But a religion which favors the rich against the poor; which exalts the proud above the humble; which divides mankind into two classes, tyrants and slaves; which says to the man in chains, *stay there;* and to the oppressor, *oppress on;* it is a religion which may be professed and enjoyed by all the robbers and enslavers of mankind; it makes God a respecter of persons, denies his fatherhood of the race, and tramples in the dust the great truth of the brotherhood of man. All this we affirm to be true of the popular church, and the popular worship of our land and nation—a religion, a church, and a worship which, on the authority of inspired wisdom, we pronounce to be an abomination in the sight of God. In the language of Isaiah, the American church might be well addressed, "Bring no more vain oblations; incense is an abomination unto me: the new moons and Sabbaths, the calling of assemblies, I cannot away with; it is iniquity, even the solemn meeting. Your new moons, and your appointed feasts my soul hateth. They are a trouble to me; I am weary to bear them; and when ye spread forth your hands I will hide mine eyes from you. Yea! when ye make many prayers, I will not hear. YOUR HANDS ARE FULL OF BLOOD; cease to do evil, learn to do well; seek judgment; relieve the oppressed; judge for the fatherless; plead for the widow."

The American church is guilty, when viewed in connection with what it is doing to uphold slavery; but it is superlatively guilty when viewed in connection with its ability to abolish slavery.

The sin of which it is guilty is one of omission as well as of commission. Albert Barnes but uttered what the common sense of every man at all observant of the actual state of the case will receive as truth, when he declared that "There is no power out of the church that could sustain slavery an hour, if it were not sustained in it."

Let the religious press, the pulpit, the sunday school, the conference meeting, the great ecclesiastical, missionary, Bible and tract associations of the land array their immense powers against slavery, and slave-holding; and the whole system of crime and blood would be scattered to the winds, and that they do not do this involves them in the most awful responsibility of which the mind can conceive.

In prosecuting the anti-slavery enterprise, we have been asked to spare the church, to spare the ministry; but *how,* we ask, could such a thing be done? We are met on the threshold of our efforts for the redemption of the slave, by the church and ministry of the country, in battle arrayed against us; and we are compelled to fight or flee. From *what* quarter, I beg to know, has proceeded a fire so deadly upon our ranks, during the last two years, as from the Northern pulpit? As the champions of oppressors, the chosen men of American theology have appeared—men, honored for their so-called piety, and their real learning. The LORDS of Buffalo, the SPRINGS of New York, the LATHROPS of Auburn, the COXES and SPENCERS of Brooklyn, the GANNETS and SHARPS of Boston, the DEWEYS of Washington, and other great religious lights of the land, have, in utter denial of the authority of *Him*, by whom they professed to be called to the ministry, deliberately taught us, against the example of the Hebrews, and against the remonstrance of the Apostles, they teach *"that we ought to obey man's law before the law of God."*

My spirit wearies of such blasphemy; and how such men can be supported, as the "standing types and representatives of Jesus Christ," is a mystery which I leave others to penetrate. In speaking of the American church, however, let it be distinctly understood that I mean the *great mass* of the religious organizations of our land. There are exceptions, and I thank God that there are. Noble men may be found, scattered all over these Northern States, of whom Henry Ward Beecher of Brooklyn, Samuel J. May of Syracuse, and my esteemed friend* on the platform, are shining examples; and let me say further, that, upon these men lies the duty to inspire our ranks with high religious faith and zeal, and to cheer us on in the great mission of the slave's redemption from his chains.

RELIGION IN ENGLAND AND RELIGION IN AMERICA

One is struck with the difference between the attitude of the American church towards the anti-slavery movement, and that occupied by the churches in England towards a similar movement in that country. There, the church, true to its mission of ameliorating, elevating, and improving the condition of mankind, came forward promptly, bound up the wounds of the West Indian slave, and restored him to his liberty. There, the question of emancipation was a high religious question. It was demanded, in the name of humanity, and according to the law of the living God. The Sharps, the Clarksons, the Wilberforces, the Buxtons, and Burchells and the Knibbs, were alike famous for their piety, and for their philanthropy. The anti-slavery movement *there*, was not an anti-church movement, for the reason that the church took its full share in prosecuting that movement: and the anti-slavery movement in this country will cease to be an anti-church movement, when the church of this country shall assume a favorable, instead of a hostile position towards that movement.

Americans! your republican politics, not less than your republican religion, are flagrantly inconsistent. You boast of your love of liberty,

*Rev. R. R. Raymond.

your superior civilization, and your pure Christianity, while the whole political power of the nation, as embodied in the two great political parties, is solemnly pledged to support and perpetuate the enslavement of three millions of your countrymen. You hurl your anathemas at the crowned headed tyrants of Russia and Austria, and pride yourselves on your Democratic institutions, while you yourselves consent to be the mere *tools* and *body-guards* of the tyrants of Virginia and Carolina. You invite to your shores fugitives of oppression from abroad, honor them with banquets, greet them with ovations, cheer them, toast them, salute them, protect them, and pour out your money to them like water; but the fugitives from your own land, you advertise, hunt, arrest, shoot and kill. You glory in your refinement and your universal education; yet you maintain a system as barbarous and dreadful, as ever stained the character of a nation—a system begun in avarice, supported in pride, and perpetuated in cruelty. You shed tears over fallen Hungary, and make the sad story of her wrongs the theme of your poets, statesmen and orators, till your gallant sons are ready to fly to arms to vindicate her cause against her oppressors; but, in regard to the ten thousand wrongs of the American slave, you would enforce the strictest silence, and would hail him as an enemy of the nation who dares to make those wrongs the subject of public discourse! You are all on fire at the mention of liberty for France or for Ireland; but are as cold as an iceberg at the thought of liberty for the enslaved of America.—You discourse eloquently on the dignity of labor; yet, you sustain a system which, in its very essence, casts a stigma upon labor. You can bare your bosom to the storm of British artillery, to throw off a threepenny tax on tea; and yet wring the last hard-earned farthing from the grasp of the black laborers of your country. You profess to believe "that, of one blood, God made all nations of men to dwell on the face of all the earth." and hath commanded all men, everywhere to love one another; yet you notoriously hate, (and glory in your hatred,) all men whose skins are not colored like your own. You declare, before the world, and are understood by the world to declare, that you *"hold these truths to be self evident, that all men are created equal; and are endowed by their Creator with certain inalienable rights; and that, among these are, life, liberty, and the pursuit of happiness;"* and yet, you hold securely, in a bondage, which according to your own Thomas Jefferson, *"is worse than ages of that which your fathers rose in rebellion to oppose,"* a seventh part of the inhabitants of your country.

Fellow-citizens! I will not enlarge further on your national inconsistencies. The existence of slavery in this country brands your republicanism as a sham, your humanity as a base pretence, and your Christianity as a lie. It destroys your moral power abroad; it corrupts your politicians at home. It saps the foundation of religion; it makes your name a hissing, and a by-word to a mocking earth. It is the antagonistic force in your government, the only thing that seriously disturbs and endangers your *Union*. It fetters your progress; it is the enemy of improvement, the deadly foe of education; it fosters pride; it breeds insolence; it promotes vice; it shelters crime; it is a curse to the earth that supports it; and yet, you cling to it, as if it were the sheet anchor of all your hopes. Oh! be warned! be warned! a horrible reptile is coiled up in your nation's bosom; the venomous creature is nursing at the tender breast of your youthful republic; *for the love of God, tear away,* and fling from you the hideous monster, and *let the weight of twenty millions, crush and destroy it forever!*

THE CONSTITUTION

But it is answered in reply to all this, that precisely what I have now denounced is, in fact, guaranteed and sanctioned by the Constitution of the United States; that the right to hold, and to hunt slaves is a part of that Constitution framed by the illustrious Fathers of this Republic.

Then, I dare to affirm, notwithstanding all I have said before, your fathers stooped, basely stooped

> "To palter with us in a double sense:
> And keep the word of promise to the ear,
> But break it to the heart."

And instead of being the honest men I have before declared them to be, they were the veriest imposters that ever practised on mankind. *This* is the inevitable conclusion, and from it there is no escape; but I differ from those who charge this baseness on the framers of the Constitution of the United States. *It is a slander upon their memory,* at least, so I believe. There is not time now to argue the constitutional question at length; nor have I the ability to discuss it as it ought to be discussed. The subject has been handled with masterly power by Lysander Spooner, Esq., by William Goodell, by Samuel E. Sewall, Esq., and last, though not least, by Gerritt Smith, Esq. These gentlemen have, as I think, fully and clearly vindicated the Constitution from any design to support slavery for an hour.

Fellow-citizens! there is no matter in respect to which, the people of the North have allowed themselves to be so ruinously imposed upon, as that of the pro-slavery character of the Constitution. In *that* instrument I hold there is neither warrant, license, nor sanction of the hateful thing; but, interpreted, as it *ought* to be interpreted, the Constitution is a GLORIOUS LIBERTY DOCUMENT. Read its preamble, consider its purposes. Is slavery among them? Is it at the gateway? or is it in the temple? it is neither. While I do not intend to argue this question on the present occasion, let me ask, if it be not somewhat singular that, if the Constitution were intended to be, by its framers and adopters, a slave-holding instrument, why neither *slavery, slaveholding,* nor *slave* can anywhere be found in it. What would be thought of an instrument, drawn up, *legally* drawn up, for the purpose of entitling the city of Rochester to a track of land, in which no mention of land was made? Now, there are certain rules of interpretation, for the proper understanding of all legal instruments. These rules are well established. They are plain, common-sense rules, such as you and I, and all of us, can understand and apply, without having passed years in the study of law. I scout the idea that the question of the constitutionality, or unconstitutionality of slavery is not a question for the people. I hold that every American citizen has a right to form an opinion of the Constitution, and to propagate that opinion, and to use all honorable means to make his opinion the prevailing one. Without this right, the liberty of an American citizen would be as insecure as that of a Frenchman. Ex-Vice-President Dallas tells us that the Constitution is an object to which no American mind can be too attentive, and no American heart too devoted. He further says, the Constitution, in its words, is plain and intelligible, and is meant for the home-bred, unsophisticated understandings of our fellow-citizens. Senator Berrien tells us that the Constitution is the fundamental law, that which controls all others. The charter of our liberties, which every citizen has a personal interest in understanding thoroughly. The testimony of Senator Breese, Lewis Cass, and many others that might be named, who are everywhere esteemed as sound lawyers, so regard the Constitution. I take it, therefore, that it is not presumption in a private citizen to form an opinion of that instrument.

Now, take the Constitution according to its plain reading, and I defy the presentation of a single pro-slavery clause in it. On the other hand it will be found to contain principles and purposes, entirely hostile to the existence of slavery.

I have detained my audience entirely too long already. At some future period I will gladly avail myself of an opportunity to give this subject a full and fair discussion.

Allow me to say, in conclusion, notwithstanding the dark picture I have this day presented, of the state of the nation, I do not despair of this country. There are forces in operation, which must inevitably, work the downfall of slavery. *"The arm of the Lord is not shortened,"* and the doom of slavery is certain. I, therefore, leave off where I began, with *hope.* While drawing encouragement from the Declaration of Independence, the great principles it contains, and the genius of American Institutions, my spirit is also cheered by the obvious tendencies of the age. Nations do not now stand in the same relation to each other that they did ages ago. No nation can now shut itself up, from the surrounding world, and trot round in the same old path of its fathers without interference. The time *was* when such could be done. Long established customs of hurtful character could formerly fence themselves in, and do their evil work with social impunity. Knowledge was then confined and enjoyed by the privileged few, and the multitude walked on in mental darkness. But a change has now come over the affairs of mankind. Walled cities and empires have become unfashionable. The arm of commerce has borne away the gates of the strong city. Intelligence is penetrating the darkest corners of the globe. It makes its pathway over and under the sea, as well as on the earth. Wind, steam, and lightning are its chartered agents. Oceans no longer divide, but link nations together. From Boston to London is now a holiday excursion. Space is comparatively annihilated.—Thoughts expressed on one side of the Atlantic are distinctly heard on the other.

The far off and almost fabulous Pacific rolls in grandeur at our feet. The Celestial Empire, the mystery of ages, is being solved. The fiat of the Almighty, *"Let there be Light,"* has not yet spent its force. No abuse, no outrage whether in taste, sport or avarice, can now hide itself from the all-pervading light. The iron shoe, and crippled foot of China must be seen, in contrast with nature. *Africa must rise and put on her yet unwoven garment. "Ethiopia shall stretch out her hand unto God."* In the fervent aspirations of William Lloyd Garrison, I say, and let every heart join in saying it:

> God speed the year of jubilee
>   The wide world o'er!
> When from their galling chains set free,
> Th' oppress'd shall vilely bend the knee,
> And wear the yoke of tyranny
>   Like brutes no more.
> That year will come, and freedom's reign,
> To man his plundered rights again
>   Restore.
>
> God speed the day when human blood
>   Shall cease to flow!
> In every clime be understood,
> The claims of human brotherhood,
> And each return for evil, good,
>   Not blow for blow;
> That day will come all feuds to end,
> And change into a faithful friend
>   Each foe.
>
> God speed the hour, the glorious hour,
>   When none on earth
> Shall exercise a lordly power,

Nor in a tyrant's presence cower;
But all to manhood's stature tower,
   By equal birth!
THAT HOUR WILL COME, to each, to all,
And from his prison-house, the thrall
   Go forth.

Until that year, day, hour, arrive,
With head, and heart, and hand I'll strive,
To break the rod, and rend the gyve,
The spoiler of his prey deprive—
   So witness Heaven!
And never from my chosen post,
Whate'er the peril or the cost,
   Be driven.

CHAPTER 5

The Heroic Slave (1853)

Part of *The Heroic Slave* first appeared in *Frederick Douglass' Paper* on March 11, 1853. The earliest complete version of the novella (and the source of the present text) was published in *Autographs for Freedom* (Boston: Jewett, 1853), an antislavery anthology created as an aid for fundraising by Julia Griffiths, Douglass's friend and the financial officer of his newspaper. In his speeches during the late 1840s, Douglass helped to keep the memory of Madison Washington, the successful leader of an 1841 slave mutiny, alive. But it was not until passage of the Fugitive Slave Law in 1850 that Douglass became sufficiently militant on the justifiability of violence against slaveholders to treat Washington as the epitome of the "heroic slave."

The Heroic Slave reads in some ways like a historical novel pared down to the basic plot of the slave narrative, the quest of the bondman for freedom. Douglass's major innovation in his recreation of Madison Washington was to give this heroic slave a voice. The world knew what Madison Washington had done on board the *Creole*, but it did not know his motives, his justification, or his goals in perpetrating the uprising. Douglass wanted not only to place Washington on the stage of history but to give him an extensive speaking part so that he could articulate himself in a fashion befitting true nobility of mind and spirit. To late twentieth-century readers, Washington's rhetoric may sound high-flown and literary to the extreme, at times almost bombastic. But in an era when virtually all African Americans in popular literature spoke in gutterals or a laughable pidgen, Douglass's oratorical slave provided a needed cultural alternative. "I forgot his blackness in the dignity of his manner, and the eloquence of his speech," Tom Grant, first mate of the *Creole*, confesses to a group of fellow sailors after the mutiny. By giving special attention to the positive effect of Washington's words, not just his deeds, on the minds and hearts of ordinary whites from the North and South, Douglass's novella established a lasting tradition in African American fiction of the black hero as master wordsmith, a liberator through language.

❖ ❖ ❖

PART I

Oh! child of grief, why weepest thou?
Why droops thy sad and mournful brow?
Why is thy look so like despair?
What deep, sad sorrow lingers there?

The State of Virginia is famous in American annals for the multitudinous array of her statesmen and heroes. She has been dignified by some the mother of statesmen. History has not been sparing in recording their names, or in blazoning their deeds. Her high position in this respect, has given her an enviable distinction among her sister States. With Virginia for his birth-place, even a man of ordinary parts, on account of the general partiality for her sons, easily rises to eminent stations. Men, not great enough to attract special attention in their native States, have, like a certain distinguished citizen in the State of New York, sighed and repined that they were not born in Virginia. Yet not all the great ones of the Old Dominion have, by the fact of their birth-place, escaped undeserved obscurity. By some strange neglect, *one* of the truest, manliest, and bravest of her children,—one who, in after years, will, I think, command the pen of genius to set his merits forth, holds now no higher place in the records of that grand old Commonwealth than is held by a horse or an ox. Let those account for it who can, but there stands the fact, that a man who loved liberty as well as did Patrick Henry,—who deserved it as much as Thomas Jefferson,—and who fought for it with a valor as high, an arm as strong, and against odds as great, as he who led all the armies of the American colonies through the great war for freedom and independence, lives now only in the chattel records of his native State.

Glimpses of this great character are all that can now be presented. He is brought to view only by a few transient incidents, and these afford but partial satisfaction. Like a guiding star on a stormy night, he is seen through the parted clouds and the howling tempests; or, like the gray peak of a menacing rock on a perilous coast, he is seen by the quivering flash of angry lightning, and he again disappears covered with mystery.

Curiously, earnestly, anxiously we peer into the dark, and wish even for the blinding flash, or the light of northern skies to reveal him. But alas! he is still enveloped in darkness, and we return from the pursuit like a wearied and disheartened mother, (after a tedious and unsuccessful search for a lost child,) who returns weighed down with disappointment and sorrow. Speaking of marks, traces, possibles, and probabilities, we come before our readers.

In the spring of 1835, on a Sabbath morning, within hearing of the solemn peals of the church bells at a distant village a Northern traveller through the State of Virginia drew up his horse to drink at a sparkling brook, near the edge of a dark pine forest. While his weary and thirsty steed drew in the grateful water, the rider caught the sound of a human voice, apparently engaged in earnest conversation.

Following the direction of the sound, he descried, among the tall pines, the man whose voice had arrested his attention. "To whom can he be speaking?" thought the traveller. "He seems to be alone." The circumstance interested him much, and he became intensely curious to know what thoughts and feelings, or, it might be, high aspirations, guided those rich and mellow accents. Tieing his horse at a short distance from the brook, he stealthily drew near the solitary speaker; and, concealing himself by the side of a huge fallen tree, he distinctly heard the following soliloquy:—

"What, then, is life to me? it is aimless and worthless, and worse than worthless. Those birds, perched on yon swinging boughs, in friendly conclave, sounding forth their merry notes in seeming worship of the rising sun, though liable to the sportsman's fowling-piece, are still my superiors. They *live free*, though they may die slaves. They fly where they list by day, and retire in freedom at night. But what is freedom to me, or I to it? I am a *slave*,—born a slave, an abject slave,— even before I [was] made part of this breathing world, the scourge was platted for my back; the fetters were forged for my limbs. How mean a thing am I. That accursed and crawling snake, that miserable reptile, that has just glided into its slimy home, is freer and better off than I. He escaped my blow, and is safe. But here am I, a man,—yes, *a man!*— with thoughts and wishes, with powers and faculties as far as angel's flight above that hated reptile,—yet he is my superior, and scorns to own me as his master, or to stop to take my blows. When he saw my uplifted arm, he darted beyond my reach, and turned to give me battle. I dare not do as much as that. I neither run nor fight, but do meanly stand, answering each heavy blow of a cruel master with doleful wails and piteous cries. I am galled with irons; but even these are more tolerable than the consciousness, the *galling* consciousness of cowardice and indecision. Can it be that I *dare* not run away? *Perish the thought*, I *dare* do anything which may be done by another. When that young man struggled with the waves *for life*, and others stood back appalled in helpless horror, did I not plunge in, forgetful of life, to save his? The raging bull from whom all others fled, pale with fright, did I not keep at bay with a single pitchfork? Could a coward do that? *No,—no,*—I wrong myself,—I am no coward. *Liberty* I will have, or die in the attempt to gain it. This working that others may live in idleness! This cringing submission to insolence and curses! This living under the constant dread and apprehension of being sold and transferred, like a mere brute, is *too* much for me. I will stand it no longer. What others have done, I will do. These trusty legs, or these sinewy arms shall place me among the free. Tom escaped; so can I. The North Star will not be less kind to me than to him. I will follow it. I will at least make the trial. I have nothing to lose. If I am caught, I shall only be a slave. If I am shot, I shall only lose a life which is a burden and a curse. If I get clear, (as something tells me I shall,) liberty, the inalienable birth-right of every man, precious and priceless, will be mine. My resolution is fixed. *I shall be free.*"

At these words the traveller raised his head cautiously and noise-lessly, and caught, from his hiding-place, a full view of the unsus-pecting speaker. Madison (for that was the name of our hero) was standing erect, a smile of satisfaction rippled upon his expressive coun-tenance, like that which plays upon the face of one who has but just solved a difficult problem, or vanquished a malignant foe; for at that moment he was free, at least in spirit. The future gleamed brightly before him, and his fetters lay broken at his feet. His air was trium-phant.

Madison was of manly form. Tall, symmetrical, round, and strong. In his movements he seemed to combine, with the strength of the lion, a lion's elasticity. His torn sleeves disclosed arms like polished iron. His face was "black, but comely." His eye, lit with emotion, kept guard under a brow as dark and as glossy as the raven's wing. His whole appearance betokened Herculean strength; yet there was nothing sav-age or forbidding in his aspect. A child might play in his arms, or dance on his shoulders. A giant's strength but not a giant's heart was in him. His broad mouth and nose spoke only of good nature and kindness. But his voice, that unfailing index of the soul, though full and melodious, had that in it which could terrify as well as charm. He was just the man you would choose when hardships were to be en-dured, or danger to be encountered,—intelligent and brave. He had the head to conceive, and the hand to execute. In a word, he was one to be sought as a friend, but to be dreaded as an enemy.

As our traveller gazed upon him, he almost trembled at the thought of his dangerous intrusion. Still he could not quit the place. He had long desired to sound the mysterious depths of the thoughts and feelings of a slave. He was not, therefore, disposed to allow so providential an opportunity to pass unimproved. He resolved to hear more; so he listened again for those mellow and mournful accents which, he says, made such an impression upon him as can never be erased. He did not have to wait long. There came another gush from the same full fountain; now bitter, and now sweet. Scathing denuncia-tions of the cruelty and injustice of slavery; heart-touching narrations of his own personal suffering, intermingled with prayers to the God of the oppressed for help and deliverance, were followed by presenta-tions of the dangers and difficulties of escape, and formed the burden of his eloquent utterances; but his high resolution clung to him,—for he ended each speech by an emphatic declaration of his purpose to be free. It seemed that the very repetition of this imparted a glow to his countenance. The hope of freedom seemed to sweeten, for a season, the bitter cup of slavery, and to make it, for a time, tolerable; for when in the very whirlwind of anguish,—when his heart's cord seemed screwed up to snapping tension, hope sprung up and soothed his troubled spirit. Fitfully he would exclaim, "How can I leave her? Poor thing! what can she do when I am gone? Oh! oh! 'tis impossible that I can leave poor Susan!"

A brief pause intervened. Our traveller raised his head, and saw again the sorrow-smitten slave. His eye was fixed upon the ground. The strong man staggered under a heavy load. Recovering himself, he argued thus aloud: "All is uncertain here. To-morrow's sun may not rise before I am sold, and separated from her I love. What, then, could I do for her? I should be in more hopeless slavery, and she no nearer to liberty,—whereas if I were free,—my arms my own,—I might devise the means to rescue her."

This said, Madison cast around a searching glance, as if the thought of being overheard had flashed across his mind. He said no more, but, with measured steps, walked away, and was lost to the eye of our traveller amidst the wildering woods.

Long after Madison had left the ground, Mr. Listwell (our traveller) remained in motionless silence, meditating on the extraordinary revelations to which he had listened. He seemed fastened to the spot, and stood half hoping, half fearing the return of the sable preacher to his solitary temple. The speech of Madison rung through the chambers of his soul, and vibrated through his entire frame. "Here is indeed a man," thought he, "of rare endowments, a child of God,—guilty of no crime but the color of his skin,—hiding away from the face of humanity, and pouring out his thoughts and feelings, his hopes and resolutions to the lonely woods; to him those distant church bells have no grateful music. He shuns the church, the altar, and the great congregation of christian worshippers, and wanders away to the gloomy forest, to utter in the vacant air complaints and griefs, which the religion of his times and his country can neither console nor relieve. Goaded almost to madness by the sense of the injustice done him, he resorts hither to give vent to his pent up feelings, and to debate with himself the feasibility of plans, plans of his own invention, for his own deliverance. From this hour I am an abolitionist. I have seen enough and heard enough, and I shall go to my home in Ohio resolved to atone for my past indifference to this ill-starred race, by making such exertions as I shall be able to do, for the speedy emancipation of every slave in the land."

PART II

"The gaudy, babbling and remorseful day
Is crept into the bosom of the sea;
And now loud-howling wolves arouse the jades
That drag the tragic melancholy night;
Who with their drowsy, slow, and flagging wings
Clip dead men's graves, and from their misty jaws
Breathe foul contagions, darkness in the air."
Shakespeare.

Five years after the foregoing singular occurrence, in the winter of 1840, Mr. and Mrs. Listwell sat together by the fireside of their own happy home, in the State of Ohio. The children were all gone to bed. A single lamp burnt brightly on the centre-table. All was still and comfortable within; but the night was cold and dark; a heavy wind sighed and moaned sorrowfully around the house and barn, occasionally bringing against the clattering windows a stray leaf from the large oak trees that embowered their dwelling. It was a night for strange noises and for strange fancies. A whole wilderness of thought might pass through one's mind during such an evening. The smouldering embers, partaking of the spirit of the restless night, became fruitful of varied and fantastic pictures, and revived many bygone scenes and old impressions. The happy pair seemed to sit in silent fascination, gazing on the fire. Suddenly this *reverie* was interrupted by a heavy growl. Ordinarily such an occurrence would have scarcely provoked a single word, or excited the least apprehension. But there are certain seasons when the slightest sound sends a jar through all the subtle chambers of the mind; and such a season was this. The happy pair started up, as if some sudden danger had come upon them. The growl was from their trusty watch-dog.

"What can it mean? Certainly no one can be out on such a night as this," said Mrs. Listwell.

"The wind has deceived the dog, my dear; he has mistaken the noise of falling branches, brought down by the wind, for that of the footsteps of persons coming to the house. I have several times to-night thought that I heard the sound of footsteps. I am sure, however, that it was but the wind. Friends would not be likely to come out at such an hour, or such a night; and thieves are too lazy and self-indulgent to expose themselves to this biting frost; but should there be any one about, our brave old Monte, who is on the look-out, will not be slow in sounding the alarm."

Saying this they quietly left the window, whither they had gone to learn the cause of the menacing growl, and re-seated themselves by the fire, as if reluctant to leave the slowly expiring embers, although the hour was late. A few minutes only intervened after resuming their seats, when again their sober meditations were disturbed. Their faithful dog now growled and barked furiously, as if assailed by an advancing foe. Simultaneously the good couple arose, and stood in mute expectation. The contest without seemed fierce and violent. It was, however, soon over,—the barking ceased, for, with true canine instinct, Monte quickly discovered that a friend, not an enemy of the family, was coming to the house, and instead of rushing to repel the supposed intruder, he was now at the door, whimpering and dancing for the admission of himself and his newly made friend.

Mr. Listwell knew by this movement that all was well; he advanced and opened the door, and saw by the light that streamed out into the darkness, a tall man advancing slowly towards the house, with a stick in one hand, and a small bundle in the other. "It is a traveller," thought he, "who has missed his way, and is coming to inquire the road. I am glad we did not go to bed earlier,—I have felt all the evening as if somebody would be here to-night."

The man had now halted a short distance from the door, and looked prepared alike for flight or battle. "Come in, sir, don't be alarmed, you have probably lost your way."

Slightly hesitating, the traveller walked in; not, however, without regarding his host with a scrutinizing glance. "No, sir," said he, "I have come to ask you a greater favor."

Instantly Mr. Listwell exclaimed, (as the recollection of the Virginia forest scene flashed upon him,) "Oh, sir, I know not your name, but I have seen your face, and heard your voice before. I am glad to see you. *I know all.* You are flying for your liberty,—be seated,—be seated,—banish all fear. You are safe under my roof."

This recognition, so unexpected, rather disconcerted and disquieted the noble fugitive. The timidity and suspicion of persons escaping from slavery are easily awakened, and often what is intended to dispel the one, and to allay the other, has precisely the opposite effect. It was so in this case. Quickly observing the unhappy impression made by his words and action, Mr. Listwell assumed a more quiet and inquiring aspect, and finally succeeded in removing the apprehensions which his very natural and generous salutation had aroused.

Thus assured, the stranger said, "Sir, you have rightly guessed, I am, indeed, a fugitive from slavery. My name is Madison,—Madison Washington my mother used to call me. I am on my way to Canada, where I learn that persons of my color are protected in all the rights of men; and my object in calling upon you was, to beg the privilege of resting my weary limbs for the night in your barn. It was my purpose to have continued my journey till morning; but the piercing cold, and the frowning darkness compelled me to seek shelter; and, seeing a light through the lattice of your window, I was encouraged to come here to beg the privilege named. You will do me a great favor by affording me shelter for the night."

"A resting-place, indeed, sir, you shall have; not, however, in my barn, but in the best room of my house. Consider yourself, if you please, under the roof of a friend; for such I am to you, and to all your deeply injured race."

While this introductory conversation was going on, the kind lady had revived the fire, and was diligently preparing supper; for she, not less than her husband, felt for the sorrows of the oppressed and hunted ones of earth, and was always glad of an opportunity to do them a service. A bountiful repast was quickly prepared, and the hungry and toil-worn bondman was cordially invited to partake thereof. Gratefully he acknowledged the favor of his benevolent benefactress; but appeared scarcely to understand what such hospitality could mean. It was the first time in his life that he had met so humane and friendly a greeting at the hands of persons whose color was unlike his own; yet it was impossible for him to doubt the charitableness of his new friends, or the genuiness of the welcome so freely given; and he therefore, with many thanks, took his seat at the table with Mr. and Mrs. Listwell, who, desirous to make him feel at home, took a cup of tea themselves, while urging upon Madison the best that the house could afford.

Supper over, all doubts and apprehensions banished, the three drew around the blazing fire, and a conversation commenced which lasted till long after midnight.

"Now," said Madison to Mr. Listwell, "I was a little surprised and alarmed when I came in, by what you said; do tell me, sir, *why* you thought you had seen my face before, and by what you knew me to be a fugitive from slavery; for I am sure that I never was before in this neighborhood, and I certainly sought to conceal what I supposed to be the manner of a fugitive slave."

Mr. Listwell at once frankly disclosed the secret; describing the place where he first saw him; rehearsing the language which he (Madison) had used; referring to the effect which his manner and speech had made upon him; declaring the resolution he there formed to be an abolitionist; telling how often he had spoken of the circumstance, and the deep concern he had ever since felt to know what had become of him; and whether he had carried out the purpose to make his escape, as in the woods he declared he would do.

"Ever since that morning," said Mr. Listwell, "you have seldom been absent from my mind, and though now I did not dare to hope that I should ever see you again, I have often wished that such might be my fortune; for, from that hour, your face seemed to be daguerreotyped on my memory."

Madison looked quite astonished, and felt amazed at the narration to which he had listened. After recovering himself he said, "I well remember that morning, and the bitter anguish that wrung my heart; I will state the occasion of it. I had, on the previous Saturday, suffered a cruel lashing; had been tied up to the limb of a tree, with my feet chained together, and a heavy iron bar placed between my ankles. Thus suspended, I received on my naked back forty stripes, and was kept in this distressing position three or four hours, and was then let down, only to have my torture increased; for my bleeding back, gashed by the cow-skin, was washed by the overseer with old brine, partly to augment my suffering, and partly, as he said, to prevent inflammation. My crime was that I had stayed longer at the mill, the day previous, than it was thought I ought to have done, which, I assured my master and the overseer, was no fault of mine; but no excuses were allowed. 'Hold your tongue, you impudent rascal,' met my every explanation. Slave-holders are so imperious when their passions are excited, as to construe every word of the slave into insolence. I could do nothing but submit to the agonizing infliction. Smarting still from the wounds, as well as from the consciousness of being whipt for no cause, I took advantage of the absence of my master, who had gone to church, to spend the time in the woods, and brood over my wretched lot. Oh, sir, I remember it well,—and can never forget it."

"But this was five years ago; where have you been since?"

"I will try to tell you," said Madison. "Just four weeks after that Sabbath morning, I gathered up the few rags of clothing I had, and started, as I supposed, for the North and for freedom. I must not stop to describe my feelings on taking this step. It seemed like taking a leap into the dark. The thought of leaving my poor wife and two little children caused me indescribable anguish; but consoling myself with the reflection that once free, I could, possibly, devise ways and means to gain their freedom also, I nerved myself up to make the attempt. I started, but ill-luck attended me; for after being out a whole week, strange to say, I still found myself on my master's grounds; the third night after being out, a season of clouds and rain set in, wholly preventing me from seeing the North Star, which I had trusted as my guide, not dreaming that clouds might intervene between us.

"This circumstance was fatal to my project, for in losing my star, I lost my way; so when I supposed I was far towards the North, and had almost gained my freedom, I discovered myself at the very point from which I had started. It was a severe trial, for I arrived at home in great destitution; my feet were sore, and in travelling in the dark, I had dashed my foot against a stump, and started a nail, and lamed myself. I was wet and cold; one week had exhausted all my stores; and when I landed on my master's plantation, with all my work to do over again,—hungry, tired, lame, and bewildered,—I almost cursed the day that I was born. In this extremity I approached the quarters. I did so stealthily, although in my desperation I hardly cared whether I was

139

discovered or not. Peeping through the rents of the quarters, I saw my fellow-slaves seated by a warm fire, merrily passing away the time, as though their hearts knew no sorrow. Although I envied their seeming contentment, all wretched as I was, I despised the cowardly acquiescence in their own degradation which it implied, and felt a kind of pride and glory in my own desperate lot. I dared not enter the quarters,—for where there is seeming contentment with slavery, there is certain treachery to freedom. I proceeded towards the great house, in the hope of catching a glimpse of my poor wife, whom I knew might be trusted with my secrets even on the scaffold. Just as I reached the fence which divided the field from the garden, I saw a woman in the yard, who in the darkness I took to be my wife; but a nearer approach told me it was not she. I was about to speak; had I done so, I would not have been here this night; for an alarm would have been sounded, and the hunters been put on my track. Here were hunger, cold, thirst, disappointment, and chagrin, confronted only by the dim hope of liberty. I tremble to think of that dreadful hour. To face the deadly cannon's mouth in warm blood unterrified, is, I think, a small achievement, compared with a conflict like this with gaunt starvation. The gnawings of hunger conquers by degrees, till all that a man has he would give in exchange for a single crust of bread. Thank God, I was not quite reduced to this extremity.

"Happily for me, before the fatal moment of utter despair, my good wife made her appearance in the yard. It was she; I knew her step. All was well now. I was, however, afraid to speak, lest I should frighten her. Yet speak I did; and, to my great joy, my voice was known. Our meeting can be more easily imagined than described. For a time hunger, thirst, weariness, and lameness were forgotten. But it was soon necessary for her to return to the house. She being a house-servant, her absence from the kitchen, if discovered, might have excited suspicion. Our parting was like tearing the flesh from my bones; yet it was the part of wisdom for her to go. She left me with the purpose of meeting me at midnight in the very forest where you last saw me. She knew the place well, as one of my melancholy resorts, and could easily find it, though the night was dark.

"I hastened away, therefore, and concealed myself, to await the arrival of my good angel. As I lay there among the leaves, I was strongly tempted to return again to the house of my master and give myself up; but remembering my solemn pledge on that memorable Sunday morning, I was able to linger out the two long hours between ten and midnight. I may well call them long hours. I have endured much hardship; I have encountered many perils; but the anxiety of those two hours, was the bitterest I ever experienced. True to her word, my wife came laden with provisions, and we sat down on the side of a log, at that dark and lonesome hour of the night. I cannot say we talked; our feelings were too great for that; yet we came to an understanding that I should make the woods my home, for if I gave myself up, I should be whipped and sold away; and if I started for the North, I should leave a wife doubly dear to me. We mutually determined, therefore, that I should remain in the vicinity. In the dismal swamps I lived, sir, five long years,—a cave for my home during the day. I wandered about at night with the wolf and the bear,—sustained by the promise that my good Susan would meet me in the pine woods at least once a week. This promise was redeemed, I assure you, to the letter, greatly to my relief. I had partly become contented with my mode of life, and had made up my mind to spend my days there; but the wilderness that sheltered me thus long took fire, and refused longer to be my hiding-place.

"I will not harrow up your feelings by portraying the terrific scene of this awful conflagration. There is nothing to which I can liken it. It was horribly and indescribably grand. The whole world seemed on fire, and it appeared to me that the day of judgment had come; that the burning bowels of the earth had burst forth, and that the end of all things was at hand. Bears and wolves scorched from their mysterious hiding-places in the earth, and all the wild inhabitants of the untrodden forest, filled with a common dismay, ran forth, yelling, howling, bewildered amidst the smoke and flame. The very heavens seemed to rain down fire through the towering trees; it was by the merest chance that I escaped the devouring element. Running before it, and stopping occasionally to take breath, I looked back to behold its frightful ravages, and to drink in its savage magnificence. It was awful, thrilling, solemn, beyond compare. When aided by the fitful wind, the merciless tempest of fire swept on, sparkling, creaking, cracking, curling, roaring, out-doing in its dreadful splendor a thousand thunderstorms at once. From tree to tree it leaped, swallowing them up in its lurid, baleful glare; and leaving them leafless, limbless, charred, and lifeless behind. The scene was overwhelming, stunning,—nothing was spared,—cattle, tame and wild, herds of swine and of deer, wild beasts of every name and kind,—huge night-birds, bats, and owls, that had retired to their homes in lofty tree-tops to rest, perished in that fiery storm. The long-winged buzzard and croaking raven mingled their dismal cries with those of the countless myriads of small birds that rose up to the skies, and were lost to the sight in clouds of smoke and flame. Oh, I shudder when I think of it! Many a poor wandering fugitive, who, like myself, had sought among wild beasts the mercy denied by our fellow men, saw, in helpless consternation, his dwelling-place and city of refuge reduced to ashes forever. It was this grand conflagration that drove me hither; I ran alike from fire and from slavery."

After a slight pause, (for both speaker and hearers were deeply moved by the above recital,) Mr. Listwell, addressing Madison, said, "If it does not weary you too much, do tell us something of your journeyings since this disastrous burning,—we are deeply interested in everything which can throw light on the hardships of persons escaping from slavery; we could hear you talk all night; are there no incidents that you could relate of your travels hither? or are they such that you do not like to mention them?"

"For the most part, sir, my course has been uninterrupted; and, considering the circumstances, at times even pleasant. I have suffered little for want of food; but I need not tell you how I got it. Your moral code may differ from mine, as your customs and usages are different. The fact is, sir, during my flight, I felt myself robbed by society of all my just rights; that I was in an enemy's land, who sought both my life and my liberty. They had transformed me into a brute; made merchandise of my body, and, for all the purposes of my flight, turned day into night,—and guided by my own necessities, and in contempt of their conventionalities, I did not scruple to take bread where I could get it."

"And just there you were right," said Mr. Listwell; "I once had doubts on this point myself, but a conversation with Gerrit Smith, (a man, by the way, that I wish you could see, for he is a devoted friend of your race, and I know he would receive you gladly,) put an end to all my doubts on this point. But do not let me interrupt you."

"I had but one narrow escape during my whole journey," said Madison.

"Do let us hear of it," said Mr. Listwell.

"Two weeks ago," continued Madison, "after travelling all night, I was overtaken by daybreak, in what seemed to me an almost interminable wood. I deemed it unsafe to go farther, and, as usual, I looked around for a suitable tree in which to spend the day. I liked one with a bushy top, and found one just to my mind. Up I climbed, and hiding myself as well as I could, I, with this strap, (pulling one out of his old coat-pocket,) lashed myself to a bough, and flattered myself that I should get a *good night's* sleep that day; but in this I was soon disappointed. I had scarcely got fastened to my natural hammock, when I heard the voices of a number of persons, apparently approaching the part of the woods where I was. Upon my word, sir, I dreaded more these human voices than I should have done those of wild beasts. I was at a loss to know what to do. If I descended, I should probably be discovered by the men; and if they had dogs I should, doubtless, be 'treed.' It was an anxious moment, but hardships and dangers have been the accompaniments of my life; and have, perhaps, imparted to me a certain hardness of character, which, to some extent, adapts me to them. In my present predicament, I decided to hold my place in the tree-top, and abide the consequences. But here I must disappoint you; for the men, who were all colored, halted at least a hundred yards from me, and began with their axes, in right good earnest, to attack the trees. The sound of their laughing axes was like the report of as many well-charged pistols. By and by there came down at least a dozen trees with a terrible crash. They leaped upon the fallen trees with an air of victory. I could see no dog with them, and felt myself comparatively safe, though I could not forget the possibility that some freak or fancy might bring the axe a little nearer my dwelling than comported with my safety.

"There was no sleep for me that day, and I wished for night. You may imagine that the thought of having the tree attacked under me was far from agreeable, and that it very easily kept me on the look-out. The day was not without diversion. The men at work seemed to be a gay set; and they would often make the woods resound with that uncontrolled laughter for which we, as a race, are remarkable. I held my place in the tree till sunset,—saw the men put on their jackets to be off. I observed that all left the ground except one, whom I saw sitting on the side of a stump, with his head bowed, and his eyes apparently fixed on the ground. I became interested in him. After sitting in the position to which I have alluded ten or fifteen minutes, he left the stump, walked directly towards the tree in which I was secreted, and halted almost under the same. He stood for a moment and looked around, deliberately and reverently took off his hat, by which I saw that he was a man in the evening of life, slightly bald and quite gray. After laying down his hat carefully, he knelt and prayed aloud, and such a prayer, the most fervent, earnest, and solemn, to which I think I ever listened. After reverently addressing the Almighty, as the all-wise, all-good, and the common Father of all mankind, he besought God for grace, for strength, to bear up under, and to endure, as a good soldier, all the hardships and trials which beset the journey of life, and to enable him to live in a manner which accorded with the gospel of Christ. His soul now broke out in humble supplication for deliverance from bondage. 'O thou,' said he, 'that hearest the raven's cry, take pity on poor me! O deliver me! O deliver me! in mercy, O God, deliver me from the chains and manifold hardships of slavery! With thee, O Father, all things are possible. Thou canst stand and measure the earth. Thou hast beheld and drove asunder the nations,—all power is in thy hand,—thou didst say of old, "I have seen the affliction of my people, and am come to deliver them,"—Oh look down upon our afflictions, and have mercy upon us.' But I cannot repeat his prayer, nor can I give you an idea of its deep pathos. I had given but little attention to religion, and had but little faith in it; yet, as the old man prayed, I felt almost like coming down and kneel[ing] by his side, and mingl[ing] my broken complaint with his.

"He had already gained my confidence; as how could it be otherwise? I knew enough of religion to know that the man who prays in secret is far more likely to be sincere than he who loves to pray standing in the street, or in the great congregation. When he arose from his knees, like another Zacheus, I came down from the tree. He seemed a little alarmed at first, but I told him my story, and the good man embraced me in his arms, and assured me of his sympathy.

"I was now about out of provisions, and thought I might safely ask him to help me replenish my store. He said he had no money; but if he had, he would freely give it me. I told him I had *one dollar*; it was all the money I had in the world. I gave it to him, and asked him to purchase some crackers and cheese, and to kindly bring me the balance; that I would remain in or near that place, and would come to him on his return, if he would whistle. He was gone only about an hour. Meanwhile, from some cause or other, I know not what, (but as you shall see very wisely,) I changed my place. On his return I started to meet him; but it seemed as if the shadow of approaching danger fell upon my spirit, and checked my progress. In a very few minutes, closely on the heels of the old man, I distinctly saw *fourteen men*, with something like guns in their hands."

"Oh! the old wretch!" exclaimed Mrs. Listwell "he had betrayed you, had he?"

"I think not," said Madison, "I cannot believe that the old man was to blame. He probably went into a store, asked for the articles for which I sent, and presented the bill I gave him; and it is so unusual for slaves in the country to have money, that fact, doubtless, excited suspicion, and gave rise to inquiry, I can easily believe that the truthfulness of the old man's character compelled him to disclose the facts; and thus were these blood-thirsty men put on my track. Of course I did not present myself; but hugged my hiding-place securely. If discovered and attacked, I resolved to sell my life as dearly as possible.

"After searching about the woods silently for a time, the whole company gathered around the old man; one charged him with lying, and called him an old villain; said he was a thief; charged him with stealing money; said if he did not instantly tell where he got it, they would take the shirt from his old back, and give him thirty-nine lashes.

" 'I did *not* steal the money,' said the old man, 'it was given me, as I told you at the store; and if the man who gave it me is not here, it is not my fault.'

" 'Hush! you lying old rascal; we'll make you smart for it. You shall not leave this spot until you have told where you got that money.'

"They now took hold of him, and began to strip him; while others went to get sticks with which to beat him. I felt, at the moment, like rushing out in the midst of them; but considering that the old man would be whipped the more for having aided a fugitive slave, and that, perhaps, in the *melee* he might be killed outright, I disobeyed this impulse. They tied him to a tree, and began to whip him. My own flesh crept at every blow, and I seem to hear the old man's piteous cries even now. They laid thirty-nine lashes on his bare back, and were going to repeat that number, when one of the company besought his comrades to desist. 'You'll kill the d—d old scoundrel! You've already whipt a dollar's worth out of him, even if he stole it!' 'O yes,' said another, 'let him down. He'll never tell us another lie, I'll warrant ye!' With this, one of the company untied the old man, and bid him go about his business.

"The old man left, but the company remained as much as an hour, scouring the woods. Round and round they went, turning up the underbrush, and peering about like so many bloodhounds. Two or three times they came within six feet of where I lay. I tell you I held my stick with a firmer grasp than I did in coming up to your house to-night. I expected to level one of them at least. Fortunately, however, I eluded their pursuit, and they left me alone in the woods.

"My last dollar was now gone, and you may well suppose I felt the loss of it; but the thought of being once again free to pursue my journey, prevented that depression which a sense of destitution causes; so swinging my little bundle on my back, I caught a glimpse of the *Great Bear* (which ever points the way to my beloved star,) and I started again on my journey. What I lost in money I made up at a hen-roost that same night, upon which I fortunately came."

"But you didn't eat your food raw? How did you cook it?" said Mrs. Listwell.

"O no, Madam," said Madison, turning to his little bundle;—"I had the means of cooking." Here he took out of his bundle an old-fashioned tinder-box, and taking up a piece of a file, which he brought with him, he struck it with a heavy flint, and brought out at least a dozen sparks at once. "I have had this old box," said he, "more than five years. It is the *only* property saved from the fire in the dismal swamp. It has done me good service. It has given me the means of broiling many a chicken!"

It seemed quite a relief to Mrs. Listwell to know that Madison had, at least, lived upon cooked food. Women have a perfect horror of eating uncooked food.

By this time thoughts of what was best to be done about getting Madison to Canada, began to trouble Mr. Listwell; for the laws of Ohio were very stringent against any one who should aid, or who were found aiding a slave to escape through that State. A citizen, for the simple act of taking a fugitive slave in his carriage, had just been stripped of all his property, and thrown penniless upon the world. Notwithstanding this, Mr. Listwell was determined to see Madison safely on his way to Canada. "Give yourself no uneasiness," said he to Madison, "for if it cost my farm, I shall see you safely out of the States, and on your way to a land of liberty. Thank God that there is *such* a land so near us! You will spend to-morrow with us, and to-morrow night I will take you in my carriage to the lake. Once upon that, and you are safe."

"Thank you! thank you," said the fugitive; "I will commit myself to your care."

For the *first* time during *five* years, Madison enjoyed the luxury of resting his limbs on a comfortable bed, and inside a human habitation. Looking at the white sheets, he said to Mr. Listwell, "What, sir! you don't mean that I shall sleep in that bed?"

"Oh yes, oh yes."

After Mr. Listwell left the room, Madison said he really hesitated whether or not he should lie on the floor; for that was *far* more comfortable and inviting than any bed to which he had been used.

We pass over the thoughts and feelings, the hopes and fears, the plans and purposes, that revolved in the mind of Madison during the day that he was secreted at the house of Mr. Listwell. The reader will be content to know that nothing occurred to endanger his liberty, or to excite alarm. Many were the little attentions bestowed upon him in his quiet retreat and hiding-place. In the evening, Mr. Listwell, after treating Madison to a new suit of winter clothes, and replenishing his exhausted purse with five dollars, all in silver, brought out his two-horse wagon, well provided with buffaloes, and silently started off with him to Cleveland. They arrived there without interruption, a few minutes before sunrise the next morning. Fortunately the steamer Admiral lay at the wharf, and was to start for Canada at nine o'clock. Here the last anticipated danger was surmounted. It was feared that just at this point the hunters of men might be on the look-out, and, possibly, pounce upon their victim. Mr. Listwell saw the captain of the boat; cautiously sounded him on the matter of carrying liberty-loving passengers, before he introduced his precious charge. This done, Madison was conducted on board. With usual generosity this true subject of the emancipating queen welcomed Madison in and assured him that he should be safely landed in Canada, free of charge. Madison now felt himself no more a piece of merchandise, but a passenger, and, like any other passenger, going about his business, carrying with him what belonged to him, and nothing which rightfully belonged to anybody else.

Wrapped in his new winter suit, snug and comfortable, a pocket full of silver, safe from his pursuers, embarked for a free country, Madison gave every sign of sincere gratitude, and bade his kind benefactor farewell, with such a grip of the hand as bespoke a heart full of honest manliness, and a soul that knew how to appreciate kindness. It need scarcely be said that Mr. Listwell was deeply moved by the gratitude and friendship he had excited in a nature so noble as that of the fugitive. He went to his home that day with a joy and gratification which knew no bounds. He had done something "to deliver the spoiled out of the hands of the spoiler," he had given bread to the hungry, and clothes to the naked; he had befriended a man to whom the laws of his country forbade all friendship,—and in proportion to the odds against his righteous deed, was the delightful satisfaction that gladdened his heart. On reaching home, he exclaimed, *"He is safe,—he is safe,—he is safe,"*—and the cup of his joy was shared by his excellent lady. The following letter was received from Madison a few days after.

My dear Friend,—for such you truly are:—

Madison is out of the woods at last; I nestle in the mane of the British lion, protected by the mighty paw from the talons and the beak of the American eagle. I AM FREE, and breathe an atmosphere too pure for *slaves,* slave-hunters, or slave-holders. My heart is full. As many thanks to you, sir, and to your kind lady, as there are pebbles on the shores of lake Erie; and may the blessing of God rest upon you both. You will never be forgotten by your profoundly grateful friend,
MADISON WASHINGTON."

PART III

————His head was with his heart,
And that was far away!
Childe Harold.

Just upon the edge of the great road from Petersburg, Virginia, to Richmond, and only about fifteen miles from the latter place, there stands a somewhat ancient and famous public tavern, quite notorious in its better days, as being the grand resort for most of the leading gamblers, horse-racers, cock-fighters, and slave-traders from all the country round about. This old rookery, the nucleus of all sorts of birds, mostly those of ill omen, has, like everything else peculiar to Virginia, lost much of its ancient consequence and splendor; yet it keeps up some appearance of gaiety and high life, and is still frequented, even by respectable travellers, who are unacquainted with its past history and present condition. Its fine old portico looks well at a distance, and gives the building an air of grandeur. A nearer view, however, does little to sustain this pretension. The house is large, and its style imposing, but time and dissipation, unfailing in their results, have made ineffaceable marks upon it, and it must, in the common course of events, soon be numbered with things that were. The gloomy mantle of ruin is, already, outspread to envelop it, and its remains, even but now remind one of a human skull, after the flesh has mingled with the earth. Old hats and rags fill the places in the upper windows once occupied by large panes of glass, and the molding boards along the roofing have dropped off from their places, leaving holes and crevices in the rented wall for bats and swallows to build their nests in. The platform of the portico, which fronts the highway is a rickety affair, its planks are loose, and in some places entirely gone, leaving effective mantraps in their stead for nocturnal ramblers. The wooden pillars, which once supported it, but which now hang as encumbrances, are all rotten, and tremble with the touch. A part of the stable, a fine old structure in its day, which has given comfortable shelter to hundreds of the noblest steeds of "the Old Dominion" at once, was blown down many years ago, and never has been, and probably never will be, re-built. The doors of the barn are in wretched condition; they will shut with a little human strength to help their worn out hinges, but not otherwise. The side of the great building seen from the road is much discolored in sundry places by slops poured from the upper windows, rendering it unsightly and offensive in other respects. Three or four great dogs, looking as dull and gloomy as the mansion itself, lie stretched out along the door-sills under the portico; and double the number of loafers, some of them completely rum-ripe, and others rip-ening, dispose themselves like so many sentinels about the front of the house. These latter understand the science of scraping acquaintance to perfection. They know every-body, and almost every-body knows them. Of course, as their title implies, they have no regular employ-ment. They are (to use an expressive phrase) *hangers on,* or still better, they are what sailors would denominate *holders-on to the slack, in every-body's mess, and in nobody's watch.* They are, however, as good as the newspaper for the events of the day, and they sell their knowledge almost as cheap. Money they seldom have; yet they always have capi-tal the most reliable. They make their way with a succeeding traveller by intelligence gained from a preceding one. All the great names of Virginia they know by heart, and have seen their owners often. The history of the house is folded in their lips, and they rattle off stories in connection with it, equal to the guides at Dryburgh Abbey. He must be a shrewd man, and well skilled in the art of evasion, who gets out of the hands of these fellows without being at the expense of a treat.

It was at this old tavern, while on a second visit to the State of Virginia in 1841, that Mr. Listwell, unacquainted with the fame of the place, turned aside, about sunset, to pass the night. Riding up to the house, he had scarcely dismounted, when one of the half dozen bar-room fraternity met and addressed him in a manner exceedingly bland and accommodating.

"Five evening, sir."

"Very fine," said Mr. Listwell. "This is a tavern, I believe?"

"O yes, sir, yes; although you may think it looks a little the worse for wear, it was once as good a house as any in Virginy. I make no doubt if ye spend the night here, you'll think it a good house yet; for there aint a more accommodating man in the country than you'll find the landlord."

Listwell. "The most I want is a good bed for myself, and a full manger for my horse. If I get these, I shall be quite satisfied."

Loafer. "Well, I alloys like to hear a gentleman talk for his horse; and just because the horse can't talk for itself. A man that don't care about his beast, and don't look arter it when he's travelling, aint much in my eye anyhow. Now, sir, I likes a horse, and I'll guarantee your horse will be taken good care on here. That old stable, for all you see it looks so shabby now, once sheltered the great *Eclipse*, when he run here agin *Batchelor* and *Jumping Jemmy*. Them was fast horses, but he beat 'em both."

Listwell. "Indeed."

Loafer. "Well I rather reckon you've travelled a right smart distance to-day, from the look of your horse?"

Listwell. "Forty miles only."

Loafer. "Well! I'll be darned if that aint a pretty good *only*. Mister, that beast of your is a singed cat, I warrant you. I never see'd a creature like that that wasn't good on the road. You've come about forty miles, then?"

Listwell. "Yes, yes, and a pretty good pace at that."

Loafer. "You're somewhat in a hurry, then, I make no doubt? I reckon I could guess if I would, what you're going to Richmond for? It wouldn't be much of a guess either; for it's rumored hereabouts, that there's to be the greatest sale of niggers at Richmond to-morrow that has taken place there in a long time; and I'll be bound you're a going there to have a hand in it."

Listwell. "Why, you must think, then, that there's money to be made at that business?"

Loafer. "Well, 'pon my honor, sir, I never made any that way myself; but it stands to reason that it's a money making business; for almost all other business in Virginia is dropped to engage in this. One thing is sartain, I never see'd a nigger-buyer yet that hadn't a plenty of money, and he wasn't as free with it as water. I has known one on 'em to treat as high as twenty times in a night; and, ginerally speaking, they's men of edication, and knows all about the government. The fact is, sir, I alloys like to hear 'em talk, bekase I alloys can learn something from them."

Listwell. "What may I call your name, sir?"

Loafer. "Well, now, they calls me Wilkes. I'm known all around by the gentlemen that comes here. They all knows old Wilkes."

Listwell. "Well, Wilkes, you seem to be acquainted here, and I see you have a strong liking for a horse. Be so good as to speak a kind word for mine to the hostler to-night, and you'll not lose anything by it."

Loafer. "Well, sir, I see you don't say much, but you've got an insight into things. It's alloys wise to get the good will of them that's acquainted about a tavern; for a man don't know when he goes into a house what may happen, or how much he may need a friend." Here the loafer gave Mr. Listwell a significant grin, which expressed a sort of triumphant pleasure at having, as he supposed, by his tact succeeded in placing so fine appearing a gentleman under obligations to him.

The pleasure, however, was mutual; for there was something so insinuating in the glance of this loquacious customer, that Mr. Listwell was very glad to get quit of him, and to do so more successfully, he ordered his supper to be brought to him in his private room, private to the eye, but not to the ear. This room was directly over the bar, and the plastering being off, nothing but pine boards and naked laths separated him from the disagreeable company below,—he could easily hear what was said in the bar-room, and was rather glad of the advantage it afforded, for, as you shall see, it furnished him important hints as to the manner and deportment he should assume during his stay at that tavern.

Mr. Listwell says he had got into his room but a few moments, when he heard the officious Wilkes below, in a tone of disappointment, exclaim, "Whar's that gentleman?" Wilkes was evidently expecting to meet with his friend at the bar-room, on his return, and had no doubt of his doing the handsome thing. "He has gone to his room," answered the landlord, "and has ordered his supper to be brought to him."

Here some one shouted out, "Who is he, Wilkes? Where's he going?"

"Well, now, I'll be hanged if I know; but I'm willing to make any man a bet of this old hat agin a five dollar bill, that that gent is as full of money as a dog is of fleas. He's going down to Richmond to buy niggers, I make no doubt. He's no fool, I warrant ye."

"Well, he acts d——d strange," said another, "anyhow. I likes to see a man, when he comes up to a tavern, to come straight into the bar-room, and show that he's a man among men. Nobody was going to bite him."

"Now, I don't blame him a bit for not coming in here. That man knows his business, and means to take care on his money," answered Wilkes.

"Wilkes, you're a fool. You only say that, because you hope to get a few coppers out on him."

"You only measure my corn by your half-bushel, I won't say that you're only mad bekase I got the chance of speaking to him first."

"O Wilkes! you're known here. You'll praise up anybody that will give you a copper; besides, 't is my opinion that that fellow who took his long slab-sides up stairs, for all the world just like a half-scared woman, afraid to look honest men in the face, is a *Northerner*, and as mean as dish-water."

"Now what will you bet of that," said Wilkes.

The speaker said, "I make no bets with you, 'kase you can get that fellow up stairs there to say anything."

"Well," said Wilkes, "I am willing to bet any man in the company that *that* gentleman is a *nigger*-buyer. He didn't tell me so right down, but I reckon I knows enough about men to give a pretty clean guess as to what they are arter."

The dispute as to *who* Mr. Listwell was, what his business, where he was going, etc., was kept up with much animation for some time, and more than once threatened a serious disturbance of the peace. Wilkes had his friends as well as his opponents. After this sharp debate, the company amused them selves by drinking whiskey, and telling stories. The latter consisting of quarrels, fights, *recontres*, and duels, in which distinguished persons of that neighborhood, and frequenters of that house, had been actors. Some of these stories were frightful enough, and were told, too, with a relish which bespoke the pleasure of the parties with the horrid scenes they portrayed. It would not be proper here to give the reader any idea of the vulgarity and dark profanity which rolled, as "a sweet morsel," under these corrupt tongues. A more brutal set of creatures, perhaps, never congregated.

Disgusted, and a little alarmed withal, Mr. Listwell, who was not accustomed to such entertainment, at length retired, but not to sleep. He was *too* much wrought upon by what he had heard to rest quietly, and what snatches of sleep he got, were interrupted by dreams which were anything than pleasant. At eleven o'clock, there seemed to be several hundreds of persons crowding into the house. A loud and confused clamor, cursing and cracking of whips, and the noise of chains startled him from his bed; for a moment he would have given the half of his farm in Ohio to have been at home. This uproar was kept up with undulating course, till near morning. There was loud laughing,— loud singing,—loud cursing,—and yet there seemed to be weeping and mourning in the midst of all. Mr. Listwell said he had heard enough during the forepart of the night to convince him that a buyer of men and women stood the best chance of being respected. And he, therefore, thought it best to say nothing which might undo the favorable opinion that had been formed of him in the bar-room by at least one of the fraternity that swarmed about it. While he would not avow himself a purchaser of slaves, he deemed it not prudent to disavow it. He felt that he might, properly, refuse to cast such a pearl before parties which, to him, were worse than swine. To reveal himself, and to impart a knowledge of his real character and sentiments would, to say the least, be imparting intelligence with the certainty of seeing it and himself both abused. Mr. Listwell confesses, that this reasoning did not altogether satisfy his conscience, for, hating slavery as he did, and regarding it to be the immediate duty of every man to cry out against it, "without compromise and without concealment," it was hard for him to admit to himself the possibility of circumstances wherein a man might, properly, hold his tongue on the subject. Having as little of the spirit of a martyr as Erasmus, he concluded, like the latter, that it was wiser to trust the mercy of God for his soul, than the humanity of slave-traders for his body. Bodily fear, not conscientious scruples, prevailed.

In this spirit he rose early in the morning, manifesting no surprise at what he had heard during the night. His quondam friend was soon at his elbow, boring him with all sorts of questions. All, however, directed to find out his character, business, residence, purposes, and destination. With the most perfect appearance of good nature and carelessness, Mr. Listwell evaded these meddlesome inquiries, and turned conversation to general topics, leaving himself and all that specially pertained to him, out of discussion. Disengaging himself from their troublesome companionship, he made his way towards an old bowling-alley, which was connected with the house, and which, like all the rest, was in very bad repair.

On reaching the alley Mr. Listwell saw, for the first time in his life, a slave-gang on their way to market. A sad sight truly. Here were one hundred and thirty human beings,—children of a common Creator—guilty of no crime—men and women, with hearts, minds, and deathless spirits, chained and fettered, and bound for the market, in a christian country,—in a country boasting of its liberty, independence, and high civilization! Humanity converted into merchandise, and linked in iron bands, with no regard to decency or humanity! All sizes, ages, and sexes, mothers, fathers, daughters, brothers, sisters,—all huddled together, on their way to market to be sold and separated from home, and from each other *forever*. And all to fill the pockets of men too lazy to work for an honest living, and who gain their fortune by plundering the helpless, and trafficking in the souls and sinews of men. As he gazed upon this revolting and heart-rending scene, our informant said he almost doubted the existence of a God of justice! And he stood wondering that the earth did not open and swallow up such wickedness.

In the midst of these recollections, and while running his eye up and down the fettered ranks, he met the glance of one whose face he thought he had seen before. To be resolved, he moved towards the spot. It was MADISON WASHINGTON! Here was a scene for the pencil! Had Mr. Listwell been confronted by one risen from the dead, he could not have been more appalled. He was completely stunned. A thunderbolt could not have struck him more dumb. He stood, for a few moments as motionless as one petrified; collecting himself, he at length exclaimed, *"Madison, is that you?"*

The noble fugitive, but little less astonished than himself, answered cheerily, "O yes, sir, they've got me again."

Thoughtless of consequences for the moment, Mr. Listwell ran up to his old friend, placing his hands upon his shoulders, and looked him in the face! Speechless they stood gazing at each other as if to be doubly resolved that there was no mistake about the matter, till Madison motioned his friend away, intimating a fear lest the keepers should find him there, and suspect him of tampering with the slaves.

"They will soon be out to look after us. You can come when they go to breakfast, and I will tell you all."

Pleased with this arrangement, Mr. Listwell passed out of the alley; but only just in time to save himself, for, while near the door, he observed three men making their way to the alley. The thought occurred to him to await their arrival, as the best means of diverting the ever ready suspicions of the guilty.

While the scene between Mr. Listwell and his friend Madison was going on, the other slaves stood as mute spectators,—at a loss to know what all this could mean. As he left, he heard the man chained to Madison ask, "Who is that gentleman?"

"He is a friend of mine. I cannot tell you now. Suffice it to say he is a friend. You shall hear more of him before long, but mark me! whatever shall pass between that gentleman and me, in your hearing, I pray you will say nothing about it. We are chained here together,—ours is a common lot; and that gentleman is not less *your* friend than *mine*." At these words, all mysterious as they were, the unhappy company gave signs of satisfaction and hope. It seems that Madison, by that mesmeric power which is the invariable accompaniment of genius, had already won the confidence of the gang, and was a sort of general-in-chief among them.

By this time the keepers arrived. A horrid trio, well fitted for their demoniacal work. Their uncombed hair came down over foreheads "*villainously low,*" and with eyes, mouths, and noses to match. "Hallo! hallo!" they growled out as they entered. "Are you all there!"

"All here," said Madison.

"Well, well, that's right! your journey will soon be over. You'll be in Richmond by eleven to-day, and then you'll have an easy time on it."

"I say, gal, what in the devil are you crying about?" said one of them. "I'll give you something to cry about, if you don't mind." This was said to a girl, apparently not more than twelve years old, who had been weeping bitterly. She had, probably, left behind her a loving mother, affectionate sisters, brothers, and friends, and her tears were but the natural expression of her sorrow, and the only solace. But the dealers in human flesh have *no* respect for such sorrow. They look upon it as a protest against their cruel injustice, and they are prompt to punish it.

This is a puzzle not easily solved. *How* came he here? what can I do for him? may I not even now be in some way compromised in this affair? were thoughts that troubled Mr. Listwell, and made him eager for the promised opportunity of speaking to Madison.

The bell now sounded for breakfast, and keepers and drivers, with pistols and bowie-knives gleaming from their belts, hurried in, as if to get the best places. Taking the chance now afforded, Mr. Listwell has-tened back to the bowling-alley. Reaching Madison, he said, "Now *do* tell me all about the matter. Do you know me?"

"Oh, yes," said Madison, "I know you well, and shall never forget you nor that cold and dreary night you gave me shelter. I must be short," he continued, "for they'll soon be out again. This, then, is the story in brief. On reaching Canada, and getting over the excitement of making my escape, sir, my thoughts turned to my poor wife, who had well de-served my love by her virtuous fidelity and undying affection for me. I could not bear the thought of leaving her in the cruel jaws of slavery, without making an effort to rescue her. First, I tried to get money to her; but oh! the process was *too slow*. I despaired of accomplishing it. She was in all my thoughts by day, and my dreams by night. At times I could al-most hear her voice, saying, 'O Madison! Madison! will you then leave me here? can you leave me here to die? No! no! you will come! you will come!' I was wretched. I lost my appetite. I could neither work, eat, nor sleep, till I resolved to hazard my own liberty, to gain that of my wife! But I must be short. Six weeks ago I reached my old master's place. I laid about the neighborhood nearly a week, watching my chance, and, fi-nally, I ventured upon the desperate attempt to reach my poor wife's room by means of a ladder. I reached the window, but the noise in rais-ing it frightened my wife, and she screamed and fainted. I took her in my arms, and was descending the ladder, when the dogs began to bark furiously, and before I could get to the woods the white folks were roused. The cool night air soon restored my wife, and she readily recog-nized me. We made the best of our way to the woods, but it was now *too* late,—the dogs were after us as though they would have torn us to pieces. It was all over with me now! My old master and his two sons ran out with loaded rifles, and before we were out of gunshot, our ears were assailed with '*Stop! stop! or be shot down.*' Nevertheless we ran on. Seeing that we gave no heed to their calls, they fired, and my poor wife fell by my side dead, while I received but a slight flesh wound. I now became desperate, and stood my ground, and awaited their attack over her dead body. They rushed upon me, with their rifles in hand. I parried their blows, and fought them 'till I was knocked down and overpowered."

"Oh! it was madness to have returned," said Mr. Listwell.

"Sir, I could not be free with the galling thought that my poor wife was still a slave. With her in slavery, my body, not my spirit, was free. I was taken to the house,—chained to a ring-bolt,—my wounds dressed. I was kept there three days. All the slaves, for miles around, were brought to see me. Many slave-holders came with their slaves, using me as proof of the completeness of their power, and of the im-possibility of slaves getting away. I was taunted, jeered at, and berated by them, in a manner that pierced me to the soul. Thank God, I was able to smother my rage, and to bear it all with seeming composure. After my wounds were nearly healed, I was taken to a tree and stripped, and I received sixty lashes on my naked back. A few days after, I was sold to a slave-trader, and placed in this gang for the New Orleans market."

"Do you think your master would sell you to me?"

"O no, sir! I was sold on condition of my being taken South. Their motive is revenge."

"Then, then," said Mr. Listwell, "I fear I can do nothing for you. Put your trust in God, and bear your sad lot with the manly fortitude which becomes a man. I shall see you at Richmond, but don't recognize me." Saying this, Mr. Listwell handed Madison ten dollars; said a few words to the other slaves; received their hearty "God bless you," and made his way to the house.

Fearful of exciting suspicion by too long delay, our friend went to the breakfast table, with the air of one who half reproved the greediness of those who rushed in at the sound of the bell. A cup of coffee was all that he could manage. His feelings were too bitter and excited, and his heart was too full with the fate of poor Madison (whom he loved as well as admired) to relish his breakfast; and although he sat long after the company had left the table, he really did little more than change the position of his knife and fork. The strangeness of meeting again one whom he had met on two several occasions before, under extraordinary circumstances, was well calculated to suggest the idea that a supernatural power, a wakeful providence, or an inexorable fate, had linked their destiny together; and that no efforts of his could disentangle him from the mysterious web of circumstances which enfolded him.

On leaving the table, Mr. Listwell nerved himself up and walked firmly into the bar-room. He was at once greeted again by that talkative chatter-box, Mr. Wilkes.

"Them's a likely set of niggers in the alley there," said Wilkes.

"Yes, they're fine looking fellows, one of them I should like to purchase, and for him I would be willing to give a handsome sum."

Turning to one of his comrades, and with a grin of victory, Wilkes said, "Aha, Bill, did you hear that? I told you I know'd that gentleman wanted to buy niggers, and would bid as high as any purchaser in the market."

"Come, come," said Listwell, "don't be too loud in your praise, you are old enough to know that prices rise when purchasers are plenty."

"That's a fact," said Wilkes, "I see you knows the ropes—and there's not a man in old Virginy whom I'd rather help to make a good bargain than you, sir."

Mr. Listwell here threw a dollar at Wilkes, (which the latter caught with a dexterous hand,) saying, "Take that for your kind good will." Wilkes held up the dollar to his right eye, with a grin of victory, and turned to the morose grumbler in the corner who had questioned the liberality of a man of whom he knew nothing.

Mr. Listwell now stood as well with the company as any other occupant of the bar-room.

We pass over the hurry and bustle, the brutal vociferations of the slave-drivers in getting their unhappy gang in motion for Richmond; and we need not narrate every application of the lash to those who faltered in the journey. Mr. Listwell followed the train at a long distance, with a sad heart; and on reaching Richmond, left his horse at a hotel, and made his way to the wharf in the direction of which he saw the slave-coffle driven. He was just in time to see the whole company embark for New Orleans. The thought struck him that, while mixing with the multitude, he might do his friend Madison one last service, and he stept into a hardware store and purchased three strong *files*. These he took with him, and standing near the small boat, which lay in waiting to bear the company by parcels to the side of the brig that lay in the stream, he managed, as Madison passed him, to slip the files into his pocket, and at once darted back among the crowd.

All the company now on board, the imperious voice of the captain sounded, and instantly a dozen hardy seamen were in the rigging, hurrying aloft to unfurl the broad canvas of our Baltimore built American Slaver. The sailors hung about the ropes, like so many black cats, now in the round-tops, now in the cross-trees, now on the yard-arms, all was bluster and activity. Soon the broad fore topsail, the royal and top gallant sail were spread to the breeze. Round went the heavy windlass, clank, clank went the fall-bit,—the anchors weighed,—jibs, mainsails, and topsails hauled to the wind, and the long, low, black slaver, with her cargo of human flesh, careened and moved forward to the sea.

Mr. Listwell stood on the shore, and watched the slaver till the last speck of her upper sails faded from sight, and announced the limit of human vision. "Farewell! farewell! brave and true man! God grant that brighter skies may smile upon your future than have yet looked down upon your thorny pathway."

Saying this to himself, our friend lost no time in completing his business, and in making his way homewards, gladly shaking off from his feet the dust of Old Virginia.

PART IV

Oh, where's the slave so lowly
Condemn'd to chains unholy,
   Who could he burst
   His bonds at first
Would pine beneath them slowly?
                    Moore.

——Know ye not
Who would be free, *themselves* must strike the blow.
    Childe Harold.

What a world of inconsistency, as well as of wickedness, is suggested by the smooth and gliding phrase, AMERICAN SLAVE TRADE; and how strange and perverse is that moral sentiment which loathes, execrates, and brands as piracy and as deserving of death the carrying away into captivity men, women, and children from the *African coast;* but which is neither shocked nor disturbed by a similar traffic, carried on with the same motives and purposes, and characterized by even *more* odious peculiarities on the coast of our MODEL REPUBLIC. We execrate and hang the wretch guilty of this crime on the coast of Guinea, while we respect and applaud the guilty participators in this murderous business on the enlightened shores of the Chesapeake. The inconsistency is so flagrant and glaring, that it would seem to cast a doubt on the doctrine of the innate moral sense of mankind.

Just two months after the sailing of the Virginia slave brig, which the reader has seen move off to sea so proudly with her human cargo for the New Orleans market, there chanced to meet, in the Marine Coffee-house at Richmond, a company of *ocean birds,* when the following conversation, which throws some light on the subsequent history, not only of Madison Washington, but of the hundred and thirty human beings with whom we last saw him chained.

"I say, shipmate, you had rather rough weather on your late passage to Orleans?" said Jack Williams, a regular old salt, tauntingly, to a trim, compact, manly looking person, who proved to be the first mate of the slave brig in question.

"Foul play, as well as foul weather," replied the firmly knit personage, evidently but little inclined to enter upon a subject which terminated so ingloriously to the captain and officers of the American slaver.

"Well, betwixt you and me," said Williams, "that whole affair on board of the *Creole* was miserably and disgracefully managed. Those black rascals got the upper hand of ye altogether; and, in my opinion, the whole disaster was the result of ignorance of the real character of *darkies* in general. With half a dozen *resolute* white men, (I say it not boastingly,) I could have had the rascals in irons in ten minutes, not because I'm so strong, but I know how to manage 'em. With my back against the *caboose,* I could, myself, have flogged a dozen of them; and had I been on board, by every monster of the deep, every black devil of 'em all would have had his neck stretched from the yard-arm. Ye made a mistake in yer manner of fighting 'em. All that is needed in dealing with a set of rebellious *darkies,* is to show that yer not afraid of 'em. For my own part, I would not honor a dozen niggers, by pointing a gun at one on 'em,—a good stout whip, or a stiff rope's end, is better than all the guns at Old Point to quell a *nigger* insurrection. Why, sir, to take a gun to a *nigger* is the best way you can select to tell him you are afraid of him, and the best way of inviting his attack."

This speech made quite a sensation among the company, and a part of them indicated solicitude for the answer which might be made to it. Our first mate replied, "Mr. Williams, all that you've now said sounds very well *here* on shore, where, perhaps, you have studied ne-gro character. I do not profess to understand the subject as well as yourself; but it strikes me, you apply the same rule in dissimilar cases. It is quite easy to talk of flogging niggers here on land, where you have the sympathy of the community, and the whole physical force of the government, State and national, at your command, and where, if a negro shall lift his hand against a white man, the whole community, with one accord, are ready to unite in shooting him down. I say, in such circumstances, it's easy to talk of flogging negroes and of negro cowardice; but, sir, I deny that the negro is, naturally, a coward, or that your theory of managing slaves will stand the test of *salt* water. It may do very well for an overseer, a contemptible hireling, to take ad-vantage of fears already in existence, and which his presence has no power to inspire; to swagger about whip in hand, and discourse on the timidity and cowardice of negroes; for they have a smooth sea and a fair wind. It is one thing to manage a company of slaves on a Virginia plantation, and quite another thing to quell an insurrection on the lonely billows of the Atlantic, where every breeze speaks of courage and liberty. For the negro to act cowardly on shore, may be to act wisely; and I've some doubts whether *you*, Mr. Williams, would find it very convenient were you a slave in Algiers, to raise your hand against the bayonets of a whole government."

"By George, shipmate," said Williams, "you're coming rather *too* near. Either I've fallen very low in your estimation, or your notions of negro courage have got up a button-hole too high. Now I more than ever wish I'd been on board of that luckless craft. I'd have given ye practical evidence of the truth of my theory. I don't doubt there's some difference in being at sea. But a nigger's a nigger, on sea or land; and is a coward, find him where you will; a drop of blood from one on 'em will skeer a hundred. A knock on the nose, or a kick on the shin, will tame the wildest '*darkey*' you can fetch me. I say again, and will stand by it, I could, with half a dozen good men, put the whole nineteen on 'em in irons, and have carried them safe to New Orleans too. Mind, I don't blame you, but I do say, and every gentleman here will bear me out in it, that the fault was somewhere, or them niggers would never have got off as they have done. For my part I feel ashamed to have the idea go abroad, that a ship load of slaves can't be safely taken from Richmond to New Orleans. I should like, merely to redeem the charac-ter of Virginia sailors, to take charge of a ship load on 'em to-morrow."

Williams went on in this strain, occasionally casting an imploring glance at the company for applause for his wit, and sympathy for his contempt of negro courage. He had, evidently, however, waked up the wrong passenger; for besides being in the right, his opponent carried that in his eye which marked him a man not to be trifled with.

"Well, sir," said the sturdy mate, "you can select your own method for distinguishing yourself;—the path of ambition in this direction is quite open to you in Virginia, and I've no doubt that you will be highly appreciated and compensated for all your valiant achievements in that line; but for myself, while I do not profess to be a giant, I have resolved never to set my foot on the deck of a slave ship, either as officer, or common sailor again; I have got enough of it."

"Indeed! indeed!" exclaimed Williams, derisively.

"Yes, *indeed*," echoed the mate; "but don't misunderstand me. It is not the high value that I set upon my life that makes me say what I have said; yet I'm resolved never to endanger my life again in a cause which my conscience does not approve. I dare say *here* what many men *feel*, but *dare not speak*, that this whole slave-trading business is a disgrace and scandal to Old Virginia."

"Hold! hold on! shipmate," said Williams, "I hardly thought you'd have shown your colors so soon,—I'll be hanged if you're not as good an abolitionist as Garrison himself."

The mate now rose from his chair, manifesting some excitement. "What do you mean, sir," said he, in a commanding tone. *"That man does not live who shall offer me an insult with impunity."*

The effect of these words was marked; and the company clustered around. Williams, in an apologetic tone, said, "Shipmate! keep your temper. I meant no insult. We all know that Tom Grant is no coward, and what I said about your being an abolitionist was simply this: you *might* have put down them black mutineers and murderers, but your conscience held you back."

"In that, too," said Grant, "you were mistaken. I did all that any man with equal strength and presence of mind could have done. The fact is, Mr. Williams, you underrate the courage as well as the skill of these negroes, and further, you do not seem to have been correctly informed about the case in hand at all."

"All I know about it is," said Williams, "that on the ninth day after you left Richmond, a dozen or two of the niggers ye had on board, came on deck and took the ship from you;—had her steered into a British port, where, by the by, every woolly head of them went ashore and was free. Now I take this to be a discreditable piece of business, and one demanding explanation."

"There are a great many discreditable things in the world," said Grant. "For a ship to go down under a calm sky is, upon the first flush of it, disgraceful either to sailors or caulkers. But when we learn, that by some mysterious disturbance in nature, the waters parted beneath, and swallowed the ship up, we lose our indignation and disgust in lamentation of the disaster, and in awe of the Power which controls the elements."

"Very true, very true," said Williams, "I should be very glad to have an explanation which would relieve the affair of its present discreditable features. I have desired to see you ever since you got home, and to learn from you a full statement of the facts in the case. To me the whole thing seems unaccountable. I cannot see how a dozen or two of ignorant negroes, not one of whom had ever been to sea before, and all of them were closely ironed between decks, should be able to get their fetters off, rush out of the hatchway in open daylight, kill two white men, the one the captain and the other their master, and then carry the ship into a British port, where every 'darkey' of them was set free. There must have been great carelessness, or cowardice somewhere!"

The company, which had listened in silence during most of this discussion, now became much excited. One said, I agree with Williams; and several said the thing looks black enough. After the temporary tumultuous exclamations had subsided,—

"I see," said Grant, "how you regard this case, and how difficult it will be for me to render our ship's company blameless in your eyes. Nevertheless, I will state the fact[s] precisely as they came under my own observation. Mr. Williams speaks of 'ignorant negroes,' and, as a general rule, they are ignorant; but had he been on board the *Creole* as I was, he would have seen cause to admit that there are exceptions to this general rule. The leader of the mutiny in question was just as shrewd a fellow as ever I met in my life, and was as well fitted to lead in a dangerous enterprise as any one white man in ten thousand. The name of this man, strange to say, (ominous of greatness,) was MADISON WASHINGTON. In the short time he had been on board, he had secured the confidence of every officer. The negroes fairly worshipped him. His manner and bearing were such, that no one could suspect him of a murderous purpose. The only feeling with which we regarded him was, that he was a powerful, good-disposed negro. He seldom spake to anyone, and when he did speak, it was with the utmost propriety. His words were well chosen, and his pronunciation equal to that of any schoolmaster. It was a mystery to us *where* he got his knowledge of language; but as little was said to him, none of us knew the extent of his intelligence and ability till it was too late. It seems he brought three files with him on board, and must have gone to work upon his fetters the first night out; and he must have worked well at that; for on the day of the rising, he got the irons *off eighteen* besides himself.

"The attack began just about twilight in the evening. Apprehending a squall, I had commanded the second mate to order all hands on deck, to take in sail. A few minutes before this I had seen Madison's head above the hatchway, looking out upon the white-capped waves at the leeward. I think I never saw him look more good-natured. I stood just about midship, on the larboard side. The captain was pacing the quarter-deck on the starboard side, in company with Mr. Jameson, the owner of most of the slaves on board. Both were armed. I had just told the men to lay aloft, and was looking to see my orders obeyed, when I heard the discharge of a pistol on the starboard side; and turning suddenly around, the very deck seemed covered with fiends from the pit. The nineteen negroes were all on deck, with their broken fetters in their hands, rushing in all directions. I put my hand quickly in my pocket to draw out my jack-knife; but before I could draw it, I was knocked senseless to the deck. When I came to myself, (which I did in a few minutes, I suppose, for it was yet quite light,) there was not a white man on deck. The sailors were all aloft in the rigging, and dared not come down. Captain Clarke and Mr. Jameson lay stretched on the quarter-deck,—both dying,—while Madison himself stood at the helm unhurt.

"I was completely weakened by the loss of blood, and had not recovered from the stunning blow which felled me to the deck; but it was a little too much for me, even in my prostrate condition, to see our good brig commanded by a *black murderer*. So I called out to the men to come down and take the ship, or die in the attempt. Suiting the action to the word, I started aft. 'You murderous villain,' said I, to the imp at the helm, and rushed upon him to deal him a blow, when he pushed me back with his strong, black arm, as though I had been a boy of twelve. I looked around for the men. They were still in the rigging. Not one had come down. I started towards Madison again. The rascal now told me to stand back. 'Sir,' said he, 'your life is in my hands. I could have killed you a dozen times over during this last half hour, and could kill you now. You call me a *black murderer*. I am not a murderer. God is my witness that LIBERTY, not *malice*, is the motive for this night's work. I have done no more to those dead men yonder, than they would have done to me in like circumstances. We have struck for our freedom, and if a true man's heart be in you, you will honor us for the deed. We have done that which you applaud your fathers for doing, and if we are murderers, *so were they.*'

"I felt little disposition to reply to this impudent speech. By heaven, it disarmed me. The fellow loomed up before me. I forgot his blackness in the dignity of his manner, and the eloquence of his speech. It seemed as if the souls of both the great dead (whose names he bore) had entered him. To the sailors in the rigging he said: 'Men! the battle is over,—your captain is dead. I have complete command of this vessel. All resistance to my authority will be in vain. My men have won their liberty, with no other weapons but their OWN BROKEN FETTERS. We are nineteen in number. We do not thirst for your blood, we demand only our rightful freedom. Do not flatter yourselves that I am ignorant of chart or compass. I know both. We are now only about sixty miles from Nassau. Come down, and do your duty. Land us in Nassau, and not a hair of your heads shall be hurt.'

"I shouted, *'Stay where you are, men,'*—when a sturdy black fellow ran at me with a handspike, and would have split my head open, but for the interference of Madison, who darted between me and the blow. 'I know what you are up to,' said the latter to me. 'You want to navigate this brig into a slave port, where you would have us all hanged; but you'll miss it; before this brig shall touch a slave-cursed shore while I am on board, I will myself put a match to the magazine, and blow her, and be blown with her, into a thousand fragments. Now I have saved your life twice within these last twenty minutes,—for, when you lay helpless on deck, my men were about to kill you. I held them in check. And if you now (seeing I am your friend and not your enemy) persist in your resistance to my authority, I give you fair warning, YOU SHALL DIE.'

"Saying this to me, he cast a glance into the rigging where the terror-stricken sailors were clinging, like so many frightened monkeys, and commanded them to come down, in a tone from which there was no appeal; for four men stood by with muskets in hand, ready at the word of command to shoot them down.

"I now became satisfied that resistance was out of the question; that my best policy was to put the brig into Nassau, and secure the assistance of the American consul at the port. I felt sure that the authorities would enable us to secure the murderers, and bring them to trial.

"By this time the apprehended squall had burst upon us. The wind howled furiously,—the ocean was white with foam, which, on account of the darkness, we could see only by the quick flashes of lightning that darted occasionally from the angry sky. All was alarm and confusion. Hideous cries came up from the slave women. Above the roaring billows a succession of heavy thunder rolled along, swelling the terrific din. Owing to the great darkness, and a sudden shift of the wind, we found ourselves in the trough of the sea. When shipping a heavy sea over the starboard bow, the bodies of the captain and Mr. Jameson were washed overboard. For awhile we had dearer interests to look after than slave property. A more savage thunder-gust never swept the ocean. Our brig rolled and creaked as if every bolt would be started, and every thread of oakum would be pressed out of the seams. 'To the pumps! to the pumps!' I cried, but not a sailor would quit his grasp. Fortunately this squall soon passed over, or we must have been food for sharks.

"During all the storm, Madison stood firmly at the helm,—his keen eye fixed upon the binnacle. He was not indifferent to the dreadful hurricane; yet he met it with the equanimity of an old sailor. He was silent but not agitated. The first words he uttered after the storm had slightly subsided, were characteristic of the man. 'Mr. mate, you cannot write the bloody laws of slavery on those restless billows. The ocean, if not the land, is free.' I confess, gentlemen, I felt myself in the presence of a superior man; one who, had he been a white man, I would have followed willingly and gladly in any honorable enterprise. Our difference of color was the only ground for difference of action. It was not that his principles were wrong in the abstract; for they are the principles of 1776. But I could not bring myself to recognize their application to one whom I deemed my inferior.

"But to my story. What happened now is soon told. Two hours after the frightful tempest had spent itself, we were plump at the wharf in Nassau. I sent two of our men immediately to our consul with a statement of facts, requesting his interference in our behalf. What he did, or whether he did anything, I don't know; but, by order of the authorities, a company of *black* soldiers came on board, for the purpose, as they said, of protecting the property. These impudent rascals, when I called on them to assist me in keeping the slaves on board, sheltered themselves adroitly under their instructions only to protect property,—and said they did not recognize *persons* as *property*. I told them that by the laws of Virginia and the laws of the United States, the slaves on board were as much property as the barrels of flour in the hold. At this the stupid blockheads showed their *ivory*, rolled up their white eyes in horror, as if the idea of putting men on a footing with merchandise were revolting to their humanity. When these instructions were understood among the negroes, it was impossible for us to keep them on board. They deliberately gathered up their baggage before our eyes, and, against our remonstrances, poured through the gangway,—formed themselves into a procession on the wharf,—bid farewell to all on board, and, uttering the wildest shouts of exultation, they marched, amidst the deafening cheers of a multitude of sympathizing spectators, under the triumphant leadership of their heroic chief and deliverer, MADISON WASHINGTON."

CHAPTER 6

From *My Bondage and My Freedom* (1855)

I n August 1855, Douglass's second autobiography, *My Bondage and My Freedom,* was published by Miller, Orton, and Mulligan of Auburn, New York. Reliable evidence suggests that within the first two months of publication, *My Bondage and My Freedom* had sold 15,000 copies. The book continued to be popular for the remainder of the decade; in 1860 Douglass's friend Ottilia Assing translated it into German. In the twentieth century *My Bondage and My Freedom* has been overshadowed alternately by Douglass's third autobiography and, more recently, by his first. Nevertheless, the second autobiography has attracted considerable attention, particularly among the growing number of critics who see it as key to an understanding of the development of Douglass's mind and art in the critical mid-century era.

My Bondage and My Freedom received many favorable reviews for reasons similar to those that made the *Narrative* a best-seller. In the wake of Harriet Beecher Stowe's immensely popular *Uncle Tom's Cabin* (1852), Douglass's second autobiography struck the *New York Tribune*'s reviewer as "one of the most striking illustrations of American Slavery, which either fact or fiction has presented to the public." The unusual scope and power of *My Bondage and My Freedom* was also cited in *Putnam's Monthly,* one of the more prominent literary magazines of the era. Despite admonishing Douglass for writing "bitterly," the *Putnam's* reviewer granted the ex-slave preeminence among the most celebrated men of "genius struggling against adversity" in English literature.

The opening three chapters of *My Bondage and My Freedom* illustrate the author's decision to represent his origins in such a way as to call attention to the sustaining slave community, headed by his grandmother, Betsy Bailey, that gave him his first sense of home and identity. In his rendition of the famous battle with Covey in Chapter 17 of *My Bondage and My Freedom* Douglass offered a more complete perspective on that incident, stressing the important role of the female slave Caroline, and infusing the entire account with comic asides, so that the image of the grand rebel-individualist in the 1845 *Narrative* is reshaped more in accordance with common humanity. Douglass's treatment of his life in freedom in the final chapters of *My Bondage and My Freedom* is designed to speak much more freely about struggles with northern racism than the *Narrative* does. The exposé of the Garrisonians is not presented as cause for despair about reforming America, however. "Progress is still possible," Douglass asserts. But by 1855 his notion of progress owes less to the abstract ideals of abolitionism than to his renewing sense of reintegration into the northern African American community and the empowered selfhood that representing that community seemed to promise for him.

❖ ❖ ❖

EDITOR'S PREFACE

If the volume now presented to the public were a mere work of ART, the history of its misfortune might be written in two very simple words—TOO LATE. The nature and character of slavery have been subjects of an almost endless variety of artistic representation; and after the brilliant achievements in that field, and while those achievements are yet fresh in the memory of the million, he who would add another to the legion, must possess the charm of transcendent excellence, or apologize for something worse than rashness. The reader is, therefore, assured, with all due promptitude, that his attention is not invited to a work of ART, but to a work of FACTS—Facts, terrible and almost incredible, it may be—yet FACTS, nevertheless.

I am authorized to say that there is not a fictitious name nor place in the whole volume; but that names and places are literally given, and that every transaction therein described actually transpired.

Perhaps the best Preface to this volume is furnished in the following letter of Mr. Douglass, written in answer to my urgent solicitation for such a work:

ROCHESTER, N.Y. *July* 2, 1855.

DEAR FRIEND: I have long entertained, as you very well know, a somewhat positive repugnance to writing or speaking anything for the public, which could, with any degree of plausibility, make me liable to the imputation of seeking personal notoriety, for its own sake. Entertaining that feeling very sincerely, and permitting its control, perhaps, quite unreasonably, I have often refused to narrate my personal experience in public antislavery meetings, and in sympathizing circles, when urged to do so by friends, with whose views and wishes, ordinarily, it were a pleasure to comply. In my letters and speeches, I have generally aimed to discuss the question of Slavery in the light of fundamental principles, and upon facts, notorious and open to all; making, I trust, no more of the fact of my own former enslavement, than circumstances seemed absolutely to require. I have never placed my opposition to slavery on a basis so narrow as my own enslavement, but rather upon the indestructible and unchangeable laws of human nature, every one of which is perpetually and flagrantly violated by the slave system. I have also felt that it was best for those having histories worth the writing—or supposed to be so—to commit such work to hands other than their own. To write of one's self, in such a manner as not to incur the imputation of weakness, vanity, and egotism, is a work within the ability of but few; and I have little reason to believe that I belong to that fortunate few.

These considerations caused me to hesitate, when first you kindly urged me to prepare for publication a full account of my life as a slave, and my life as a freeman.

Nevertheless, I see, with you, many reasons for regarding my autobiography as exceptional in its character, and as being, in some sense, naturally beyond the reach of those reproaches which honorable and sensitive minds dislike to incur. It is not to illustrate any heroic achievements of a man, but to vindicate a just and beneficent principle, in its application to the whole human family, by letting in the light of truth upon a system, esteemed by some as a blessing, and by others as a curse and a crime. I agree with you, that this system is now at the bar of public opinion—not only of this country, but of the whole civilized world—for judgment. Its friends have made for it the usual plea—"not guilty;" the case must, therefore, proceed. Any facts, either from slaves, slaveholders, or by-standers, calculated to enlighten the public mind, by revealing the true nature, character, and tendency of the slave system, are in order, and can scarcely be innocently withheld.

I see, too, that there are special reasons why I should write my own biography, in preference to employing another to do it. Not only is slavery on trial, but unfortunately, the enslaved people are also on trial. It is alleged, that they are, naturally, inferior; that they are *so low* in the scale of humanity, and so utterly stupid, that they are unconscious of their wrongs, and do not apprehend their rights. Looking, then, at your request, from this stand-point, and wishing everything of which you think me capable to go to the benefit of my afflicted people, I part with my doubts and hesitation, and proceed to furnish you with the desired manuscript; hoping that you may be able to make such arrangements for its publication as shall be best adapted to accomplish that good which you so enthusiastically anticipate.

FREDERICK DOUGLASS

There was little necessity for doubts and hesitation on the part of Mr. Douglass, as to the propriety of his giving to the world a full account of himself. A man who was born and brought up in slavery, a living witness of its horrors; who often himself experienced its cruelties; and who, despite the depressing influences surrounding his birth, youth and manhood, has risen, from a dark and almost absolute obscurity, to the distinguished position which he now occupies, might very well assume the existence of a commendable curiosity, on the part of the public, to know the facts of his remarkable history.

EDITOR.

INTRODUCTION

When a man raises himself from the lowest condition in society to the highest, mankind pay him the tribute of their admiration; when he accomplishes this elevation by native energy, guided by prudence and wisdom, their admiration is increased; but when his course, onward and upward, excellent in itself, furthermore proves a possible, what had hitherto been regarded as an impossible, reform, then he becomes a burning and a shining light, on which the aged may look with gladness, the young with hope, and the down-trodden, as a representative of what they may themselves become. To such a man, dear reader, it is my privilege to introduce you.

The life of Frederick Douglass, recorded in the pages which follow, is not merely an example of self-elevation under the most adverse circumstances; it is, moreover, a noble vindication of the highest aims of the American anti-slavery movement. The real object of that movement is not only to disenthrall, it is, also, to bestow upon the negro the exercise of all those rights, from the possession of which he has been so long debarred.

But this full recognition of the colored man to the right, and the entire admission of the same to the full privileges, political, religious and social, of manhood, requires powerful effort on the part of the enthralled, as well as on the part of those who would disenthrall them. The people at large must feel the conviction, as well as admit the abstract logic, of human equality; the negro, for the first time in the world's history, brought in full contact with high civilization, must prove his title to all that is demanded for him; in the teeth of unequal chances, he must prove himself equal to the mass of those who oppress him—therefore, absolutely superior to his apparent fate, and to their relative ability. And it is most cheering to the friends of freedom, to-day, that evidence of this equality is rapidly accumulating, not from the ranks of the half-freed colored people of the free states, but from the very depths of slavery itself; the indestructible equality of man to man is demonstrated by the ease with which black men, scarce one remove from barbarism—if slavery can be honored with such a distinction—vault into the high places of the most advanced and painfully acquired civilization. Ward and Garnett, Wells Brown and Pennington, Loguen and Douglass, are banners on the outer wall, under which abolition is fighting its most successful battles, because they are living exemplars of the practicability of the most radical abolitionism; for, they were all of them born to the doom of slavery, some of them remained slaves until adult age, yet they all have not only won equality to their white fellow citizens, in civil, religious, political and social rank, but they have also illustrated and adorned our common country by their genius, learning and eloquence.

The characteristics whereby Mr. Douglass has won first rank among these remarkable men, and is still rising toward highest rank among living Americans, are abundantly laid bare in the book before us. Like the autobiography of Hugh Miller, it carries us so far back into early childhood, as to throw light upon the question, "when positive and persistent memory begins in the human being." And, like Hugh Miller, he must have been a shy old fashioned child, occasionally oppressed by what he could not well account for, peering and poking about among the layers of right and wrong, of tyrant and thrall, and the wonderfulness of that hopeless tide of things which brought power to one race, and unrequited toil to another, until, finally, he stumbled upon his "first-found Ammonite," hidden away down in the depths of his own nature, and which revealed to him the fact that liberty and right, for all men, were anterior to slavery and wrong. When his knowledge of the world was bounded by the visible horizon on Col. Lloyd's plantation, and while every thing around him bore a fixed, iron stamp, as if it had always been so, this was, for one so young, a notable discovery.

To his uncommon memory, then, we must add a keen and accurate insight into men and things; an original breadth of common sense which enabled him to see, and weigh, and compare whatever passed before him, and which kindled a desire to search out and define their relations to other things not so patent, but which never succumbed to the marvelous nor the supernatural; a sacred thirst for liberty and for learning, first as a means of attaining liberty, then as an end in itself most desirable; a will; an unfaltering energy and determination to obtain what his soul pronounced desirable; a majestic self-hood; determined courage; a deep and agonizing sympathy with his embruted, crushed and bleeding fellow slaves, and an extraordinary depth of passion, together with that rare alliance between passion and intellect, which enables the former, when deeply roused, to excite, develop and sustain the latter.

With these original gifts in view, let us look at his schooling; the fearful discipline through which it pleased God to prepare him for the high calling on which he has since entered—the advocacy of emancipation by the people who are not slaves. And for this special mission, his plantation education was better than any he could have acquired in any lettered school. What he needed, was facts and experiences, welded to acutely wrought up sympathies, and these he could not elsewhere have obtained, in a manner so peculiarly adapted to his nature. His physical being was well trained, also, running wild until advanced into boyhood; hard work and light diet, thereafter, and a skill in handicraft in youth.

For his special mission, then, this was, considered in connection with his natural gifts, a good schooling; and, for his special mission, he doubtless "left school" just at the proper moment. Had he remained longer in slavery—had he fretted under bonds until the ripening of manhood and its passions, until the drear agony of slave-wife and slave-children had been piled upon his already bitter experiences—then, not only would his own history have had another termination, but the drama of American slavery would have been essentially varied; for I cannot resist the belief, that the boy who learned to read and write as he did, who taught his fellow slaves these precious acquirements as he did, who plotted for their mutual escape as he did, would, when a man at bay, strike a blow which would make slavery reel and stagger. Furthermore, blows and insults he bore, at the moment, without resentment; deep but suppressed emotion rendered him insensible to their sting; but it was afterward, when the memory of them went seething through his brain, breeding a fiery indignation at his injured self-hood, that the resolve came to resist, and the time fixed when to resist, and the plot laid, how to resist; and he always kept his self-pledged word. In what he undertook, in this line, he looked fate in the face, and had a cool, keen look at the relation of means to ends. Henry Bibb, to avoid chastisement, strewed his master's bed with charmed leaves—and *was whipped*. Frederick Douglass quietly pocketed a like *fetiche*, compared his muscles with those of Covey—and *whipped him*.

In the history of his life in bondage, we find, well developed, that inherent and continuous energy of character which will ever render him distinguished. What his hand found to do, he did with his might; even while conscious that he was wronged out of his daily earnings, he worked, and worked hard. At his daily labor he went with a will; with keen, well set eye, brawny chest, lithe figure, and fair sweep of arm, he would have been king among calkers, had that been his mission.

It must not be overlooked, in this glance at his education, that Mr. Douglass lacked one aid to which so many men of mark have been deeply indebted—he had neither a mother's care, nor a mother's culture, save that which slavery grudgingly meted out to him. Bitter nurse! may not even her features relax with human feeling, when she gazes at such offspring! How susceptible he was to the kindly influences of mother-culture, may be gathered from his own words, on page 155: "It has been a life-long, standing grief to me, that I know so little of my mother, and that I was so early separated from her. The counsels of her love must have been beneficial to me. The side view of her face is imaged on my memory, and I take few steps in life, without feeling her presence; but the image is mute, and I have no striking words of hers treasured up."

From the depths of chattel slavery in Maryland, our author escaped into the caste-slavery of the north, in New Bedford, Massachusetts. Here he found oppression assuming another, and hardly less bitter, form; of that very handicraft which the greed of slavery had taught him, his half-freedom denied him the exercise for an honest living; he found himself one of a class—free colored men—whose position he has described in the following words:

"Aliens are we in our native land. The fundamental principles of the republic, to which the humblest white man, whether born here or elsewhere, may appeal with confidence, in the hope of awakening a favorable response, are held to be inapplicable to us. The glorious doctrines of your revolutionary fathers, and the more glorious teachings of the Son of God, are construed and applied against us. We are literally scourged beyond the beneficent range of both authorities, human and divine. . . . American humanity hates us, scorns us, disowns and denies, in a thousand ways, our very personality. The outspread wing of American christianity, apparently broad enough to give shelter to a perishing world, refuses to cover us. To us, its bones are brass, and its features iron. In running thither for shelter and succor, we have only fled from the hungry blood-hound to the devouring wolf—from a corrupt and selfish world, to a hollow and hypocritical church."—*Speech before American and Foreign Anti-Slavery Society, May, 1854.*

Four years or more, from 1837 to 1841, he struggled on, in New Bedford, sawing wood, rolling casks, or doing what labor he might, to support himself and young family; four years he brooded over the scars which slavery and semi-slavery had inflicted upon his body and soul; and then, with his wounds yet unhealed, he fell among the Garrisonians—a glorious waif to those most ardent reformers. It happened one day, at Nantucket, that he, diffidently and reluctantly, was led to address an anti-slavery meeting. He was about the age when the younger Pitt entered the House of Commons; like Pitt, too, he stood up a born orator.

William Lloyd Garrison, who was happily present, writes thus of Mr. Douglass' maiden effort; "I shall never forget his first speech at the convention—the extraordinary emotion it excited in my own mind—the powerful impression it created upon a crowded auditory, completely taken by surprise. . . . I think I never hated slavery so intensely as at that moment; certainly, my perception of the enormous outrage which is inflicted by it on the godlike nature of its victims, was rendered far more clear than ever. There stood one in physical proportions and stature commanding and exact—in intellect richly endowed—in natural eloquence a prodigy."*

It is of interest to compare Mr. Douglass's account of this meeting with Mr. Garrison's. Of the two, I think the latter the most correct. It must have been a grand burst of eloquence! The pent up agony, indignation and pathos of an abused and harrowed boyhood and youth, bursting out in all their freshness and overwhelming earnestness!

This unique introduction to its great leader, led immediately to the employment of Mr. Douglass as an agent by the American Anti-Slavery Society. So far as his self-relying and independent character would per-

*Letter, Introduction to Life of Frederick Douglass, Boston, 1845.

mit, he became, after the strictest sect, a Garrisonian. It is not too much to say, that he formed a complement which they needed, and they were a complement equally necessary to his "make-up." With his deep and keen sensitiveness to wrong, and his wonderful memory, he came from the land of bondage full of its woes and its evils, and painting them in characters of living light; and, on his part, he found, told out in sound Saxon phrase, all those principles of justice and right and liberty, which had dimly brooded over the dreams of his youth, seeking definite forms and verbal expression. It must have been an electric flashing of thought, and a knitting of soul, granted to but few in this life, and will be a life-long memory to those who participated in it. In the society, moreover, of Wendell Phillips, Edmund Quincy, William Lloyd Garrison, and other men of earnest faith and refined culture, Mr. Douglass enjoyed the high advantage of their assistance and counsel in the labor of self-culture, to which he now addressed himself with wonted energy. Yet, these gentlemen, although proud of Frederick Douglass, failed to fathom, and bring out to the light of day, the highest qualities of his mind; the force of their own education stood in their own way: they did not delve into the mind of a colored man for capacities which the pride of race led them to believe to be restricted to their own Saxon blood. Bitter and vindictive sarcasm, irresistible mimicry, and a pathetic narrative of his own experiences of slavery, were the intellectual manifestations which they encouraged him to exhibit on the platform or in the lecture desk.

A visit to England, in 1845, threw Mr. Douglass among men and women of earnest souls and high culture, and who, moreover, had never drank of the bitter waters of American caste. For the first time in his life, he breathed an atmosphere congenial to the longings of his spirit, and felt his manhood free and unrestricted. The cordial and manly greetings of the British and Irish audiences in public, and the refinement and elegance of the social circles in which he mingled, not only as an equal, but as a recognized man of genius, were, doubtless genial and pleasant resting places in his hitherto thorny and troubled journey through life. There are joys on the earth, and, to the wayfaring fugitive from American slavery or American caste, this is one of them.

But his sojourn in England was more than a joy to Mr. Douglass. Like the platform at Nantucket, it awakened him to the consciousness of new powers that lay in him. From the pupilage of Garrisonism he rose to the dignity of a teacher and a thinker; his opinions on the broader aspects of the great American question were earnestly and incessantly sought, from various points of view, and he must, perforce, bestir himself to give suitable answer. With that prompt and truthful

---

*One of these ladies, impelled by the same noble spirit which carried Miss Nightingale to Scutari, has devoted her time, her untiring energies, to a great extent her means, and her high literary abilities, to the advancement and support of Frederick Douglass' Paper, the only organ of the downtrodden, edited and published by one of themselves, in the United States.

perception which has led their sisters in all ages of the world to gather at the feet and support the hands of reformers, the gentlewomen of England* were foremost to encourage and strengthen him to carve out for himself a path fitted to his powers and energies, in the life-battle against slavery and caste to which he was pledged. And one stirring thought, inseparable from the British idea of the evangel of freedom, must have smote his ear from every side—

> "Hereditary bondmen! know ye not
> Who would be free, themselves must strike the blow?"

The result of this visit was, that on his return to the United States, he established a newspaper. This proceeding was sorely against the wishes and the advice of the leaders of the American Anti-Slavery Society, but our author had fully grown up to the conviction of a truth which they had once promulged, but now forgotten, to wit: that in their own elevation—self-elevation—colored men have a blow to strike "on their own hook," against slavery and caste. Differing from his Boston friends in this matter, diffident in his own abilities, reluctant at their dissuadings, how beautiful is the loyalty with which he still clung to their principles in all things else, and even in this.

Now came the trial hour. Without cordial support from any large body of men or party on this side the Atlantic, and too far distant in space and immediate interest to expect much more, after the much already done, on the other side, he stood up, almost alone, to the arduous labor and heavy expenditure of editor and lecturer. The Garrison party, to which he still adhered, did not want a *colored* newspaper—there was an odor of *caste* about it; the Liberty party could hardly be expected to give warm support to a man who smote their principles as with a hammer; and the wide gulf which separated the free colored people from the Garrisonians, also separated them from their brother, Frederick Douglass.

The arduous nature of his labors, from the date of the establishment of his paper, may be estimated by the fact, that anti-slavery papers in the United States, even while the organs of, and when supported by, anti-slavery parties, have, with a single exception, failed to pay expenses. Mr. Douglass has maintained, and does maintain, his paper without the support of any party, and even in the teeth of the opposition of those from whom he had reason to expect counsel and encouragement. He has been compelled, at one and the same time, and almost constantly, during the past seven years, to contribute matter to its columns as editor, and to raise funds for its support as lecturer. It is within bounds to say, that he has expended twelve thousand dollars of his own hard earned money, in publishing this paper, a larger sum than has been contributed by any one individual for the general advancement of the colored people. There had been many other papers published and edited by colored men, beginning as far back as 1827, when the Rev. Samuel E. Cornish and John B. Russworm (a graduate of Bowdoin college, and afterward Governor of Cape Palmas) published the FREEDOM'S JOURNAL, in New York city; probably not less than one hundred newspaper enterprises have been started in the United States, by free colored men, born free, and some of them of liberal education and fair talents for this work; but, one after another, they have fallen through, although, in several instances, antislavery friends contributed to their support.* It had almost been given up, as an impracticable thing, to maintain a colored newspaper, when Mr. Douglass, with fewest early advantages of all his competitors, essayed, and has proved the thing perfectly practicable, and, moreover, of great public benefit. This paper, in addition to its power in holding up the hands of those to whom it is especially devoted, also affords irrefutable evidence of the justice, safety and practicability of Immediate Emancipation; it further proves the immense loss which slavery inflicts on the land while it dooms such energies as his to the hereditary degradation of slavery.

It has been said in this Introduction, that Mr. Douglass had raised himself by his own efforts to the highest position in society. As a successful editor, in our land, he occupies this position. Our editors rule the land, and he is one of them. As an orator and thinker, his position is equally high, in the opinion of his countrymen. If a stranger in the United States would seek its most distinguished men—the movers of public opinion—he will find their names mentioned, and their movements chronicled, under the head of "By MAGNETIC TELEGRAPH," in the daily papers. The keen caterers for the public attention, set down, in this column, such men only as have won high mark in the public esteem. During the past winter—1854–5—very frequent mention of Frederick Douglass was made under this head in the daily papers; his name glided as often—this week from Chicago, next week from Boston— over the lightning wires, as the name of any other man, of whatever note. To no man did the people more widely nor more earnestly say, *"Tell me thy thought!"* And, somehow or other, revolution seemed to follow in his wake. His were not the mere words of eloquence which Kossuth speaks of, that delight the ear and then pass away. No! They were *work*-able, *do*-able words, that brought forth fruits in the revolution in Illinois, and in the passage of the franchise resolutions by the Assembly of New York.

And the secret of his power, what is it? He is a Representative American man—a type of his countrymen. Naturalists tell us that a full grown man is a resultant or representative of all animated nature on this globe; beginning with the early embryo state, then representing

*Mr. Stephen Myers, of Albany, deserves mention as one of the most persevering among the colored editorial fraternity.

†The German physiologists have even discovered vegetable matter—starch—in the human body. See Med. Chirurgical Rev., Oct., 1854, p. 339.

the lowest forms of organic life,† and passing through every subordinate grade or type, until he reaches the last and highest—manhood. In like manner, and to the fullest extent, has Frederick Douglass passed through every gradation of rank comprised in our national make-up, and bears upon his person and upon his soul every thing that is American. And he has not only full sympathy with every thing American; his proclivity or bent, to active toil and visible progress, are in the strictly national direction, delighting to outstrip "all creation."

Nor have the natural gifts, already named as his, lost anything by his severe training. When unexcited, his mental processes are probably slow, but singularly clear in perception, and wide in vision, the unfailing memory bringing up all the facts in their every aspect; incongruities he lays hold of incontinently, and holds up on the edge of his keen and telling wit. But this wit never descends to frivolity; it is rigidly in the keeping of his truthful common sense, and always used in illustration or proof of some point which could not so readily be reached any other way. "Beware of a Yankee when he is feeding," is a shaft that strikes home in a matter never so laid bare by satire before. "The Garrisonian views of disunion, if carried to a successful issue, would only place the people of the north in the same relation to American slavery which they now bear to the slavery of Cuba or the Brazils," is a statement, in a few words, which contains the result and the evidence of an argument which might cover pages, but could not carry stronger conviction, nor be stated in less pregnable form. In proof of this, I may say, that having been submitted to the attention of the Garrisonians in print, in March, it was repeated before them at their business meeting in May—the platform, *par excellence*, on which they invite free fight, *a l'outrance*, to all comers. It was given out in the clear, ringing tones, wherewith the hall of shields was wont to resound of old, yet neither Garrison, nor Phillips, nor May, nor Remond, nor Foster, nor Burleigh, with his subtle steel of "the ice brook's temper," ventured to break a lance upon it! The doctrine of the dissolution of the Union, as a means for the abolition of American slavery, was silenced upon the lips that gave it birth, and in the presence of an array of defenders who compose the keenest intellects in the land.

"The man who is right is a majority," is an aphorism struck out by Mr. Douglass in that great gathering of the friends of freedom, at Pittsburgh, in 1852, where he towered among the highest, because, with abilities inferior to none, and moved more deeply than any, there was neither policy nor party to trammel the outpourings of his soul. Thus we find, opposed to all the disadvantages which a black man in the United States labors and struggles under, is this one vantage ground—when the chance comes, and the audience where he may have a say, he stands forth the freest, most deeply moved and most earnest of all men.

It has been said of Mr. Douglass, that his descriptive and declamatory powers, admitted to be of the very highest order, take precedence of his logical force. Whilst the schools might have trained him to the exhibition of the formulas of deductive logic, nature and circumstances forced him into the exercise of the higher faculties required by induction. The first ninety pages of this "Life in Bondage," afford specimens of observing, comparing, and careful classifying, of such superior character, that it is difficult to believe them the results of a child's thinking; he questions the earth, and the children and the slaves around him again and again, and finally looks to *"God in the sky"* for the why and the wherefore of the unnatural thing, slavery. *"Yere, if indeed thou art, wherefore dost thou suffer us to be slain?"* is the only prayer and worship of the God-forsaken Dodos in the heart of Africa. Almost the same was his prayer. One of his earliest observations was that white children should know their ages, while the colored children were ignorant of theirs; and the songs of the slaves grated on his inmost soul, because a something told him that harmony in sound, and music of the spirit, could not consociate with miserable degradation.

To such a mind, the ordinary processes of logical deduction are like proving that two and two make four. Mastering the intermediate steps by an intuitive glance, or recurring to them as Ferguson resorted to geometry, it goes down to the deeper relation of things, and brings out what may seem, to some, mere statements, but which are new and brilliant generalizations, each resting on a broad and stable basis. Thus, Chief Justice Marshall gave his decisions, and then told Brother Story to look up the authorities—and they never differed from him. Thus, also, in his "Lecture on the Anti-Slavery Movement," delivered before the Rochester Ladies' Anti-Slavery Society, Mr. Douglass presents a mass of thoughts, which, without any showy display of logic on his part, requires an exercise of the reasoning faculties of the reader to keep pace with him. And his "Claims of the Negro Ethnologically Considered," is full of new and fresh thoughts on the dawning science of race-history.

If, as has been stated, his intellection is slow, when unexcited, it is most prompt and rapid when he is thoroughly aroused. Memory, logic, wit, sarcasm, invective, pathos and bold imagery of rare structural beauty, well up as from a copious fountain, yet each in its proper place, and contributing to form a whole, grand in itself, yet complete in the minutest proportions. It is most difficult to hedge him in a corner, for his positions are taken so deliberately, that it is rare to find a point in them undefended aforethought. Professor Reason tells me the following: "On a recent visit of a public nature, to Philadelphia, and in a meeting composed mostly of his colored brethren, Mr. Douglass proposed a comparison of views in the matters of the relations and duties of 'our people;' he holding that prejudice was the result of condition, and could be conquered by the efforts of the degraded themselves. A gentleman present, distinguished for logical acumen and subtlety, and who had devoted no small portion of the last twenty-five years to the study and elucidation of this very question, held the opposite view, that prejudice is innate and unconquerable. He terminated a series of well dove-tailed, Socratic questions to Mr. Douglass, with the following: 'If the legislature at Harrisburgh should awaken, to-morrow morning, and find each man's skin turned black and his hair woolly, what could they do to remove prejudice?' 'Immediately pass laws entitling black men to all civil, political and social privileges,' was the instant reply—and the questioning ceased."

The most remarkable mental phenomenon in Mr. Douglass, is his style in writing and speaking. In March 1855, he delivered an address in the assembly chamber before the members of the legislature of the state of New York. An eye witness* describes the crowded and most intelligent audience, and their rapt attention to the speaker, as the grandest scene he ever witnessed in the capitol. Among those whose eyes were riveted on the speaker full two hours and a half, were Thurlow Weed and Lieutenant Governor Raymond; the latter, at the conclusion of the address, exclaimed to a friend, "I would give twenty thousand dollars, if I could deliver that address in that manner." Mr. Raymond is a first class graduate of Dartmouth, a rising politician, ranking foremost in the legislature; of course, his ideal of oratory must be of the most polished and finished description.

The style of Mr. Douglass in writing, is to me an intellectual puzzle. The strength, affluence and terseness may easily be accounted for, because the style of a man is the man; but how are we to account for that rare polish in his style of writing, which, most critically examined, seems the result of careful early culture among the best classics of our language; it equals if it do not surpass the style of Hugh Miller, which was the wonder of the British literary public, until he unraveled the mystery in the most interesting of autobiographies. But Frederick Douglass was still calking the seams of Baltimore clippers, and had only written a "pass," at the age when Miller's style was already formed.

I asked William Whipper, of Pennsylvania, the gentleman alluded to above, whether he thought Mr. Douglass's power inherited from the Negroid, or from what is called the Caucasian side of his make-up? After some reflection, he frankly answered, "I must admit, although sorry to do so, that the Caucasian predominates." At that time, I almost agreed with him; but, facts narrated in the first part of this work, throw a different light on this interesting question.

We are left in the dark as to who was the paternal ancestor of our author; a fact which generally holds good of the Romuluses and Remuses who are to inaugurate the new birth of our republic. In the absence of testimony from the Caucasian side, we must see what evidence is given on the other side of the house.

"My grandmother, though advanced in years, . . . was yet a

*Mr. Wm. H. Topp, of Albany.

woman of power and spirit. She was marvelously straight in figure, elastic and muscular." (p. 148).

After describing her skill in constructing nets, her perseverance in using them, and her wide-spread fame in the agricultural way, he adds, "It happened to her—as it will happen to any careful and thrifty person residing in an ignorant and improvident neighborhood—to enjoy the reputation of being born to good luck." And his grandmother was a black woman.

"My mother was tall, and finely proportioned; of deep black, glossy complexion; had regular features; and among other slaves was remarkably sedate in her manners." "Being a field hand, she was obliged to walk twelve miles and return, between nightfall and daybreak, to see her children" (p. 153.) "I shall never forget the indescribable expression of her countenance when I told her that I had had no food since morning. . . . There was pity in her glance at me, and a fiery indignation at Aunt Katy at the same time; . . . . she read Aunt Katy a lecture which she never forgot." (p. 154.) "I learned, after my mother's death, that she could read, and that she was the *only* one of all the slaves and colored people in Tuckahoe who enjoyed that advantage. How she acquired this knowledge, I know not, for Tuckahoe is the last place in the world where she would be apt to find facilities for learning." (p. 155.) "There is, in *'Prichard's Natural History of Man,'* the head of a figure—on page 157—the features of which so resemble those of my mother, that I often recur to it with something of the feeling which I suppose others experience when looking upon the pictures of dear departed ones." (p. 152.)

The head alluded to is copied from the statue of Ramses the Great, an Egyptian king of the nineteenth dynasty. The authors of the "Types of Mankind" give a side view of the same on page 148, remarking that the profile, "like Napoleon's, is superbly European!" The nearness of its resemblance to Mr. Douglass' mother, rests upon the evidence of his memory, and judging from his almost marvelous feats of recollection of forms and outlines recorded in this book, this testimony may be admitted.

These facts show that for his energy, perseverance, eloquence, invective, sagacity, and wide sympathy, he is indebted to his negro blood. The very marvel of his style would seem to be a development of that other marvel,—how his mother learned to read. The versatility of talent which he wields, in common with Dumas, Ira Aldridge, and Miss Greenfield, would seem to be the result of the grafting of the Anglo-Saxon on good, original, negro stock. If the friends of "Caucasus" choose to claim, for that region, what remains after this analysis— to wit: combination—they are welcome to it. They will forgive me for reminding them that the term "Caucasian" is dropped by recent writers on Ethnology; for the people about Mount Caucasus, are, and have ever been, Mongols. The great "white race" now seek paternity, according to Dr. Pickering, in Arabia—"Arida Nutrix" of the best breed of horses &c. Keep on, gentlemen; you will find yourselves in Africa, by-and-by. The Egyptians, like the Americans, were a *mixed race*, with some negro blood circling around the throne, as well as in the mud hovels.

This is the proper place to remark of our author, that the same strong self-hood, which led him to measure strength with Mr. Covey, and to wrench himself from the embrace of the Garrisonians, and which has borne him through many resistances to the personal indignities offered him as a colored man, sometimes becomes a hypersensitiveness to such assaults as men of his mark will meet with, on paper. Keen and unscrupulous opponents have sought, and not unsuccessfully, to pierce him in this direction; for well they know, that if assailed, he will smite back.

It is not without a feeling of pride, dear reader, that I present you with this book. The son of a self-emancipated bond-woman, I feel joy in introducing to you my brother, who has rent his own bonds, and who, in his every relation—as a public man, as a husband and as a father—is such as does honor to the land which gave him birth. I shall place this book in the hands of the only child spared me, bidding him to strive and emulate its noble example. You may do likewise. It is an American book, for Americans, in the fullest sense of the idea. It shows that the worst of our institutions, in its worst aspect, cannot keep down energy, truthfulness, and earnest struggle for the right. It proves the justice and practicability of Immediate Emancipation. It shows that any man in our land, "no matter in what battle his liberty may have been cloven down, ... no matter what complexion an Indian or an African sun may have burned upon him," not only may "stand forth redeemed and disenthralled," but may also stand up a candidate for the highest suffrage of a great people—the tribute of their honest, hearty admiration. Reader, *Vale!*

New York, May 23, 1855.   JAMES M'CUNE SMITH.

LIFE AS A SLAVE

CHAPTER I

The Author's Childhood

In Talbot county, Eastern Shore, Maryland, near Easton, the county town of that county, there is a small district of country, thinly populated, and remarkable for nothing that I know of more than for the worn-out, sandy, desert-like appearance of its soil, the general dilapidation of its farms and fences, the indigent and spiritless character of its inhabitants, and the prevalence of ague and fever.

The name of this singularly unpromising and truly famine stricken district is Tuckahoe, a name well known to all Marylanders, black and white. It was given to this section of country probably, at the first, merely in derision; or it may possibly have been applied to it, as I have heard, because some one of its earlier inhabitants had been guilty of the petty meanness of stealing a hoe—or taking a hoe—that did not belong to him. Eastern Shore men usually pronounce the word *took*, as *tuck; Took-a-hoe*, therefore, is, in Maryland parlance, *Tuckahoe*. But, whatever may have been its origin—and about this I will not be positive—that name has stuck to the district in question; and it is seldom mentioned but with contempt and derision, on account of the barrenness of its soil, and the ignorance, indolence, and poverty of its people. Decay and ruin are everywhere visible, and the thin population of the place would have quitted it long ago, but for the Choptank river, which runs through it, from which they take abundance of shad and herring, and plenty of ague and fever.

It was in this dull, flat, and unthrifty district, or neighborhood, surrounded by a white population of the lowest order, indolent and drunken to a proverb, and among slaves, who seemed to ask, *"Oh! what's the use?"* every time they lifted a hoe, that I—without any fault of mine—was born, and spent the first years of my childhood.

The reader will pardon so much about the place of my birth, on the score that it is always a fact of some importance to know where a man is born, if, indeed, it be important to know anything about him. In regard to the *time* of my birth, I cannot be as definite as I have been respecting the *place*. Nor, indeed, can I impart much knowledge concerning my parents. Genealogical trees do not flourish among slaves. A person of some consequence here in the north, sometimes designated *father*, is literally abolished in slave law and slave practice. It is only once in a while that an exception is found to this statement. I never met with a slave who could tell me how old he was. Few slave-mothers know anything of the months of the year, nor of the days of the month. They keep no family records, with marriages, births, and deaths. They measure the ages of their children by spring time, winter time, harvest time, planting time, and the like; but these soon become undistinguishable and forgotten. Like other slaves, I cannot tell how old I am. This destitution was among my earliest troubles. I learned when I grew up, that my master—and this is the case with masters generally—allowed no questions to be put to him, by which a slave might learn his age. Such questions are deemed evidence of impatience, and even of impudent curiosity. From certain events, however, the dates of which I have since learned , I suppose myself to have been born about the year 1817.

The first experience of life with me that I now remember—and I remember it but hazily—began in the family of my grandmother and grandfather, Betsey and Isaac Baily. They were quite advanced in life, and had long lived on the spot where they then resided. They were considered old settlers in the neighborhood, and, from certain circumstances, I infer that my grandmother, especially, was held in high esteem, far higher than is the lot of most colored persons in the slave states. She was a good nurse, and a capital hand at making nets for catching shad and herring; and these nets were in great demand, not only in Tuckahoe, but at Denton and Hillsboro, neighboring villages. She was not only good at making the nets, but was also somewhat famous for her good fortune in taking the fishes referred to. I have known her to be in the water half the day. Grandmother was likewise more provident than most of her neighbors in the preservation of seedling sweet potatoes, and it happened to her—as it will happen to any careful and thrifty person residing in an ignorant and improvident community—to enjoy the reputation of having been born to "good luck." Her "good luck" was owing to the exceeding care which she took in preventing the succulent root from getting bruised in the digging, and in placing it beyond the reach of frost, by actually burying it under the hearth of her cabin during the winter months. In the time of planting sweet potatoes, "Grandmother Betty," as she was familiarly called, was sent for in all directions, simply to place the seedling potatoes in the hills; for superstition had it, that if "Grandmamma Betty but touches them at planting, they will be sure to grow and flourish." This high reputation was full of advantage to her, and to the children around her. Though Tuckahoe had but few of the good things of life, yet of such as it did possess grandmother got a full share, in the way of presents. If good potato crops came after her planting, she was not forgotten by those for whom she planted; and as she was remembered by others, so she remembered the hungry little ones around her.

The dwelling of my grandmother and grandfather had few pretensions. It was a log hut, or cabin, built of clay, wood, and straw. At a distance it resembled—though it was much smaller, less commodious and less substantial—the cabins erected in the western states by the first settlers. To my child's eye, however, it was a noble structure, admirably adapted to promote the comforts and conveniences of its inmates. A few rough, Virginia fence-rails, flung loosely over the rafters above, answered the triple purpose of floors, ceilings, and bedsteads. To be sure, this upper apartment was reached only by a ladder—but what in the world for climbing could be better than a ladder? To me, this ladder was really a high invention, and possessed a sort of charm as I played with delight upon the rounds of it. In this little hut there was a large family of children: I dare not say how many. My grandmother—whether because too old for field service, or because she had so faithfully discharged the duties of her station in early life, I know not—enjoyed the high privilege of living in a cabin, separate from the quarter, with no other burden than her own support, and the necessary care of the little children, imposed. She evidently esteemed it a great fortune to live so. The children were not her own, but her grandchildren—the children of her daughters. She took delight in having them around her, and in attending to their few wants. The practice of separating children from their mothers, and hiring the latter out at distances too great to admit of their meeting, except at long intervals, is a marked feature of the cruelty and barbarity of the slave system. But it is in harmony with the grand aim of slavery, which, always and everywhere, is to reduce man to a level with the brute. It is a successful method of obliterating from the mind and heart of the slave, all just ideas of the sacredness of *the family*, as an institution.

Most of the children, however, in this instance, being the children of my grandmother's daughters, the notions of family, and the reciprocal duties and benefits of the relation, had a better chance of being understood than where children are placed—as they often are—in the hands of strangers, who have no care for them, apart from the wishes of their masters. The daughters of my grandmother were five in number. Their names were JENNY, ESTHER, MILLY, PRISCILLA, and HARRIET. The daughter last named was my mother, of whom the reader shall learn more by-and-by.

Living here, with my dear old grandmother and grandfather, it was a long time before I knew myself to be *a slave*. I knew many other things before I knew that. Grandmother and grandfather were the greatest people in the world to me; and being with them so snugly in their own little cabin—I supposed it be their own—knowing no higher authority over me or the other children than the authority of grandmamma, for a time there was nothing to disturb me; but, as I grew larger and older, I learned by degrees the sad fact, that the "little hut," and the lot on which it stood, belonged not to my dear old grandparents, but to some person who lived a great distance off, and who was called, by grandmother, "OLD MASTER." I further learned the sadder fact, that not only the house and lot, but that grandmother herself, (grandfather was free,) and all the little children around her, belonged to this mysterious personage, called by grandmother, with every mark of reverence, "Old Master." Thus early did clouds and shadows begin to fall upon my path. Once on the track—troubles never come singly— I was not long in finding out another fact, still more grievous to my childish heart. I was told that this "old master," whose name seemed ever to be mentioned with fear and shuddering, only allowed the children to live with grandmother for a limited time, and that in fact as soon as they were big enough, they were promptly taken away, to live with the said "old master." These were distressing revelations indeed; and though I was quite too young to comprehend the full import of the intelligence, and mostly spent my childhood days in gleesome sports with the other children, a shade of disquiet rested upon me.

The absolute power of this distant "old master" had touched my young spirit with but the point of its cold, cruel iron, and left me something to brood over after the play and in moments of repose. Grandmammy was, indeed, at that time, all the world to me; and the thought of being separated from her, in any considerable time, was more than an unwelcome intruder. It was intolerable.

Children have their sorrows as well as men and women; and it would be well to remember this in our dealings with them. SLAVE-children *are* children, and prove no exceptions to the general rule. The liability to be separated from my grandmother, seldom or never to see her again, haunted me. I dreaded the thought of going to live with that mysterious "old master," whose name I never heard mentioned with affection, but always with fear. I look back to this as among the heaviest of my childhood's sorrows. My grandmother! my grandmother! and the little hut, and the joyous circle under her care, but especially *she*, who made us sorry when she left us but for an hour, and glad on her return,—how could I leave her and the good old home?

But the sorrows of childhood, like the pleasures of after life, are transient. It is not even within the power of slavery to write *indelible* sorrow, at a single dash, over the heart of a child.

> "The tear down childhood's cheek that flows,
> Is like the dew-drop on the rose,—
> When next the summer breeze comes by,
> And waves the bush,—the flower is dry."

There is, after all, but little difference in the measure of contentment felt by the slave-child neglected and the slaveholder's child cared for and petted. The spirit of the All Just mercifully holds the balance for the young.

The slaveholder, having nothing to fear from impotent childhood, easily affords to refrain from cruel inflictions; and if cold and hunger do not pierce the tender frame, the first seven or eight years of the slave-boy's life are about as full of sweet content as those of the most favored and petted *white* children of the slaveholder. The slave-boy escapes many troubles which befall and vex his white brother. He seldom has to listen to lectures on propriety of behavior, or on anything else. He is never chided for handling his little knife and fork improperly or awkwardly, for he uses none. He is never reprimanded for soiling the table-cloth, for he takes his meals on the clay floor. He never has the misfortune, in his games or sports, of soiling or tearing his clothes, for he has almost none to soil or tear. He is never expected to act like a nice little gentleman, for he is only a rude little slave. Thus, freed from all restraint, the slave-boy can be, in his life and conduct, a genuine boy, doing whatever his boyish nature suggests; enacting, by turns, all the strange antics and freaks of horses, dogs, pigs, and barn-door fowls, without in any manner compromising his dignity, or incurring reproach of any sort. He literally runs wild; has no pretty little verses to learn in the nursery; no nice little speeches to make for aunts, uncles, or cousins, to show how smart he is; and, if he can only manage to keep out of the way of the heavy feet and fists of the older slave boys, he may trot on, in his joyous and roguish tricks, as happy as any little heathen under the palm trees of Africa. To be sure, he is occasionally reminded, when he stumbles in the path of his master—and this he early learns to avoid—that he is eating his *"white bread,"* and that he will be made to *"see sights"* by-and-by. The threat is soon forgotten; the shadow soon passes, and our sable boy continues to roll in the dust, or play in the mud, as bests suits him, and in the veriest freedom. If he feels uncomfortable, from mud or from dust, the coast is clear; he can plunge into the river or the pond, without the ceremony of undressing, or the fear of wetting his clothes; his little tow-linen shirt—for that is all he has on—is easily dried; and it needed ablution as much as did his skin. His food is of the coarsest kind, consisting for the most part of corn-meal mush, which often finds its way from the wooden tray to his mouth in an oyster shell. His days, when the weather is warm, are spent in the pure, open air, and in the bright sunshine. He always sleeps in airy apartments; he seldom has to take powders, or to be paid to swallow pretty little sugar-coated pills, to cleanse his blood, or to quicken his appetite. He eats no candies; gets no lumps of loaf sugar; always relishes his food; cries but little, for nobody cares for his crying; learns to esteem his bruises but slight, because others so esteem them. In a word, he is, for the most part of the first eight years of his life, a spirited, joyous, uproarious, and happy boy, upon whom troubles fall only like water on a duck's back. And such a boy, so far as I can now remember, was the boy whose life in slavery I am now narrating.

CHAPTER II

The Author Removed From His First Home

That mysterious individual referred to in the first chapter as an object of terror among the inhabitants of our little cabin, under the ominous title of "old master," was really a man of some consequence. He owned several farms in Tuckahoe; was the chief clerk and butler on the home plantation of Col. Edward Lloyd; had overseers on his own farms; and gave directions to overseers on the farms belonging to Col. Lloyd. This plantation is situated on Wye river—the river receiving its name, doubtless, from Wales, where the Lloyds originated. They (the Lloyds) are an old and honored family in Maryland, exceedingly wealthy. The home plantation, where they have resided, perhaps for a century or more, is one of the largest, most fertile, and best appointed, in the state.

About this plantation, and about that queer old master—who must be something more than a man, and something worse than an angel—the reader will easily imagine that I was not only curious, but eager, to know all that could be known. Unhappily for me, however, all the information I could get concerning him but increased my great dread of being carried thither—of being separated from and deprived of the protection of my grandmother and grandfather. It was, evidently, a great thing to go to Col. Lloyd's; and I was not without a little curiosity to see the place; but no amount of coaxing could induce in me the wish to remain there. The fact is, such was my dread of leaving the little cabin, that I wished to remain little forever, for I knew the taller I grew the shorter my stay. The old cabin, with its rail floor and rail bedsteads up stairs, and its clay floor down stairs, and its dirt chimney, and windowless sides, and that most curious piece of workmanship of all the rest, the ladder stairway, and the hole curiously dug in front of the fire-place, beneath which grandmammy placed the sweet potatoes to keep them from the frost, was MY HOME—the only home I ever had; and I loved it, and all connected with it. The old fences around it, and the stumps in the edge of the woods near it, and the squirrels that ran, skipped, and played upon them, were objects of interest and affection. There, too, right at the side of the hut, stood the old well, with its stately and skyward-pointing beam, so aptly placed between the limbs of what had once been a tree, and so nicely balanced that I could move it up and down with only one hand, and could get a drink myself without calling for help. Where else in the world could such a well be found, and where could such another home be met with? Nor were these all the attractions of the place. Down in a little valley, not far from grandmammy's cabin, stood Mr. Lee's mill, where the people came often in large numbers to get their corn ground. It was a water-mill; and I never shall be able to tell the many things thought and felt, while I sat on the bank and watched that mill, and the turning of that ponderous wheel. The mill-pond, too, had its charms; and with my pin-hook, and thread line, I could get *nibbles*, if I could catch no fish. But, in all my sports and plays, and in spite of them, there would, occasionally, come the painful foreboding that I was not long to remain there, and that I must soon be called away to the home of old master.

I was a SLAVE—born a slave—and though the fact was incomprehensible to me, it conveyed to my mind a sense of my entire dependence on the will of *somebody* I had never seen; and, from some cause or other, I had been made to fear this somebody above all else on earth. Born for another's benefit, as the *firstling* of the cabin flock I was soon to be selected as a meet offering to the fearful and inexorable *demi-god,* whose huge image on so many occasions haunted my childhood's imagination. When the time of my departure was decided upon, my grandmother, knowing my fears, and in pity for them, kindly kept me ignorant of the dreaded event about to transpire. Up to the morning (a beautiful summer morning) when we were to start, and, indeed, during the whole journey—a journey which, child as I was, I remember as well as if it were yesterday—she kept the sad fact hidden from me. This reserve was necessary; for, could I have known all, I should have given grandmother some trouble in getting me started. As it was, I was helpless, and she—dear woman!—led me along by the hand, resisting, with the reserve and solemnity of a priestess, all my inquiring looks to the last.

The distance from Tuckahoe to Wye river—where my old master lived—was full twelve miles, and the walk was quite a severe test of the endurance of my young legs. The journey would have proved too severe for me, but that my dear old grandmother—blessings on her memory!—afforded occasional relief by "toting" me (as Marylanders have it) on her shoulder. My grandmother, though advanced in years—as was evident from more than one gray hair, which peeped from between the ample and graceful folds of her newly-ironed bandana turban—was yet a woman of power and spirit. She was marvelously straight in figure, elastic, and muscular. I seemed hardly to be a burden to her. She would have "toted" me farther, but that I felt myself too much of a man to allow it, and insisted on walking. Releasing dear grandmamma from carrying me, did not make me altogether independent of her, when we happened to pass through portions of the somber woods which lay between Tuckahoe and Wye river. She often found me increasing the energy of my grip, and holding her clothing, lest something should come out of the woods and eat me up. Several old logs and stumps imposed upon me, and got themselves taken for wild beasts. I could see their legs, eyes, and ears, or I could see something like eyes, legs, and ears, till I got close enough to them to see that the eyes were knots, washed white with rain, and the legs were broken limbs, and the ears, only ears owing to the point from which they were seen. Thus early I learned that the point from which a thing is viewed is of some importance.

As the day advanced the heat increased; and it was not until the afternoon that we reached the much dreaded end of the journey. I found myself in the midst of a group of children of many colors; black, brown, copper colored, and nearly white. I had not seen so many children before. Great houses loomed up in different directions, and a great many men and women were at work in the fields. All this hurry, noise, and singing was very different from the stillness of Tuckahoe. As a new comer, I was an object of special interest; and, after laughing and yelling around me, and playing all sorts of wild tricks, they (the children) asked me to go out and play with them. This I refused to do, preferring to stay with grandmamma. I could not help feeling that our being there boded no good to me. Grandmamma looked sad. She was soon to lose another object of affection, as she had lost many before. I knew she was unhappy, and the shadow fell from her brow on me, though I knew not the cause.

All suspense, however, must have an end; and the end of mine, in this instance, was at hand. Affectionately patting me on the head, and exhorting me to be a good boy, grandmamma told me to go and play with the little children. "They are kin to you," said she; "go and play with them." Among a number of cousins were Phil, Tom, Steve, and Jerry, Nance and Betty.

Grandmother pointed out my brother PERRY, my sister SARAH, and my sister ELIZA, who stood in the group. I had never seen my brother nor my sisters before; and, though I had sometimes heard of them, and felt a curious interest in them, I really did not understand what they were to me, or I to them. We were brothers and sisters, but what of that? Why should they be attached to me, or I to them? Brothers and sisters we were by blood; but *slavery* had made us strangers. I heard the words brother and sisters, and knew they must mean something; but slavery had robbed these terms of their true meaning. The experience through which I was passing, they had passed through before. They had already been initiated into the mysteries of the old master's domicile, and they seemed to look upon me with a certain degree of compassion; but my heart clave to my grandmother. Think it not strange, dear reader, that so little sympathy of feeling existed between us. The conditions of brotherly and sisterly feeling were wanting—we had never nestled and played together. My poor mother, like many other slave-women, had *many children*, but NO FAMILY! The domestic hearth, with its holy lessons and precious endearments, is abolished in the case of a slave-mother and her children. "Little children, love one another," are words seldom heard in a slave cabin.

I really wanted to play with my brother and sisters, but they were strangers to me, and I was full of fear that grandmother might leave without taking me with her. Entreated to do so, however, and that, too, by my dear grandmother, I went to the back part of the house, to play with them and the other children. *Play*, however, I did not, but stood with my back against the wall, witnessing the playing of the others. At last, while standing there, one of the children, who had been in the kitchen, ran up to me, in a sort of roguish glee, exclaiming, "Fed, Fed! grandmammy gone! grandmammy gone!" I could not believe it; yet, fearing the worst, I ran into the kitchen, to see for myself, and found it even so. Grandmammy had indeed gone, and was now far away, "clean" out of sight. I need not tell all that happened now. Almost heart-broken at the discovery, I fell upon the ground, and wept a boy's bitter tears, refusing to be comforted. My brother and sisters came around me, and said, "Don't cry," and gave me peaches and pears, but I flung them away, and refused all their kindly advances. I had never been deceived before; and I felt not only grieved at parting— as I supposed forever—with my grandmother, but indignant that a trick had been played upon me in a matter so serious.

It was now late in the afternoon. The day had been an exciting and wearisome one, and I knew not how or where, but I suppose I sobbed myself to sleep. There is a healing in the angel wing of sleep, even for the slave-boy; and its balm was never more welcome to any wounded soul than it was to mine, the first night I spent at the domicile of old master. The reader may be surprised that I narrate so minutely an incident apparently so trivial, and which must have occurred when I was not more than seven years old; but as I wish to give a faithful history of my experience in slavery, I cannot withhold a circumstance which, at the time, affected me so deeply. Besides, this was, in fact, my first introduction to the realities of slavery.

CHAPTER III

The Author's Parentage

If the reader will now be kind enough to allow me time to grow bigger, and afford me an opportunity for my experience to become greater, I will tell him something, by-and-by, of slave life, as I saw, felt, and heard it, on Col. Edward Lloyd's plantation, and at the house of old master, where I had now, despite of myself, most suddenly, but not unexpectedly, been dropped. Meanwhile, I will redeem my promise to say something more of my dear mother.

I say nothing of *father*, for he is shrouded in a mystery I have never been able to penetrate. Slavery does away with fathers, as it does away with families. Slavery has no use for either fathers or families, and its laws do not recognize their existence in the social arrangements of the plantation. When they *do* exist, they are not the outgrowths of slavery, but are antagonistic to that system. The order of civilization is reversed here. The name of the child is not expected to be that of its father, and his condition does not necessarily affect that of the child. He may be the slave of Mr. Tilgman; and his child, when born, may be the slave of Mr. Gross. He may be a *freeman;* and yet his child may be a *chattel*. He may be white, glorying in the purity of his Anglo-Saxon blood; and his child may be ranked with the blackest slaves. Indeed, he *may* be, and often *is*, master and father to the same child. He can be father without being a husband, and may sell his child without incurring reproach, if the child be by a woman in whose veins courses one thirty-second part of African blood. My father was a white man, or nearly white. It was sometimes whispered that my master was my father.

But to return, or rather, to begin. My knowledge of my mother is very scanty, but very distinct. Her personal appearance and bearing are ineffaceably stamped upon my memory. She was tall, and finely proportioned; of deep black, glossy complexion; had regular features, and among the other slaves, was remarkably sedate in her manners. There is in *"Prichard's Natural History of Man,"* the head of a figure—on page 157—the features of which so resemble those of my mother, that

187

I often recur to it with something of the feeling which I suppose others experience when looking upon the pictures of dear departed ones.

Yet I cannot say that I was very deeply attached to my mother; certainly not so deeply as I should have been had our relations in childhood been different. We were separated, according to the common custom, when I was but an infant, and, of course, before I knew my mother from any one else.

The germs of affection with which the Almighty, in his wisdom and mercy, arms the helpless infant against the ills and vicissitudes of his lot, had been directed in their growth toward that loving old grandmother, whose gentle hand and kind deportment it was the first effort of my infantile understanding to comprehend and appreciate. Accordingly, the tenderest affection which a beneficent Father allows, as a partial compensation to the mother for the pains and lacerations of her heart, incident to the maternal relation, was, in my case, diverted from its true and natural object, by the envious, greedy, and treacherous hand of slavery. The slave-mother can be spared long enough from the field to endure all the bitterness of a mother's anguish, when it adds another name to a master's ledger, but *not* long enough to receive the joyous reward afforded by the intelligent smiles of her child. I never think of this terrible interference of slavery with my infantile affections, and its diverting them from their natural course, without feelings to which I can give no adequate expression.

I do not remember to have seen my mother at my grandmother's at any time. I remember her only in her visits to me at Col. Lloyd's plantation, and in the kitchen of my old master. Her visits to me there were few in number, brief in duration, and mostly made in the night. The pains she took, and the toil she endured, to see me, tells me that a true mother's heart was hers, and that slavery had difficulty in paralyzing it with unmotherly indifference.

My mother was hired out to a Mr. Stewart, who lived about twelve miles from old master's, and, being a field hand, she seldom had leisure, by day, for the performance of the journey. The nights and the distance were both obstacles to her visits. She was obliged to walk, unless chance flung into her way an opportunity to ride; and the latter was sometimes her good luck. But she always had to walk one way or the other. It was a greater luxury than slavery could afford, to allow a black slave-mother a horse or a mule, upon which to travel twenty-four miles, when she could walk the distance. Besides, it is deemed a foolish whim for a slave-mother to manifest concern to see her children, and, in one point of view, the case is made out—she can do nothing for them. She has no control over them; the master is even more than the mother, in all matters touching the fate of her child. Why, then, should she give herself any concern? She has no responsibility. Such is the reasoning, and such the practice. The iron rule of the plantation, always passionately and violently enforced in that neighborhood, makes flogging the penalty of failing to be in the field before sunrise in the morning, unless special permission be given to the absenting slave. "I went to see my child," is no excuse to the ear or heart of the overseer.

One of the visits of my mother to me, while at Col. Lloyd's, I remember very vividly, as affording a bright gleam of a mother's love, and the earnestness of a mother's care.

I had on that day offended "Aunt Katy," (called "Aunt" by way of respect,) the cook of old master's establishment. I do not now remember the nature of my offense in this instance, for my offenses were numerous in that quarter, greatly depending, however, upon the mood of Aunt Katy, as to their heinousness; but she had adopted, that day, her favorite mode of punishing me, namely, making me go without food all day—that is, from after breakfast. The first hour or two after dinner, I succeeded pretty well in keeping up my spirits; but though I made an excellent stand against the foe, and fought bravely during the afternoon, I knew I must be conquered at last, unless I got the accustomed reënforcement of a slice of corn bread, at sundown. Sundown came, but *no bread*, and, in its stead, there came the threat, with a scowl well suited to its terrible import, that she "meant to *starve the life out of me!*" Brandishing her knife, she chopped off the heavy slices for the other children, and put the loaf away, muttering, all the while, her savage designs upon myself. Against this disappointment, for I was expecting that her heart would relent at last, I made an extra effort to maintain my dignity; but when I saw all the other children around me with merry and satisfied faces, I could stand it no longer. I went out behind the house, and cried like a fine fellow! When tired of this, I returned to the kitchen, sat by the fire, and brooded over my hard lot. I was too hungry to sleep. While I sat in the corner, I caught sight of an ear of Indian corn on an upper shelf of the kitchen. I watched my chance, and got it, and, shelling off a few grains, I put it back again. The grains in my hand, I quickly put in some ashes, and covered them with embers, to roast them. All this I did at the risk of getting a brutal thumping, for Aunt Katy could beat, as well as starve me. My corn was not long in roasting, and, with my keen appetite, it did not matter even if the grains were not exactly done. I eagerly pulled them out, and placed them on my stool, in a clever little pile. Just as I began to help myself to my very dry meal, in came my dear mother. And now, dear reader, a scene occurred which was altogether world beholding, and to me it was instructive as well as interesting. The friendless and hungry boy, in his extremest need—and when he did not dare to look for succor—found himself in the strong, protecting arms of a mother; a mother who was, at the moment (being endowed with high powers of manner as well as matter) more than a match for all his enemies. I shall never forget the indescribable expression of her countenance, when I told her that I had had no food since morning; and that Aunt Katy said she "meant to starve the life out of me." There was pity in her glance at me, and a fiery indignation at Aunt Katy at the same time; and, while she took the corn from me, and gave me a large ginger cake, in its stead, she read Aunt Katy a lecture which she never forgot. My mother threatened her with complaining to old master in my behalf; for the latter, though harsh and cruel himself, at times, did not sanction the meanness, injustice, partiality and oppressions enacted by Aunt Katy in the kitchen. That night I learned the fact, that I was not only a child, but *somebody's* child. The "sweet cake" my mother gave me was in the shape of a heart, with a rich, dark ring glazed upon the edge of it. I was victorious, and well off for the moment; prouder, on my mother's knee, than a king upon his throne. But my triumph was short. I dropped off to sleep, and waked in the morning only to find my mother gone, and myself left at the mercy of the sable virago, dominant in my old master's kitchen, whose fiery wrath was my constant dread.

I do not remember to have seen my mother after this occurrence. Death soon ended the little communication that had existed between us; and with it, I believe, a life—judging from her weary, sad, downcast countenance and mute demeanor—full of heart-felt sorrow. I was not allowed to visit her during any part of her long illness; nor did I see her for a long time before she was taken ill and died. The heartless and ghastly form of *slavery* rises between mother and child, even at the bed of death. The mother, at the verge of the grave, may not gather her children, to impart to them her holy admonitions, and invoke for them her dying benediction. The bondwoman lives as a slave, and is left to die as a beast; often with fewer attentions than are paid to a favorite horse. Scenes of sacred tenderness, around the death-bed, never forgotten, and which often arrest the vicious and confirm the virtuous during life, must be looked for among the free, though they sometimes occur among the slaves. It has been a life-long, standing grief to me, that I knew so little of my mother; and that I was so early separated from her. The counsels of her love must have been beneficial to me. The side view of her face is imaged on my memory, and I take few steps in life, without feeling her presence; but the image is mute, and I have no striking words of her's treasured up.

I learned, after my mother's death, that she could read, and that she was the *only* one of all the slaves and colored people in Tuckahoe who enjoyed that advantage. How she acquired this knowledge, I know not, for Tuckahoe is the last place in the world where she would be apt to find facilities for learning. I can, therefore, fondly and proudly ascribe to her an earnest love of knowledge. That a "field hand" should learn to read, in any slave state, is remarkable; but the achievement of my mother, considering the place, was very extraordinary; and, in view of that fact, I am quite willing, and even happy, to attribute any love of letters I possess, and for which I have got—despite of prejudices—only too much credit, *not* to my admitted Anglo-

Saxon paternity, but to the native genius of my sable, unprotected, and uncultivated *mother*—a woman, who belonged to a race whose mental endowments it is, at present, fashionable to hold in disparagement and contempt.

Summoned away to her account, with the impassible gulf of slavery between us during her entire illness, my mother died without leaving me a single intimation of *who* my father was. There was a whisper, that my master was my father; yet it was only a whisper, and I cannot say that I ever gave it credence. Indeed, I now have reason to think he was not; nevertheless, the fact remains, in all its glaring odiousness, that, by the laws of slavery, children, in all cases, are reduced to the condition of their mothers. This arrangement admits of the greatest license to brutal slaveholders, and their profligate sons, brothers, relations and friends, and gives to the pleasure of sin, the additional attraction of profit. A whole volume might be written on this single feature of slavery, as I have observed it.

One might imagine, that the children of such connections, would fare better, in the hands of their masters, than other slaves. The rule is quite the other way; and a very little reflection will satisfy the reader that such is the case. A man who will enslave his own blood, may not be safely relied on for magnanimity. Men do not love those who remind them of their sins—unless they have a mind to repent—and the mulatto child's face is a standing accusation against him who is master and father to the child. What is still worse, perhaps, such a child is a constant offense to the wife. She hates its very presence, and when a slaveholding woman hates, she wants not means to give that hate telling effect. Women—white women, I mean—are IDOLS at the south, not WIVES, for the slave woman are preferred in many instances; and if these *idols* but nod, or lift a finger, woe to the poor victim: kicks, cuffs and stripes are sure to follow. Masters are frequently compelled to sell this class of their slaves, out of deference to the feelings of their white wives; and shocking and scandalous as it may seem for a man to sell his own blood to the traffickers in human flesh, it is often an act of humanity toward the slave-child to be thus removed from his merciless tormentors.

It is not within the scope of the design of my simple story, to comment upon every phase of slavery not within my experience as a slave.

But, I may remark, that, if the lineal descendants of Ham are only to be enslaved, according to the scriptures, slavery in this country will soon become an unscriptual institution; for thousands are ushered into the world, annually, who—like myself—owe their existence to white fathers, and, most frequently, to their masters, and master's sons. The slave-woman is at the mercy of the fathers, sons or brothers of her master. The thoughtful know the rest.

After what I have now said of the circumstances of my mother, and my relations to her, the reader will not be surprised, nor be disposed to censure me, when I tell but the simple truth, viz: that I received the tidings of her death with no strong emotions of sorrow for her, and with very little regret for myself on account of her loss. I had to learn the value of my mother long after her death, and by witnessing the devotion of other mothers to their children.

There is not, beneath the sky, an enemy to filial affection so destructive as slavery. It had made my brothers and sisters strangers to me; it converted the mother that bore me, into a myth; it shrouded my father in mystery, and left me without an intelligible beginning in the world.

My mother died when I could not have been more than eight or nine years old, on one of old master's farms in Tuckahoe, in the neighborhood of Hillsborough. Her grave is, as the grave of the dead at sea, unmarked, and without stone or stake.

CHAPTER XVII

The Last Flogging

Sleep itself does not always come to the relief of the weary in body, and the broken in spirit; especially when past troubles only foreshadow coming disasters. The last hope had been extinguished. My master, who I did not venture to hope would protect me as *a man*, had even now refused to protect me as *his property;* and had cast me back, covered with reproaches and bruises, into the hands of a stranger to that mercy which was the soul of the religion he professed. May the reader never spend such a night as that allotted to me, previous to the morning which was to herald my return to the den of horrors from which I had made a temporary escape.

I remained all night—sleep I did not—at St. Michael's; and in the morning (Saturday) I started off, according to the order of Master Thomas, feeling that I had no friend on earth, and doubting if I had one in heaven. I reached Covey's about nine o'clock; and just as I stepped into the field, before I had reached the house, Covey, true to his snakish habits, darted out at me from a fence corner, in which he had secreted himself, for the purpose of securing me. He was amply provided with a cowskin and a rope; and he evidently intended to *tie me up,* and to wreak his vengeance on me to the fullest extent. I should have been an easy prey, had he succeeded in getting his hands upon me, for I had taken no refreshment since noon on Friday; and this, together with the pelting, excitement, and the loss of blood, had reduced my strength. I, however, darted back into the woods, before the ferocious hound could get hold of me, and buried myself in a thicket, where he lost sight of me. The corn-field afforded me cover, in getting to the woods. But for the tall corn, Covey would have overtaken me, and made me his captive. He seemed very much chagrined that he did not catch me, and gave up the chase, very reluctantly; for I could see his angry movements, toward the house from which he had sallied, on his foray.

Well, now I am clear of Covey, and of his wrathful lash, for the present. I am in the wood, buried in its somber gloom, and hushed in its solemn silence; hid from all human eyes; shut in with nature and nature's God, and absent from all human contrivances. Here was a good place to pray; to pray for help for deliverance—a prayer I had often made before. But how could I pray? Covey could pray—Capt. Auld could pray—I would fain pray; but doubts (arising partly from my own neglect of the means of grace, and partly from the sham religion which everywhere prevailed, cast in my mind a doubt upon all religion, and led me to the conviction that prayers were unavailing and delusive) prevented my embracing the opportunity, as a religious one. Life, in itself, had almost become burdensome to me. All my outward relations were against me; I must stay here and starve, (I was already hungry,) or go home to Covey's, and have my flesh torn to pieces, and my spirit humbled under the cruel lash of Covey. This was the painful alternative presented to me. The day was long and irksome. My physical condition was deplorable. I was weak, from the toils of the previous day, and from the want of food and rest; and had been so little concerned about my appearance, that I had not yet washed the blood from my garments. I was an object of horror, even to myself. Life, in Baltimore, when most oppressive, was a paradise to this. What had I done, what had my parents done, that such a life as this should be mine? That day, in the woods, I would have exchanged my manhood for the brutehood of an ox.

Night came. I was still in the woods, unresolved what to do. Hunger had not yet pinched me to the point of going home, and I laid down in the leaves to rest; for I had been watching for hunters all day, but not being molested during the day. I expected no disturbance during the night. I had come to the conclusion that Covey relied upon hunger to drive me home; and in this I was quite correct—the facts showed that he had made no effort to catch me, since morning.

During the night, I heard the step of a man in the woods. He was coming toward the place where I lay. A person lying still has the advantage over one walking in the woods, in the day time, and this advantage is much greater at night. I was not able to engage in a physical struggle, and I had recourse to the common resort of the weak. I hid myself in the leaves to prevent discovery. But, as the night rambler in the woods drew nearer, I found him to be a *friend*, not an enemy; it was a slave of Mr. William Groomes, of Easton, a kind hearted fellow, named "Sandy." Sandy lived with Mr. Kemp that year, about four miles from St. Michael's. He, like myself, had been hired out by the year; but, unlike myself, had not been hired out to be broken. Sandy was the husband of a free woman, who lived in the lower part of *"Pot-pie Neck,"* and he was now on his way through the woods, to see her, and to spend the Sabbath with her.

As soon as I had ascertained that the disturber of my solitude was not an enemy, but the good-hearted Sandy—a man as famous among the slaves of the neighborhood for his good nature, as for his good sense—I came out from my hiding place, and made myself known to him. I explained the circumstances of the past two days, which had driven me to the woods, and he deeply compassionated my distress. It was a bold thing for him to shelter me, and I could not ask him to do so; for, had I been found in his hut, he would have suffered the penalty of thirty-nine lashes on his bare back, if not something worse. But, Sandy was too generous to permit the fear of punishment to prevent his relieving a brother bondman from hunger and exposure; and, therefore, on his own motion, I accompanied him to his home, or rather to the home of his wife—for the house and lot were hers. His wife was called up—for it was now about midnight—a fire was made, some Indian meal was soon mixed with salt and water, and an ash cake was baked in a hurry to relieve my hunger. Sandy's wife was not behind him in kindness—both seemed to esteem it a privilege to succor me; for, although I was hated by Covey and by my master, I was loved by the colored people, because *they* thought I was hated for my knowledge, and persecuted because I was feared. I was the *only* slave *now* in that region who could read and write. There had been one other man, belonging to Mr. Hugh Hamilton, who could read, (his name was "Jim,") but he, poor fellow, had, shortly after my coming into the neighborhood, been sold off to the far south. I saw Jim ironed, in the cart, to be carried to Easton for sale,—pinioned like a yearling for the slaughter. My knowledge was now the pride of my brother slaves; and, no doubt, Sandy felt something of the general interest in me on that account. The supper was soon ready, and though I have feasted since, with honorables, lord mayors and aldermen, over the sea, my supper on ash cake and cold water, with Sandy, was the meal, of all my life, most sweet to my taste, and now most vivid in my memory.

Supper over, Sandy and I went into a discussion of what was *possible* for me, under the perils and hardships which now overshadowed my path. The question was, must I go back to Covey, or must I now attempt to run away? Upon a careful survey, the latter was found to be impossible; for I was on a narrow neck of land, every avenue from which would bring me in sight of pursuers. There was the Chesapeake bay to the right, and "Pot-pie" river to the left, and St. Michael's and its neighborhood occupying the only space through which there was any retreat.

I found Sandy an old adviser. He was not only a religious man, but he professed to believe in a system for which I have no name. He was a genuine African, and had inherited some of the so called magical powers, said to be possessed by African and eastern nations. He told me that he could help me; that, in those very woods, there was an herb, which in the morning might be found, possessing all the powers required for my protection, (I put his thoughts in my own language;) and that, if I would take his advice, he would procure me the root of the herb of which he spoke. He told me further, that if I would take that root and wear it on my right side, it would be impossible for Covey to strike me a blow; that with this root about my person, no white man could whip me. He said he had carried it for years, and that he had fully tested its virtues. He had never received a blow from a slaveholder since he carried it; and he never expected to receive one, for he always meant to carry that root as a protection. He knew Covey well, for Mrs. Covey was the daughter of Mr. Kemp; and he (Sandy) had heard of the barbarous treatment to which I was subjected, and he wanted to do something for me.

Now all this talk about the root, was, to me, very absurd and ridiculous, if not positively sinful. I at first rejected the idea that the simple carrying a root on my right side, (a root, by the way, over which I walked every time I went into the woods,) could possess any such magic power as he ascribed to it, and I was, therefore, not disposed to cumber my pocket with it. I had a positive aversion to all pretenders to "*divination.*" It was beneath one of my intelligence to countenance such dealings with the devil, as this power implied. But, with all my learning—it was really precious little—Sandy was more than a match for me. "My book learning," he said, "had not kept Covey off me," (a powerful argument just then,) and he entreated me, with flashing eyes, to try this. If it did me no good, it could do me no harm, and it would cost me nothing, any way. Sandy was so earnest, and so confident of the good qualities of this weed, that, to please him, rather than from any conviction of its excellence, I was induced to take it. He had been to me the good Samaritan, and had, almost providentially, found me, and helped me when I could not help myself; how did I know but that the hand of the Lord was in it? With thoughts of this sort, I took the roots from Sandy, and put them in my right hand pocket.

This was, of course, Sunday morning. Sandy now urged me to go home, with all speed, and to walk up bravely to the house, as though nothing had happened. I saw in Sandy too deep an insight into human nature, with all his superstition, not to have some respect for his advice; and perhaps, too, a slight gleam or shadow of his superstition had fallen upon me. At any rate, I started off toward Covey's, as directed by Sandy. having, the previous night, poured my griefs into Sandy's ears, and got him enlisted in my behalf, having made his wife a sharer in my sorrows, and having, also, become well refreshed by sleep and food, I moved off, quite courageously, toward the much dreaded Covey's. Singularly enough, just as I entered his yard gate, I met him and his wife, dressed in their Sunday best—looking as smiling as angels—on their way to church. The manner of Covey astonished me. There was something really benignant in his countenance. He spoke to me as never before; told me that the pigs had got into the lot, and he wished me to drive them out; inquired how I was, and seemed an altered man. This extraordinary conduct of Covey, really made me begin to think that Sandy's herb had more virtue in it than I, in my pride, had been willing to allow; and, had the day been other than Sunday, I should have attributed Covey's altered manner solely to the magic power of the root. I suspected, however, that the *Sabbath*, and not the *root*, was the real explanation of Covey's manner. His religion hindered him from breaking the Sabbath, but not from breaking my skin. He had more respect for the *day* than for the *man*, for whom the day was mercifully given; for while he would cut and slash my body during the week, he would not hesitate, on Sunday, to teach me the value of my soul, or the way of life and salvation by Jesus Christ.

All went well with me till Monday morning; and then, whether the root had lost its virtue, or whether my tormentor had gone deeper into the black art than myself, (as was sometimes said of him,) or whether he had obtained a special indulgence, for his faithful Sabbath day's worship, it is not necessary for me to know, or to inform the reader; but, this much I *may* say,—the pious and benignant smile which graced Covey's face on *Sunday*, wholly disappeared on *Monday*. Long before daylight, I was called up to go and feed, rub, and curry the horses. I obeyed the call, and I would have so obeyed it, had it been made at an earlier hour, for I had brought my mind to a firm resolve, during that Sunday's reflection, viz: to obey every order, however unreasonable, if it were possible, and, if Mr. Covey should then undertake to beat me, to defend and protect myself to the best of my ability. My religious views on the subject of resisting my master, had suffered a serious shock, by the savage persecution to which I had been subjected, and my hands were no longer tied by my religion. Master Thomas's indifference had severed the last link. I had now to this extent "backslidden" from this point in the slave's religious creed; and I soon had occasion to make my fallen state known to my Sunday-pious brother, Covey.

Whilst I was obeying his order to feed and get the horses ready for the field, and when in the act of going up the stable loft for the purpose of throwing down some blades, Covey sneaked into the stable, in his peculiar snake-like way, and seizing me suddenly by the leg, he brought me to the stable floor, giving my newly mended body a fearful jar. I now forgot my *roots*, and remembered my pledge to *stand up in my own defense*. The brute was endeavoring skillfully to get a slipknot on my legs, before I could draw up my feet. As soon as I found what he was up to, I gave a sudden spring, (my two day's rest had been of much service to me,) and by that means, no doubt, he was able to bring me to the floor so heavily. He was defeated in his plan of tying me. While down, he seemed to think he had me very securely in his power. He little thought he was—as the rowdies say—"in" for a "rough and tumble" fight; but such was the fact. Whence came the daring spirit necessary to grapple with a man who, eight-and-forty hours before, could, with his slightest word have made me tremble like a leaf in a storm, I do not know; at any rate, *I was resolved to fight*, and, what was better still, I was actually hard at it. The fighting madness had come upon me, and I found my strong fingers firmly attached to the throat of my cowardly tormentor; as heedless of consequences, at the moment, as though we stood as equals before the law. The very color of the man was forgotten. I felt as supple as a cat, and was ready for the snakish creature at every turn. Every blow of his was parried, though I dealt no blows in turn. I was strictly on the *defensive*, preventing him from injuring me, rather than trying to injure him. I flung him on the ground several times, when he meant to have hurled me there. I held him so firmly by the throat, that his blood followed my nails. He held me, and I held him.

All was fair, thus far, and the contest was about equal. My resistance was entirely unexpected, and Covey was taken all aback by it, for he trembled in every limb. *"Are you going to resist*, you scoundrel?" said he. To which, I returned a polite *"yes sir;"* steadily gazing my interrogator in the eye, to meet the first approach or dawning of the blow, which I expected my answer would call forth. But, the conflict did not long remain thus equal. Covey soon cried out lustily for help; not that I was obtaining any marked advantage over him, or was injuring him, but because he was gaining none over me, and was not able, single handed, to conquer me. He called for his cousin Hughes, to come to his assistance, and now the scene was changed. I was compelled to give blows, as well as to parry them; and, since I was, in any case, to suffer for resistance, I felt (as the musty proverb goes) that "I might as well be hanged for an old sheep as a lamb." I was still *defensive* toward Covey, but *aggressive* toward Hughes; and, at the first approach of the latter, I dealt a blow, in my desperation, which fairly sickened my youthful assailant. He went off, bending over with pain, and manifesting no disposition to come within my reach again. The poor fellow was in the act of trying to catch and tie my right hand, and while flattering himself with success, I gave him the kick which sent him staggering away in pain, at the same time that I held Covey with a firm hand.

Taken completely by surprise, Covey seemed to have lost his usual strength and coolness. He was frightened, and stood puffing and blowing, seemingly unable to command words or blows. When he saw that poor Hughes was standing half bent with pain—his courage quite gone—the cowardly tyrant asked if I "meant to persist in my resistance." I told him "I *did mean to resist, come what might*;" that I had been by him treated like a *brute*, during the last six months; and that I should stand it *no longer*. With that, he gave me a shake, and attempted to drag me toward a stick of wood, that was lying just outside the stable door. He meant to knock me down with it; but, just as he leaned over to get the stick, I seized him with both hands by the collar, and, with a vigorous and sudden snatch, I brought my assailant harmlessly, his full length, on the *not over* clean ground—for we were now in the cow yard. He had selected the place for the fight, and it was but right that he should have all the advantages of his own selection.

By this time, Bill, the hired man, came home. He had been to Mr. Hemsley's, to spend the Sunday with his nominal wife, and was coming home on Monday morning, to go to work. Covey and I had been skirmishing from before daybreak, till now, that the sun was almost shooting his beams over the eastern woods, and we were still at it. I could not see where the matter was to terminate. He evidently was afraid to let me go, lest I should again make off to the woods; otherwise, he would probably have obtained arms from the house, to frighten me. Holding me, Covey called upon Bill for assistance. The scene here, had something comic about it. "Bill," who knew *precisely* what Covey wished him to do, affected ignorance, and pretended he did not know what to do. "What shall I do, Mr. Covey," said Bill. "Take hold of him—take hold of him!" said Covey. With a toss of his head, peculiar to Bill, he said, "indeed, Mr. Covey, I want to go to work." "*This is* your work," said Covey; "take hold of him." Bill replied, with spirit, "My master hired me here, to work, and *not* to help you whip Frederick." It was now my turn to speak. "Bill," said I, "don't put your hands on me." To which he replied, "MY GOD! Frederick, I ain't goin' to tech ye," and Bill walked off, leaving Covey and myself to settle our matters as best we might.

But, my present advantage was threatened when I saw Caroline (the slave-woman of Covey) coming to the cow yard to milk, for she was a powerful woman, and could have mastered me very easily, exhausted as I now was. As soon as she came into the yard, Covey attempted to rally her to his aid. Strangely—and, I may add, fortunately—Caroline was in no humor to take a hand in any such sport. We were all in open rebellion, that morning. Caroline answered the command of her master to "*take hold of me*," precisely as Bill had answered, but in *her*, it was at greater peril so to answer; she was the slave of Covey, and he could do what he pleased with her. It was *not* so with Bill, and Bill knew it. Samuel Harris, to whom Bill belonged, did not allow his slaves to be beaten, unless they were guilty of some crime which the law would punish. But, poor Caroline, like myself, was at the mercy of the merciless Covey; nor did she escape the dire effects of her refusal. He gave her several sharp blows.

Covey at length (two hours had elapsed) gave up the contest. Letting me go, he said,—puffing and blowing at a great rate—"now, you scoundrel, go to your work; I would not have whipped you half so much as I have had you not resisted." The fact was, *he had not whipped me at all.* He had not, in all the scuffle, drawn a single drop of blood from me. I had drawn blood from him; and, even without this satisfaction, I should have been victorious, because my aim had not been to injure him, but to prevent his injuring me.

During the whole six months that I lived with Covey, after this transaction, he never laid on me the weight of his finger in anger. He would, occasionally, say he did not want to have to get hold of me again—a declaration which I had no difficulty in believing; and I had a secret feeling, which answered, "you need not wish to get hold of me again, for you will be likely to come off worse in a second fight than you did in the first."

Well, my dear reader, this battle with Mr. Covey,—undignified as it was, and as I fear my narration of it is—was the turning point in my *"life as a slave."* It rekindled in my breast the smouldering embers of liberty; it brought up my Baltimore dreams, and revived a sense of my own manhood. I was a changed being after that fight. I was *nothing* before: I WAS A MAN NOW. It recalled to life my crushed self-respect and my self-confidence, and inspired me with a renewed determination to be A FREEMAN. A man, without force, is without the essential dignity of humanity. Human nature is so constituted, that it cannot *honor* a helpless man, although it can *pity* him; and even this it cannot do long, if the signs of power do not arise.

He only can understand the effect of this combat on my spirit, who has himself incurred something, hazarded something, in repelling the unjust and cruel aggressions of a tyrant. Covey was a tyrant, and a cowardly one, withal. After resisting him, I felt as I had never felt before. It was a resurrection from the dark and pestiferous tomb of slavery, to the heaven of comparative freedom. I was no longer a servile coward, trembling under the frown of a brother worm of the dust, but, my long-cowed spirit was roused to an attitude of manly independence. I had reached the point, at which I was *not afraid to die.* This spirit made me a freeman in *fact,* while I remained a slave in *form.* When a slave cannot be flogged he is more than half free. He has a domain as broad as his own manly heart to defend, and he is really *"a power on earth."* While slaves prefer their lives, with flogging, to instant death, they will always find christians enough, like unto Covey, to accommodate that preference. From this time, until that of my escape from slavery, I was never fairly whipped. Several attempts were made to whip me, but they were always unsuccessful. Bruises I did get, as I shall hereafter inform the reader; but the case I have been describing, was the end of the brutification to which slavery had subjected me.

The reader will be glad to know why, after I had so grievously offended Mr. Covey, he did not have me taken in hand by the authorities; indeed, why the law of Maryland, which assigns hanging to the slave who resists his master, was not put in force against me; at any rate, why I was not taken up, as is usual in such cases, and publicly whipped, for an example to other slaves, and as a means of deterring me from committing the same offense again. I confess, that the easy manner in which I got off, was, for a long time, a surprise to me, and I cannot, even now, fully explain the cause.

The only explanation I can venture to suggest, is the fact, that Covey was, probably, ashamed to have it known and confessed that he had been mastered by a boy of sixteen. Mr. Covey enjoyed the unbounded and very valuable reputation, of being a first rate overseer and *negro breaker*. By means of this reputation, he was able to procure his hands for *very trifling* compensation, and with very great ease. His interest and his pride mutually suggested the wisdom of passing the matter by, in silence. The story that he had undertaken to whip a lad, and had been resisted, was, of itself, sufficient to damage him; for his bearing should, in the estimation of slaveholders, be of that imperial order that should make such an occurrence *impossible*. I judge from these circumstances, that Covey deemed it best to give me the go-by. It is, perhaps, not altogether creditable to my natural temper, that, after this conflict with Mr. Covey, I did, at times, purposely aim to provoke him to an attack, by refusing to keep with the other hands in the field, but I could never bully him to another battle. I had made up my mind to do him serious damage, if he ever again attempted to lay violent hands on me.

"Hereditary bondmen, know ye not
Who would be free, themselves must strike the blow?"

LIFE AS A FREEMAN

CHAPTER XXII

Liberty Attained

There is no necessity for any extended notice of the incidents of this part of my life. There is nothing very striking or peculiar about my career as a freeman, when viewed apart from my life as a slave. The relation subsisting between my early experience and that which I am now about to narrate, is, perhaps, my best apology for adding another chapter to this book.

Disappearing from the kind reader, in a flying cloud or balloon, (pardon the figure,) driven by the wind, and knowing not where I should land—whether in slavery or in freedom—it is proper that I should remove, at once, all anxiety, by frankly making known where I alighted. The flight was a bold and perilous one; but here I am, in the great city of New York, safe and sound, without loss of blood or bone. In less than a week after leaving Baltimore, I was walking amid the hurrying throng, and gazing upon the dazzling wonders of Broadway. The dreams of my childhood and the purposes of my manhood were now fulfilled. A free state around me, and a free earth under my feet! What a moment was this to me! A whole year was pressed into a single day. A new world burst upon my agitated vision. I have often been asked, by kind friends to whom I have told my story, how I felt when first I found myself beyond the limits of slavery; and I must say here, as I have often said to them, there is scarcely anything about which I could not give a more satisfactory answer. It was a moment of joyous excitement, which no words can describe. In a letter to a friend, written soon after reaching New York, I said I felt as one might be supposed to feel, on escaping from a den of hungry lions. But, in a moment like that, sensations are too intense and too rapid for words. Anguish and grief, like darkness and rain, may be described, but joy and gladness, like the rainbow of promise, defy alike the pen and pencil.

For ten or fifteen years I had been dragging a heavy chain, with a huge block attached to it, cumbering my every motion. I had felt myself doomed to drag this chain and this block through life. All efforts, before, to separate myself from the hateful encumbrance, had only seemed to rivet me the more firmly to it. Baffled and discouraged at times, I had asked myself the question, May not this, after all, be God's work? May He not, for wise ends, have doomed me to this lot? A contest had been going on in my mind for years, between the clear consciousness of right and the plausible errors of superstition; between the wisdom of manly courage, and the foolish weakness of timidity. The contest was now ended; the chain was severed; God and right stood vindicated. I WAS A FREEMAN, and the voice of peace and joy thrilled my heart.

Free and joyous, however, as I was, joy was not the only sensation I experienced. It was like the quick blaze, beautiful at first, but which subsiding, leaves the building charred and desolate. I was soon taught that I was still in an enemy's land. A sense of loneliness and insecurity oppressed me sadly. I had been but a few hours in New York, before I was met in the streets by a fugitive slave, well known to me, and the information I got from him respecting New York, did nothing to lessen my apprehension of danger. The fugitive in question was "Allender's Jake," in Baltimore; but, said he, I am "WILLIAM DIXON," in New York! I knew Jake well, and knew when Tolly Allender and Mr. Price (for the latter employed Master Hugh as his foreman, in his shipyard on Fell's Point) made an attempt to recapture Jake, and failed. Jake told me all about his circumstances, and how narrowly he escaped being taken back to slavery; that the city was now full of southerners, returning from the springs; that the black people in New York were not to be trusted; that there were hired men on the lookout for fugitives from slavery, and who, for a few dollars, would betray me into the hands of the slave-catchers; that I must trust no man with my secret; that I must not think of going either on the wharves to work, or to a boarding-house to board; and, worse still, this same Jake told me it was not in his power to help me. He seemed, even while cautioning me, to be fearing lest, after all, I might be a party to a second attempt to recapture him. Under the inspiration of his thought, I must suppose it was, he gave signs of a wish to get rid of me, and soon left me—his whitewash brush in hand—as he said, for his work. He was soon lost to sight among the throng, and I was alone again, an easy prey to the kidnappers, if any should happen to be on my track.

New York, seventeen years ago, was less a place of safety for a runaway slave than now, and all know how unsafe it now is, under the new fugitive slave bill. I was much troubled. I had very little money—enough to buy me a few loaves of bread, but not enough to pay board, outside a lumber yard. I saw the wisdom of keeping away from the ship yards, for if Master Hugh pursued me, he would naturally expect to find me looking for work among the calkers. For a time, every door seemed closed against me. A sense of my loneliness and helplessness crept over me, and covered me with something bordering on despair. In the midst of thousands of my fellowmen, and yet a perfect stranger! In the midst of human brothers, and yet more fearful of them than of hungry wolves! I was without home, without friends, without work, without money, and without any definite knowledge of which way to go, or where to look for succor.

Some apology can easily be made for the few slaves who have, after making good their escape, turned back to slavery, preferring the actual rule of their masters, to the life of loneliness, apprehension, hunger, and anxiety, which meets them on their first arrival in a free state. It is difficult for a freeman to enter into the feelings of such fugitives. He cannot see things in the same light with the slave, because he does not, and cannot, look from the same point from which the slave does. "Why do you tremble," he says to the slave—"you are in a free state;" but the difficulty is, in realizing that he is in a free state, the slave might reply. A freeman cannot understand why the slave-master's shadow is bigger, to the slave, than the might and majesty of a free state; but when he reflects that the slave knows more about the slavery of his master than he does of the might and majesty of the free state, he has the explanation. The slave has been all his life learning the power of his master—being trained to dread his approach—and only a few hours learning the power of the state. The master is to him a stern and flinty reality, but the state is little more than a dream. He has been accustomed to regard every white man as the friend of his master, and every colored man as more or less under the control of his master's friends—the white people. It takes stout nerves to stand up, in such circumstances. A man, homeless, shelterless, breadless, friendless, and moneyless, is not in a condition to assume a very proud or joyous tone; and in just this condition was I, while wandering about the streets of New York city, and lodging, at least one night, among the barrels on one of its wharves. I was not only free from slavery, but I was free from home, as well. The reader will easily see that I had something more than the simple fact of being free to think of, in this extremity.

I kept my secret as long as I could, and at last was forced to go in search of an honest man—a man sufficiently *human* not to betray me into the hands of slave-catchers. I was not a bad reader of the human face, nor long in selecting the right man, when once compelled to disclose the facts of my condition to some one.

I found my man in the person of one who said his name was Stewart. He was a sailor, warm-hearted and generous, and he listened to my story with a brother's interest. I told him I was running for my freedom—knew not where to go—money almost gone—was hungry—thought it unsafe to go the shipyards for work, and needed a friend. Stewart promptly put me in the way of getting out of my trouble. He took me to his house, and went in search of the late David Ruggles, who was then the secretary of the New York Vigilance Committee, and a very active man in all anti-slavery works. Once in the hands of Mr. Ruggles, I was comparatively safe. I was hidden with Mr. Ruggles several days. In the meantime, my intended wife, Anna, came on from Baltimore—to whom I had written, informing her of my safe arrival at New York—and, in the presence of Mrs. Mitchell and Mr. Ruggles, we were married, by Rev. James W. C. Pennington.

Mr. Ruggles* was the first officer on the under-ground railroad with whom I met after reaching the north, and, indeed, the first of whom I ever heard anything. Learning that I was a calker by trade, he promptly decided that New Bedford was the proper place to send me. "Many ships," said he, "are there fitted out for the whaling business, and you may there find work at your trade, and make a good living." Thus, in one fortnight after my flight from Maryland, I was safe in New Bedford, regularly entered upon the exercise of the rights, responsibilities, and duties of a freeman.

I may mention a little circumstance which annoyed me on reaching New Bedford. I had not a cent of money, and lacked two dollars toward paying our fare from Newport, and our baggage—not very

---

*He was a whole-souled man, fully imbued with a love of his afflicted and hunted people, and took pleasure in being to me, as was his wont, "Eyes to the blind, and legs to the lame." This brave and devoted man suffered much from the persecutions common to all who had been prominent benefactors. He at last became blind, and needed a friend to guide him, even as he had been a guide to others. Even in his blindness, he exhibited his manly character. In search of health, he became a physician. When hope of gaining his own was gone, he had hope for others. Believing in hydropathy, he established at Northampton, Massachusetts, a large *"Water Cure,"* and became one of the most successful of all engaged in that mode of treatment.

costly—was taken by the stage driver, and held until I could raise the money to redeem it. This difficulty was soon surmounted. Mr. Nathan Johnson, to whom we had a line from Mr. Ruggles, not only received us kindly and hospitably, but, on being informed about our baggage, promptly loaned me two dollars with which to redeem my little property. I shall ever be deeply grateful, both to Mr. and Mrs. Nathan Johnson, for the lively interest they were pleased to take in me, in this the hour of my extremest need. They not only gave myself and wife bread and shelter, but taught us how to begin to secure those benefits for ourselves. Long may they live, and may blessings attend them in this life and in that which is to come!

Once initiated into the new life of freedom, and assured by Mr. Johnson that New Bedford was a safe place, the comparatively unimportant matter, as to what should be my name, came up for consideration. It was necessary to have a name in my new relations. The name given me by my beloved mother was no less pretentious than "Frederick Augustus Washington Bailey." I had, however, before leaving Maryland, dispensed with the *Augustus Washington,* and retained the name *Frederick Bailey.* Between Baltimore and New Bedford, however, I had several different names, the better to avoid being overhauled by the hunters, which I had good reason to believe would be put on my track. Among honest men an honest man may well be content with one name, and to acknowledge it at all times and in all places; but toward fugitives, Americans are not honest. When I arrived at New Bedford, my name was Johnson; and finding that the Johnson family in New Bedford were already quite numerous—sufficiently so to produce some confusion in attempts to distinguish one from another—there was the more reason for making another change in my name. In fact, "Johnson" had been assumed by nearly every slave who had arrived in New Bedford from Maryland, and this, much to the annoyance of the original "Johnsons" (of whom there were many) in that place. Mine host, unwilling to have another of his own name added to the community in this unauthorized way, after I spent a night and a day at his house, gave me my present name. He had been reading the "Lady of the Lake," and was pleased to regard me as a suitable person to wear this, one of Scotland's many famous names. Considering the noble hospitality and manly character of Nathan Johnson, I have felt that he, better than I, illustrated the virtues of the great Scottish chief. Sure I am, that had any slave-catcher entered his domicile, with a view to molest any one of his household, he would have shown himself like him of the "stalwart hand."

The reader will be amused at my ignorance, when I tell the notions I had of the state of northern wealth, enterprise, and civilization. Of wealth and refinement, I supposed the north had none. My Columbian Orator, which was almost my only book, had not done must to enlighten me concerning northern society. The impressions I had received were all wide of the truth. New Bedford, especially, took me by surprise, in the solid wealth and grandeur there exhibited. I had formed my notions respecting the social condition of the free states, by what I had seen and known of free, white, non-slaveholding people in the slave states. Regarding slavery as the basis of wealth, I fancied that no people could become very wealthy without slavery. A free white man, holding no slaves, in the country, I had known to be the most ignorant and poverty-stricken of men, and the laughing stock even of slaves themselves—called generally by them, in derision, *"poor white trash."* Like the non-slaveholders at the south, in holding no slave, I supposed the northern people like them, also, in poverty and degradation. Judge, then, of my amazement and joy, when I found—as I did find—the very laboring population of New Bedford living in better houses, more elegantly furnished—surrounded by more comfort and refinement—than a majority of the slaveholders on the Eastern Shore of Maryland. There was my friend, Mr. Johnson, himself a colored man, (who at the south would have been regarded as a proper marketable commodity,) who lived in a better house—dined at a richer board—was the owner of more books—the reader of more newspapers—was more conversant with the political and social condition of this nation and the world—than nine-tenths of all the slaveholders of Talbot county, Maryland. Yet Mr. Johnson was a working man, and his hands were hardened by honest toil. Here, then, was something for observation and study. Whence the difference? The explanation was soon furnished, in the superiority of mind over simple brute force. Many pages might be given to the contrast, and in explanation of its causes. But an incident or two will suffice to show the reader as to how the mystery gradually vanished before me.

My first afternoon, on reaching New Bedford, was spent in visiting the wharves and viewing the shipping. The sight of the broad brim and the plain, Quaker dress, which met me at every turn, greatly increased my sense of freedom and security. "I am among the Quakers," thought I, "and am safe." Lying at the wharves and riding in the stream, were full-rigged ships of finest model, ready to start on whaling voyages. Upon the right and the left, I was walled in by large granite-fronted warehouses, crowded with the good things of this world. On the wharves, I saw industry without bustle, labor without noise, and heavy toil without the whip. There was no loud singing, as in southern ports, where ships are loading or unloading—no loud cursing or swearing—but everything went on as smoothly as the works of a well adjusted machine. How different was all this from the noisily fierce and clumsily absurd manner of labor-life in Baltimore and St. Michael's! One of the first incidents which illustrated the superior mental character of northern labor over that of the south, was the manner of unloading a ship's cargo of oil. In a southern port, twenty or thirty hands would have been employed to do what five or six did here, with the aid of a single ox attached to the end of a fall. Main strength, unassisted by skill, is slavery's method of labor. An old ox, worth eighty dollars, was doing, in New Bedford, what would have required fifteen thousand dollars worth of human bones and muscles to have performed in a southern port. I found that everything was done here with a scrupulous regard to economy, both in regard to men and things, time and strength. The maid servant, instead of spending at least a tenth part of her time in bringing and carrying water, as in Baltimore, had the pump at her elbow. The wood was dry, and snugly piled away for winter. Wood-houses, in-door pumps, sinks, drains, self-shutting gates, washing machines, pounding barrels, were all new things, and told me that I was among a thoughtful and sensible people. To the ship-repairing dock I went, and saw the same wise prudence. The carpenters struck where they aimed, and the calkers wasted no blows in idle flourishes of the mallet. I learned that men went from New Bedford to Baltimore, and bought old ships, and brought them here to repair, and made them better and more valuable than they ever were before. Man talked here of going whaling on a four *years'* voyage with more coolness than sailors where I came from talked of going a four *months'* voyage.

I now find that I could have landed in no part of the United States, where I should have found a more striking and gratifying contrast to the condition of the free people of color in Baltimore, than I found here in New Bedford. No colored man is really free in a slaveholding state. He wears the badge of bondage while nominally free, and is often subjected to hardships to which the slave is a stranger; but here in New Bedford, it was my good fortune to see a pretty near approach to freedom on the part of the colored people. I was taken all aback when Mr. Johnson—who lost no time in making me acquainted with the fact— told me that there was nothing in the constitution of Massachusetts to prevent a colored man from holding any office in the state. There, in New Bedford, the black man's children—although anti-slavery was then far from popular—went to school side by side with the white children, and apparently without objection from any quarter. To make me at home, Mr. Johnson assured me that no slaveholder could take a slave from New Bedford; that there were men there who would lay down their lives, before such an outrage could be perpetrated. The colored people themselves were of the best metal, and would fight for liberty to the death.

Soon after my arrival in New Bedford, I was told the following story, which was said to illustrate the spirit of the colored people in that goodly town: A colored man and a fugitive slave happened to have a little quarrel, and the former was heard to threaten the latter with informing his master of his whereabouts. As soon as this threat became known, a notice was read from the desk of what was then the only colored church in the place, stating that business of importance was to be then and there transacted. Special measures had been taken to secure the attendance of the would-be Judas, and had proved successful. Accordingly, at the hour appointed, the people came, and the betrayer also. All the usual formalities of public meetings were scrupulously gone through, even to the offering prayer for Divine direction in the duties of the occasion. The president himself performed this part of the ceremony, and I was told that he was unusually fervent. Yet, at the close of his prayer, the old man (one of the numerous family of Johnsons) rose from his knees, deliberately surveyed his audience, and then said, in a tone of solemn resolution, *"Well, friends, we have got him here, and I would now recommend that you young men should just take him outside the door and kill him."* With this, a large body of the congregation, who well understood the business they had come there to transact, made a rush at the villian, and doubtless would have killed him, had he not availed himself of an open sash, and made good his escape. He has never shown his head in New Bedford since that time. This little incident is perfectly characteristic of the spirit of the colored people in New Bedford. A slave could not be taken from that town seventeen years ago, any more than he could be so taken away now. The reason is, that the colored people in that city are educated up to the point of fighting for their freedom, as well as speaking for it.

Once assured of my safety in New Bedford, I put on the habiliments of a common laborer, and went on the wharf in search of work. I had no notion of living on the honest and generous sympathy of my colored brother, Johnson, or that of the abolitionists. My cry was like that of Hood's laborer, "Oh! only give me work." Happily for me, I was not long in searching. I found employment, the third day after my arrival in New Bedford, in stowing a sloop with a load of oil for the New York market. It was new, hard, and dirty work, even for a calker, but I went at it with a glad heart and a willing hand. I was now my own master—a tremendous fact—and the rapturous excitement with which I seized the job, may not easily be understood, except by some one with an experience something like mine. The thoughts—"I can work! I can work for a living; I am not afraid of work; I have no Master Hugh to rob me of my earnings"—placed me in a state of independence, beyond seeking friendship or support of any man. That day's work I considered the real starting point of something like a new existence. Having finished this job and got my pay for the same, I went next in pursuit of a job at calking. It so happened that Mr. Rodney French, late mayor of the city of New Bedford, had a ship fitting out for sea, and to which there was a large job of calking and coppering to be done. I applied to that noble-hearted man for employment, and he promptly told me to go to work; but going on the float-stage for the purpose, I was informed that every white man would leave the ship if I struck a blow upon her. "Well, well," thought I, "this is a hardship, but yet not a very serious one for me." The difference between the wages of a calker and that of a common day laborer, was an hundred per cent, in favor of the former; but then I was free, and free to work, though not at my trade. I now prepared myself to do anything which came to hand in the way of turning an honest penny; sawed wood—dug cellars—shoveled coal—swept chimneys with Uncle Lucas Debuty—rolled oil casks on the wharves—helped to load and unload vessels—worked in Ricketson's candle works—in Richmond's brass foundery, and elsewhere; and thus supported myself and family for three years.

The first winter was unusually severe, in consequence of the high prices of food; but even during that winter we probably suffered less than many who had been free all their lives. During the hardest of the winter, I hired out for nine dollars a month; and out of this rented two rooms for nine dollars per quarter, and supplied my wife—who was unable to work—with food and some necessary articles of furniture. We were closely pinched to bring our wants within our means; but the jail stood over the way, and I had a wholesome dread of the consequences of running in debt. This winter past, and I was up with the times—got plenty of work—got well paid for it—and felt that I had not done a foolish thing to leave Master Hugh and Master Thomas. I was now living in a new world, and was wide awake to its advantages. I early began to attend the meetings of the colored people of New Bedford, and to take part in them. I was somewhat amazed to see colored men drawing up resolutions and offering them for consideration. Several colored young men of New Bedford, at that period, gave promise of great usefulness. They were educated, and possessed what seemed to me, at that time, very superior talents. Some of them have been cut down by death, and others have removed to different parts of the world, and some remain there now, and justify, in their present activities, my early impressions of them.

Among my first concerns on reaching New Bedford, was to become united with the church, for I had never given up, in reality, my religious faith. I had become lukewarm and in a backslidden state, but I was still convinced that it was my duty to join the Methodist church. I was not then aware of the powerful influence of that religious body in favor of the enslavement of my race, nor did I see how the northern churches could be responsible for the conduct of southern churches; neither did I fully understand how it could be my duty to remain separate from the church, because bad men were connected with it. The slaveholding church, with its Coveys, Weedens, Aulds, and Hopkins, I could see through at once, but I could not see how Elm Street church, in New Bedford, could be regarded as sanctioning the christianity of these characters in the church at St. Michael's. I therefore resolved to join the Methodist church in New Bedford, and to enjoy the spiritual advantage of public worship. The minister of the Elm Street Methodist church, was the Rev. Mr. Bonney; and although I was not allowed a seat in the body of the house, and was proscribed on account of my color, regarding this proscription simply as an accommodation of the unconverted congregation who had not yet been won to Christ and his brotherhood, I was willing thus to be proscribed, lest sinners should be driven away from the saving power of the gospel. Once converted, I though they would be sure to treat me as a man and a brother. "Surely," thought I, "these christian people have none of this feeling against color. They, at least, have renounced this unholy feeling." Judge, then, dear reader, of my astonishment and mortification, when I found, as soon I did find, all my charitable assumptions at fault.

An opportunity was soon afforded me for ascertaining the exact position of Elm Street church on that subject. I had a chance of seeing the religious part of the congregation by themselves; and although they disowned, in affect, their black brothers and sisters, before the world, I did think that where none but the saints were assembled, and no offense could be given to the wicked, and the gospel could not be "blamed," they would certainly recognize us as children of the same Father, and heirs of the same salvation, on equal terms with them-selves.

The occasion to which I refer, was the sacrament of the Lord's Supper, that most sacred and most solemn of all the ordinances of the christian church. Mr. Bonney had preached a very solemn and search-ing discourse, which really proved him to be acquainted with the in-most secrets of the human heart. At the close of his discourse, the congregation was dismissed, and the church remained to partake of the sacrament. I remained to see, as I thought, this holy sacrament celebrated in the spirit of its great Founder.

There were only about a half dozen colored members attached to the Elm Street church, at this time. After the congregation was dis-missed, these descended from the gallery, and took a seat against the wall most distant from the altar. Brother Bonney was very animated, and sung very sweetly, "Salvation 'tis a joyful sound," and soon began to administer the sacrament. I was anxious to observe the bearing of the colored members, and the result was most humiliating. During the whole ceremony, they looked like sheep without a shepherd. The white members went forward to the altar by the bench full; and when it was evident that all the whites had been served with the bread and wine, Brother Bonney—pious Brother Bonney—after a long pause, as if inquiring whether all the white members had been served, and fully assuring himself on that important point, then raised his voice to an unnatural pitch, and looking to the corner where his black sheep seemed penned, beckoned with his hand, exclaiming, "Come forward, colored friends!—come forward! You, too, have an interest in the blood of Christ. God is no respecter of persons. Come forward, and take this holy sacrament to your comfort." The colored members—poor, slavish souls—went forward, as invited. I went *out*, and have never been in that church since, although I honestly went there with a view to joining that body. I found it impossible to respect the religious profession of any who were under the dominion of this wicked prejudice, and I could not, therefore, feel that in joining them, I was joining a christian church, at all. I tried other churches in New Bedford, with the same result, and, finally, I attached myself to a small body of colored Methodists, known as the Zion Methodists. Favored with the affection and confidence of the members of this humble communion, I was soon made a class-leader and a local preacher among them. Many seasons of peace and joy I experienced among them, the remembrance of which is still precious, although I could not see it to be my duty to remain with that body, when I found that it consented to the same spirit which held my brethren in chains.

In four or five months after reaching New Bedford, there came a young man to me, with a copy of the "Liberator," the paper edited by WILLIAM LLOYD GARRISON, and published by ISAAC KNAPP, and asked me to subscribe for it. I told him I had but just escaped from slavery, and was of course very poor, and remarked further, that I was unable to pay for it then; the agent, however, very willingly took me as a subscriber, and appeared to be much pleased with securing my name to his list. From this time I was brought in contact with the mind of William Lloyd Garrison. His paper took its place with me next to the bible.

The Liberator was a paper after my own heart. It detested slavery—exposed hypocrisy and wickedness in high places—made no truce with the traffickers in the bodies and souls of men; it preached human brotherhood, denounced oppression, and, with all the solemnity of God's word, demanded the complete emancipation of my race. I not only liked—I *loved* this paper, and its editor. He seemed a match for all the opponents of emancipation, whether they spoke in the name of the law, or the gospel. His words were few, full of holy fire, and straight to the point. Learning to love him, through his paper, I was prepared to be pleased with his presence. Something of a hero worshiper, by nature, here was one, on first sight, to excite my love and reverence.

Seventeen years ago, few men possessed a more heavenly countenance than William Lloyd Garrison, and few men evinced a more genuine or a more exalted piety. The bible was his text book—held sacred, as the word of the Eternal Father—sinless perfection—complete submission to insults and injuries—literal obedience to the injunction, if smitten on one side to turn the other also. Not only was Sunday a Sabbath, but all days were Sabbaths, and to be kept holy. All sectarism false and mischievous—the regenerated, throughout the world, members of one body, and the HEAD Christ Jesus. Prejudice against color was rebellion against God. Of all men beneath the sky, the slaves, because most neglected and despised, were nearest and dearest to his great heart. Those ministers who defended slavery from the bible, were of their "father the devil;" and those churches which fellowshiped slaveholders as christians, were synagogues of Satan, and our nation was a nation of liars. Never loud or noisy—calm and serene as a summer sky, and as pure. "You are the man, the Moses, raised up by God, to deliver his modern Israel from bondage," was the spontaneous feeling of my heart, as I sat away back in the hall and listened to his mighty words; mighty in truth—mighty in their simple earnestness.

I had not long been a reader of the Liberator, and listener to its editor, before I got a clear apprehension of the principles of the anti-slavery movement. I had already the spirit of the movement, and only needed to understand its principles and measures. These I got from the Liberator, and from those who believed in that paper. My acquaintance with the movement increased my hope for the ultimate freedom of my race, and I united with it from a sense of delight, as well as duty.

Every week the Liberator came, and every week I made myself master of its contents. All the anti-slavery meetings held in New Bedford I promptly attended, my heart burning at every true utterance against the slave system, and every rebuke of its friends and supporters. Thus passed the first three years of my residence in New Bedford. I had not then dreamed of the possibility of my becoming a public advocate of the cause so deeply imbedded in my heart. It was enough for me to listen—to receive and applaud the great words of others, and only whisper in private, among the white laborers on the wharves, and elsewhere, the truths which burned in my breast.

CHAPTER XXIII

Introduced to the Abolitionists

In the summer of 1841, a grand anti-slavery convention was held in Nantucket, under the auspices of Mr. Garrison and his friends. Until now, I had taken no holiday since my escape from slavery. Having worked very hard that spring and summer, in Richmond's brass foundery—sometimes working all night as well as all day—and needing a day or two of rest, I attended this convention, never supposing that I should take part in the proceedings. Indeed, I was not aware that any one connected with the convention even so much as knew my name. I was, however, quite mistaken. Mr. William C. Coffin, a prominent abolitionist in those days of trial, had heard me speaking to my colored friends, in the little school-house on Second street, New Bedford, where we worshiped. He sought me out in the crowd, and invited me to say a few words to the convention. Thus sought out, and thus invited, I was induced to speak out the feelings inspired by the occasion, and the fresh recollection of the scenes through which I had passed as a slave. My speech on this occasion is about the only one I ever made, of which I do not remember a single connected sentence. It was with the utmost difficulty that I could stand erect, or that I could command and articulate two words without hesitation and stammering. I trembled in every limb. I am not sure that my embarrassment was not the most effective part of my speech, if speech it could be called. At any rate, this is about the only part of my performance that I now distinctly remember. But excited and convulsed as I was, the audience, though remarkably quiet before, became as much excited as myself. Mr. Garrison followed me, taking me as his text; and now, whether I had made an eloquent speech in behalf of freedom or not, his was one never to be forgotten by those who heard it. Those who had heard Mr. Garrison oftenest, and had known him longest, were astonished. It was an effort of unequaled power, sweeping down, like a very tornado, every opposing barrier, whether of sentiment or opinion. For a moment, he possessed that almost fabulous inspiration, often referred to but seldom attained, in which a public meeting is transformed, as it were, into a single individuality—the orator wielding a thousand heads and hearts at once, and by the simple majesty of his all controlling thought, converting his hearers into the express image of his own soul. That night there were at least one thousand Garrisonians in Nantucket! At the close of this great meeting, I was duly waited on by Mr. John A. Collins—then the general agent of the Massachusetts anti-slavery society—and urgently solicited by him to become an agent of that society, and to publicly advocate its anti-slavery principles. I was reluctant to take the proffered position. I had not been quite three years from slavery—was honestly distrustful of my ability—wished to be excused; publicity exposed me to discovery and arrest by my master; and other objections came up, but Mr. Collins was not to be put off, and I finally consented to go out for three months, for I supposed that I should have got to the end of my story and my usefulness, in that length of time.

Here opened upon me a new life—a life for which I had had no preparation. I was a "graduate from the peculiar institution," Mr. Collins used to say, when introducing me, *with my diploma written on my back!* The three years of my freedom had been spent in the hard school of adversity. My hands had been furnished by nature with something like a solid leather coating, and I had bravely marked out for myself a life of rough labor, suited to the hardness of my hands, as a means of supporting myself and rearing my children.

Now what shall I say of this fourteen years' experience as a public advocate of the cause of my enslaved brothers and sisters? The time is but as a speck, yet large enough to justify a pause for retrospection—and a pause it must only be.

Young, ardent, and hopeful, I entered upon this new life in the full gush of unsuspecting enthusiasm. The cause was good; the men engaged in it were good; the means to attain its triumph, good; Heaven's blessing must attend all, and freedom must soon be given to the pining millions under a ruthless bondage. My whole heart went with the holy cause, and my most fervent prayer to the Almighty Disposer of the hearts of men, were continually offered for its early triumph. "Who or what," thought I, "can withstand a cause so good, so holy, so indescribably glorious. The God of Israel is with us. The might of the Eternal is on our side. Now let but the truth be spoken, and a nation will start forth at the sound!" In this enthusiastic spirit, I dropped into the ranks of freedom's friends, and went forth to the battle. For a time I was made to forget that my skin was dark and my hair crisped. For a time I regretted that I could not have shared the hardships and dangers endured by the earlier workers for the slave's release. I soon, however, found that my enthusiasm had been extravagant; that hardships and dangers were not yet passed; and that the life now before me, had shadows as well as sunbeams.

Among the first duties assigned me, on entering the ranks, was to travel, in company with Mr. George Foster, to secure subscribers to the "Anti-slavery Standard" and the "Liberator." With him I traveled and lectured through the eastern counties of Massachusetts. Much interest was awakened—large meetings assembled. Many came, no doubt, from curiosity to hear what a negro could say in his own cause. I was generally introduced as a *"chattel"*—a *"thing"*—a piece of southern *"property"*—the chairman assuring the audience that *it* could speak. Fugitive slaves, at that time, were not so plentiful as now; and as a fugitive slave lecturer, I had the advantage of being a *"brand new fact"*—the first one out. Up to that time, a colored man was deemed a fool who confessed himself a runaway slave, not only because of the danger to which he exposed himself of being retaken, but because it was a confession of a very *low* origin! Some of my colored friends in New Bedford thought very badly of my wisdom for thus exposing and degrading myself. The only precaution I took, at the beginning, to prevent Master Thomas from knowing where I was, and what I was about, was the withholding my former name, my master's name, and the name of the state and country from which I came. During the first three or four months, my speeches were almost exclusively made up of narrations of my own personal experience as a slave. "Let us have the facts," said the people. So also said Friend George Foster, who always wished to pin me down to my simple narrative. "Give us the facts," said Collins, "we will take care of the philosophy." Just here arose some embarrassment. It was impossible for me to repeat the same old story month after month, and to keep up my interest in it. It was new to the people, it is true, but it was an old story to me; and to go through with it night after night, was a task altogether too mechanical for my nature. "Tell your story, Frederick," would whisper my then revered friend, William Lloyd Garrison, as I stepped upon the platform. I could not always obey, for I was now reading and thinking. New views of the subject were presented to my mind. It did not entirely satisfy me to *narrate* wrongs; I felt like *denouncing* them. I could not always curb my moral indignation for the perpetrators for slaveholding villainy, long enough for a circumstantial statement of the facts which I felt almost everybody must know. Besides, I was growing, and needed room. "People won't believe you ever was a slave, Frederick, if you keep on this way," said Friend Foster. "Be yourself," said Collins, "and tell your story." It was said to me, "Better have a *little* of the plantation manner of speech than not; 'tis not best that you seem too learned." These excellent friends were actuated by the best of motives, and were not altogether wrong in their advice; and still I must speak just the word that seemed to *me* the word to be spoken *by* me.

At last the apprehended trouble came. People doubted if I had ever been a slave. They said I did not talk like a slave, look like a slave, nor act like a slave, and that they believed I had never been south of Mason and Dixon's line. "He don't tell us where he came from—what his master's name was—how he got away—nor the story of his experience. Besides, he is educated, and is, in this, a contradiction of all the facts we have concerning the ignorance of the slaves." Thus, I was in a pretty fair way to be denounced as an impostor. The committee of the Massachusetts anti-slavery society knew all the facts in my case, and agreed with me in the prudence of keeping them private. They, therefore, never doubted my being a genuine fugitive; but going down the aisles of the churches in which I spoke, and hearing the free spoken Yankees saying, repeatedly, *"He's never been a slave, I'll warrant ye,"* I resolved to dispel all doubt, at no distant day, by such a revelation of facts as could not be made by any other than a genuine fugitive.

In a little less than four years, therefore, after becoming a public lecturer, I was induced to write out the leading facts connected with my experience in slavery, giving names of persons, places, and dates—thus putting it in the power of any who doubted, to ascertain the truth or falsehood of my story of being a fugitive slave. This statement soon became known in Maryland, and I had reason to believe that an effort would be made to recapture me.

It is not probable that any open attempt to secure me as a slave could have succeeded, further than the obtainment, by my master, of the money value of my bones and sinews. Fortunately for me, in the four years of my labors in the abolition cause, I had gained many friends, who would have suffered themselves to be taxed to almost any extent to save me from slavery. It was felt that I had committed the double offense of running away, and exposing the secrets and crimes of slavery and slaveholders. There was a double motive for seeking my reënslavement—avarice and vengeance; and while, as I have said, there was little probability of successful recapture, if attempted openly, I was constantly in danger of being spirited away, at a moment when my friends could render me no assistance. In traveling about from place to place—often alone—I was much exposed to this sort of attack. Any one cherishing the design to betray me, could easily do so, by simply tracing my whereabouts through the anti-slavery journals, for my meetings and movements were promptly made known in advance. My true friends, Mr. Garrison and Mr. Phillips, had no faith in the power of Massachusetts to protect me in my right to liberty. Public sentiment and the law, in their opinion, would hand me over to the tormentors. Mr. Phillips, especially, considered me in danger, and said, when I showed him the manuscript of my story, if in my place, he would throw it into the fire. Thus, the reader will observe, the settling of one difficulty only opened the way for another; and that though I had reached a free state, and had attained a position for public usefulness, I was still tormented with the liability of losing my liberty. How this liability was dispelled, will be related, with other incidents, in the next chapter.

CHAPTER XXV

Various Incidents

I have now given the reader an imperfect sketch of nine years' experience in freedom—three years as a common laborer on the wharves of New Bedford, four years as a lecturer in New England, and two years of semi-exile in Great Britain and Ireland. A single ray of light remains to be flung upon my life during the last eight years, and my story will be done.

A trial awaited me on my return from England to the United States, for which I was but very imperfectly prepared. My plans for my then future usefulness as an anti-slavery advocate were all settled. My friends in England had resolved to raise a given sum to purchase for me a press and printing materials; and I already saw myself wielding my pen, as well as my voice, in the great work of renovating the public mind, and building up a public sentiment which should, at least, send slavery and oppression to the grave, and restore to "liberty and the pursuit of happiness" the people with whom I had suffered, both as a slave and as a freeman. Intimation had reached my friends in Boston of what I intended to do, before my arrival, and I was prepared to find them favorably disposed toward my much cherished enterprise. In this I was mistaken. I found them very earnestly opposed to the idea of my starting a paper, and for several reasons. First, the paper was not needed; secondly, it would interfere with my usefulness as a lecturer; thirdly, I was better fitted to speak than to write; fourthly, the paper could not succeed. This opposition, from a quarter so highly esteemed, and to which I had been accustomed to look for advice and direction, caused me not only to hesitate, but inclined me to abandon the enterprise. All previous attempts to establish such a journal having failed, I felt that probably I should but add another to the list of failures, and thus contribute another proof of the mental and moral deficiencies of my race. Very much that was said to me in respect to my imperfect literary acquirements, I felt to be most painfully true. The unsuccessful projectors of all the previous colored newspapers were my superiors in point of education, and if they failed, how could I hope for success? Yet I did hope for success, and persisted in the undertaking. Some of my English friends greatly encouraged me to go forward, and I shall never cease to be grateful for their words of cheer and generous deeds.

I can easily pardon those who have denounced me as ambitious and presumptuous, in view of my persistance in this enterprise. I was but nine years from slavery. In point of mental experience, I was but nine years old. That one, in such circumstances, should aspire to establish a printing press, among an educated people, might well be considered, if not ambitious, quite silly. My American friends looked at me with astonishment! "A wood-sawyer" offering himself to the public as an editor! A slave, brought up in the very depths of ignorance, assuming to instruct the highly civilized people of the north in the principles of liberty, justice, and humanity! The thing looked absurd. Nevertheless, I persevered. I felt that the want of education, great as it was, could be overcome by study, and that knowledge would come by experience; and further, (which was perhaps the most controlling consideration,) I thought that an intelligent public, knowing my early history, would easily pardon a large share of the deficiencies which I was sure that my paper would exhibit. The most distressing thing, however, was the offense which I was about to give my Boston friends, by what seemed to them a reckless disregard of their sage advice. I am not sure that I was not under the influence of something like a slavish adoration of my Boston friends, and I labored hard to convince them of the wisdom of my undertaking, but without success. Indeed, I never expect to succeed, although time has answered all their original objections. The paper has been successful. It is a large sheet, costing eighty dollars per week—has three thousand subscribers—has been published regularly nearly eight years—and bids fair to stand eight years longer. At any rate, the eight years to come are as full of promise as were the eight that are past.

It is not to be concealed, however, that the maintenance of such a journal, under the circumstances, has been a work of much difficulty; and could all the perplexity, anxiety, and trouble attending it, have been clearly foreseen, I might have shrunk from the undertaking. As it is, I rejoice in having engaged in the enterprise, and count it joy to have been able to suffer, in many ways, for its success, and for the success of the cause to which it has been faithfully devoted. I look upon the time, money, and labor bestowed upon it, as being amply rewarded, in the development of my own mental and moral energies, and in the corresponding development of my deeply injured and oppressed people.

From motives of peace, instead of issuing my paper in Boston, among my New England friends, I came to Rochester, Western New York, among strangers, where the circulation of my paper could not interfere with the local circulation of the Liberator and the Standard; for at that time I was, on the anti-slavery question, a faithful disciple of William Lloyd Garrison, and fully committed to his doctrine touching the pro-slavery character of the constitution of the United States, and the *non-voting principle*, of which he is the known and distinguished advocate. With Mr. Garrison, I held it to be the first duty of the non-slaveholding states to dissolve the union with the slaveholding states; and hence my cry, like his, was, "No union with slaveholders." With these views, I came into Western New York; and during the first four years of my labor here, I advocated them with pen and tongue, according to the best of my ability.

About four years ago, upon a reconsideration of the whole subject, I became convinced that there was no necessity for dissolving the "union between the northern and southern states;" that to seek this dissolution was no part of my duty as an abolitionist; that to abstain from voting, was to refuse to exercise a legitimate and powerful means for abolishing slavery; and that the constitution of the United States not only contained no guarantees in favor of slavery, but, on the contrary, it is, in its letter and spirit, an anti-slavery instrument, demanding the abolition of slavery as a condition of its own existence, as the supreme law of the land.

Here was a radical change in my opinions, and in the action logically resulting from that change. To those with whom I had been in agreement and in sympathy, I was now in opposition. What they held to be a great and important truth, I now looked upon as a dangerous error. A very painful, and yet a very natural, thing now happened. Those who could not see any honest reasons for changing their views, as I had done, could not easily see any such reasons for my change, and the common punishment of apostates was mine.

The opinions first entertained were naturally derived and honestly entertained, and I trust that my present opinions have the same claims to respect. Brought directly, when I escaped from slavery, into contact with a class of abolitionists regarding the constitution as a slaveholding instrument, and finding their views supported by the united and entire history of every department of the government, it is not strange that I assumed the constitution to be just what their interpretation made it. I was bound, not only by their superior knowledge, to take their opinions as the true ones, in respect to the subject, but also because I had no means of showing their unsoundness. But for the responsibility of conducting a public journal, and the necessity imposed upon me of meeting opposite views from abolitionists in this state, I should in all probability have remained as firm in my disunion views as any other disciple of William Lloyd Garrison.

My new circumstances compelled me to re-think the whole subject, and to study, with some care, not only the just and proper rules of legal interpretation, but the origin, design, nature, rights, powers, and duties of civil government, and also the relations which human beings sustain to it. By such a course of thought and reading, I was conducted to the conclusion that the constitution of the United States—inaugurated "to form a more perfect union, establish justice, insure domestic tranquillity, provide for the common defense, promote the general welfare, and secure the blessings of liberty"—could not well have been designed at the same time to maintain and perpetuate a system of rapine and murder like slavery; especially, as not one word can be found in the constitution to authorize such a belief. Then, again, if the declared purposes of an instrument are to govern the meaning of all its parts and details, as they clearly should, the constitution of our country is our warrant for the abolition of slavery in every state in the American Union. I mean, however, not to argue, but simply to state my views. It would require very many pages of a volume like this, to set forth the arguments demonstrating the unconstitutionality and the complete illegality of slavery in our land; and as my experience, and not my arguments, is within the scope and contemplation of this volume, I omit the latter and proceed with the former.

I will now ask the kind reader to go back a little in my story, while I bring up a thread left behind for convenience sake, but which, small as it is, cannot be properly omitted altogether; and that thread is American prejudice against color, and its varied illustrations in my own experience.

When I first went among the abolitionists of New England, and began to travel, I found this prejudice very strong and very annoying. The abolitionists themselves were not entirely free from it, and I could see that they were nobly struggling against it. In their eagerness, sometimes, to show their contempt for the feeling, they proved that they had not entirely recovered from it; often illustrating the saying, in their conduct, that a man may "stand up so straight as to lean backward." When it was said to me, "Mr. Douglass, I will walk to meeting with you; I am not afraid of a black man," I could not help thinking—seeing nothing very frightful in my appearance—"And why should you be?" The children at the north had all been educated to believe that if they were bad, the old *black* man—not the old *devil*—would get them; and it was evidence of some courage, for any so educated to get the better of their fears.

The custom of providing separate cars for the accommodation of colored travelers, was established on nearly all the railroads of New England, a dozen years ago. Regarding this custom as fostering the spirit of caste, I made it a rule to seat myself in the cars for the accommodation of passengers generally. Thus seated, I was sure to be called upon to betake myself to the *"Jim Crow car."* Refusing to obey, I was often dragged out of my seat, beaten, and severely bruised, by conductors and brakemen. Attempting to start from Lynn, one day, for Newburyport, on the Eastern railroad, I went, as my custom was, into one of the best railroad carriages on the road. The seats were very luxuriant and beautiful. I was soon waited upon by the conductor, and ordered out; whereupon I demanded the reason for my invidious removal. After a good deal of parleying, I was told that it was because I was black. This I denied, and appealed to the company to sustain my denial; but they were evidently unwilling to commit themselves, on a point so delicate, and requiring such nice powers of discrimination, for they remained as dumb as death. I was soon waited on by half a dozen fellows of the baser sort, (just such as would volunteer to take a bull-dog out of a meeting-house in time of public worship,) and told that I must move out of that seat, and if I did not, they would drag me out. I refused to move, and they clutched me, head, neck, and shoulders. But, in anticipation of the stretching to which I was about to be subjected, I had interwoven myself among the seats. In dragging me out, on this occasion, it must have cost the company twenty-five or thirty dollars, for I tore up seats and all. So great was the excitement in Lynn, on the subject, that the superintendent, Mr. Stephen A. Chase, ordered the trains to run through Lynn without stopping, while I remained in that town; and this ridiculous farce was enacted. For several days the trains went dashing through Lynn without stopping. At the same time that they excluded a free colored man from their cars, this same company allowed slaves, in company with their masters and mistresses, to ride unmolested.

After many battles with the railroad conductors, and being roughly handled in not a few instances, proscription was at last abandoned; and the "Jim Crow car"—set up for the degradation of colored people—is nowhere found in New England. This result was not brought about without the intervention of the people, and the threatened enactment of a law compelling railroad companies to respect the rights of travelers. Hon. Charles Francis Adams performed signal service in the Massachusetts legislature, in bringing about this reformation; and to him the colored citizens of that state are deeply indebted.

Although often annoyed, and sometimes outraged, by this prejudice against color, I am indebted to it for many passages of quiet amusement. A half-cured subject of it is sometimes driven into awkward straits, especially if he happens to get a genuine specimen of the race into his house.

In the summer of 1843, I was traveling and lecturing, in company with William A. White, Esq., through the state of Indiana. Anti-slavery friends were not very abundant in Indiana, at that time, and beds were not more plentiful than friends. We often slept out, in preference to sleeping in the houses, at some points. At the close of one of our meetings, we were invited home with a kindly-disposed old farmer, who, in the generous enthusiasm of the moment, seemed to have forgotten that he had but one spare bed, and that his guests were an ill-matched pair. All went on pretty well, till near bed time, when signs of uneasiness began to show themselves, among the unsophisticated sons and daughters. White is remarkably fine looking, and very evidently a born gentleman; the idea of putting us in the same bed was hardly to be tolerated; and yet, there we were, and but the one bed for us, and that, by the way, was in the same room occupied by the other members of the family. White, as well as I, perceived the difficulty, for yonder slept the old folks, there the sons, and a little farther along slept the daughters; and but one other bed remained. Who should have this bed, was the puzzling question. There was some whispering between the old folks, some confused looks among the young, as the time for going to bed approached. After witnessing the confusion as long as I liked, I relieved the kindly-disposed family by playfully saying, "Friend White, having got entirely rid of my prejudice against color, I think, as a proof of it, I must allow you to sleep with me to-night." White kept up the joke, by seeming to esteem himself the favored party, and thus the difficulty was removed. If we went to a hotel, and called for dinner, the landlord was sure to set one table for White and another for me, always taking him to be master, and me the servant. Large eyes were generally made when the order was given to remove the dishes from my table to that of White's. In those days, it was thought strange that a white man and a colored man could dine peaceably at the same table, and in some parts the strangeness of such a sight has not entirely subsided.

Some people will have it that there is a natural, an inherent, and an invincible repugnance in the breast of the white race toward dark-colored people; and some very intelligent colored men think that their proscription is owing solely to the color which nature has given them. They hold that they are rated according to their color, and that it is impossible for white people ever to look upon dark races of men, or men belonging to the African race, with other than feelings of aversion. My experience, both serious and mirthful, combats this conclusion. Leaving out of sight, for a moment, grave facts, to this point, I will state one or two, which illustrate a very interesting feature of American character as well as American prejudice. Riding from Boston to Albany, a few years ago, I found myself in a large car, well filled with passengers. The seat next to me was about the only vacant one. At every stopping place we took in new passengers, all of whom, on reaching the seat next to me, cast a disdainful glance upon it, and passed to another car, leaving me in the full enjoyment of a whole form. For a time, I did not know but that my riding there was prejudicial to the interest of the railroad company. A circumstance occurred, however, which gave me an elevated position at once. Among the passengers on this train was Gov. George N. Briggs. I was not acquainted with him, and had no idea that I was known to him. Known to him, however, I was, for upon observing me, the governor left his place, and making his way toward me, respectfully asked the privilege of a seat by my side; and upon introducing himself, we entered into a conversation very pleasant and instructive to me. The despised seat now became honored. His excellency had removed all the prejudice against sitting by the side of a negro; and upon his leaving it, as he did, on reaching Pittsfield, there were at least one dozen applicants for the place. The governor had, without changing my skin a single shade, made the place respectable which before was despicable.

A similar incident happened to me once on the Boston and New Bedford railroad, and the leading party to it has since been governor of the state of Massachusetts. I allude to Col. John Henry Clifford. Lest the reader may fancy I am aiming to elevate myself, by claiming too much intimacy with great men, I must state that my only acquaintance with Col. Clifford was formed while I was *his hired servant*, during the first winter of my escape from slavery. I owe it him to say, that in that relation I found him always kind and gentlemanly. But to the incident. I entered a car at Boston, for New Bedford, which, with the exception of a single seat, was full, and found I must occupy this, or stand up, during the journey. Having no mind to do this, I stepped up to the man having the next seat, and who had a few parcels on the seat, and gently asked leave to take a seat by his side. My fellow-passenger gave me a look made up of reproach and indignation, and asked me why I should come to that particular seat. I assured him, in the gentlest manner, that of all others this was the seat for me. Finding that I was actually about to sit down, he sang out, "O! stop, stop! and let me get out!" Suiting the action to the word, up the agitated man got, and sauntered to the other end of the car, and was compelled to stand for most of the way thereafter. Half-way to New Bedford, or more, Col. Clifford, recognizing me, left his seat, and not having seen me before since I had ceased to wait on him, (in everything except hard arguments against his pro-slavery position,) apparently forgetful of his rank, manifested, in greeting me, something of the feeling of an old friend. This demonstration was not lost on the gentleman whose dignity I had, an hour before, most seriously offended. Col. Clifford was known to be about the most aristocratic gentleman in Bristol county; and it was evidently thought that I must be somebody, else I should not have been thus noticed, by a person so distinguished. Sure enough, after Col. Clifford left me, I found myself surrounded with friends; and among the number, my offended friend stood nearest, and with an apology for his rudeness, which I could not resist, although it was one of the lamest ever offered. With such facts as these before me— and I have many of them—I am inclined to think that pride and fashion have much to do with the treatment commonly extended to colored people in the United States. I once heard a very plain man say, (and he was cross-eyed, and awkwardly flung together in other respects,) that he should be a handsome man when public opinion shall be changed.

Since I have been editing and publishing a journal devoted to the cause of liberty and progress, I have had my mind more directed to the condition and circumstances of the free colored people than when I was the agent of an abolition society. The result has been a corresponding change in the disposition of my time and labors. I have felt it to be a part of my mission—under a gracious Providence—to impress my sable brothers in this country with the conviction that, not withstanding the ten thousand discouragements and the powerful hinderances, which beset their existence in this country—notwithstanding the blood-written history of Africa, and her children, from whom we have descended, or the clouds and darkness, (whose stillness and gloom are made only more awful by wrathful thunder and lightning,) now overshadowing them—progress is yet possible, and bright skies shall yet shine upon their pathway; and that "Ethiopia shall yet reach forth her hand unto God."

Believing that one of the best means of emancipating the slaves of the south is to improve and elevate the character of the free colored people of the north, I shall labor in the future, as I have labored in the past, to promote the moral, social, religious, and intellectual elevation of the free colored people; never forgetting my own humble origin, nor refusing, while Heaven lends me ability, to use my voice, my pen, or my vote, to advocate the great and primary work of the universal and unconditional emancipation of my entire race.

CHAPTER 7

"Men of Color, To Arms!" (1863)

A rallying cry that was reprinted in newspapers and in broadside form, "Men of Color, To Arms!" appeared in *Douglass' Monthly* in March 1863. In this address Douglass expressed his enthusiasm, echoed in speech after speech since the onset of the Civil War, for the engagement of the African American as a soldier in the cause of freedom. The assurances that Douglass the recruiter gave prospective black troops—that they would "receive the same wages, the same rations, the same equipments, the same protection, the same treatment, and the same bounty" as their white counterparts—turned out to be unreliable, not because Douglass misled his black followers, but because the United States government reneged on its promises to Douglass. Nevertheless, fervent appeals such as this to the patriotism and self-sacrifice of African Americans enabled Douglass to play a crucial role in attracting thousands of blacks to the Union Army. Through them he would finally deal a death blow to American slavery.

❖ ❖ ❖

When first the rebel cannon shattered the walls of Sumter, and drove away its starving garrison, I predicted that the war, then and there inaugurated would not be fought out entirely by white men. Every month's experience during these two dreary years, has confirmed that opinion. A war undertaken and brazenly carried on for the perpetual enslavement of colored men, calls logically and loudly upon colored men to help suppress it. Only a moderate share of sagacity was needed to see that the arm of the slave was the best defence against the arm of the slaveholder. Hence with every reverse to the National arms, with every exulting shout of victory raised by the slaveholding rebels, I have implored the imperrilled nation to unchain against her foes her powerful black hand. Slowly and reluctantly that appeal is beginning to be heeded. Stop not now to complain that it was not heeded sooner. It may, or it may not have been best that it should not. This is not the time to discuss that question. Leave it to the future. When the war is over, the country is saved, peace is established, and the black man's rights are secured, as they will be, history with an impartial hand, will dispose of that and sundry other questions. Action! action! not criticism, is the plain duty of this hour. Words are now useful only as they stimulate to blows. The office of speech now is only to point out when, [w]here and how, to strike to the best advantage. There is no time for delay. The tide is at its flood that leads on to fortune. From East to West, from North to South, the sky is written all over "NOW OR NEVER." Liberty won by white men would lose half its lustre. Who would be free themselves must strike the blow. Better even to die free, than to live slaves. This is the sentiment of every brave colored man amongst us. There are weak and cowardly men in all nations. We have them amongst us. They tell you that this is the "white man's war";— that you will be no "better off after, than before the war"; that the getting of you into the army is to "sacrifice you on the first opportunity." Believe them not—cowards themselves, they do not wish to have their cowardice shamed by your brave example. Leave them to their timidity, or to whatever motive may hold them back.

I have not thought lightly of the words I am now addressing to you. The counsel I give comes of close observations of the great struggle now in progress—and of the deep conviction that this is your hour, and mine.

In good earnest then, and after the best deliberation, I now for the first time during this war feel at liberty to call and counsel you to arms. By every consideration which binds you to your enslaved fellow country-men, and the peace and welfare of your country; by every aspiration which you cherish for the freedom and equality of yourselves and your children; by all the ties of blood and identity which make us one with the brave black men, now fighting our battles in Louisiana, in South Carolina, I urge you to fly to arms, and smite with death the power that would bury the Government and your Liberty in the same hopeless grave. I wish I could tell you that the State of New York calls you to this high honor. For the moment her constituted authorities are silent on the subject. They will speak by and by, and doubtless on the right side; but we are not compelled to wait for her. We can get at the throat of treason and slavery, through the State of Massachusetts.

She was first in the war of Independence: first to break the chains of her slaves; first to make the black man equal before the law; first to admit colored children to her common schools, and she was first to answer with her blood the alarm cry of the nation—when its capital was menaced by rebels. You know her patriotic Governor, and you know Charles Sumner—I need not add more.

Massachusetts now welcomes you to arms as her soldiers. She has but a small colored population from which to recruit. She has full leave of the General Government to send one regiment to the war, and she has undertaken to do it. Go quickly and help fill up this first colored regiment from the North. I am authorized to assure you that you will receive the same wages, the same rations, the same equipments, the same protection, the same treatment and the same bounty secured to white soldiers. You will be led by able and skillful officers—men who will take especial pride in your efficiency and success. They will be quick to accord to you all the honor you shall merit by your valor— and see that your rights and feelings are respected by other soldiers. I have assured myself on these points—and can speak with authority. More than twenty years unswerving devotion to our common cause, may give me some humble claim to be trusted at this momentous crisis.

I will not argue. To do so implies hesitation and doubt, and you do not hesitate. You do not doubt. The day dawns—the morning star is bright upon the horizon! The Iron gate of our prison stands half open. One gallant rush from the North will fling it wide open, while four millions of our brothers and sisters, shall march out into Liberty! The chance is now given you to end in a day the bondage of centuries, and to rise in one bound from social degradation to the plane of common equality with all other varieties of men. Remember Denmark Vesey of Charleston.—Remember Nathaniel Turner of South Hampton, remember Shields Green, and Cope and who followed noble John Brown, and fell as glorious martyrs for the cause of the slave.—Remember that in a contest with oppression the Almighty has no attribute which can take sides with oppressors. The case is before you. This is our golden opportunity—let us accept it—and forever wipe out the dark reproaches unsparingly hurled against us by our enemies. Win for ourselves the gratitude of our Country—and the best blessings of our posterity through all time. The nucleus of this first regiment is now in camp at Readville, a short distance from Boston. I will undertake to forward to Boston all persons adjudged fit to be mustered into the regiment, who shall apply to me at any time within the next two weeks.

Frederick Douglass.
Rochester, March 2d. 1863

CHAPTER 8

From *Life and Times of Frederick Douglass* (1892)

M aking minimal substantive changes in the account of his slave experience in *My Bondage and My Freedom* (except for finally revealing how he escaped from slavery), Douglass enlarged the freedom section of his second autobiography by an additional fifteen chapters to create the *Life and Times of Frederick Douglass* (Hartford, Conn.: Park, 1881). Introduced by George L. Ruffin, a Harvard-educated black attorney, the third autobiography was almost half again as large as the second. The new material in the *Life and Times* was designed to show how Douglass's dedication to social justice and progress committed him to a "life of conflict and battle" not only in the tempestuous mid-century decades but thereafter. Yet, Douglass affirmed confidently in the conclusion of the *Life and Times,* his had also been a "life of victory, if not complete, at least assured."

The *Life and Times* was the least popular of Douglass's autobiographies, selling only 463 copies in its first seven years of existence, according to Benjamin Quarles. Douglass complained to his publisher about the illustrations and appearance of the *Life and Times.* Perhaps in response to this dissatisfaction, Park Publishing Company brought out a new edition in 1882, with some stylistic revisions by Douglass. Still, few of the major literary magazines in the United States noticed the appearance of the *Life and Times. The Critic* called Douglass's book "unique" and worthy of acceptance "without carping or criticism," but deplored the volume's poor printing and Douglass's "child-like self-complacency" in daring to publish his story "before there is five feet of good solid earth over him." According to the well-meaning reviewer for the *Catholic World,* the *Life and Times* shed light on "a most important period in the history of the Republic." But Douglass's third autobiography also revealed, in the *Catholic World's* delicate phrasing, "those deeply-hidden causes from which has sprung the present transition-state of the nation." In other words, the *Life and Times* spoke perhaps more forthrightly than post-Reconstruction America wanted to hear about the origins of the nation's ongoing racial problems. It is worth noting, however, that the *Life and Times* was published in England in 1882 and translated into French in 1883.

The following chapters from *Life and Times of Frederick Douglass* represent Douglass in the roles he relished most in his third memoir: (1) historian of the antislavery movement recalling first-hand the legendary figures and events of that time ("John Brown and Mrs. Stowe," "The Beginning of the End"), (2) chronicler of personal successes in the new era of freedom ("Vast Changes," "Weighed in the Balance"), and (3) exponent of healing and hopeful cooperation between the races ("Weighed in the Balance," " 'Time Makes All Things Even' "). The chapters here are reprinted from the 1892 edition of *Life and Times of Frederick Douglass,* which reflects Douglass's final revisions of the Second Part of his *Life and Times.*

❖ ❖ ❖

SECOND PART

CHAPTER I

Escape from Slavery

In the first narrative of my experience in slavery, written nearly forty years ago, and in various writings since, I have given the public what I considered very good reasons for withholding the manner of my escape. In substance these reasons were, first, that such publication at any time during the existence of slavery might be used by the master against the slave, and prevent the future escape of any who might adopt the same means that I did. The second reason was, if possible, still more binding to silence—for publication of details would certainly have put in peril the persons and property of those who assisted. Murder itself was not more sternly and certainly punished in the State of Maryland than was the aiding and abetting the escape of a slave. Many colored men, for no other crime than that of giving aid to a fugitive slave, have, like Charles T. Torrey, perished in prison. The abolition of slavery in my native State and throughout the country, and the lapse of time, render the caution hitherto observed no longer necessary. But, even since the abolition of slavery, I have sometimes thought it well enough to baffle curiosity by saying that while slavery existed there were good reasons for not telling the manner of my escape, and since slavery had ceased to exist there was no reason for telling it. I shall now, however, cease to avail myself of this formula, and, as far as I can, endeavor to satisfy this very natural curiosity. I should perhaps have yielded to that feeling sooner, had there been anything very heroic or thrilling in the incidents connected with my escape, for I am sorry to say I have nothing of that sort to tell; and yet the courage that could risk betrayal and the bravery which was ready to encounter death if need be, in pursuit of freedom, were essential features in the undertaking. My success was due to address rather than to courage; to good luck rather than to bravery. My means of escape were provided for me by the very men who were making laws to hold and bind me more securely in slavery. It was the custom in the State of Maryland to require of the free colored people to have what were called free papers. This instrument they were required to renew very often, and by charging a fee for this writing, considerable sums from time to time were collected by the State. In these papers the name, age, color, height and form of the free man were described, together with any scars or other marks upon his person which would assist in his identification. This device of slaveholding ingenuity, like other devices of wickedness, in some measure defeated itself—since more than one man could be found to answer the same general description. Hence many slaves could escape by personating the owner of one set of papers; and this was often done as follows: A slave nearly or sufficiently answering the description set forth in the papers, would borrow or hire them till he could by their means escape to a free state, and then, by mail or otherwise, return them to the owner. The operation was a hazardous one for the lender as well as for the borrower. A failure on the part of the fugitive to send back the papers would imperil his benefactor, and the discovery of the papers in possession of the wrong man would imperil both the fugitive and his friend. It was therefore an act of supreme trust on the part of a freeman of color thus to put in jeopardy his own liberty that another might be free. It was, however, not unfrequently bravely done, and was seldom discovered. I was not so fortunate as to sufficiently resemble any of my free acquaintances as to answer the description of their papers. But I had one friend—a sailor—who owned a sailor's protection, which answered somewhat the purpose of free papers—describing his person and certifying to the fact that he was a free American sailor. The instrument had at its head the American eagle, which at once gave it the appearance of an authorized document. This protection did not, when in my hands, describe its bearer very accurately. Indeed, it called for a man much darker than myself, and close examination of it would have caused my arrest at the start. In order to avoid this fatal scrutiny on the part of the railroad official, I had arranged with Isaac Rolls, a hackman, to bring my baggage to the train just on the moment of starting, and jumped upon the car myself when the train was already in motion. Had I gone into the station and offered to purchase a ticket, I should have been instantly and carefully examined, and undoubtedly arrested. In choosing this plan upon which to act, I considered the jostle of the train, and the natural haste of the conductor in a train crowded with passengers, and relied upon my skill and address in playing the sailor as described in my protection, to do the rest. One element in my favor was the kind feeling which prevailed in Baltimore and other seaports at the time, towards "those who go down to the sea in ships." "Free trade and sailors' rights" expressed the sentiment of the country just then. In my clothing I was rigged out in sailor style. I had on a red shirt and a tarpaulin hat and black cravat, tied in sailor fashion, carelessly and loosely about my neck. My knowledge of ships and sailor's talk came much to my assistance, for I knew a ship from stem to stern, and from keelson to cross-trees, and could talk sailor like an "old salt." On sped the train, and I was well on the way to Havre de Grace before the conductor came into the negro car to collect tickets and examine the papers of his black passengers. This was a critical moment in the drama. My whole future depended upon the decision of this conductor. Agitated I was while this ceremony was proceeding, but still, externally at least, I was apparently calm and self-possessed. He went on with his duty—examining several colored passengers before reaching me. He was somewhat harsh in tone and peremptory in manner until he reached me, when, strangely enough, and to my surprise and relief, his whole manner changed. Seeing that I did not readily produce my free papers, as the other colored persons in the car had done, he said to me in a friendly contrast with that observed towards the others: "I suppose you have your free papers?" To which I answered: "No, sir; I never carry my free papers to sea with me." "But you have something to show that you are a free man, have you not?" "Yes, sir," I answered; "I have a paper with the American eagle on it, that will carry me round the world." With this I drew from my deep sailor's pocket my seaman's protection, as before described. The merest glance at the paper satisfied him, and he took my fare and went on about his business. This moment of time was one of the most anxious I ever experienced. Had the conductor looked closely at the paper, he could not have failed to discover that it called for a very different looking person from myself, and in that case it would have been his duty to arrest me on the instant and send me back to Baltimore from the first station. When he left me with the assurance that I was all right, though much relieved, I realized that I was still in great danger: I was still in Maryland, and subject to arrest at any moment. I saw on the train several persons who would have known me in any other clothes, and I feared they might recognize me, even in my sailor "rig," and report me to the conductor, who would then subject me to a closer examination, which I knew well would be fatal to me.

Though I was not a murderer fleeing from justice, I felt, perhaps, quite as miserable as such a criminal. The train was moving at a very high rate of speed for that time of railroad travel, but to my anxious mind, it was moving far too slowly. Minutes were hours, and hours were days during this part of my flight. After Maryland I was to pass through Delaware—another slave State, where slave-catchers generally awaited their prey, for it was not in the interior of the State, but on its borders, that these human hounds were most vigilant and active. The border lines between slavery and freedom were the dangerous ones, for the fugitives. The heart of no fox or deer, with hungry hounds on his trail, in full chase, could have beaten more anxiously or noisily than did mine from the time I left Baltimore till I reached Philadelphia. The passage of the Susquehanna river at Havre de Grace was at that time made by ferry-boat, on board of which I met a young colored man by the name of Nichols, who came very near betraying me. He was a "hand" on the boat, but instead of minding his business, he insisted upon knowing me, and asking me dangerous questions as to where I was going, and when I was coming back, etc. I got away from my old and inconvenient acquaintance as soon as I could decently do so, and went to another part of the boat. Once across the river I encountered a new danger. Only a few days before I had been at work on a revenue cutter, in Mr. Price's ship-yard, under the care of Captain McGowan. On the meeting at this point of the two trains, the one going south stopped on the track just opposite to the one going north, and it so happened that this Captain McGowan sat at a window where he could see me very distinctly, and would certainly have recognized me had he looked at me but for a second. Fortunately, in the hurry of the moment, he did not see me, and the trains soon passed each other on their respective ways. But this was not the only hair-breadth escape. A German blacksmith, whom I knew well, was on the train with me, and looked at me very intently, as if he thought he had seen me somewhere before in his travels. I really believe he knew me, but had no heart to betray me. At any rate he saw me escaping and held his peace.

The last point of imminent danger, and the one I dreaded most, was Wilmington. Here we left the train and took the steamboat for Philadelphia. In making the change I again apprehended arrest, but no one disturbed me, and I was soon on the broad and beautiful Delaware, speeding away to the Quaker City. On reaching Philadelphia in the afternoon I inquired of a colored man how I could get on to New York? He directed me to the Willow street depot, and thither I went, taking the train that night. I reached New York Tuesday morning, having completed the journey in less than twenty-four hours. Such is briefly the manner of my escape from slavery—and the end of my experience as a slave. Other chapters will tell the story of my life as a freeman.

CHAPTER VIII

John Brown and Mrs. Stowe

About the time I began my enterprise in Rochester I chanced to spend a night and a day under the roof of a man whose character and conversation, and whose objects and aims in life, made a very deep impression upon my mind and heart. His name had been mentioned to me by several prominent colored men, among whom were the Rev. Henry Highland Garnet and J. W. Loguen. In speaking of him their voices would drop to a whisper, and what they said of him made me very eager to see and to know him. Fortunately, I was invited to see him in his own house. At the time to which I now refer this man was a respectable merchant in a populous and thriving city, and our first place of meeting was at his store. This was a substantial brick building on a prominent, busy street. A glance at the interior, as well as at the massive walls without, gave me the impression that the owner must be a man of considerable wealth. My welcome was all that I could have asked. Every member of the family, young and old, seemed glad to see me, and I was made much at home in a very little while. I was, however, a little disappointed with the appearance of the house and its location. After seeing the fine store I was prepared to see a fine residence in an eligible locality, but this conclusion was completely dispelled by actual observation. In fact, the house was neither commodious nor elegant, nor its situation desirable. It was a small wooden building on a back street, in a neighborhood chiefly occupied by laboring men and mechanics; respectable enough, to be sure, but not quite the place, I thought, where one would look for the residence of a flourishing and successful merchant. Plain as was the outside of this man's house, the inside was plainer. Its furniture would have satisfied a Spartan. It would take longer to tell what was not in this house than what was in it. There was an air of plainness about it which almost suggested destitution. My first meal passed under the misnomer of tea, though there was nothing about it resembling the usual significance of that term. It consisted of beef-soup, cabbage, and potatoes—a meal such as a man might relish after following the plow all day or performing a forced march of a dozen miles over a rough road in frosty weather. Innocent of paint, veneering, varnish, or table-cloth, the table announced itself unmistakably of pine and of the plainest workmanship. There was no hired help visible. The mother, daughters, and sons did the serving, and did it well. They were evidently used to it, and had no thought of any impropriety or degradation in being their own servants. It is said that a house in some measure reflects the character of its occupants; this one certainly did. In it there were no disguises, no illusions, no make-believes. Everything implied stern truth, solid purpose, and rigid economy. I was not long in company with the master of this house before I discovered that he was indeed the master of it, and was likely to become mine too if I stayed long enough with him. He fulfilled St. Paul's idea of the head of the family. His wife believed in him, and his children observed him with reverence. Whenever he spoke his words commanded earnest attention. His arguments, which I ventured at some points to oppose, seemed to convince all; his appeals touched all, and his will impressed all. Certainly I never felt myself in the presence of a stronger religious influence than while in this man's house.

In person he was lean, strong, and sinewy, of the best New England mold, built for times of trouble and fitted to grapple with the flintiest hardships. Clad in plain American woolen, shod in boots of cowhide leather, and wearing a cravat of the same substantial material, under six feet high, less than 150 pounds in weight, aged about fifty, he presented a figure straight and symmetrical as a mountain pine. His bearing was singularly impressive. His head was not large, but compact and high. His hair was coarse, strong, slightly gray and closely trimmed, and grew low on his forehead. His face was smoothly shaved, and revealed a strong, square mouth, supported by a broad and prominent chin. His eyes were bluish-gray, and in conversation they were full of light and fire. When on the street, he moved with a long, springing, race-horse step, absorbed by his own reflections, neither seeking nor shunning observation. Such was the man whose name I had heard in whispers; such was the spirit of his house and family; such was the house in which he lived; and such was Captain John Brown, whose name has now passed into history, as that of one of the most marked characters and greatest heroes known to American fame.

After the strong meal already described, Captain Brown cautiously approached the subject which he wished to bring to my attention; for he seemed to apprehend opposition to his views. He denounced slavery in look and language fierce and bitter, thought that slaveholders had forfeited their right to live, that the slaves had the right to gain their liberty in any way they could, did not believe that moral suasion would ever liberate the slave, or that political action would abolish the system. He said that he had long had a plan which could accomplish this end, and he had invited me to his house to lay that plan before me. He said he had been for some time looking for colored men to whom he could safely reveal his secret, and at times he had almost despaired of finding such men; but that now he was encouraged, for he saw heads of such rising up in all directions. He had observed my course at home and abroad, and he wanted my coöperation. His plan as it then lay in his mind had much to commend it. It did not, as some suppose, contemplate a general rising among slaves, and a general slaughter of the slave-masters. An insurrection, he thought, would only defeat the object; but his plan did contemplate the creating of an armed force which should act in the very heart of the South. He was not averse to the shedding of blood, and thought the practice of carrying arms would be a good one for the colored people to adopt, as it would give them a sense of their manhood. No people, he said, could have self-respect, or be respected, who would not fight for their freedom. He called my attention to a map of the United States, and pointed out to me the far-reaching Alleghanies, which stretch away from the borders of New York into the Southern States. "These mountains," he said, "are the basis of my plan. God has given the strength of the hills to freedom; they were placed here for the emancipation of the negro race; they are full of natural forts, where one man for defence will be equal to a hundred for attack; they are full also of good hiding-places, where large numbers of brave men could be concealed, and baffle and elude pursuit for a long time. I know these mountains well, and could take a body of men into them and keep them there despite of all the efforts of Virginia to dislodge them. The true object to be sought is first of all to destroy the money value of slave property; and that can only be done by rendering such property insecure. My plan, then, is to take at first about twenty-five picked men, and begin on a small scale; supply them with arms and ammunition and post them in squads of fives on a line of twenty-five miles. The most persuasive and judicious of these shall go down to the fields from time to time, as opportunity offers, and induce the slaves to join them, seeking and selecting the most restless and daring."

He saw that in this part of the work the utmost care must be used to avoid treachery and disclosure. Only the most conscientious and skillful should be sent on this perilous duty. With care and enterprise he thought he could soon gather a force of one hundred hardy men, men who would be content to lead the free and adventurous life to which he proposed to train them; when these were properly drilled, and each man had found the place for which he was best suited, they would begin work in earnest; they would run off the slaves in large numbers, retain the brave and strong ones in the mountains, and send the weak and timid to the north by the underground railroad. His operations would be enlarged with increasing numbers and would not be confined to one locality.

When I asked him how he would support these men, he said emphatically that he would subsist them upon the enemy. Slavery was a state of war, and the slave had a right to anything necessary to his freedom. "But," said I, "suppose you succeed in running off a few slaves, and thus impress the Virginia slaveholders with a sense of insecurity in their slaves, the effect will be only to make them sell their slaves further south." "That," said he, "will be what I want first to do; then I would follow them up. If we could drive slavery out of *one county*, it would be a great gain; it would weaken the system throughout the State." "But they would employ bloodhounds to hunt you out of the mountains." "That they might attempt," said he, "but the chances are, we should whip them, and when we should have whipped one squad, they would be careful how they pursued." "But you might be surrounded and cut off from your provisions or means of subsistence." He thought that this could not be done so they could not cut their way out, but even if the worst came he could but be killed, and he had no better use for his life than to lay it down in the cause of the slave. When I suggested that we might convert the slaveholders, he became much excited, and said that could never be, "he knew their proud hearts and that they would never be induced to give up their slaves, until they felt a big stick about their heads." He observed that I might have noticed the simple manner in which he lived, adding that he had adopted this method in order to save money to carry out his purposes. This was said in no boastful tone, for he felt that he had delayed already too long, and had no room to boast either his zeal or his self-denial. Had some men made such display of rigid virtue, I should have rejected it, as affected, false, and hypocritical, but in John Brown, I felt it to be real as iron or granite. From this night spent with John Brown in Springfield, Mass., 1847, while I continued to write and speak against slavery, I became all the same less hopeful of its peaceful abolition. My utterances became more and more tinged by the color of this man's strong impressions. Speaking at an anti-slavery convention in Salem, Ohio, I expressed this apprehension that slavery could only be destroyed by blood-shed, when I was suddenly and sharply interrupted by my good old friend Sojourner Truth with the question, "Frederick, is God dead?" "No," I answered, "and because God is not dead slavery can only end in blood." My quaint old sister was of the Garrison school of non-resistants, and was shocked at my sanguinary doctrine, but she too became an advocate of the sword, when the war of the maintenance of the Union was declared.

In 1848 it was my privilege to attend, and in some measure to participate in the famous Free-Soil Convention held in Buffalo, New York. It was a vast and variegated assemblage, composed of persons from all sections of the North, and may be said to have formed a new departure in the history of forces organized to resist the growing and aggressive demands of slavery and the slave power. Until this Buffalo convention, anti-slavery agencies had been mainly directed to the work of changing public sentiment by exposing through the press and on the platform the nature of the slave system. Anti-slavery thus far had only been sheet-lightning; the Buffalo convention sought to make it a thunder-bolt. It is true the Liberty party, a political organization, had been in existence since 1840, when it cast seven thousand votes for James G. Birney, a former slaveholder, but who, in obedience to an enlightened conscience, had nobly emancipated his slaves, and was now devoting his time and talents to the overthrow of slavery. It is true that this little party of brave men had increased their numbers at one time to sixty thousand voters. It, however, had now apparently reached its culminating point, and was no longer able to attract to itself and combine all the available elements at the North capable of being marshaled against the growing and aggressive measures and aims of the slave power. There were many in the old Whig party known as Conscience-Whigs, and in the Democratic party known as Barn-burners and Free Democrats, who were anti-slavery in sentiment and utterly opposed to the extension of the slave system to territory hitherto uncursed by its presence, but who, nevertheless, were not willing to join the Liberty party. It was held to be deficient in numbers and wanting in prestige. Its fate was the fate of all pioneers. The work it had been required to perform had exposed it to assaults from all sides, and it wore on its front the ugly marks of conflict. It was unpopular for its very fidelity to the cause of liberty and justice. No wonder that some of its members, such as Gerrit Smith, William Goodell, Beriah Green, and Julius Lemoyne, refused to quit the old for the new. They felt that the Free-Soil party was a step backward, a lowering of the standard; that the people should come to them, not they to the people. The party which had been good enough for them ought to be good enough for all others. Events, however, overruled this reasoning. The conviction became general that the time had come for a new organization which should embrace all who were in any manner opposed to slavery and the slave power, and this Buffalo Free-Soil convention was the result of that conviction. It is easy to say that this or that measure would have been wiser and better than the one adopted. But any measure is vindicated by its necessity and good results. It was impossible for the mountain to go to Mahomet, or for the Free-Soil element to go to the old Liberty party; so the latter went to the former. "All is well that ends well." This Buffalo convention of free-soilers, however low was their standard, did lay the foundation of a grand superstructure. It was a powerful link in the chain of events by which the slave system has been abolished, the slave emancipated and the country saved from dismemberment.

It is nothing against the actors in this new movement that they did not see the end from the beginning; that they did not at first take the high ground that further on in the conflict their successors felt themselves called upon to take, or that their Free-Soil party, like the old Liberty party, was ultimately required to step aside and make room for the great Republican party. In all this and more it illustrates the experience of reform in all ages, and conforms to the laws of human progress. Measures change, principles never.

I was not the only colored man well known to the country who was present at this convention. Samuel Ringgold Ward, Henry Highland Garnet, Charles L. Remond, and Henry Bibb were there and made speeches which were received with surprise and gratification by the thousands there assembled. As a colored man I felt greatly encouraged and strengthened for my cause while listening to these men, in the presence of the ablest men of the Caucasian race. Mr. Ward especially attracted attention at that convention. As an orator and thinker he was vastly superior, I thought, to any of us, and being perfectly black and of unmixed African descent, the splendors of his intellect went directly to the glory of race. In depth of thought, fluency of speech, readiness of wit, logical exactness, and general intelligence,

Samuel R. Ward has left no successor among the colored men amongst us, and it was a sad day for our cause when he was laid low in the soil of a foreign country.

After the Free-Soil party, with "Free Soil," "Free Labor," "Free States," "Free Speech," and "Free Men"' on its banner, had defeated the almost permanently victorious Democratic party under the leadership of so able and popular a standard-bearer as General Lewis Cass, Mr. Calhoun and other southern statesmen were more than ever alarmed at the rapid increase of anti-slavery feeling in the North, and devoted their energies more and more to the work of devising means to stay the torrents and tie up the storm. They were not ignorant of whereunto this sentiment would grow if unsubjected and unextinguished. Hence they became fierce and furious in debate, and more extravagant than ever in their demands for additional safeguards for their system of robbery and murder. Assuming that the Constitution guaranteed their rights of property in their fellow-men, they held it to be in open violation of the Constitution for any American citizen in any part of the United States to speak, write, or act against this right. But this shallow logic they plainly saw could do them no good unless they could obtain further safe-guards for slavery. In order to effect this the idea of so changing the Constitution was suggested that there should be two instead of one President of the United States—one from the North and the other from the South—and that no measure should become a law without the assent of both. But this device was so utterly impracticable that it soon dropped out of sight, and it is mentioned here only to show the desperation of slaveholders to prop up their system of barbarism against which the sentiment of the North was being directed with destructive skill and effect. They clamored for more slave States, more power in the Senate and House of Representatives, and insisted upon the suppression of free speech. At the end of two years, in 1850, when Clay and Calhoun, two of the ablest leaders the South ever had, were still in the Senate, we had an attempt at a settlement of differences between the North and South which our legislators meant to be final. What those measures were I need not here enumerate, except to say that chief among them was the Fugitive Slave Bill, framed by James M. Mason of Virginia and supported by Daniel Webster of Massachusetts—a bill undoubtedly more designed to involve the North in complicity with slavery and deaden its moral sentiment than to procure the return of fugitives to their so-called owners. For a time this design did not altogether fail. Letters, speeches, and pamphlets literally rained down upon the people of the North, reminding them of their constitutional duty to hunt down and return to bondage runaway slaves. In this the preachers were not much behind the press and the politicians, especially that class of preachers known as Doctors of Divinity. A long list of these came forward with their Bibles to show that neither Christ nor his holy apostles objected to returning fugitives to slavery. Now that that evil day is past, a sight of those sermons would, I doubt not, bring the red blush of shame to the cheeks of many.

Living, as I then did, in Rochester, on the border of Canada, I was compelled to see the terribly distressing effects of this cruel enactment. Fugitive slaves who had lived for many years safely and securely in western New York and elsewhere, some of whom had by industry and economy saved money and bought little homes for themselves and their children, were suddenly alarmed and compelled to flee to Canada for safety as from an enemy's land—a doomed city—and take up a dismal march to a new abode, empty-handed, among strangers. My old friend Ward, of whom I have just now spoken, found it necessary to give up the contest and flee to Canada, and thousands followed his example. Bishop Daniel A. Payne of the African Methodist Episcopal Church came to me about this time to consult me as to whether it was best to stand our ground or flee to Canada. When I told him I could not desert my post until I saw I could not hold it, adding that I did not wish to leave while Garnet and Ward remained, "Why," said he, "Ward? Ward, he is already gone. I saw him crossing from Detroit to Windsor." I asked him if he were going to stay, and he answered: "Yes; we are whipped, we are whipped, and we might as well retreat in order." This was indeed a stunning blow. This man had power to do more to defeat this inhuman enactment than any other colored man in the land, for no other could bring such brain power to bear against it. I felt like a besieged city at news that its defenders had fallen at its gates. The hardships imposed by this atrocious and shameless law were cruel and shocking, and yet only a few of all the fugitives of the Northern States were returned to slavery under its infamously wicked provisions. As a means of recapturing their runaway property in human flesh the law was an utter failure. Its efficiency was destroyed by its enormity. Its chief effect was to produce alarm and terror among the class subject to its operation, and this it did most effectually and distressingly. Even colored people who had been free all their lives felt themselves very insecure in their freedom, for under this law the oaths of any two villains were sufficient to consign a free man to slavery for life. While the law was a terror to the free, it was a still greater terror to the escaped bondman. To him there was no peace. Asleep or awake, at work or at rest, in church or market, he was liable to surprise and capture. By the law the judge got ten dollars a head for all he could consign to slavery, and only five dollars apiece for any which he might adjudge free. Although I was now myself free, I was not without apprehension. My purchase was of doubtful validity, having been bought when out of the possession of my owner and when he must take what was given or take nothing. It was a question whether my claimant could be estopped by such a sale from asserting certain or supposable equitable rights in my body and soul. From rumors that reached me my house was guarded by my friends several nights, when kidnappers, had they come, would have got anything but a cool reception, for there would have been "blows to take as well as blows to give." Happily this reign of terror did not continue long. Despite the efforts of Daniel Webster and Millard Fillmore and our Doctors of Divinity, the law fell rapidly into disrepute. The rescue of Shadrack resulting in the death of one of the kidnappers, in Boston, the cases of Simms and Anthony Burns, in the same place, created the deepest feeling against the law and its upholders. But the thing which more than all else destroyed the fugitive slave law was the resistance made to it by the fugitives themselves. A decided check was given to the execution of the law at Christiana, Penn., where three colored men, being pursued by Mr. Gorsuch and his son, slew the father, wounded the son, and drove away the officers, and made their escape to my house in Rochester. The work of getting these men safely into Canada was a delicate one. They were not only fugitives from slavery but charged with murder, and officers were in pursuit of them. There was no time for delay. I could not look upon them as murderers. To me, they were heroic defenders of the just rights of man against manstealers and murderers. So I fed them, and sheltered them in my house. Had they been pursued then and there, my home would have been stained with blood, for these men who had already tasted blood were well armed and prepared to sell their lives at any expense to the lives and limbs of their probable assailants. What they had already done at Christiana and the cool determination which showed very plainly especially in Parker, (for that was the name of the leader,) left no doubt on my mind that their courage was genuine and that their deeds would equal their words. The situation was critical and dangerous. The telegraph had that day announced their deeds at Christiana, their escape, and that the mountains of Pennsylvania were being searched for the murderers. These men had reached me simultaneously with this news in the New York papers. Immediately after the occurrence at Christiana, they, instead of going into the mountains, were placed on a train which brought them to Rochester. They were thus almost in advance of the lightning, and much in advance of probable pursuit, unless the telegraph had raised agents already here. The hours they spent at my house were therefore hours of anxiety as well as activity. I dispatched my friend Miss Julia Griffiths to the landing three miles away on the Genesee River to ascertain if a steamer would leave that night for any port in Canada, and remained at home myself to guard my tired, dust-covered, and sleeping guests, for they had been harassed and traveling for two days and nights, and needed rest. Happily for us the suspense was not long, for it turned out that that very night a steamer was to leave for Toronto, Canada.

This fact, however, did not end my anxiety. There was danger that between my house and the landing or at the landing itself we might meet with trouble. Indeed the landing was the place where trouble was likely to occur if at all. As patiently as I could, I waited for the shades of night to come on, and then put the men in my "Democrat carriage," and started for the landing on the Genesee. It was an exciting ride, and somewhat speedy withal. We reached the boat at least fifteen minutes before the time of its departure, and that without remark or molestation. But those fifteen minutes seemed much longer than usual. I remained on board till the order to haul in the gang-plank was given; I shook hands with my friends, received from Parker the revolver that fell from the hand of Gorsuch when he died, presented now as a token of gratitude and a memento of the battle for Liberty at Christiana, and I returned to my home with a sense of relief which I cannot stop here to describe. This affair, at Christiana, and the Jerry rescue at Syracuse, inflicted fatal wounds on the fugitive slave bill. It became thereafter almost a dead letter, for slaveholders found that not only did it fail to put them in possession of their slaves, but that the attempt to enforce it brought odium upon themselves and weakened the slave system.

In the midst of these fugitive slave troubles came the book known as Uncle Tom's Cabin, a work of marvelous depth and power. Nothing could have better suited the moral and humane requirements of the hour. Its effect was amazing, instantaneous, and universal. No book on the subject of slavery had so generally and favorably touched the American heart. It combined all the power and pathos of preceding publications of the kind, and was hailed by many as an inspired production. Mrs. Stowe at once became an object of interest and admiration. She had made fortune and fame at home, and had awakened a deep interest abroad. Eminent persons in England, roused to anti-slavery enthusiasm by her "Uncle Tom's Cabin," invited her to visit that country, and promised to give her a testimonial. Mrs. Stowe accepted the invitation and the proffered testimonial. Before sailing for England, however, she invited me from Rochester, N.Y., to spend a day at her house in Andover, Mass. Delighted with an opportunity to become personally acquainted with the gifted authoress, I lost no time in making my way to Andover. I was received at her home with genuine cordiality. There was no contradiction between the author and her book. Mrs. Stowe appeared in conversation equally as well as she appeared in her writing. She made to me a nice little speech in announcing her object in sending for me. "I have invited you here," she said, "because I wish to confer with you as to what can be done for the free colored people of the country. I am going to England and expect to have a considerable sum of money placed in my hands, and I intend to use it in some way for the permanent improvement of the free colored people, and especially for that class which has become free by their own exertions. In what way I can do this most successfully is the subject about which I wish to talk with you. In any event I desire to have some monument rise after Uncle Tom's Cabin, which shall show that it produced more than a transient influence." She said several plans had been suggested, among others an educational institution pure and simple, but that she thought favorably of the establishment of an industrial school; and she desired me to express my views as to what I thought would be the best plan by which to help the free colored people. I was not slow to tell Mrs. Stowe all I knew and had thought on the subject. As to a purely educational institution, I agreed with her that it did not meet our necessities. I argued against expending money in that way. I was also opposed to an ordinary industrial school where pupils should merely "earn the means of obtaining an education in books. There were such schools, already. What I thought of as best was rather a series of workshops, where colored people could learn some of the handicrafts, learn to work in iron, wood, and leather, and where a plain English education could also be taught. I argued that the *want* of money was the root of all evil to the colored people. They were shut out from all lucrative employments and compelled to be merely barbers, waiters, coachmen, and the like, at wages so low that they could lay up little or nothing. Their poverty kept them ignorant and their ignorance kept them degraded. We needed more to learn how to make a good living than to learn Latin and Greek. After listening to me at considerable length, she was good enough to tell me that she favored my views, and would devote the money she expected to receive abroad to meeting the want I had described as the most important; by establishing an institution in which colored youth should learn trades as well as to read, write, and count. When about to leave Andover, Mrs. Stowe asked me to put my views on the subject in the form of a letter, so that she could take it to England with her and show it to her friends there, that they might see to what their contributions were to be devoted. I acceded to her request and wrote her the following letter for the purpose named:

ROCHESTER, March 8, 1853.

MY DEAR MRS. STOWE:

You kindly informed me, when at your house a fortnight ago, that you designed to do something which should permanently contribute to the improvement and elevation of the free colored people in the United States. You especially expressed an interest in such of this class as had become free by their own exertions, and desired most of all to be of service to them. In what manner and by what means you can assist this class most successfully, is the subject upon which you have done me the honor to ask my opinion. . . . I assert, then, that *poverty, ignorance,* and *degradation* are the combined evils; or in other words, these constitute the social disease of the free colored people of the United States.

To deliver them from this triple malady is to improve and elevate them, by which I mean simply to put them on an equal footing with their white fellow-countrymen in the sacred right to *"Life, Liberty,* and the pursuit of happiness." I am for no fancied or artificial elevation, but only ask fair play. How shall this be obtained? I answer, first, not by establishing for our use high schools and colleges. Such institutions are, in my judgment, beyond our immediate occasions and are not adapted to our present most pressing wants. High schools and colleges are excellent institutions, and will in due season be greatly subservient to our progress; but they are the result, as well as they are the demand, of a point of progress which we as a people have not yet attained. Accustomed as we have been to the rougher and harder modes of living, and of gaining a livelihood, we cannot and we ought not to hope that in a single leap from our low condition, we can reach that of *Ministers, Lawyers, Doctors, Editors, Merchants,* etc. These will doubtless be attained by us; but this will only be when we have patiently and laboriously, and I may add successfully, mastered and passed through the intermediate gradations of agriculture and the mechanic arts. Besides, there are (and perhaps this is a better reason for my view of the case) numerous institutions of learning in this country, already thrown open to colored youth. To my thinking, there are quite as many facilities now afforded to the colored people as they can spare the time, from the sterner duties of life, to judiciously appropriate. In their present condition of poverty, they cannot spare their sons and daughters two or three years at boarding-schools or colleges, to say nothing of finding the means to sustain them while at such institutions. I take it, therefore, that we are well provided for in this respect; and that it may be fairly inferred from the fact, that the facilities for our education, so far as schools and colleges in the Free States are concerned, will increase quite in proportion with our future wants. Colleges have been open to colored youth in this country during the last dozen years. Yet few, comparatively, have acquired a classical education; and even this few have found themselves educated far above a living condition, there being no methods by which they could turn their learning to account. Several of this latter class have entered the ministry; but you need not be told that an educated people is needed to sustain an educated ministry. There must be a certain amount of cultivation among the people, to sustain such a ministry. At present we have not that cultivation amongst us; and, therefore, we value in the preacher strong lungs rather than high learning. I do not stay that educated ministers are not needed amongst us, far from it! I wish there were more of them! but to increase their number is *not* the largest benefit you can bestow upon us.

We have two or three colored lawyers in this country; and I rejoice in the fact; for it affords very gratifying evidence of our progress. Yet it must be confessed that, in point of success, our lawyers are as great failures as our ministers. White people will not employ them to the obvious embarrassment of their causes, and the blacks, taking their *cue* from the whites, have not sufficient confidence in their abilities to employ them. Hence educated colored men, among the colored people, are at a very great discount. It would seem that education and emigration go together with us, for as soon as a man rises amongst us, capable, by his genius and learning, to do us great service, just so soon he finds that he can serve himself better by going elsewhere. In proof of this, I might instance the Russwurms, the Garnets, the Wards, the Crummells, and others, all men of superior ability and attainments, and capable of removing mountains of prejudice against their race, by their simple presence in the country; but these gentlemen, finding themselves embarrassed here by the peculiar disadvantages to which I have referred, disadvantages in part growing out of their education, being repelled by ignorance on the one hand, and prejudice on the other, and having no taste to continue a contest against such odds, have sought more congenial climes, where they can live more peaceable and quiet lives. I regret their election, but I cannot blame them; for with an equal amount of education, and the hard lot which was theirs, I might follow their example. . . .

There is little reason to hope that any considerable number of the free colored people will ever be induced to leave this country, even if such a thing were desirable. The black man (*un*like the Indian) loves civilization. He does not make very great progress in civilization himself, but he likes to be in the midst of it, and prefers to share its most galling evils, to encountering barbarism. Then the love of country, the dread of isolation, the lack of adventurous spirit, and the thought of seeming to desert their "brethren in bonds," are a powerful check upon all schemes of colonization, which look to the removal of the colored people, without the slaves. The truth is, dear madam, we are *here*, and here we are likely to remain. Individuals emigrate—nations never. We have grown up with this republic, and I see nothing in her character, or even in the character of the American people, as yet, which compels the belief that we must leave the United States. If, then, we are to remain here, the question for the wise and good is precisely that which you have submitted to me—namely: What can be done to improve the condition of the free people of color in the United States? The plan which I humbly submit in answer to this inquiry (and in the hope that it may find favor with you, and with the many friends of humanity who honor, love and coöperate with you) is the establishment in Rochester, N.Y., or in some other part of the United States equally favorable to such an enterprise, of an INDUSTRIAL COLLEGE in which shall be taught several important branches of the mechanic arts. This college shall be open to colored youth. I will pass over the details of such an institution as I propose. . . . Never having had a day's schooling in all my life, I may not be expected to map out the details of a plan so comprehensive as that involved in the idea of a college. I repeat, then, that I leave the organization and administration of the institution to the superior wisdom of yourself and the friends who second your noble efforts. The argument in favor of an Industrial College (a college to be conducted by the best men, and the best workmen which the mechanic arts can afford; a college where colored youth can be instructed to use their hands, as well as their heads; where they can be put in possession of the means of getting a living whether their lot in after life may be cast among civilized or uncivilized men; whether they choose to stay here, or prefer to return to the land of their fathers) is briefly this: Prejudice against the free colored people in the United States has shown itself nowhere so invincible as among mechanics. The farmer and the professional man cherish no feeling so bitter as that cherished by these. The latter would starve us out of the country entirely. At this moment I can more easily get my son into a lawyer's office to study law than I can into a blacksmith's shop to blow the bellows and to wield the sledge-hammer. Denied the means of learning useful trades, we are pressed into the narrowest limits to obtain a livelihood. In times past we have been the hewers of wood and drawers of water for American society, and we once enjoyed a monopoly in menial employments, but this is so no longer. Even these employments are rapidly passing away out of our hands. The fact is (every day begins with the lesson, and ends with the lesson) that colored men must learn trades; must find new employments; new modes of usefulness to society, or that they must decay under the pressing wants to which their condition is rapidly bringing them.

We must become mechanics; we must build as well as live in houses; we must make as well as use furniture; we must construct bridges as well as pass over them, before we can properly live or be respected by our fellow men. We need mechanics as well as ministers. We need workers in iron, clay, and leather. We have orators, authors, and other professional men, but these reach only a certain class, and get respect for our race in certain select circles. To live here as we ought we must fasten ourselves to our countrymen through their every-day, cardinal wants. We must not only be able to *black* boots, but to *make* them. At present we are, in the northern States, unknown as mechanics. We give no proof of genius or skill at the county, State, or national fairs. We are unknown at any of the great exhibitions of the industry of our fellow-citizens, and being unknown, we are unconsidered.

The fact that we make no show of our ability is held conclusive of our inability to make any, hence all the indifference and contempt with which incapacity is regarded fall upon us, and that too when we have had no means of disproving the infamous opinion of our natural inferiority. I have, during the last dozen years, denied before the Americans that we are an inferior race; but this has been done by arguments based upon admitted principles rather than by the presentation of facts. Now, firmly believing, as I do, that there are skill, invention, power, industry, and real mechanical genius among the colored people, which will bear favorable testimony for them, and which only need the means to develop them, I am decidedly in favor of the establishment of such a college as I have mentioned. The benefits of such an institution would not be confined to the Northern States, nor to the free colored people. They would extend over the whole Union. The slave not less than the freeman would be benefited by such an institution. It must be confessed that the most powerful argument now used by the southern slaveholder, and the one most soothing to his conscience, is that derived from the low condition of the free colored people of the North. I have long felt that too little attention has been given by our truest friends in this country to removing this stumbling-block out of the way of the slave's liberation.

The most telling, the most killing refutation of slavery is the presentation of an industrious, enterprising, thrifty, and intelligent free black population. Such a population I believe would rise in the Northern States under the fostering care of such a college as that supposed.

To show that we are capable of becoming mechanics I might adduce any amount of testimony; but, dear madam, I need not ring the changes on such a proposition. There is no question in the mind of any unprejudiced person that the Negro is capable of making a good mechanic. Indeed, even those who cherish the bitterest feelings toward us have admitted that the apprehension that negroes might be employed in their stead dictated the policy of excluding them from trades altogether. But I will not dwell upon this point, as I fear I have already trespassed too long upon your precious time, and written more than I ought to expect you to read. Allow me to say in conclusion that I believe every intelligent colored man in America will approve and rejoice at the establishment of some such institution as that now suggested. There are many respectable colored men, fathers of large families, having boys nearly grown up, whose minds are tossed by day and by night with the anxious inquiry, What shall I do with my boys? Such an institution would meet the wants of such persons. Then, too, the establishment of such an institution would be in character with the eminently practical philanthropy of your transatlantic friends. America could scarcely object to it as an attempt to agitate the public mind on the subject of slavery, or to *dissolve the Union*. It could not be tortured into a cause for hard words by the American people, but the noble and good of all classes would see in the effort an excellent motive, a benevolent object, temperately, wisely, and practically manifested.

Wishing you, dear madam, renewed health, a pleasant passage and safe return to your native land,

I am, most truly, your grateful friend,

FREDERICK DOUGLASS.

MRS. H. B. STOWE.

I was not only requested to write the foregoing letter for the purpose indicated, but I was also asked, with admirable foresight, to see and ascertain, as far as possible, the views of the free colored people themselves in respect to the proposed measure for their benefit. This I was enabled to do in July, 1853, at the largest and most enlightened colored convention that, up to that time, had ever assembled in this country. This convention warmly approved the plan of a manual labor school, as already described, and expressed high appreciation of the wisdom and benevolence of Mrs. Stowe. This convention was held in Rochester, N. Y., and will long be remembered there for the surprise and gratification it caused our friends in that city. They were not looking for such exhibitions of enlightened zeal and ability as were there displayed in speeches, addresses, and resolutions, and in the conduct of the business for which it had assembled. Its proceedings attracted widespread attention at home and abroad.

While Mrs. Stowe was abroad she was, by the pro-slavery press of our country, so persistently and vigorously attacked for receiving money for her own private use, that the Rev. Henry Ward Beecher felt called upon to notice and reply to it in the columns of the New York *Independent*, of which he was then the editor. He denied that Mrs. Stowe was gathering British gold for herself and referred her assailants to me if they would learn what she intended to do with the money. In answer to her maligners, I denounced their accusations as groundless and through the columns of my paper, assured the public that the testimonial then being raised in England by Mrs. Stowe would be sacredly devoted to the establishment of an industrial school for colored youth. This announcement was circulated by other journals, and the attacks ceased. Nobody could well object to such application of the money received from any source, at home or abroad. After her return to this country I called again on Mrs. Stowe, and was much disappointed to learn from her that she had reconsidered her plan for the industrial school. I have never been able to see any force in the reasons for this change. It is enough, however, to say that they were sufficient for her, and that she no doubt acted conscientiously, though her change of purpose was a great disappointment, and placed me in an awkward position before the colored people of this country, as well as to friends abroad, to whom I had given assurances that the money would be appropriated in the manner I have described.

CHAPTER X

The Beginning of the End

What was my connection with John Brown, and what I knew of his scheme for the capture of Harper's Ferry, I may now proceed to state. From the time of my visit to him in Springfield, Mass., in 1847, our relations were friendly and confidential. I never passed through Springfield without calling on him, and he never came to Rochester without calling on me. He often stopped over night with me, when we talked over the feasibility of his plan for destroying the value of slave property, and the motive for holding slaves in the border States. That plan, as already intimated elsewhere, was to take twenty or twenty-five discreet and trustworthy men into the mountains of Virginia and Maryland, and station them in squads of five, about five miles apart, on a line of twenty-five miles; each squad to co-operate with all, and all with each. They were to have selected for them secure and comfortable retreats in the fastnesses of the mountains, where they could easily defend themselves in case of attack. They were to subsist upon the country roundabout. They were to be well armed, but were to avoid battle or violence, unless compelled by pursuit or in self-defence. In that case, they were to make it as costly as possible to the assailing party, whether that party should be soldiers or citizens. He further proposed to have a number of stations from the line of Pennsylvania to the Canada border, where such slaves as he might, through his men, induce to run away, should be supplied with food and shelter and be forwarded from one station to another till they should reach a place of safety either in Canada or the Northern States. He proposed to add to his force in the mountains any courageous and intelligent fugitives who might be willing to remain and endure the hardships and brave the dangers of this mountain life. These, he thought, if properly selected, could, on account of their knowledge of the surrounding country, be made valuable auxiliaries. The work of going into the valley of Virginia and persuading the slaves to flee to the mountains was to be committed to the most courageous and judicious man connected with each squad.

Hating slavery as I did, and making its abolition the object of my life, I was ready to welcome any new mode of attack upon the slave system which gave any promise of success. I readily saw that this plan could be made very effective in rendering slave property in Maryland and Virginia valueless by rendering it insecure. Men do not like to buy runaway horses, or to invest their money in a species of property likely to take legs and walk off with itself. In the worse case, too, if the plan should fail, and John Brown should be driven from the mountains, a new fact would be developed by which the nation would be kept awake to the existence of slavery. Hence, I assented to this, John Brown's scheme or plan for running off slaves.

To set this plan in operation, money and men, arms and ammunition, food and clothing, were needed; and these, from the nature of the enterprise, were not easily obtained, and nothing was immediately done. Captain Brown, too, notwithstanding his rigid economy, was poor, and was unable to arm and equip men for the dangerous life he had mapped out. So the work lingered till after the Kansas trouble was over and freedom in that Territory was an accomplished fact. This left him with arms and men, for the men who had been with him in Kansas believed in him, and would follow him in any humane though dangerous enterprise he might undertake.

After the close of his Kansas work, Captain Brown came to my house in Rochester, and said he desired to stop with me several weeks; "but," he added, "I will not stay unless you will allow me to pay board." Knowing that he was no trifler and meant all he said, and desirous of retaining him under my roof, I charged three dollars a week. While here, he spent most of his time in correspondence. He wrote often to George L. Stearns of Boston, Gerrit Smith of Peterboro, N. Y., and many others, and received many letters in return. When he was not writing letters, he was writing and revising a constitution which he meant to put in operation by means of the men who should go with him into the mountains. He said that, to avoid anarchy and confusion, there should be a regularly-constituted government, which each man who came with him should be sworn to honor and support. I have a copy of this constitution in Captain Brown's own handwriting, as prepared by himself at my house.

He called his friends from Chatham (Canada) to come together, that he might lay his constitution before them for their approval and adoption. His whole time and thought were given to this subject. It was the first thing in the morning and the last thing at night, till I confess it began to be something of a bore to me. Once in a while he would say he could, with a few resolute men, capture Harper's Ferry, and supply himself with arms belonging to the government at that place; but he never announced his intention to do so. It was, however, very evidently passing in his mind as a thing he might do. I paid but little attention to such remarks, though I never doubted that he thought just what he said. Soon after his coming to me, he asked me to get for him two smoothly-planed boards, upon which he could illustrate, with a pair of dividers, by a drawing, the plan of fortification which he meant to adopt in the mountains.

These forts were to be so arranged as to connect one with the other, by secret passages, so that if one was carried another could easily be fallen back upon, and be the means of dealing death to the enemy at the very moment when he might think himself victorious. I was less interested in these drawings than my children were, but they showed that the old man had an eye to the means as well as to the end, and was giving his best thought to the work he was about to take in hand.

It was his intention to begin this work in '58 instead of '59. Why he did not will appear from the following circumstances.

While in Kansas, he made the acquaintance of one Colonel Forbes, an Englishman, who had figured somewhat in revolutionary movements in Europe, and, as it turned out, had become an adventurer—a soldier of fortune in this country. This Forbes professed to be an expert in military matters, and easily fastened upon John Brown, and, becoming master of his scheme of liberation, professed great interest in it, and offered his services to him in the preparation of his men for the work before them. After remaining with Brown a short time, he came to me in Rochester, with a letter from him, asking me to receive and assist him. I was not favorably impressed with Colonel Forbes at first, but I "conquered my prejudice," took him to a hotel and paid his board while he remained. Just before leaving, he spoke of his family in Europe as in destitute circumstances, and of his desire to send them some money. I gave him a little—I forget how much—and through Miss Assing, a German lady, deeply interested in the John Brown scheme, he was introduced to several of my German friends in New York. But he soon wore them out by his endless begging; and when he could make no more money by professing to advance the John Brown project he threatened to expose it, and all connected with it. I think I was the first to be informed of his tactics, and I promptly communicated them to Captain Brown. Through my friend Miss Assing, I found that Forbes had told of Brown's designs to Horace Greeley, and to the government officials at Washington, of which I informed Captain Brown, and this led to the postponement of the enterprise another year. It was hoped that by this delay the story of Forbes would be discredited, and this calculation was correct, for nobody believed the scoundrel, though in this he told the truth.

While at my house, John Brown made the acquaintance of a colored man who called himself by different names—sometimes "Emperor," at other times, "Shields Green." He was a fugitive slave, who had made his escape from Charleston, South Carolina; a State from which a slave found it no easy matter to run away. But Shields Green was not one to shrink from hardships or dangers. He was a man of few words, and his speech was singularly broken; but his courage and self-respect made him quite a dignified character. John Brown saw at once what "stuff" Green "was made of," and confided to him his plans and purposes. Green easily believed in Brown, and promised to go with him whenever he should be ready to move. About three weeks before the raid on Harper's Ferry, John Brown wrote to me, informing me that a beginning in his work would soon be made, and that before going forward he wanted to see me, and appointed an old stonequarry near Chambersburg, Penn., as our place of meeting. Mr. Kagi, his secretary, would be there, and they wished me to bring any money I could command, and Shields Green along with me. In the same letter, he said that his "mining tools" and stores were then at Chambersburg, and that he would be there to remove them. I obeyed the old man's summons. Taking Shields, we passed through New York city, where we called upon Rev. James Glocester and his wife, and told them where and for what we were going, and that our old friend needed money. Mrs. Glocester gave me ten dollars, and asked me to hand the same to John Brown, with her best wishes.

When I reached Chambersburg, a good deal of surprise was expressed (for I was instantly recognized) that I should come there unannounced, and I was pressed to make a speech to them, with which invitation I readily complied. Meanwhile, I called upon Mr. Henry Watson, a simple-minded and warm-hearted man, to whom Capt. Brown had imparted the secret of my visit, to show me the road to the appointed rendezvous. Watson was very busy in his barber's shop, but he dropped all and put me on the right track. I approached the old quarry very cautiously, for John Brown was generally well armed, and regarded strangers with suspicion. He was then under the ban of the government, and heavy rewards were offered for his arrest, for offenses said to have been committed in Kansas. He was passing under the name of John Smith. As I came near, he regarded me rather suspiciously, but soon recognized me, and received me cordially. He had in his hand when I met him a fishing-tackle, with which he had apparently been fishing in a stream hard by; but I saw no fish, and did not suppose that he cared much for his "fisherman's luck." The fishing was simply a disguise, and was certainly a good one. He looked every way like a man of the neighborhood, and as much at home as any of the farmers around there. His hat was old and storm-beaten, and his clothing was about the color of the stone-quarry itself—his then present dwelling-place.

His face wore an anxious expression, and he was much worn by thought and exposure. I felt that I was on a dangerous mission, and was as little desirous of discovery as himself, though no reward had been offered for me.

We—Mr. Kagi, Captain Brown, Shields Green, and myself—sat down among the rocks and talked over the enterprise which was about to be undertaken. The taking of Harper's Ferry, of which Captain Brown had merely hinted before, was now declared as his settled purpose, and he wanted to know what I thought of it. I at once opposed the measure with all the arguments at my command. To me such a measure would be fatal to running off slaves (as was the original plan), and fatal to all engaged in doing so. It would be an attack upon the federal government, and would array the whole country against us. Captain Brown did most of the talking on the other side of the question. He did not at all object to rousing the nation; it seemed to him that something startling was just what the nation needed. He had completely renounced his old plan, and thought that the capture of Harper's Ferry would serve as notice to the slaves that their friends had come, and as a trumpet to rally them to his standard. He described the place as to its means of defense, and how impossible it would be to dislodge him if once in possession. Of course I was no match for him in such matters, but I told him, and these were my words, that all his arguments, and all his descriptions of the place, convinced me that he was going into a perfect steel-trap, and that once in he would never get out alive; that he would be surrounded at once and escape would be impossible. He was not to be shaken by anything I could say, but treated my views respectfully, replying that even if surrounded he would find means for cutting his way out; but that would not be forced upon him; he should, at the start, have a number of the best citizens of the neighborhood as his prisoners and that holding them as hostages he should be able, if worse came to worse, to dictate terms of egress from the town. I looked at him with some astonishment, that he could rest upon a reed so weak and broken, and told him that Virginia would blow him and his hostages sky-high, rather than that he should hold Harper's Ferry an hour. Our talk was long and earnest; we spent the most of Saturday and a part of Sunday in this debate— Brown for Harper's Ferry, and I against it; he for striking a blow which should instantly rouse the country, and I for the policy of gradually and unaccountably drawing off the slaves to the mountains, as at first suggested and proposed by him. When I found that he had fully made up his mind and could not be dissuaded, I turned to Shields Green and told him he heard what Captain Brown had said; his old plan was changed, and that I should return home, and if he wished to go with me he could do so. Captain Brown urged us both to go with him, but I could not do so, and could but feel that he was about to rivet the fetters more firmly than ever on the limbs of the enslaved. In parting he put his arms around me in a manner more than friendly, and said: "Come with me, Douglass; I will defend you with my life. I want you for a special purpose. When I strike, the bees will begin to swarm, and I shall want you to help hive them." But my discretion or my cowardice made me proof against the dear old man's eloquence—perhaps it was something of both which determined my course. When about to leave I asked Green what he had decided to do, and was surprised by his coolly saying, in his broken way, "I b'leve I'll go wid de ole man." Here we separated; they to go to Harper's Ferry, I to Rochester. There has been some difference of opinion as to the propriety of my course in thus leaving my friend. Some have thought that I ought to have gone with him; but I have no reproaches for myself at this point, and since I have been assailed only by colored men who kept even farther from this brave and heroic man than I did, I shall not trouble myself much about their criticisms. They compliment me in assuming that I should perform greater deeds than themselves.

Such then was my connection with John Brown, and it may be asked, if this is all, why I should have objected to being sent to Virginia to be tried for the offense charged. The explanation is not difficult. I knew that if my enemies could not prove me guilty of the offense of being with John Brown, they could prove that I was Frederick Douglass; they could prove that I was in correspondence and conspiracy with Brown against slavery; they could prove that I brought Shields Green, one of the bravest of his soldiers, all the way from Rochester to him at Chambersburg; they could prove that I brought money to aid him, and in what was then the state of the public mind I could not hope to make a jury of Virginia believe I did not go the whole length he went, or that I was not one of his supporters; and I knew that all Virginia, were I once in her clutches, would say "Let him be hanged." Before I had left Canada for England, Jeremiah Anderson, one of Brown's men, who was present and took part in the raid, but escaped by the mountains, joined me, and he told me that he and Shields Green were sent out on special duty as soon as the capture of the arsenal, etc., was effected. Their business was to bring in the slaves from the surrounding country, and hence they were on the outside when Brown was surrounded. I said to him, "Why then did not Shields come with you?" "Well," he said, "I told him to come; that we could do nothing more, but he simply said he must go down to de ole man." Anderson further told me that Captain Brown was careful to keep his plans from his men, and that there was much opposition among them when they found what were the precise movements determined upon; but they were an oath-bound company, and like good soldiers were agreed to follow their captain wherever he might lead.

On the 12th of November, 1859, I took passage from Quebec on board the steamer Scotia, Captain Thompson, of the Allan line. My going to England was not at first suggested by my connection with John Brown, but the fact that I was now in danger of arrest on the ground of complicity with him made what I had intended a pleasure a necessity, for though in Canada, and under British law, it was not impossible that I might be kidnapped and taken to Virginia. England had given me shelter and protection when the slave-hounds were on my track fourteen years before, and her gates were still open to me now that I was pursued in the name of Virginia justice. I could but feel that I was going into exile, perhaps for life. Slavery seemed to be at the very top of its power; the national government, with all its powers and appliances, was in its hands, and it bade fair to wield them for many years to come. Nobody could then see that in the short space of four years this power would be broken and the slave system destroyed. So I started on my voyage with feelings far from cheerful. No one who has not himself been compelled to leave his home and country and go into permanent banishment can well imagine the state of mind and heart which such a condition brings. The voyage out was by the north passage, and at this season, as usual, it was cold, dark, and stormy. Before quitting the coast of Labrador we had four degrees below zero. Although I had crossed the Atlantic twice before, I had not experienced such unfriendly weather as during the most of this voyage. Our great ship was dashed about upon the surface of the sea as though she had been the smallest "dug-out." It seemed to tax all the seamanship of our captain to keep her in manageable condition; but after battling with the waves on an angry ocean during fourteen long days I gratefully found myself upon the soil of Great Britain, beyond the reach of Buchanan's power and Virginia's prisons. Upon reaching Liverpool I learned that England was nearly as much alive to what had happened at Harper's Ferry as was the United States, and I was immediately called upon in different parts of the country to speak on the subject of slavery, and especially to give some account of the men who had thus flung away their lives in a desperate attempt to free the slaves. My own relation to the affair was a subject of much interest, as was the fact of my presence there being in some sense to elude the demands of Governor Wise, who, having learned that I was not in Michigan, but *was* on a British steamer bound for England, publicly declared that "could he overtake that vessel he would take me from her deck at any cost."

While in England, wishing to visit France, I wrote to Mr. George M. Dallas, the American minister at the British court, to obtain a passport. The attempt upon the life of Napoleon III about that time, and the suspicion that the conspiracy against him had been hatched in England, made the French government very strict in the enforcement of its passport system. I might possibly have been permitted to visit that country without a certificate of my citizenship, but wishing to leave nothing to chance, I applied to the only competent authority; but, true to the traditions of the Democratic party, true to the slaveholding policy of his country, true to the decision of the United States Supreme Court, and true, perhaps, to the petty meanness of his own nature, Mr. George M. Dallas, the Democratic American minister, refused to grant me a passport, on the ground that I was not a citizen of the United States. I did not beg or remonstrate with this dignitary further, but simply addressed a note to the French minister in London asking for a permit to visit France, and that paper came without delay. I mention this not to belittle the civilization of my native country, but as a part of the story of my life. I could have borne this denial with more serenity could I have foreseen what has since happened, but under the circumstances it was a galling disappointment.

I had at this time been about six months out of the United States. My time had been chiefly occupied in different parts of England and Scotland, in speaking on slavery and other subjects, meeting and enjoying the while the society of many of the kind friends whose acquaintance I had made during my visit, fourteen years before, to those countries. Much of the excitement caused by the Harper's Ferry insurrection had subsided, both at home and abroad, and I should have now gratified a long-cherished desire to visit France, and availed myself for that purpose of the permit so promptly and civilly given by the French minister, had not news reached me from home of the death of my beloved daughter Annie, the light and life of my house. Deeply distressed by this bereavement, and acting upon the impulse of the moment, regardless of the peril, I at once resolved to return home, and took the first outgoing steamer for Portland, Maine. After a rough passage of seventeen days I reached home by way of Canada, and remained in my house nearly a month before the knowledge got abroad that I was again in this country. Great changes had now taken place in the public mind touching the John Brown raid. Virginia had satisfied her thirst for blood. She had executed all the raiders who had fallen into her hands. She had not given Captain Brown the benefit of a reasonable doubt, but hurried him to the scaffold in panic-stricken haste. She had made herself ridiculous by her fright and despicable by her fury. Emerson's prediction that Brown's gallows would become like the cross was already being fulfilled. The old hero, in the trial hour, had behaved so grandly that men regarded him not as a murderer but as a martyr. All over the North men were singing the John Brown song. His body was in the dust, but his soul was marching on. His defeat was already assuming the form and pressure of victory, and his death was giving new life and power to the principles of justice and liberty. He had spoken great words in the face of death and the champions of slavery. He had quailed before neither. What he had lost by the sword he had more than gained by the truth. Had he wavered, had he retreated or apologized, the case had been different. He did not even ask that the cup of death might pass from him. To his own soul he was right, and neither "principalities nor powers, life nor death, things present nor things to come," could shake his dauntless spirit or move him from his ground. He may not have stooped on his way to the gallows to kiss a little colored child, as it is reported he did, but the act would have been in keeping with the tender heart, as well as with the heroic spirit of the man. Those who looked for confession heard only the voice of rebuke and warning.

Early after the insurrection at Harper's Ferry an investigating committee was appointed by Congress, and a "drag net" was spread all over the country in the hope of inculpating many distinguished persons. They had imprisoned Thaddeus Hyatt, who denied their right to interrogate him, and had called many witnesses before them, as if the judicial power of the nation had been confided to their committee and not to the Supreme Court of the United States. But Captain Brown implicated nobody. Upon his own head he invited all the bolts of slave-holding vengeance. He said that he, and he alone, was responsible for all that had happened. He had many friends, but no instigators. In all their efforts this committee signally failed, and soon after my arrival home they gave up the search and asked to be discharged, not having half fulfilled the duty for which they were appointed.

I have never been able to account satisfactorily for the sudden abandonment of this investigation on any other ground than that the men engaged in it expected soon to be in rebellion themselves, and that, not a rebellion for liberty, like that of John Brown, but a rebellion for slavery, and that they saw that by using their senatorial power in search of rebels they might be whetting a knife for their own throats. At any rate the country was soon relieved of the congressional drag-net and was now engaged in the heat and turmoil of a presidential canvass—a canvass which had no parallel, involving as it did the question of peace or war, the integrity or the dismemberment of the Republic, and, I may add, the maintenance or destruction of slavery. In some of the Southern States the people were already organizing and arming to be ready for an apprehended contest, and with this work on their hands they had no time to spare to those they had wished to convict as instigators of the raid, however desirous they might have been to do so under other circumstances, for they had parted with none of their hate. As showing their feeling toward me, I may state that a colored man appeared about this time in Knoxville, Tenn., and was beset by a furious crowd with knives and bludgeons because he was supposed to be Fred. Douglass. But, however perilous it would have been for me to have shown myself in any Southern State, there was no especial danger for me at the North.

Though disappointed in my tour on the Continent, and called home by one of the saddest events that can afflict the domestic circle, my presence here was fortunate, since it enabled me to participate in the most important and memorable presidential canvass ever witnessed in the United States, and to labor for the election of a man who in the order of events was destined to do a greater service to his country and to mankind than any man who had gone before him in the presidential office. It is something to couple one's name with great occasions, and it was a great thing to me to be permitted to bear some humble part in this, the greatest that had thus far come to the American people. It was a great thing to achieve American independence when we numbered three millions, but it was a greater thing to save this country from dismemberment and ruin when it numbered thirty millions. He alone of all our Presidents was to have the opportunity to destroy slavery, and to lift into manhood millions of his countrymen hitherto held as chattels and numbered with the beasts of the field.

The presidential canvass of 1860 was three-sided, and each side had its distinctive doctrine as to the question of slavery and slavery extension. We had three candidates in the field. Stephen A. Douglas was the standard-bearer of what may be called the western faction of the old divided democratic party, and John C. Breckenridge was the standard-bearer of the southern or slaveholding faction of that party. Abraham Lincoln represented the then young, growing, and united republican party. The lines between these parties and candidates were about as distinctly and clearly drawn as political lines are capable of being drawn. The name of Douglas stood for territorial sovereignty, or, in other words, for the right of the people of a territory to admit or exclude, to establish or abolish, slavery, as to them might seem best. The doctrine of Breckenridge was that slaveholders were entitled to carry their slaves into any territory of the United States and to hold them there, with or without the consent of the people of the territory; that the Constitution of its own force carried slavery into any territory open for settlement in the United States, and protected it there. To both these parties, factions, and doctrines, Abraham Lincoln and the republican party stood opposed. They held that the Federal Government had the right and the power to exclude slavery from the territories of the United States, and that that right and power ought to be exercised to the extent of confining slavery inside the slave States, with a view to its ultimate extinction. The position of Mr. Douglas gave him a splendid pretext for the display of a species of oratory of which he was a distinguished master. He alone of the three candidates took the stump as the preacher of popular sovereignty, called in derision at the time, "Squatter" Sovereignty. This doctrine, if not the times, gave him a chance to play fast and loose, blow hot and cold, as occasion might require. In the South and among slaveholders he could say, "My great principle of popular sovereignty does not and was not intended by me to prevent the extension of slavery; on the contrary, it gives you the right to take your slaves into the territories and secure legislation legalizing slavery; it denies to the Federal Government all right of interfer-

ence against you, and hence is eminently favorable to your interests."
When among people known to be indifferent he could say, "I do not
care whether slavery is voted up or down in the territory," but when
addressing the known opponents of the extension of slavery, he could
say that the people of the territories were in no danger of having slavery forced upon them, since they could keep it out by adverse legislation. Had he made these representations before railroads, electric
wires, phonography, and newspapers had become the powerful auxiliaries they have done, Mr. Douglas might have gained many votes, but
they were of little avail now. The South was too sagacious to leave
slavery to the chance of defeat in a fair vote by the people of a territory.
Of all property none could less afford to take such a risk, for no property can require more strongly favoring conditions for its existence. Not
only the intelligence of the slave, but the instincts of humanity, must
be barred by positive law, hence Breckenridge and his friends erected
the flinty walls of the Constitution and the Supreme Court for the protection of slavery at the outset. Against both Douglas and Breckenridge
Abraham Lincoln proposed his grand historic doctrine of the power
and duty of the National Government to prevent the spread and perpetuity of slavery. Into this contest I threw myself, with firmer faith and
more ardent hope than ever before, and what I could do by pen or
voice was done with a will. The most remarkable and memorable feature of this canvass was, that it was prosecuted under the portentous
shadow of a threat: leading public men of the South had, with the
vehemence of fiery purpose, given it out in advance that in case of
their failure to elect their candidate (Mr. John C. Breckenridge) they
would proceed to take the slaveholding States out of the Union, and
that, in no event whatever, would they submit to the rule of Abraham
Lincoln. To many of the peace-loving friends of the Union, this was a
fearful announcement, and it doubtless cost the Republican candidates
many votes. To many others, however, it was deemed a mere bra-
vado—sound and fury signifying nothing. With a third class its effect
was very different. They were tired of the rule-or-ruin intimidation
adopted by the South, and felt then, if never before, that they had
quailed before it too often and too long. It came as an insult and a
challenge in one, and imperatively called upon them for independence,
self-assertion, and resentment. Had southern men puzzled their brains
to find the most effective means to array against slavery and slaveholding manners the solid opposition of the North, they could not have hit
upon any expedient better suited to that end than was this threat. It
was not only unfair, but insolent, and more like an address to cowardly slaves than one to independent freemen. It had in it the meanness of the horse-jockey who, on entering a race, proposes, if beaten,
to run off with the stakes. In all my speeches made during this canvass, I did not fail to take advantage of this southern bluster and bul-
lying.

As I have said, this southern threat lost many votes, but it gained more than would cover the lost. It frightened the timid, but stimulated the brave; and the result was—the triumphant election of Abraham Lincoln.

Then came the question. What will the South do about it? Will she eat her bold words, and submit to the verdict of the people, or proceed to the execution of the programme she had marked out for herself prior to the election? The inquiry was an anxious one, and the blood of the North stood still, waiting for the response. It had not to wait long, for the trumpet of war was soon sounded, and the tramp of armed men was heard in that region. During all the winter of 1860 notes of preparation for a tremendous conflict came to us from that quarter on every wind. Still the warning was not taken. Few of the North could really believe that this insolent display of arms would end in anything more substantial than dust and smoke.

The shameful and shocking course of President Buchanan and his cabinet towards this rising rebellion against the government which each and all of them had solemnly sworn to "support, defend and maintain"—the facts that the treasury was emptied; that the army was scattered; that our ships of war were sent out of the way; that our forts and arsenals in the South were weakened and crippled,—purposely left an easy prey to the prospective insurgents,—that one after another the States were allowed to secede; that these rebel measures were largely encouraged by the doctrine of Mr. Buchanan, that he found no power in the Constitution to coerce a State, are all matters of history, and need only the briefest mention here.

To arrest this tide of secession and revolution, which was sweeping over the South, the southern papers, which still had some dread of the consequences likely to ensue from the course marked out before the election, proposed as a means for promoting conciliation and satisfaction that "each northern State, through her legislature, or in convention assembled, should repeal all laws passed for the injury of the constitutional rights of the South (meaning thereby all laws passed for the protection of personal liberty); that they should pass laws for the easy and prompt execution of the fugitive-slave law; that they should pass other laws imposing penalties on all malefactors who should hereafter assist or encourage the escape of fugitive slaves; also, laws declaring and protecting the right of slaveholders to travel and sojourn in northern States, accompanied by their slaves; also, that they should instruct their representatives and senators in Congress to repeal the law prohibiting the sale of slaves in the District of Columbia, and pass laws sufficient for the full protection of slave property in the Territories of the Union."

It may indeed be well regretted that there was a class of men in the North willing to patch up a peace with this rampant spirit of disunion by compliance with these offensive, scandalous, and humiliating terms, and to do so without any guarantee that the South would then be pacified; rather with the certainty, learned by past experience, that it would by no means promote this end. I confess to a feeling allied to satisfaction at the prospect of a conflict between the North and the South. Standing outside the pale of American humanity, denied citizenship, unable to call the land of my birth my country, and adjudged by the supreme court of the United States to have no rights which white men were bound to respect, and longing for the end of the bondage of my people, I was ready for any political upheaval which should bring about a change in the existing condition of things. Whether the war of words would or would not end in blows was for a time a matter of doubt; and when it became certain that the South was wholly in earnest, and meant at all hazards to execute its threats of disruption, a visible change in the sentiment of the North was apparent.

The reaction from the glorious assertion of freedom and independence on the part of the North in the triumphant election of Abraham Lincoln, was a painful and humiliating development of its weakness. It seemed as if all that had been gained in the canvass was about to be surrendered to the vanquished, and that the South, though beaten at the polls, was to be victorious and have everything its own way in the final result. During all the intervening months, from November to the ensuing March, the drift of Northern sentiment was towards compromise. To smooth the way for this, most of the Northern legislatures repealed their personal liberty bills, as they were supposed to embarrass the surrender of fugitive slaves to their claimants. The feeling everywhere seemed to be that something must be done to convince the South that the election of Mr. Lincoln meant no harm to slavery or the slave power, and that the North was sound on the question of the right of the master to hold and hunt his slave as long as he pleased, and that even the right to hold slaves in the Territories should be submitted to the supreme court, which would probably decide in favor of the most extravagant demands of the slave States. The Northern press took on a more conservative tone towards the slavery propagandists, and a corresponding tone of bitterness towards anti-slavery men and measures. It came to be a no uncommon thing to hear men denouncing South Carolina and Massachusetts in the same breath, and in the same measure of disapproval. The old pro-slavery spirit which, in 1835, mobbed anti-slavery prayer-meetings, and dragged William Lloyd Garrison through the streets of Boston with a halter about his neck, was revived. From Massachusetts to Missouri, anti-slavery meetings were ruthlessly assailed and broken up. With others, I was roughly handled in Tremont Temple, Boston, by a mob headed by one of the wealthiest men of that city. The talk was that the blood of some abolitionist must be shed to appease the wrath of the offended South, and to restore peaceful relations between the two sections of the country. A howling mob followed Wendell Phillips for three days whenever he appeared

on the pavements of his native city, because of his ability and prominence in the propagation of anti-slavery opinions.

While this humiliating reaction was going on at the North, various
devices to bring about peace and reconciliation were suggested and
pressed at Washington. Committees were appointed to listen to southern grievances, and, if possible, devise means of redress for such as
might be alleged. Some of these peace propositions would have been
shocking to the last degree to the moral sense of the North, had not
fear for the safety of the Union overwhelmed all moral conviction.
Such men as William H. Seward, Charles Francis Adams, Henry B.
Anthony, Joshua R. Giddings, and others—men whose courage had
been equal to all other emergencies—bent before this southern storm,
and were ready to purchase peace at any price. Those who had stimulated the courage of the North before the election, and had shouted
"Who's afraid?" were now shaking in their shoes with apprehension
and dread. One was for passing laws in the northern States for the
better protection of slave-hunters, and for the greater efficiency of the
fugitive-slave bill. Another was for enacting laws to punish the inva-
sion of the slave States, and others were for so altering the Constitution of the United States that the federal government should never
abolish slavery while any one State should object to such a measure.*
Everything that could be demanded by insatiable pride and selfishness
on the part of the slave-holding South, or could be surrendered by
abject fear and servility on the part of the North, had able and eloquent advocates.

Happily for the cause of human freedom, and for the final unity
of the American nation, the South was mad, and would listen to no
concessions. It would neither accept the terms offered, nor offer others
to be accepted. It had made up its mind that under a given contingency
it would secede from the Union and thus dismember the Republic.
That contingency had happened, and it should execute its threat. Mr.
Ireson of Georgia, expressed the ruling sentiment of his section when
he told the northern peacemakers that if the people of the South were
given a blank sheet of paper upon which to write their own terms on
which they would remain in the Union, they would not stay. They had
come to hate everything which had the prefix "Free"—free soil, free
States, free territories, free schools, free speech, and freedom generally, and they would have no more such prefixes. This haughty and
unreasonable and unreasoning attitude of the imperious South saved
the slave and saved the nation. Had the South accepted our concessions and remained in the Union, the slave power would in all probability have continued to rule; the North would have become utterly
demoralized; the hands on the dial-plate of American civilization
would have been reversed, and the slave would have been dragging

*See History of American Conflict, Vol. II, by Horace Greeley.

his hateful chains to-day wherever the American flag floats to the breeze. Those who may wish to see to what depths of humility and self-abasement a noble people can be brought under the sentiment of fear, will find no chapter of history more instructive than that which treats of the events in official circles in Washington during the space between the months of November, 1859, and March, 1860.

CHAPTER XIII

Vast Changes

When the war for the Union was substantially ended, and peace had dawned upon the land, as was the case almost immediately after the tragic death of President Lincoln; when the gigantic system of American slavery which had defied the march of time and resisted all the appeals and arguments of the abolitionists and the humane testimonies of good men of every generation during two hundred and fifty years, was finally abolished and forever prohibited by the organic law of the land, a strange and, perhaps, perverse feeling came over me. My great and exceeding joy over these stupendous achievements, especially over the abolition of slavery (which had been the deepest desire and the great labor of my life), was slightly tinged with a feeling of sadness.

I felt that I had reached the end of the noblest and best part of my life; my school was broken up, my church disbanded, and the beloved congregation dispersed, never to come together again. The anti-slavery platform had performed its work, and my voice was no longer needed. "Othello's occupation was gone." The great happiness of meeting with my fellow-workers was now to be among the things of memory. Then, too, some thought of my personal future came in. Like Daniel Webster, when asked by his friends to leave John Tyler's cabinet, I naturally inquired: "Where shall I go?" I was still in the midst of my years, and had something of life before me, and as the minister (urged by my old friend George Bradburn to preach anti-slavery, when to do so was unpopular) said, "It is necessary for ministers to live," I felt it was necessary for me to live, and to live honestly. But where should I go, and what should I do? I could not now take hold of life as I did when I first landed in New Bedford, twenty-five years before; I could not go to the wharf of either Gideon or George Howland, to Richmond's brass foundry, or Richetson's candle and oil works, load and unload vessels, or even ask Governor Clifford for a place as a servant. Rolling oil-casks and shoveling coal were all well enough when I was younger, immediately after getting out of slavery. Doing this was a step up, rather than a step down; but all these avocations had had their day for me, and I had had my day for them. My public life and labors had unfitted me for the pursuits of my earlier years, and yet had not prepared me for more congenial and higher employment. Outside the question of slavery my thoughts had not been much directed, and I could hardly hope to make myself useful in any other cause than that to which I had given the best twenty-five years of my life. A man in the situation in which I found myself has not only to divest himself of the old, which is never easily done, but to adjust himself to the new, which is still more difficult. Delivering lectures under various names, John B. Gough says, "Whatever may be the title, my lecture is always on Temperance"; and such is apt to be the case with any man who has devoted his time and thoughts to one subject for any considerable length of time. But what should I do, was the question. I had a few thousand dollars (a great convenience, and one not generally so highly prized by my people as it ought to be) saved from the sale of "My Bondage and My Freedom," and the proceeds of my lectures at home and abroad, and with this sum I thought of following the noble example of my old friends Stephen and Abby Kelley Foster, purchase a little farm and settle myself down to earn an honest living by tilling the soil. My children were grown and ought to be able to take care of themselves. This question, however, was soon decided for me. I had after all acquired (a very unusual thing) a little more knowledge and aptitude fitting me for the new condition of things than I knew, and had a deeper hold upon public attention than I had supposed. Invitations began to pour in upon me from colleges, lyceums, and literary societies, offering me one hundred, and even two hundred dollars for a single lecture.

I had, some time before, prepared a lecture on "Self-made Men," and also one upon Ethnology, with special reference to Africa. The latter had cost me much labor, though, as I now look back upon it, it was a very defective production. I wrote it at the instance of my friend Doctor M. B. Anderson, President of Rochester University, himself a distinguished ethnologist, a deep thinker and scholar. I had been invited by one of the literary societies of Western Reserve College (then at Hudson, but recently removed to Cleveland, Ohio), to address it on Commencement day; and never having spoken on such an occasion, never, indeed, having been myself inside of a school-house for the purpose of an education, I hesitated about accepting the invitation, and finally called upon Prof. Henry Wayland, son of the great Doctor Wayland of Brown University, and on Doctor Anderson, and asked their advice whether I ought to accept. Both gentlemen advised me to do so. They knew me, and evidently thought well of my ability. But the puzzling question now was, what shall I say if I do go there? It won't do to give them an old-fashioned anti-slavery discourse. (I learned afterwards that such a discourse was precisely what they needed, though not what they wished; for the faculty, including the President, was in great distress because I, a colored man, had been invited, and because of the reproach this circumstance might bring upon the College.) But what shall I talk about? became the difficult question. I finally hit upon the one before mentioned. I had read, with great interest, when in England a few years before, parts of Doctor Prichard's "Natural History of Man," a large volume marvelously calm and philosophical in its discussion of the science of the origin of the races, and was thus in the line of my then convictions. I at once sought in our bookstores for this valuable book, but could not obtain it anywhere in this country. I sent to England, where I paid the sum of seven and a half dollars for it. In addition to this valuable work President Anderson kindly gave me a little book entitled "Man and His Migrations," by Dr. R. G. Latham, and loaned me the large work of Dr. Morton, the famous archaeologist, and that of Messrs. Nott and Glidden, the latter written evidently to degrade the Negro and support the then-prevalent Calhoun doctrine of the rightfulness of slavery. With these books and occasional suggestions from Dr. Anderson and Prof. Wayland I set about preparing my commencement address. For many days and nights I toiled, and succeeded at last in getting something together in due form. Written orations had not been in my line. I had usually depended upon my unsystematized knowledge and the inspiration of the hour and the occasion, but I had now got the "scholar bee in my bonnet," and supposed that inasmuch as I was to speak to college professors and students I must at least make a show of some familiarity with letters. It proved, as to its immediate effect, a great mistake, for my carefully-studied and written address, full of learned quotations, fell dead at my feet, while a few remarks I made extemporaneously at collation were enthusiastically received. Nevertheless, the reading and labor expended were of much value to me. They were needed steps preparatory to the work upon which I was about to enter. If they failed at the beginning, they helped to success in the end. My lecture on "The Races of Men" was seldom called for, but that on "Self-made Men" was in great demand, especially through the West. I found that the success of a lecturer depends more upon the quality of his stock in store than the amount. My friend Wendell Phillips (for such I esteem him), who has said more cheering words to me and in vindication of my race than any man now living, has delivered his famous lecture on the "Lost Arts" during the last forty years; and I doubt if among all his lectures, and he has many, there is one in such requisition as this. When Daniel O'Connell was asked why he did not make a new speech he playfully replied that "it would take Ireland twenty years to learn his old ones." Upon some such consideration as this I adhered pretty closely to my old lecture on "Self-made Men," retouching and shading it a little from time to time as occasion seemed to require.

Here, then, was a new vocation before me, full of advantages mentally and pecuniarily. When in the employment of the American Anti-Slavery Society my salary was about four hundred and fifty dollars a year, and I felt I was well paid for my services; but I could now make from fifty to a hundred dollars a night, and have the satisfaction, too, that I was in some small measure helping to lift my race into consideration, for no man who lives at all lives unto himself—he either helps or hinders all who are in any wise connected with him. I never rise to speak before an American audience without something of the feeling that my failure or success will bring blame or benefit to my whole race. But my activities were not now confined entirely to lectures before lyceums. Though slavery was abolished, the wrongs of my people were not ended. Though they were not slaves, they were not yet quite free. No man can be truly free whose liberty is dependent upon the thought, feeling, and action of others, and who has himself no means in his own hands for guarding, protecting, defending, and maintaining that liberty. Yet the Negro, after his emancipation, was precisely in this state of destitution. The law on the side of freedom is of great advantage only where there is power to make that law respected. I know no class of my fellow-men, however just, enlightened, and humane, which can be wisely and safely trusted absolutely with the liberties of any other class. Protestants are excellent people, but it would not be wise for Catholics to depend entirely upon them to look after their rights and interests. Catholics are a pretty good sort of people (though there is a soul-shuddering history behind them), yet no enlightened Protestants would commit their liberty to their care and keeping. And yet the government had left the freedmen in a worse condition than either of these. It felt that it had done enough for him. It had made him free, and henceforth he must make his own way in the world. Yet he had none of the conditions for self-preservation or self-protection. He was free from the individual master, but the slave of society. He had neither money, property, nor friends. He was free from the old plantation, but he had nothing but the dusty road under his feet. He was free from the old quarter that once gave him shelter, but a slave to the rains of summer and to the frosts of winter. He was, in a word, literally turned loose, naked, hungry, and destitute, to the open sky. The first feeling toward him by the old master classes was full of bitterness and wrath. They resented his emancipation as an act of hostility toward them, and, since they could not punish the emancipator, they felt like punishing the object which that act had emancipated. Hence they drove him off the old plantation, and told him he was no longer wanted there. They not only hated him because he had been freed as a punishment to them, but because they felt that they had been robbed of his labor. An element of greater bitterness still came into their hearts; the freedman had been the friend of the government, and many of his class had borne arms against them during the war. The thought of paying cash for labor that they could formerly extort by the lash did not in any wise improve their disposition to the emancipated slave, or improve his own condition. Now, since poverty has, and can have, no chance against wealth, the landless against the landowner, the ignorant against the intelligent, the freedman was powerless. He had nothing left him with which to fight the battle of life, but a slavery-distorted and diseased body and lame and twisted limbs. I therefore soon found that the Negro had still a cause, and that he needed my voice and pen with others to plead for it. The American Anti-Slavery Society under the lead of Mr. Garrison had disbanded, its newspapers were discontinued, its agents were withdrawn from the field, and all systematic efforts by abolitionists were abandoned. Many of the society, Mr. Phillips and myself amongst the number, differed from Mr. Garrison as to the wisdom of this course. I felt that the work of the society was not done and that it had not fulfilled its mission, which was, not merely to emancipate, but to elevate the enslaved class. But against Mr. Garrison's leadership, and the surprise and joy occasioned by the emancipation, it was impossible to keep the association alive, and the cause of the freedmen was left mainly to individual effort and to hastily-extemporized societies of an ephemeral character; brought together under benevolent impulse, but having no history behind them, and, being new to the work, they were not as effective for good as the old society would have been had it followed up its work and kept its old instrumentalities in operation.

From the first I saw no chance of bettering the condition of the freedman until he should cease to be merely a freedman and should become a citizen. I insisted that there was no safety for him or for anybody else in America outside the American government; that to guard, protect, and maintain his liberty the freedman should have the ballot; that the liberties of the American people were dependent upon the ballot-box, the jury-box, and the cartridge-box; that without these no class of people could live and flourish in this country; and this was now the word for the hour with me, and the word to which the people of the North willingly listened when I spoke. Hence, regarding as I did the elective franchise as the one great power by which all civil rights are obtained, enjoyed, and maintained under our form of government, and the one without which freedom to any class is delusive if not impossible, I set myself to work with whatever force and energy I possessed to secure this power for the recently-emancipated millions.

The demand for the ballot was such a vast advance upon the former objects proclaimed by the friends of the colored race, that it startled and struck men as preposterous and wholly inadmissible. Anti-slavery men themselves were not united as to the wisdom of such [a] demand. Mr. Garrison himself, though foremost for the abolition of slavery, was not yet quite ready to join this advanced movement. In this respect he was in the rear of Mr. Phillips, who saw not only the justice, but the wisdom and necessity of the measure. To his credit it may be said, that he gave the full strength of his character and eloquence to its adoption. While Mr. Garrison thought it too much to ask, Mr. Phillips thought it too little. While the one thought it might be postponed to the future, the other thought it ought to be done at once. But Mr. Garrison was not a man to lag far in the rear of truth and right, and he soon came to see with the rest of us that the ballot was essential to the freedom of the freedman. A man's head will not long remain wrong, when his heart is right. The applause awarded to Mr. Garrison by the conservatives, for his moderation both in respect of his views on this question, and the disbandment of the American Anti-Slavery Society must have disturbed him. He was at any rate soon found on the right side of the suffrage question.

The enfranchisement of the freedmen was resisted on many grounds, but mainly on these two: first, the tendency of the measure to bring the freedmen into conflict with the old master-class and the white people of the South generally; secondly, their unfitness, by reason of their ignorance, servility and degradation, to exercise over the destinies of this great nation so great a power as the ballot.

These reasons against the measure which were supposed to be unanswerable, were in some sense the most powerful arguments in its favor. The argument that the possession of suffrage would be likely to bring the negro into conflict with the old master-class at the South, had its main force in the admission that the interests of the two classes antagonized each other and that the maintenance of the one would prove inimical to the other. It resolved itself into this, that, if the negro had the means of protecting his civil rights, those who had formerly denied him these rights would be offended and make war upon him. Experience has shown in a measure the correctness of this position. The old master was offended to find the negro whom he lately possessed the right to enslave and flog to toil, casting a ballot equal to his own, and resorted to all sorts of meanness, violence, and crime, to dispossess him of the enjoyment of this point of equality. In this respect the exercise of the right of suffrage by the negro has been attended with the evil, which the opponents of the measure predicted, and they could say "I've told you so," but immeasurably and intolerably greater would have been the evil consequences resulting from the denial to one class of this natural means of protection, and granting it to the other, and hostile class. It would have been, to have committed the lamb to the care of the wolf—the arming of one class and disarming the other—protecting one interest, and destroying the other, making the rich strong, and the poor weak—the white man a tyrant, and the black man a slave. The very fact therefore that the old master-classes of the South felt that their interests were opposed to those of the freedmen, instead of being a reason against their enfranchisement, was the most powerful one in its favor. Until it shall be safe to leave the lamb in the hold of the lion, the laborer in the power of the capitalist, the poor in the hands of the rich, it will not be safe to leave a newly emancipated people completely in the power of their former masters, especially when such masters have not ceased to be such from enlightened moral convictions but by irresistible force. Then on the part of the government itself, had it denied this great right to the freedmen, it would have been another proof that "Republics are ungrateful." It would have been rewarding its enemies, and punishing its friends—embracing its foes, and spurning its allies,—setting a premium on treason, and degrading loyalty. As to the second point, viz.: the negro's ignorance and degradation, there was no disputing either. It was the nature of slavery, from whose depths he had arisen, to make him so, and it would have kept him so. It was the policy of the system to keep him both ignorant and degraded, the better and more safely to defraud him of his hard earnings. This argument never staggered me. The ballot in the hands of the negro was necessary to open the door of the school-house and to unlock to him the treasures of its knowledge. Granting all that was said of his ignorance, I used to say, "if the negro knows enough to fight for his country he knows enough to vote; if he knows enough to pay taxes for the support of the government, he knows enough to vote; if he knows as much when sober, as an Irishman knows when drunk, he knows enough to vote."

And now while I am not blind to the evils which have thus far attended the enfranchisement of the colored people, I hold that the evils from which we escaped, and the good we have derived from that act, amply vindicate its wisdom. The evils it brought are in their nature temporary, and the good is permanent. The one is comparatively small, the other absolutely great. The young child has staggered on his little legs, and he has sometimes fallen and hurt his head in the fall, but then he has learned to walk. The boy in the water came near drowning, but then he has learned to swim. Great changes in the relations of mankind can never come, without evils analogous to those which have attended the emancipation and enfranchisement of the colored people of the United States. I am less amazed at these evils, than by the rapidity with which they are subsiding, and not more astonished at the facility with which the former slave has become a free man, than at the rapid adjustment of the master-class to the new situation.

Unlike the movement for the abolition of slavery, the success of the effort for the enfranchisement of the freedmen was not long delayed. It is another illustration of how any advance in pursuance of a right principle prepares and makes easy the way to another. The way of transgression is a bottomless pit, one step in that direction invites the next, and the end is never reached; and it is the same with the path of righteous obedience. Two hundred years ago, the pious Doctor Godwin dared affirm that it was "not a sin to baptize a negro," and won for him the rite of baptism. It was a small concession to his manhood; but it was strongly resisted by the slaveholders of Jamaica and Virginia. In this they logical in their argument, but they were not logical in their object. They saw plainly that to concede the negro's right to baptism was to receive him into the Christian Church, and make him a brother in Christ; and hence they opposed the first step sternly and bitterly. So long as they could keep him beyond the circle of human brotherhood, they could scourge him to toil, as a beast of burden, with a good Christian conscience, and without reproach. "What!" said they, "baptize a negro? preposterous!" Nevertheless the negro was baptized and admitted to church fellowship; and though for a long time his soul belonged to God, his body to his master, and he, poor fellow, had nothing left for himself, he is at last not only baptized, but emancipated and enfranchised.

In this achievement, an interview with President Andrew Johnson, on the 7th of February, 1866, by a delegation consisting of George T. Downing, Lewis H. Douglass, Wm. E. Matthews, John Jones, John F. Cook, Joseph E. Otis, A. W. Ross, William Whipper, John M. Brown, Alexander Dunlop, and myself, will take its place in history as one of the first steps. What was said on that occasion brought the whole question virtually before the American people. Until that interview the country was not fully aware of the intentions and policy of President Johnson on the subject of reconstruction, especially in respect of the newly emancipated class of the South. After having heard the brief addresses made to him by Mr. Downing and myself, he occupied at least three-quarters of an hour in what seemed a set speech, and refused to listen to any reply on our part, although solicited to grant a few moments for that purpose. Seeing the advantage that Mr. Johnson would have over us in getting his speech paraded before the country in the morning papers, the members of the delegation met on the evening of that day, and instructed me to prepare a brief reply, which should go out to the country simultaneously with the President's speech to us. Since this reply indicates the points of difference between the President and ourselves, I produce it here as a part of the history of the times, it being concurred in by all the members of the delegation.

Both the speech and the reply were commented upon very extensively.

MR. PRESIDENT: In consideration of a delicate sense of propriety as well as of your own repeated intimations of indisposition to discuss or listen to a reply to the views and opinions you were pleased to express to us in your elaborate speech to-day, the undersigned would respectfully take this method of replying thereto. Believing as we do that the views and opinions you expressed in that address are entirely unsound and prejudicial to the highest interests of our race as well as to our country at large, we cannot do other than expose the same and, as far as may be in our power, arrest their dangerous influence. It is not necessary at this time to call attention to more than two or three features of your remarkable address:

I. The first point to which we feel especially bound to take exception, is your attempt to found a policy opposed to our enfranchisement, upon the alleged ground of an existing hostility on the part of the former slaves toward the poor white people of the South. We admit the existence of this hostility, and hold that it is entirely reciprocal. But you obviously commit an error by drawing an argument from an incident of slavery, and making it a basis for a policy adapted to a state of freedom. The hostility between the whites and blacks of the South is easily explained. It has its root and sap in the relation of slavery, and was incited on both sides by the cunning of the slave masters. Those masters secured their ascendency over both the poor whites and blacks by putting enmity between them.

They divided both to conquer each. There was no earthly reason why the blacks should not hate and dread the poor whites when in a state of slavery, for it was from this class that their masters received their slave catchers, slave drivers, and overseers. They were the men called in upon all occasions by the masters whenever any fiendish outrage was to be committed upon the slave. Now, sir, you cannot but perceive, that the cause of this hatred removed, the effect must be removed also. Slavery is abolished. The cause of this antagonism is removed, and you must see that it is altogether illogical (and "putting new wine into old bottles") to legislate from slaveholding and slave-driving premises for a people whom you have repeatedly declared it your purpose to maintain in freedom.

2. Besides, even if it were true, as you allege, that the hostility of the blacks toward the poor whites must necessarily project itself into a state of freedom, and that this enmity between the two races is even more intense in a state of freedom than in a state of slavery, in the name of heaven, we reverently ask how can you, in view of your professed desire to promote the welfare of the black man, deprive him of all means of defence, and clothe him whom you regard as his enemy in the panoply of political power? Can it be that you recommend a policy which would arm the strong and cast down the defenceless? Can you, by any possibility of reasoning, regard this as just, fair, or wise? Experience proves that those are most abused who can be abused with the greatest impunity. Men are whipped oftenest who are whipped easiest. Peace between races is not to be secured by degrading one race and exalting another; by giving power to one race and withholding it from another; but by maintaining a state of equal justice between all classes. First pure, then peaceable.

3. On the colonization theory you were pleased to broach, very much could be said. It is impossible to suppose, in view of the usefulness of the black man in time of peace as a laborer in the South, and in time of war as a soldier at the North, and the growing respect for his rights among the people and his increasing adaptation to a high state of civilization in his native land, that there can ever come a time when he can be removed from this country without a terrible shock to its prosperity and peace. Besides, the worst enemy of the nation could not cast upon its fair name a greater infamy than to admit that negroes could be tolerated among them in a state of the most degrading slavery and oppression, and must be cast away, driven into exile, for no other cause than having been freed from their chains.

WASHINGTON, February 7, 1866.

From this time onward the question of suffrage for the freedmen was not allowed to rest. The rapidity with which it gained strength was something quite marvelous and surprising even to its advocates. Senator Charles Sumner soon took up the subject in the Senate, and treated it in his usually able and exhaustive manner. It was a great treat to listen to his argument running through two days, abounding as it did in eloquence, learning, and conclusive reasoning. A committee of the Senate had reported a proposition giving to the States lately in rebellion, in so many words, complete option as to the enfranchisement of their colored citizens; only coupling with that proposition the condition that, to such States as chose to enfranchise such citizens, the basis of their representation in Congress should be proportionately increased; or, in other words, that only three-fifths of the colored citizens should be counted in the basis of representation in States where colored citizens were not allowed to vote, while in the States granting suffrage to colored citizens, the entire colored people should be counted in the basis of representation. Against this proposition myself and associates addressed to the Senate of the United States the following memorial:

"To the Honorable the Senate of the United States:
"The undersigned, being a delegation representing the colored people of the several States, and now sojourning in Washington, charged with the duty to look after the best interests of the recently emancipated, would most respectfully, but earnestly, pray your honorable body to favor no amendment of the Constitution of the United States which will grant any one or all of the States of this Union to disfranchise any class of citizens on the ground of race or color, for any consideration whatever. They would further respectfully represent that the Constitution as adopted by the fathers of the Republic in 1789, evidently contemplated the result which has now happened, to wit, the abolition of slavery. The men who framed it, and those who adopted it, framed and adopted it for the people, and the whole people—colored men being at that time legal voters in most of the States. In that instrument, as it now stands, there is not a sentence or a syllable conveying any shadow of right or authority by which any State may make color or race a disqualification for the exercise of the right of suffrage; and the undersigned will regard as a real calamity the introduction of any words, expressly or by implication, giving any State or States such power; and we respectfully submit that if the amendment now pending before your honorable body shall be adopted, it will enable any State to deprive any class of citizens of the elective franchise, notwithstanding it was obviously framed with a view to affect the question of negro suffrage only.

"For these and other reasons the undersigned respectfully pray that the amendment to the Constitution, recently passed by the House and now before your body, be not adopted. And as in duty bound, etc."

It was the opinion of Senator Wm. Pitt Fessenden, Senator Henry Wilson, and many others, that the measure here memorialized against would, if incorporated into the Constitution, certainly bring about the enfranchisement of the whole colored population of the South. It was held by them to be an inducement to the States to make suffrage universal, since the basis of representation would be enlarged or contracted according as suffrage should be extended or limited; but the judgment of these leaders was not the judgment of Senator Sumner, Senators Wade, Yates, Howe and others, or of the colored people. Yet, weak as this measure was, it encountered the united opposition of democratic senators. On that side the Hon. Thomas H. Hendricks, of Indiana, took the lead in appealing to popular prejudice against the negro. He contended that among other objectionable and insufferable results that would flow from its adoption, would be, that a negro would ultimately be a member of the United States Senate. I never shall forget the ineffable scorn and indignation with which Mr. Hendricks deplored the possibility of such an event. In less, however, than a decade from that debate, Senators Revels and Bruce, both colored men, had fulfilled the startling prophecy of the Indiana senator. It was not, however, by the half-way measure, which he was opposing for its radicalism, but by the fourteenth and fifteenth amendments, that these gentlemen reached their honorable positions.

In defeating the option proposed to be given to the States to extend or deny suffrage to their colored population, much credit is due to the delegation already named as visiting President Johnson. That delegation made it their business to personally see and urge upon leading republican statesmen the wisdom and duty of impartial suffrage. Day after day Mr. Downing and myself saw and conversed with those members of the Senate whose advocacy of suffrage would be likely to insure its success.

The second marked step in effecting the enfranchisement of the negro was made at the "National Loyalist's Convention," held at Philadelphia, in September, 1866. This body was composed of delegates from the South, North, and West. Its object was to diffuse clear views of the situation of affairs at the South and to indicate the principles by it deemed advisable to be observed in the reconstruction of society in the Southern States.

This convention was, as its history shows, numerously attended by the ablest and most influential men from all sections of the country, and its deliberations participated in by them.

The policy foreshadowed by Andrew Johnson (who, by the grace of the assassin's bullet, was then in Abraham Lincoln's seat)—a policy based upon the idea that the rebel States were never out of the Union, and hence had forfeited no rights which his pardon could not restore— gave importance to this convention, more than anything which was then occurring at the South; for through the treachery of this bold, bad man, we seemed then about to lose nearly all that had been gained by the war.

I was at the time residing in Rochester and was duly elected as a delegate from that city to attend this convention. The honor was a surprise and a gratification to me. It was unprecedented for a city of over sixty thousand white citizens and only about two hundred colored residents, to elect a colored man to represent them in a national political convention, and the announcement of it gave a shock of no inconsiderable violence to the country. Many Republicans, with every respect for me personally, were unable to see the wisdom of such a course. They dreaded the clamor of social equality and amalgamation which would be raised against the party, in consequence of this startling innovation. They, dear fellows, found it much more agreeable to talk of the principles of liberty as glittering generalities, than to reduce those principles to practice.

When the train on which I was going to the convention reached Harrisburg, it met and was attached to another from the West crowded with Western and Southern delegates on the way to the convention, and among them were several loyal Governors, chief among whom was the loyal Governor of Indiana, Oliver P. Morton, a man of Websterian mould in all that appertained to mental power. When my presence became known to these gentlemen, a consultation was immediately held among them, upon the question as to what was best to do with me. It seems strange now, in view of all the progress which had been made, that such a question could arise. But the circumstances of the times made me the Jonah of the Republican ship, and responsible for the contrary winds and misbehaving weather. Before we reached Lancaster, on our eastward bound trip, I was duly waited upon by a committee of my brother delegates, which had been appointed by other honorable delegates, to represent to me the undesirableness of my attendance upon the National Loyalist's Convention. The spokesman of these sub-delegates was a gentleman from New Orleans with a very French name, which has now escaped me, but which I wish I could recall, that I might credit him with a high degree of politeness and the gift of eloquence. He began by telling me that he knew my history and my works, and that he entertained a very high respect for me, that both himself and the gentlemen who sent him, as well as those who accompanied him, regarded me with admiration; that there was not among them the remotest objection to sitting in the convention with me, but their personal wishes in the matter they felt should be set aside for the sake of our common cause; that whether I should or should not go into the convention was purely a matter of expediency; that I must know that there was a very strong and bitter prejudice against my race in the North as well as at the South; and that the cry of social and political equality would not fail to be raised against the

Republican party if I should attend this loyal national convention. He insisted that it was a time for the sacrifice of my own personal feeling, for the good of the Republican cause; that there were several districts in the State of Indiana so evenly balanced that a very slight circumstance would be likely to turn the scale against us, and defeat our Congressional candidates, and thus leave Congress without a two-thirds vote to control the headstrong and treacherous man then in the presidential chair. It was urged that this was a terrible responsibility for me or any other man to take.

I listened very attentively to this address, uttering no word during its delivery; but when it was finished, I said to the speaker and the committee, with all the emphasis I could throw into my voice and manner: "Gentlemen, with all respect, you might as well ask me to put a loaded pistol to my head and blow my brains out, as to ask me to keep out of this convention, to which I have been duly elected. Then, gentlemen, what would you gain by this exclusion? Would not the charge of cowardice, certain to be brought against you, prove more damaging than that of amalgamation? Would you not be branded all over the land as dastardly hypocrites, professing principles which you have no wish or intention of carrying out? As a matter of policy or expediency, you will be wise to let me in. Everybody knows that I have been duly elected by the city of Rochester as a delegate. The fact has been broadly announced and commented upon all over the country. If I am not admitted, the public will ask, 'Where is Douglass? Why is he not seen in the convention?' and you would find that enquiry more difficult to answer than any charge brought against you for favoring political or social equality; but, ignoring the question of policy altogether, and looking at it as one of right and wrong, I am bound to go into that convention; not to do so, would contradict the principle and practice of my life." With this answer, the committee retired from the car in which I was seated, and did not again approach me on the subject; but I saw plainly enough then, as well as on the morning when the loyalist procession was to march through the streets of Philadelphia, that while I was not to be formally excluded, I was to be ignored by the Convention.

I was the ugly and deformed child of the family, and to be kept out of sight as much as possible while there was company in the house. Especially was it the purpose to offer me no inducement to be present in the ranks of the procession of its members and friends, which was to start from Independence Hall on the first morning of its meeting.

In good season, however, I was present at this grand starting point. My reception there confirmed my impression as to the policy intended to be pursued towards me. Few of the many I knew were prepared to give me a cordial recognition, and among these few I may mention Gen. Benj. F. Butler, who, whatever others may say of him, has always shown a courage equal to his convictions. Almost every-body else on the ground whom I met seemed to be ashamed or afraid of me. On the previous night I had been warned that I should not be allowed to walk through the city in the procession; fears had been ex-pressed that my presence in it would so shock the prejudices of the people of Philadelphia, as to cause the procession to be mobbed.

The members of the convention were to walk two abreast, and as I was the only colored member of the convention, the question was, as to who of my brother members would consent to walk with me? The answer was not long in coming. There was *one man* present who was broad enough to take in the whole situation, and brave enough to meet the duty of the hour; one who was neither afraid nor ashamed to own me as a man and a brother; one man of the purest Caucasian type, a poet and a scholar, brilliant as a writer, eloquent as a speaker, and holding a high and influential position—the editor of a weekly journal having the largest circulation of any weekly paper in the city or State of New York—and that man was *Mr. Theodore Tilton*. He came to me in my isolation, seized me by the hand in a most brotherly way, and proposed to walk with me in the procession.

I have in my life been in many awkward and disagreeable positions when the presence of a friend would have been highly valued, but I think I never appreciated an act of courage and generous sentiment more highly than I did that of this brave young man when we marched through the streets of Philadelphia on this memorable day.

Well! what came of all these dark forebodings of timid men? How was my presence regarded by the populace? and what effect did it produce? I will tell you. The fears of the loyal governors who wished me excluded to propitiate the favor of the crowd, met with a signal reproof. Their apprehensions were shown to be groundless, and they were compelled, as many of them confessed to me afterwards, to own themselves entirely mistaken. The people were more enlightened and had made more progress than their leaders had supposed. An act for which those leaders expected to be pelted with stones, only brought to them unmeasured applause. Along the whole line of march my pres-ence was cheered repeatedly and enthusiastically. I was myself utterly surprised by the heartiness and unanimity of the popular approval. We were marching through a city remarkable for the depth and bitterness of its hatred of the abolition movement; a city whose populace had mobbed anti-slavery meetings, burned temperance halls and churches owned by colored people and burned down Pennsylvania Hall because it had opened its doors upon terms of equality to people of different colors. But now the children of those who had committed these out-rages and follies were applauding the very principles which their fa-thers had condemned. After the demonstrations of this first day, I found myself a welcome member of the convention, and cordial greeting took the place of cold aversion. The victory was short, signal, and complete.

During the passage of the procession, as we were marching through Chestnut street, an incident occurred which excited some interest in the crowd, and was noticed by the press at the time, and may perhaps be properly related here as a part of the story of my eventful life. It was my meeting Mrs. Amanda Sears, the daughter of my old mistress, Miss Lucretia Auld, the same Lucretia to whom I was indebted for so many acts of kindness when under the rough treatment of Aunt Katy, at the "old plantation home" of Col. Edward Lloyd. Mrs. Sears now resided in Baltimore, and as I saw her on the corner of Ninth and Chestnut streets, I hastily ran to her, and expressed my surprise and joy at meeting her. "But what brought you to Philadelphia at this time?" I asked. She replied, with animated voice and countenance, "I heard you were to be here, and I came to see you walk in this procession." The dear lady, with her two children, had been following us for hours. There was the daughter of the owner of a slave, following with enthusiasm that slave as a free man, and listening with joy to the plaudits he received as he marched along through the crowded streets of the great city. And here I may relate another circumstance which should have found place earlier in this story, which will further explain the feeling subsisting between Mrs. Sears and myself.

Seven years prior to our meeting, as just described, I delivered a lecture in National Hall, Philadelphia, and at its close a gentleman approached me and said, "Mr. Douglass, do you know that your once mistress has been listening to you tonight?" I replied that I did not, nor was I inclined to believe it. I had four or five times before had a similar statement made to me by different individuals in different States and this made me skeptical in this instance. The next morning, however, I received from a Mr. Wm. Needles a very elegantly written note, which stated that she who was Amanda Auld, daughter of Thomas and Lucretia Auld, and granddaughter to my old master, Capt. Aaron Anthony, was now married to Mr. John L. Sears, a coal merchant in West Philadelphia. The street and number of Mr. Sears's office was given, so that I might, by seeing him, assure myself of the facts in the case, and perhaps learn something of the relatives whom I left in slavery. This note, with the intimation given me the night before, convinced me there was something in it, and I resolved to know the truth. I had now been out of slavery twenty years, and no word had come to me from my sisters, or my brother Perry, or my grandmother. My separation had been as complete as if I had been an inhabitant of another planet. A law of Maryland at that time visited with heavy fine and imprisonment any colored person who should come into the State; so I could not go to them any more than they could come to me.

Eager to know if my kinsfolk still lived, and what was their condition, I made my way to the office of Mr. Sears, found him in, and handed him the note I had received from Mr. Needles, and asked him to be so kind as to read it and to tell me if the facts were as there stated. After reading the note, he said it was true but he must decline any conversation with me, since not to do so would be a sacrifice to the feelings of his father-in-law. I deeply regretted his decision, spoke of my long separation from my relations and appealed to him to give me some information concerning them. I saw that my words were not without their effect. Presently he said, "You publish a newspaper, I believe?" "I do," I said, "but if that is your objection to speaking with me, no word of our conversation shall go into its columns." To make a long story short, we had then quite a long conversation, during which Mr. Sears said that in my "Narrative" I had done his father-in-law injustice, for he was really a kind-hearted man, and a good master. I replied that there must be two sides to the relation of master and slave, and what was deemed kind and just to the one was the opposite to the other. Mr. Sears was not disposed to be unreasonable and the longer we talked the nearer we came together. I finally asked permission to see Mrs. Sears, the little girl of seven or eight years when I left the eastern shore of Maryland. This request was at first a little too much for him, and he put me off by saying that she was a mere child when I last saw her and that she was now the mother of a large family of children and I would not know her. He, as well as she, could tell me everything about my people. I pressed my suit, however, insisting that I could select Miss Amanda out of a thousand other ladies, my recollection of her was so perfect, and begged him to test my memory at this point. After much parley of this nature, he at length consented to my wishes, giving me the number of his house and name of street, with permission to call at three o'clock P.M. on the next day. I left him, delighted, and prompt to the hour was ready for my visit. I dressed myself in my best, and hired the finest carriage I could get to take me, partly because of the distance, and partly to make the contrast between the slave and the free man as striking as possible. Mr. Sears had been equally thoughtful. He had invited to his house a number of friends to witness the meeting between Mrs. Sears and myself.

I was somewhat disconcerted when I was ushered into the large parlors occupied by about thirty ladies and gentlemen, to all of whom I was a perfect stranger. I saw the design to test my memory by making it difficult for me to guess who of the company was "Miss Amanda." In her girlhood she was small and slender, and hence a thin and delicately-formed lady was seated in a rocking-chair near the center of the room with a little girl by her side. The device was good, but it did not succeed. Glancing around the room, I saw in an instant the lady who was a child twenty-five years before, and the wife and mother now. Satisfied of this, I said, "Mr. Sears, if you will allow me,

I will select Miss Amanda from this company." I started towards her, and she, seeing that I recognized her, bounded to me with joy in every feature, and expressed her great happiness at seeing me. All thought of slavery, color, or what might seem to belong to the dignity of her position vanished, and the meeting was as the meeting of friends long separated, yet still present in each other's memory and affection.

Amanda made haste to tell me that she agreed with me about slavery, and that she had freed all her slaves as they had become of age. She brought her children to me, and I took them in my arms, with sensations which I could not if I would stop here to describe. One explanation of the feeling of this lady towards me was, that her mother, who died when she was yet a tender child, had been briefly described by me in a little "Narrative of my life," published many years before our meeting, and when I could have had no motive but the highest for what I said of her. She had read my story and had through me learned something of the amiable qualities of her mother. She also recollected that as I had had trials as a slave she had had her trials under the care of a stepmother, and that when she was harshly spoken to by her father's second wife she could always read in my dark face the sympathy of one who had often received kind words from the lips of her beloved mother. Mrs. Sears died three years ago in Baltimore, but she did not depart without calling me to her bedside, that I might tell her as much as I could about her mother, whom she was firm in the faith that she should meet in another and better world. She especially wished me to describe to her the personal appearance of her mother, and desired to know if any of her own children then present resembled her. I told her that the young lady standing in the corner of the room was the image of her mother in form and features. She looked at her daughter and said, "Her name is Lucretia—after my mother." After telling me that her life had been a happy one, and thanking me for coming to see her on her death-bed, she said she was ready to die. We parted to meet no more in life. The interview touched me deeply, and [was,] I could not help thinking, a strange one—another proof that "truth is often stranger than fiction."

If any reader of this part of my life shall see in it the evidence of a want of manly resentment for wrongs inflicted by slavery upon myself and race, and by the ancestors of this lady, so it must be. No man can be stronger than nature, one touch of which, we are told, makes all the world akin. I esteem myself a good, persistent hater of injustice and oppression, but my resentment ceases when they cease, and I have no heart to visit upon children the sins of their fathers.

It will be noticed that when I first met Mr. Sears in Philadelphia he declined to talk with me, on the ground that I had been unjust to Captain Auld, his father-in-law. Soon after that meeting Captain Auld had occasion to go to Philadelphia, and, as usual, went straight to the house of his son-in-law. He had hardly finished the ordinary salutations when he said: "Sears, I see by the papers that Frederick has recently been in Philadelphia. Did you go to hear him?" "Yes, sir," was the reply. After asking something about my lecture he said, "Well, Sears, did Frederick come to see you?" "Yes, sir," said Sears. "Well, how did you receive him?" Mr. Sears then told him all about my visit, and had the satisfaction of hearing the old man say that he had done right in giving me welcome to his house. This last fact I have from Rev. J. D. Long, who, with his wife, was one of the party invited to meet me at the house of Mr. Sears on the occasion of my visit to Mrs. Sears.

But I must now return from this digression and further relate my experience in the loyalist national convention, and how, from that time, there was an impetus given to the enfranchisement of the freedmen which culminated in the fifteenth amendment to the Constitution of the United States. From the first the members of the convention were divided in their views of the proper measures of reconstruction, and this division was in some sense sectional. The men from the far South, strangely enough, were quite radical, while those from the border States were mostly conservative, and unhappily, these last had from the first the control of the convention. A Kentucky gentleman was made president. Its other officers were for the most part Kentuckians and all were in sentiment opposed to colored suffrage. There was a "whole heap" (to use a Kentucky phrase) of "halfness" in that State during the war for the Union, and there was much more there after the war. The Maryland delegates, with the exception of Hon. John L. Thomas, were in sympathy with Kentucky. Those from Virginia, except Hon. John Minor Botts, were unwilling to entertain the question. The result was that the convention was broken square in two. The Kentucky president declared it adjourned, and left the chair, against the earnest protests of the friends of manhood suffrage.

But the friends of this measure were not to be outgeneraled and suppressed in this way, and instantly reorganized, elected Hon. John M. Botts of Virginia president, discussed and passed resolutions in favor of enfranchising the freedmen, and thus placed the question before the country in such a manner that it could not be ignored. The delegates from the Southern States were quite in earnest, and bore themselves grandly in support of the measure; but the chief speakers and advocates of suffrage on that occasion were Mr. Theodore Tilton and Miss Anna E. Dickinson. Of course, on such a question, I could not be expected to be silent. I was called forward and responded with all the energy of my soul, for I looked upon suffrage to the Negro as the only measure which could prevent him from being thrust back into slavery.

From this time onward the question of suffrage had no rest. The rapidity with which it gained strength was more than surprising to me.

In addition to the justice of the measure, it was soon commended by events, as a political necessity. As in the case of the abolition of slavery, the white people of the rebellious States have themselves to thank for its adoption. Had they accepted with moderate grace the decision of the court to which they appealed, and the liberal conditions of peace offered to them, and united heartily with the national government in its efforts to reconstruct their shattered institutions, instead of sullenly refusing as they did their counsel and their votes to that end, they might easily have defeated the argument based upon the necessity for the measure. As it was, the question was speedily taken out of the hands of colored delegations and mere individual efforts and became a part of the policy of the Republican party, and President U.S. Grant, with his characteristic nerve and clear perception of justice, promptly recommended the great amendment to the Constitution by which colored men are to-day invested with complete citizenship—the right to vote and to be voted for in the American Republic.

CHAPTER XV

Weighed in the Balance

The most of my story is now before the reader. Whatever of good or ill the future may have in store for me, the past at least is secure. As I review the last decade up to the present writing, I am impressed with a sense of completeness; a sort of rounding up of the arch to the point where the keystone may be inserted, the scaffolding removed, and the work, with all its perfections or faults, left to speak for itself. This decade, from 1871 to 1881, has been crowded, if time is capable of being thus described, with incidents and events which may well enough be accounted remarkable. To me they certainly appear strange, if not wonderful. My early life not only gave no visible promise, but no hint of such experience. On the contrary, that life seemed to render it, in part at least, impossible. In addition to what is narrated in the foregoing chapter, I have, as belonging to this decade, to speak of my mission to Santo Domingo; of my appointment as a member of the council for the government of the District of Columbia; of my election as elector at large for the State of New York; of my invitation to speak at the monument of the unknown loyal dead, at Arlington, on Decoration day; of my address on the unveiling of Lincoln monument, at Lincoln Park, Washington; of my appointment to bring the electoral vote from New York to the national capital; of my invitation to speak near the statue of Abraham Lincoln, Madison Square, New York; of my accompanying the body of Vice-President Wilson from Washington to Boston; of my conversations with Senator Sumner and President Grant; of my welcome to the receptions of Secretary Hamilton Fish; of my appointment by President R. B. Hayes to the office of Marshal of the District of Columbia; of my visit to Thomas Auld, the man who claimed me as his slave, and from whom I was purchased by my English friends; of my visit, after an absence of fifty-six years, to Lloyd's plantation, the home of my childhood; and of my appointment by President James A. Garfield to the office of Recorder of Deeds of the District of Columbia.

Those who knew of my more than friendly relations with Hon. Charles Sumner, and of his determined opposition to the annexation of Santo Domingo to the United States, were surprised to find me earnestly taking sides with General Grant upon that question. Some of my white friends, and a few of those of my own color—who, unfortunately, allow themselves to look at public questions more through the medium of feeling than of reason, and who follow the line of what is grateful to their friends rather than what is consistent with their own convictions—thought my course was an ungrateful return for the eminent services of the Massachusetts senator. I am free to say that, had I been guided only by the promptings of my heart, I should in this controversy have followed the lead of Charles Sumner. He was not only the most clear-sighted, brave, and uncompromising friend of my race who had ever stood upon the floor of the Senate, but was to me a loved, honored, and precious personal friend; a man possessing the exalted and matured intellect of a statesman, with the pure and artless heart of a child. Upon any issue, as between him and others, when the right seemed in anywise doubtful, I should have followed his counsel and advice. But the annexation of Santo Domingo, to my understanding, did not seem to be any such question. The reasons in its favor were many and obvious; and those against it, as I thought, were easily answered. To Mr. Sumner, annexation was a measure to extinguish a colored nation, and to do so by dishonorable means and for selfish motives. To me it meant the alliance of a weak and defenceless people, having few or none of the attributes of a nation, torn and rent by internal feuds and unable to maintain order at home or command respect abroad, to a government which would give it peace, stability, prosperity, and civilization, and make it helpful to both countries. To favor annexation at the time when Santo Domingo asked for a place in our union, was a very different thing from what it was when Cuba and Central America were sought by fillibustering expeditions. When the slave power bore rule, and a spirit of injustice and oppression animated and controlled every part of our government, I was for limiting our dominion to the smallest possible margin; but since liberty and equality have become the law of our land, I am for extending our dominion whenever and wherever such extension can peaceably and honorably, and with the approval and desire of all the parties concerned, be accomplished. Santo Domingo wanted to come under our government upon the terms thus described; and for more reasons that I can stop here to give, I then believed, and do now believe, it would have been wise to have received her into our sisterhood of States.

The idea that annexation meant degradation to a colored nation was altogether fanciful; there was no more dishonor to Santo Domingo in making her a State of the American Union, than in making Kansas, Nebraska, or any other territory such a State. It was giving to a part the strength of the whole, and lifting what must be despised for its isolation into an organization and relationship which would compel consideration and respect.

Although I differed from Mr. Sumner in respect of this measure and although I told him that I thought he was unjust to President Grant, it never disturbed our friendship. After his great speech against annexation, which occupied six hours in its delivery, and in which he arraigned the President in a most bitter and fierce manner, being at the White House one day, I was asked by President Grant what I "now thought of my friend, Mr. Sumner"? I replied that I believed Mr. Sumner sincerely thought, that in opposing annexation, he was defending the cause of the colored race as he always had done, but that I thought he was mistaken. I saw that my reply was not very satisfactory, and said: "What do you, Mr. President, think of Senator Sumner"? He answered, with some feeling: "I think he is mad."

The difference in opinion on this question between these two great men was the cause of bitter personal estrangement, and one which I intensely regretted. The truth is, that neither one was entirely just to the other, because neither saw the other in his true character; and having once fallen asunder, the occasion never came when they could be brought together.

Variance between great men finds no healing influence in the atmosphere of Washington. Interested parties are ever ready to fan the flame of animosity and magnify the grounds of hostility in order to gain the favor of one or the other. This is perhaps true in some degree in every community; but it is especially so of the national capital, and this for the reason that there is ever a large class of people here dependent for their daily bread upon the influence and favor of powerful public men.

My selection to visit Santo Domingo with the commission sent thither, was another point indicating the difference between the OLD TIME and the NEW. It placed me on the deck of an American man-of-war, manned by one hundred marines and five hundred men-of-wars-men, under the national flag, which I could now call mine, in common with other American citizens, and gave me a place not in the forecastle, among the hands, nor in the caboose with the cooks, but in the captain's saloon and in the society of gentlemen, scientists and statesmen. It would be a pleasing task to narrate the varied experiences and the distinguished persons encountered in this Santo Domingo tour, but the material is too boundless for the limits of these pages. I can only say that it was highly interesting and instructive. The conversations at the Captain's table (at which I had the honor of a seat) were usually led by Messrs. Wade, Howe and White—the three commissioners; and by Mr. Hurlburt of the *New York World*. The last-named gentleman impressed me as one remarkable for knowledge and refinement, in which he was no whit behind Messrs. Howe and White. As for Hon. Benj. F. Wade, he was there, as everywhere, abundant in knowledge and experience, fully able to take care of himself in the discussion of any subject in which he chose to take a part. In a circle so brilliant, it is no affectation of modesty to say that I was for the most part a listener and a learner. The commander of our good ship on this voyage, Capt. Temple, now promoted to the position of Commodore, was a very imposing man, and deported himself with much dignity towards us all. For his treatment to me I am especially grateful. A son of the United States navy as he was—a department of our service considerably distinguished for its aristocratic tendencies—I expected to find something a little forbidding in his manner; but I am bound to say that in this I was agreeably disappointed. Both the commander and the officers under him bore themselves in a friendly manner towards me during all the voyage; and this is saying a great thing for them, for the spectacle presented by a colored man seated at the captain's table was not only unusual, but had never before occurred in the history of the United States navy. If, during this voyage, there was anything to complain of, it was not in the men in authority, or in the conduct of the thirty gentlemen who went out as the honored guests of the expedition, but in the colored waiters. My presence and position seemed to trouble them for its incomprehensibility, and they did not know exactly how to deport themselves towards me. Possibly they may have detected in me something of the same sort in respect of themselves; at any rate, we seemed awkwardly related to each other during several weeks of the voyage. In their eyes I was Fred. Douglass, suddenly, and possibly undeservedly, lifted above them. The fact that I was colored and they were colored had so long made us equal, that the contradiction now presented was too much for them. After all, I have no blame for Sam and Garrett. They were trained in the school of servility to believe that white men alone were entitled to be waited upon by colored men; and the lesson taught by my presence on the "Tennessee" was not to be learned upon the instant, without thought and experience. I refer to the matter simply as an incident quite commonly met with in the lives of colored men who, by their own exertions or otherwise, have happened to occupy positions of respectability and honor. While the rank and file of our race quote, with much vehemence, the doctrine of human equality, they are often among the first to deny and denounce it in practice. Of course this is true only of the more ignorant. Intelligence is a great leveler here as elsewhere. It sees plainly the real worth of men and things, and is not easily imposed upon by the dressed-up emptiness of human pride.

With a colored man on a sleeping-car as its conductor, the last to have his bed made up at night, and the last to have his boots blacked in the morning, and the last to be served in any way, is the colored passenger. This conduct is the homage which the black man pays to the white man's prejudice, whose wishes, like a well-trained servant, he is taught to anticipate and obey. Time, education, and circumstances are rapidly destroying these mere color distinctions, and men will be valued in this country, as well as in others, for what they are and for what they can do.

My appointment at the hands of President Grant to a seat in the council—by way of eminence sometimes called the upper house of the territorial legislature of the District of Columbia—must be taken as, at the time it was made, a signal evidence of his high sense of justice, fairness, and impartiality. The colored people of the district constituted then, as now, about one-third of the whole population. They were given by Gen. Grant, three members of this legislative council—a representation more proportionate than any that has existed since the government has passed into the hands of commissioners, for they have all been white men.

It has sometimes been asked why I am called "Honorable." My appointment to this council must explain this, as it explains the impartiality of Gen. Grant, though I fear it will hardly sustain this prodigious handle to my name, as well as it does the former part of this proposition. The members of this district council were required to be appointed by the President, with the advice and consent of the United States Senate. This is the ground, and only ground that I know of, upon which anybody has claimed this title for me. I do not pretend that the foundation is a very good one, but as I have generally allowed people to call me what they have pleased, and as there is nothing necessarily dishonorable in this, I have never taken the pains to dispute its application and propriety; and yet I confess that I am never so spoken of without feeling a trifle uncomfortable—about as much so as when I am called, as I sometimes am, the *Rev.* Frederick Douglass. My stay in this legislative body was of short duration. My vocation abroad left me little time to study the many matters of local legislation; hence my resignation, and the appointment of my son Lewis to fill out my term.

I have thus far told my story without copious quotations from my letters, speeches, or other writings, and shall not depart from this rule in what remains to be told, except to insert here my speech, delivered at Arlington, near the monument to the "Unknown Loyal Dead," on Decoration Day, 1871. It was delivered under impressive circumstances, in presence of President Grant, his Cabinet, and a great multitude of distinguished people, and expresses, as I think, the true view which should be taken of the great conflict between slavery and freedom to which it refers.

"Friends and Fellow Citizens: Tarry here for a moment. My words shall be few and simple. The solemn rites of this hour and place call for no lengthened speech. There is, in the very air of this resting-ground of the unknown dead a silent, subtle and all-pervading eloquence, far more touching, impressive, and thrilling than living lips have ever uttered. Into the measureless depths of every loyal soul it is now whispering lessons of all that is precious, priceless, holiest, and most enduring in human existence.

"Dark and sad will be the hour to this nation when it forgets to pay grateful homage to its greatest benefactors. The offering we bring to-day is due alike to the patriot soldiers dead and their noble comrades who still live; for, whether living or dead, whether in time or eternity, the loyal soldiers who imperiled all for country and freedom are one and inseparable.

"Those unknown heroes whose whitened bones have been piously gathered here, and whose green graves we now strew with sweet and beautiful flowers, choice emblems alike of pure hearts and brave spirits, reached, in their glorious career that last highest point of nobleness beyond which human power cannot go. They died for their country.

"No loftier tribute can be paid to the most illustrious of all the benefactors of mankind than we pay to these unrecognized soldiers when we write above their graves this shining epitaph.

"When the dark and vengeful spirit of slavery, always ambitious, preferring to rule in hell than to serve in heaven, fired the Southern heart and stirred all the malign elements of discord, when our great Republic, the hope of freedom and self-government throughout the world, had reached the point of supreme peril, when the Union of these States was torn and rent asunder at the center, and the armies of a gigantic rebellion came forth with broad blades and bloody hands to destroy the very foundation of American society, the unknown braves who flung themselves into the yawning chasm, where cannon roared and bullets whistled, fought and fell. They died for their country.

"We are sometimes asked, in the name of patriotism, to forget the merits of this fearful struggle, and to remember with equal admiration those who struck at the nation's life and those who struck to save it, those who fought for slavery and those who fought for liberty and justice.

"I am no minister of malice. I would not strike the fallen. I would not repel the repentant; but may my 'right hand forget her cunning and my tongue cleave to the roof of my mouth,' if I forget the difference between the parties to that terrible, protracted, and bloody conflict.

"If we ought to forget a war which has filled our land with widows and orphans; which has made stumps of men of the very flower of our youth; which has sent them on the journey of life armless, legless, maimed and mutilated; which has piled up a debt heavier than a mountain of gold, swept uncounted thousands of men into bloody graves and planted agony at a million hearthstones—I say, if this war is to be forgotten, I ask, in the name of all things sacred, what shall men remember?

"The essence and significance of our devotions here to-day are not to be found in the fact that the men whose remains fill these graves were brave in battle. If we met simply to show our sense of bravery, we should find enough on both sides to kindle admiration. In the raging storm of fire and blood, in the fierce torrent of shot and shell, of sword and bayonet, whether on foot or on horse, unflinching courage marked the rebel not less than the loyal soldier.

"But we are not here to applaud manly courage, save as it has been displayed in a noble cause. We must never forget that victory to the rebellion meant death to the republic. We must never forget that the loyal soldiers who rest beneath this sod flung themselves between the nation and the nation's destroyers. If to-day we have a country not boiling in an agony of blood, like France, if now we have a united country, no longer cursed by the hell-black system of human bondage, if the American name is no longer a by-word and a hissing to a mocking earth, if the star-spangled banner floats only over free American citizens in every quarter of the land, and our country has before it a long and glorious career of justice, liberty, and civilization, we are indebted to the unselfish devotion of the noble army who rest in these honored graves all around us."

In the month of April, 1872, I had the honor to attend and preside over a national convention of colored citizens held in New Orleans. It was a critical period in the history of the Republican party, as well as in that of the country. Eminent men who had hitherto been looked upon as the pillars of republicanism had become dissatisfied with President Grant's administration, and determined to defeat his nomination for a second term. The leaders in this unfortunate revolt were Messrs. Trumbull, Schurz, Greeley, and Sumner. Mr. Schurz had already succeeded in destroying the Republican party in the State of Missouri. It seemed to be his ambition to be the founder of a new party; and to him more than to any other man belongs the credit of what was once known as the Liberal-Republican party, which made Horace Greeley its standard-bearer in the campaign of that year.

At the time of the convention in New Orleans the elements of this new combination were just coming together. The division in the Republican ranks seemed to be growing deeper and broader every day. The colored people of the country were much affected by the threatened disruption, and their leaders were much divided as to the side upon which they should give their voice and their votes. The names of Greeley and Sumner, on account of their long and earnest advocacy of justice and liberty to the blacks, had powerful attractions for the newly-enfranchised class, and there was in this convention at New Orleans naturally enough a strong disposition to fraternize with the new party and follow the lead of their old friends. Against this policy I exerted whatever influence I possessed, and, I think, succeeded in holding back that convention from what I felt sure then would have been a fatal political blunder, and time has proved the correctness of that position. My speech on taking the chair on that occasion was telegraphed in full from New Orleans to the New York *Herald*, and the key-note of it was that there was no path out of the Republican party that did not lead directly into the Democratic party—away from our friends and directly to our enemies. Happily this convention pretty largely agreed with me, and its members have not since regretted that agreement.

From this convention onward, until the nomination and election of Grant and Wilson, I was actively engaged on the stump, a part of the time in Virginia with Hon. Henry Wilson, in North Carolina with John M. Langston and John H. Smyth, and in the State of Maine with Senator Hamlin, Gen. B. F. Butler, Gen. Woodford, and Hon. James G. Blaine.

Since 1872 I have been regularly what my old friend Parker Pillsbury would call a "field hand" in every important political campaign, and at each national convention have sided with what has been called the stalwart element of the Republican party. It was in the Grant presidential campaign that New York took an advanced step in the renunciation of a timid policy. The Republicans of that State, not having the fear of popular prejudice before their eyes, placed my name as an elector at large at the head of their presidential ticket. Considering the deep-rooted sentiment of the masses against Negroes, the noise and tumult likely to be raised, especially among our adopted citizens of Irish descent, this was a bold and manly proceeding, and one for which the Republicans of the State of New York deserve the gratitude of every colored citizen of the Republic, for it was a blow at popular prejudice in a quarter where it was capable of making the strongest resistance. The result proved not only the justice and generosity of the measure, but its wisdom. The Republicans carried the Sate by a majority of fifty thousand over the heads of the Liberal-Republican and Democratic parties combined.

Equally significant of the turn now taken in the political sentiment of the country was the action of the Republican electoral college at its meeting in Albany, when it committed to my custody the sealed-up electoral vote of the great State of New York and commissioned me to bring that vote to the national capital. Only a few years before this any colored man was forbidden by law to carry a United States mail bag from one post-office to another. He was not allowed to touch the sacred leather, though locked in "triple steel," but now not a mail bag, but a document which was to decide the presidential question with all its momentous interests, was committed to the hands of one of this despised class, and around him, in the execution of his high trust, was thrown all the safeguards provided by the Constitution and the laws of the land. Though I worked hard and long to secure the nomination and election of Gen. Grant in 1872, I neither received nor sought office from him. He was my choice upon grounds altogether free from selfish or personal considerations. I supported him because he had done all, and would do all, he could to save not only the country from ruin but the emancipated class from oppression and ultimate destruction, and because Mr. Greeley, with the Democratic party behind him, would not have the power, even if he had the disposition, to afford us the needed protection which our peculiar condition required. I could easily have secured the appointment as minister to Hayti, but preferred to urge the claims of my friend Ebenezer Bassett, a gentleman and a scholar, and a man well fitted by his good sense and amiable qualities to fill the position with credit to himself and his country. It is with a certain degree of pride that I am able to say that my opinion of the wisdom of sending Mr. Bassett to Hayti has been fully justified by the creditable manner in which, for eight years, he discharged the difficult duties of that position, for I have the assurance of Hon. Hamilton Fish, Secretary of State of the United States, that Mr. Bassett was a good minister. In so many words the ex-Secretary told me that he "wished that one-half of his ministers abroad performed their duties as well as Mr. Bassett." To those who know Hon. Hamilton Fish this compliment will not be deemed slight, for few men are less given to exaggeration and are more scrupulously exact in the observance of law and in the use of language than is that gentleman. While speaking in this strain of complacency in reference to Mr. Bassett, I take pleasure also in bearing my testimony, based upon knowledge obtained at the State Department, that Mr. John Mercer Langston, the present minister to Hayti, has acquitted himself with equal wisdom and ability to that of Mr. Bassett in the same position. Having known both these gentlemen in their youth, when the one was at Yale and the other at Oberlin College, and witnessed their efforts to qualify themselves for positions of usefulness, it has afforded me no limited satisfaction to see them rise in the world. Such men increase the faith of all in the possibilities of their race, and make it easier for those who are to come after them.

The unveiling of Lincoln monument in Lincoln Park, Washington, April 14, 1876, and the part taken by me in the ceremonies of that grand occasion, takes rank among the most interesting incidents of my life, since it brought me into mental communication with a greater number of the influential and distinguished men of the country than any I had before known. There were present the President of the United States and his Cabinet, judges of the Supreme Court, the Senate and House of Representatives, and many thousands of citizens to listen to my address upon the illustrious man to whose memory the colored people of the United States had, as a mark of their gratitude, erected that impressive monument. Occasions like this have done wonders in the removal of popular prejudice and lifting into consideration the colored race, and I reckon it one of the high privileges of my life that I was permitted to have a share in this and several other like celebrations.

The progress of a nation is sometimes indicated by small things. When Henry Wilson, an honored Senator and Vice-President of the United States, died in the Capitol of the nation, it was a significant and telling indication of national advance, that three colored citizens, Mr. Robert Purvis, Mr. James Wormley and myself, were selected with the Senate Committee, to accompany his honored remains from Washington to the grand old commonwealth he loved so well, and whom in turn she had so greatly loved and honored. It was meet and right that we should be represented in the long procession that met those remains in every State between here and Massachusetts, for Henry Wilson was among the foremost friends of the colored race in this country, and this was the first time in its history that a colored man had been made a pall-bearer at the funeral, as I was in this instance, of a Vice-President of the United States.

An appointment to any important and lucrative office under the United States government usually brings its recipient a large measure of praise and congratulation on the one hand, and much abuse and disparagement on the other; and he may think himself singularly fortunate if the censure does not exceed the praise. I need not dwell upon the causes of this extravagance, but I may say that there is no office of any value in the country which is not desired and sought by many persons equally meritorious and equally deserving. But as only one person can be appointed to any office, only one can be pleased, while many are offended. Unhappily, resentment follows disappointment, and this resentment often finds expression in disparagement and abuse of the successful man. As in most else that I have said, I borrow this reflection from my own experience.

My appointment as United States Marshal of the District of Columbia, was in keeping with the rest of my life, as a freeman. It was an innovation upon long established usage, and opposed to the general current of sentiment in the community. It came upon the people of the District as a gross surprise, and almost a punishment; and provoked something like a scream—I will not say a *yell*—of popular displeasure. As soon as I was named by President Hayes for the place, efforts were made by members of the bar to defeat my confirmation before the Senate. All sorts of reasons against my appointment, but the true one, were given, and that was withheld more from a sense of shame, than from a sense of justice. The apprehension doubtless was, that if appointed marshal, I would surround myself with colored deputies, colored bailiffs and colored messengers and pack the jury-box with colored jurors; in a word, Africanize the courts. But the most dreadful thing threatened, was a colored man at the *Executive Mansion* in white kid gloves, sparrow-tailed coat, patent-leather boots, and alabaster cravat, performing the ceremony—a very empty one—of introducing the aristocratic citizens of the republic to the President of the United States. This was something entirely too much to be borne; and men asked themselves in view of it, To what is the world coming? and where will these things stop? Dreadful! Dreadful!

It is creditable to the manliness of the American Senate, that it was moved by none of these things, and that it lost no time in the matter of my confirmation. I learn, and believe my information correct, that foremost among those who supported my confirmation against the objections made to it, was Hon. Roscoe Conkling of New York. His speech in executive session is said by the senators who heard it, to have been one of the most masterly and eloquent ever delivered on the floor of the Senate; and this too I readily believe, for Mr. Conkling possesses the ardor and fire of Henry Clay, the subtlety of Calhoun, and the massive grandeur of Daniel Webster.

The effort to prevent my confirmation having failed, nothing could be done but to wait for some overt act to justify my removal; and for this my *un*friends had not long to wait. In the course of one or two months I was invited by a number of citizens of Baltimore to deliver a lecture in that city, in Douglass Hall—a building named in honor of myself, and devoted to educational purposes. With this invitation I complied, giving the same lecture which I had two years before delivered in the city of Washington, and which was at the time published in full in the newspapers, and very highly commended by them. The subject of the lecture was, "Our National Capital," and in it I said many complimentary things of the city, which were as true as they were complimentary. I spoke of what it had been in the past, what it was at that time, and what I thought it destined to become in the future; giving it all credit for its good points, and calling attention to some of its ridiculous features. For this I got myself pretty roughly handled. The newspapers worked themselves up to a frenzy of passion, and committees were appointed to procure names to a petition to President Hayes demanding my removal. The tide of popular feeling was so violent, that I deemed it necessary to depart from my usual custom when assailed, so far as to write the following explanatory letter, from which the reader will be able to measure the extent and quality of my offense:

"To the Editor of the Washington Evening *Star:*

"Sir:—You were mistaken in representing me as being off on a lecturing tour, and, by implication, neglecting my duties as United States Marshal of the District of Columbia. My absence from Washington during two days was due to an invitation by the managers to be present on the occasion of the inauguration of the International Exhibition in Philadelphia.

"In complying with this invitation, I found myself in company with other members of the government who went thither in obedience to the call of patriotism and civilization. No[t] one interest of the Marshal's office suffered by my temporary absence, as I had seen to it that those upon whom the duties of the office devolved were honest, capable, industrious, painstaking, and faithful. My Deputy Marshal is a man every way qualified for his position, and the citizens of Washington may rest assured that no unfaithful man will be retained in any position under me. Of course I can have nothing to say as to my own fitness for the position I hold. You have a right to say what you please on that point; yet I think it would be only fair and generous to wait for some dereliction of duty on my part before I shall be adjudged as incompetent to fill the place.

"You will allow me to say also that the attacks upon me on account of the remarks alleged to have been made by me in Baltimore, strike me as both malicious and silly. Washington is a great city, not a village nor a hamlet, but the capital of a great nation, and the manners and habits of its various classes are proper subjects for presentation and criticism, and I very much mistake if this great city can be thrown into a tempest of passion by any humorous reflections I may take the liberty to utter. The city is too great to be small, and I think it will laugh at the ridiculous attempt to rouse it to a point of furious hostility to me for anything said in my Baltimore lecture.

"Had the reporters of that lecture been as careful to note what I said in praise of Washington as what I said, if you please, in disparagement of it, it would have been impossible to awaken any feeling against me in this community for what I said. It is the easiest thing in the world, as all editors know, to pervert the meaning and give a one-sided impression of a whole speech by simply giving isolated passages from the speech itself, without any qualifying connections. It would hardly be imagined from anything that has appeared here that I had said one word in that lecture in honor of Washington, and yet the lecture itself, as a whole, was decidedly in the interest of the national capital. I am not such a fool as to decry a city in which I have invested my money and made my permanent residence.

"After speaking of the power of the sentiment of patriotism I held this language: 'In the spirit of this noble sentiment I would have the American people view the national capital. It is our national center. It belongs to us; and whether it is mean or majestic, whether arrayed in glory or covered with shame, we cannot but share its character and its destiny. In the remotest section of the republic, in the most distant parts of the globe, amid the splendors of Europe or the wilds of Africa, we are still held and firmly bound to this common center. Under the shadow of Bunker Hill monument, in the peerless eloquence of his diction, I once heard the great Daniel Webster give welcome to all American citizens, assuring them that wherever else they might be strangers, they were all at home there. The same boundless welcome is given to all American citizens by Washington. Elsewhere we may belong to individual States, but here we belong to the whole United States. Elsewhere we may belong to a section, but here we belong to a whole country, and the whole country belongs to us. It is national territory, and the one place where no American is an intruder or a carpet-bagger. The new comer is not less at home than the old resident. Under its lofty domes and stately pillars, as under the broad blue sky, all races and colors of men stand upon a footing of common equality.

" 'The wealth and magnificence which elsewhere might oppress the humble citizen has an opposite effect here. They are felt to be a part of himself and serve to ennoble him in his own eyes. He is an owner of the marble grandeur which he beholds about him,—as much so as any of the forty millions of this great nation. Once in his life every American who can should visit Washington: not as the Mohametan to Mecca; not as the

Catholic to Rome; not as the Hebrew to Jerusalem, nor as the Chinaman to the Flowery kingdom, but in the spirit of enlightened patriotism, knowing the value of free institutions and how to perpetuate and maintain them.

" 'Washington should be contemplated not merely as an assemblage of fine buildings; not merely as the chosen resort of the wealth and fashion of the country; not merely as the honored place where the statesmen of the nation assemble to shape the policy and frame the laws; not merely as the point at which we are most visibly touched by the outside world, and where the diplomatic skill and talent of the old continent meet and match themselves against those of the new, but as the national flag itself—a glorious symbol of civil and religious liberty, leading the world in the race of social science, civilization, and renown.'

"My lecture in Baltimore required more than an hour and a half for its delivery, and every intelligent reader will see the difficulty of doing justice to such a speech when it is abbreviated and compressed into a half or three-quarters of a column. Such abbreviation and condensation has been resorted to in this instance. A few stray sentences, culled out from their connections, would be deprived of much of their harshness if presented in the form and connection in which they were uttered; but I am taking up too much space, and will close with the last paragraph of the lecture, as delivered in Baltimore. 'No city in the broad world has a higher or more beneficient mission. Among all the great capitals of the world it is preeminently the capital of free institutions. Its fall would be a blow to freedom and progress throughout the world. Let it stand then where it does now stand—where the father of his country planted it, and where it has stood for more than half a century; no longer sandwiched between two slave States; no longer a contradiction to human progress; no longer the hot-bed of slavery and the slave trade; no longer the home of the duelist, the gambler, and the assassin; no longer the frantic partisan of one section of the country against the other; no longer anchored to a dark and semi-barbarous past, but a redeemed city, beautiful to the eye and attractive to the heart, a bond of perpetual union, an angel of peace on earth and good will to men, a common ground upon which Americans of all races and colors, all sections, North and South, may meet and shake hands, not over a chasm of blood, but over a free, united, and progressive republic.' "

I have already alluded to the fact that much of the opposition to my appointment to the office of United States Marshal of the District of Columbia was due to the possibility of my being called to attend President Hayes at the Executive Mansion upon state occasions, and having the honor to introduce the guests on such occasions. I now wish to refer to the reproaches liberally showered upon me for holding the office of Marshal while denied this distinguished honor, and to show that the complaint against me at this point is not a well founded complaint.

1st. Because the office of United States Marshal is distinct and separate and complete in itself, and must be accepted or refused upon its own merits. If, when offered to any person, its duties are such as he can properly fulfill, he may very properly accept it; or, if otherwise, he may as properly refuse it.

2d. Because the duties of the office are clearly and strictly defined in the law by which it was created; and because nowhere among these duties is there any mention or intermention that the Marshal may or shall attend upon the President of the United States at the Executive Mansion on state occasions.

3d. Because the choice as to who shall have the honor and privilege of such attendance upon the President belongs exclusively and reasonably to the President himself, and that therefore no one, however distinguished, or in whatever office, has any just cause to complain of the exercise by the President of this right of choice, or because he is not himself chosen.

In view of these propositions, which I hold to be indisputable, I should have presented to the country a most foolish and ridiculous figure had I, as absurdly counseled by some of my colored friends, resigned the office of Marshal of the District of Columbia, because President Rutherford B. Hayes, for reasons that must have been satisfactory to his judgment, preferred some person other than myself to attend upon him at the Executive Mansion and perform the ceremony of introducing on state occasions. But it was said, that this statement did not cover the whole ground; that it was customary for the United States Marshal of the District of Columbia to perform this social office; and that the usage had come to have almost the force of law. I met this at the time, and I meet it now by denying the binding force of this custom. No President has any right or power to make his example the rule for his successor. The custom of inviting the Marshal to perform the duty mentioned was made by a President and could be as properly unmade by a President. Besides, the usage is altogether a modern one and had its origin in peculiar circumstances and was justified by those circumstances. It was introduced by President Lincoln in the time of war when he made his old law partner and intimate acquaintance Marshal of the District, and was continued by Gen. Grant when he appointed a relative of his, Gen. Sharp, to the same office. But again, it was said that President Hayes only departed from this custom because the Marshal in my case was a colored man. The answer I made to this, and now make to it, is, that it is a gratuitous assumption and entirely begs the question. It may or may not be true that my complexion was the cause of this departure, but no man has any right to assume that position in advance of a plain declaration to that effect by President Hayes himself. Never have I heard from him any such declaration or intimation. In so far as my intercourse with him is concerned, I can say that I at no time discovered in him a feeling of aversion to me on account of my complexion, or on any other account, and, unless I am greatly deceived, I was ever a welcome visitor at the Executive Mansion on state occasions and all others, while Rutherford B. Hayes was President of the United States. I have further to say that I have many times during his administration had the honor to introduce distinguished strangers to him, both of native and foreign birth, and never had reason to feel myself slighted by himself or his amiable wife; and I think he would be a very unreasonable man who could desire for himself, or for any other, a larger measure of respect and consideration than this at the hands of a man and woman occupying the exalted positions of Mr. and Mrs. Hayes.

I should not do entire justice to the Honorable ex-President if I did not bear additional testimony to his noble and generous spirit. When all Washington was in an uproar, and a wild clamor rent the air for my removal from the office of Marshal on account of the lecture delivered by me in Baltimore and when petitions were flowing in upon him demanding my degradation, he nobly rebuked the mad spirit of persecution by openly declaring his purpose to retain me in my place.

One other word. During the tumult raised against me in consequence of this lecture on the "National Capital," Mr. Columbus Alexander, one of the old and wealthy citizens of Washington, who was on my bond for twenty thousand dollars, was repeatedly besought to withdraw his name, and thus leave me disqualified; but like the President, both he and my other bondsman, Mr. George Hill, Jr., were steadfast and immovable. I was not surprised that Mr. Hill stood bravely by me, for he was a Republican; but I was surprised and gratified that Mr. Alexander, a Democrat, and, I believe, once a slaveholder, had not only the courage, but the magnanimity to give me fair play in this fight. What I have said of these gentlemen, can be extended to very few others in this community, during that period of excitement, among either the white or colored citizens, for, with the exception of Dr. Charles B. Purvis, no colored man in the city uttered one public word in defence or extenuation of me or of my Baltimore speech.

This violent hostility kindled against me was singularly evanescent. It came like a whirlwind, and like a whirlwind departed. I soon saw nothing of it, either in the courts among the lawyers, or on the streets among the people; for it was discovered that there was really in my speech at Baltimore nothing which made me "worthy of stripes or of bonds."

I can say of my experience in the office of United States Marshal of the District of Columbia that it was every way agreeable. When it was an open question whether I should take the office or not, it was apprehended and predicted that, if I should accept it in face of the opposition of the lawyers and judges of the courts, I should be subjected to numberless suits for damages and so vexed and worried that the office would be rendered valueless to me and that it would not only eat up my salary, but possibly endanger what little I might have laid up for a rainy day. I have now to report that this apprehension was in no sense realized. What might have happened had the members of the District bar been half as malicious and spiteful as they had been industriously represented as being, or if I had not secured as my assistant a man so capable, industrious, vigilant, and careful as Mr. L. P. Williams, of course I cannot know. But I am bound to praise the bridge that carries me safely over it. I think it will ever stand as a witness to my fitness for the position of Marshal, that I had the wisdom to select for my assistant a gentleman so well instructed and competent. I also take pleasure in bearing testimony to the generosity of Mr. Phillips, the Assistant Marshal who preceded Mr. Williams in that office, in giving the new assistant valuable information as to the various duties he would be called upon to perform. I have further to say of my experience in the Marshal's office, that while I have reason to know that the eminent Chief Justice of the District of Columbia and some of his associates were not well pleased with my appointment, I was always treated by them, as well as by the chief clerk of the courts, Hon. J. R. Meigs, and the subordinates of the latter (with a single exception), with the respect and consideration due to my office. Among the eminent lawyers of the District I believe I had many friends, and there were those of them to whom I could always go with confidence in an emergency for sound advice and direction, and this fact, after all the hostility felt in consequence of my appointment, and revived by my speech at Baltimore, is another proof of the vincibility of all feelings arising out of popular prejudices.

In all my forty years of thought and labor to promote the freedom and welfare of my race, I never found myself more widely and painfully at variance with leading colored men of the country than when I opposed the effort to set in motion a wholesale exodus of colored people of the South to the Northern States; and yet I never took a position in which I felt myself better fortified by reason and necessity. It was said of me, that I had deserted to the old master class, and that I was a traitor to my race; that I had run away from slavery myself, and yet I was opposing others in doing the same. When my opponents condescended to argue, they took the ground that the colored people of the South needed to be brought into contact with the freedom and civilization of the North; that no emancipated and persecuted people ever had or ever could rise in the presence of the people by whom they had been enslaved, and that the true remedy for the ills which the freedmen were suffering, was to initiate the Israelitish departure from our modern Egypt to a land abounding, if not in "milk and honey," certainly in pork and hominy.

Influenced, no doubt, by the dazzling prospects held out to them by the advocates of the exodus movement, thousands of poor, hungry, naked and destitute colored people were induced to quit the South amid the frosts and snows of a dreadful winter in search of a better country. I regret to say that there was something sinister in this so-called exodus, for it transpired that some of the agents most active in promoting it had an understanding with certain railroad companies, by which they were to receive one dollar per head upon all such passengers. Thousands of these poor people, traveling only so far as they had money to bear their expenses, were dropped in the extremest destitution on the levees of St. Louis, and their tales of woe were such as to move a heart much less sensitive to human suffering than mine. But while I felt for these poor deluded people, and did what I could to put a stop to their ill-advised and ill-arranged stampede, I also did what I could to assist such of them as were within my reach, who were on their way to this land of promise. Hundreds of these people came to Washington, and at one time there were from two to three hundred lodged here unable to get further for the want of money. I lost no time in appealing to my friends for the means of assisting them. Conspicuous among these friends was Mrs. Elizabeth Thompson of New York city—the lady who, several years ago, made the nation a present of Carpenter's great historical picture of the "Signing of the Emancipation Proclamation," and who had expended large sums of her money in investigating the causes of yellow-fever, and in endeavors to discover means for preventing its ravages in New Orleans and elsewhere. I found Mrs. Thompson consistently alive to the claims of humanity in this, as in other instances, for she sent me, without delay, a draft for two hundred and fifty dollars, and in doing so expressed the wish that I would promptly inform her of any other opportunity of doing good. How little justice was done me by those who accused me of indifference to the welfare of the colored people of the South on account of my opposition to the so-called exodus will be seen by the following extracts from a paper on that subject laid before the Social Science Congress at Saratoga, when the question was before the country:

"Important as manual labor everywhere is, it is nowhere more important and absolutely indispensable to the existence of society than in the more southern of the United States. Machinery may continue to do, as it has done, much of the work of the North, but the work of the South requires for its performance bone, sinew and muscle of the strongest and most enduring kind. Labor in that section must know no pause. Her soil is pregnant and prolific with life and energy. All the forces of nature within her borders are wonderfully vigorous, persistent, and active. Aided by an almost perpetual summer, abundantly supplied with heat and moisture, her soil readily and rapidly covers itself with noxious weeds, dense forests, and impenetrable jungles. Only a few years of non-tillage would be needed to give the sunny and fruitful South to the bats and owls of a desolate wilderness. From this condition, shocking for a southern man to contemplate, it is now seen that nothing less powerful than the naked iron arm of the negro can save her. For him, as a Southern laborer there is no competitor or substitute. The thought of filling his place by any other variety of the human family, will be found delusive and utterly impracticable. Neither Chinaman, German, Norwegian, nor Swede can drive him from the sugar and cotton fields of Louisiana and Mississippi. They would certainly perish in the black bottoms of these States if they could be induced, which they cannot, to try the experiment.

"Nature itself, in those States, comes to the rescue of the negro, fights his battles, and enables him to exact conditions from those who would unfairly treat and oppress him. Besides being dependent upon the roughest and flintiest kind of labor, the climate of the South makes such labor uninviting and harshly repulsive to the white man. He dreads it, shrinks from it, and refuses it. He shuns the burning sun of the fields, and seeks the shade of the verandas. On the contrary, the negro walks, labors, and sleeps in the sunlight unharmed. The standing apology for slavery was based upon a knowledge of this fact. It was said that the world must have cotton and sugar, and that only the negro could supply this want; and that he could be induced to do it only under the 'beneficent whip' of some bloodthirsty *Legree*. The last part of this argument has been happily disproved by the large crops of these productions since Emancipation; but the first part of it stands firm, unassailed, and unassailable.

"Even if climate and other natural causes did not protect the negro from all competition in the labor-market of the South, inevitable social causes would probably effect the same result. The slave system of that section has left behind it, as in the nature of the case it must, manners, customs, and conditions to which free white laboring men will be in no haste to submit themselves and their families. They do not emigrate from the free North, where labor is respected, to a lately enslaved South, where labor has for centuries been whipped, chained and degraded. Naturally enough such emigration follows the lines of latitude in which they who compose it were born. Not from South to North, but from East to West 'the Star of Empire takes its way.'

"Hence it is seen that the dependence upon the negro of the planters, land-owners, and the old master-class of the South, however galling and humiliating to Southern pride and power, is nearly complete and perfect. There is only one mode of escape for them, and that mode they will certainly not adopt. It is to take off their own coats, cease to whittle sticks and talk politics at cross-roads, and go themselves to work in their broad and sunny fields of cotton and sugar. An invitation to do this is about as harsh and distasteful to all their inclinations as would be an invitation to step down into their graves. With the negro all this is different. Neither natural, artificial nor traditional causes stand in the way of the freedman's laboring in the South. Neither the heat nor the fever-demon which lurks in her tangled and oozy swamps affrights him, and he stands to-day the admitted author of whatever prosperity, beauty, and civilization are now possessed by the South, and the admitted arbiter of her destiny.

"This, then, is the high vantage ground of the negro; he has labor; the South wants it, and must have it or perish. Since he is free he can now give it or withhold it; use it where he is, or take it elsewhere as he pleases. His labor made him a slave, and his labor can, if he will, make him free, comfortable, and independent. It is more to him than fire, swords, ballot-boxes, or bayonets. It touches the heart of the South through its pocket. This power served him well years ago, when in the bitterest extremity of destitution. But for it he would have perished when he dropped out of slavery. It saved him then, and it will save him again. Emancipation came to him surrounded by extremely unfriendly circumstances. It was not the choice or consent of the people among whom he lived, but against their will and a death struggle on their part to prevent it. His chains were broken in the tempest and whirlwind of civil war. Without food, without shelter, without land, without money, and without friends, he, with his children, his sick, his aged and helpless ones, were turned loose and naked to the open sky. The announcement of his freedom was instantly followed by an order from his master to quit his old quarters, and to seek bread thereafter from the hands of those who had given him his freedom. A desperate extremity was thus forced upon him at the outset of his freedom, and the world watched with humane anxiety to see what would become of him. His peril was imminent. Starvation and death stared him in the face and marked him for their victim.

"It will not soon be forgotten that, at the close of a five-hours' speech by the late Senator Sumner, in which he advocated, with unequaled learning and eloquence, the enfranchisement of the freed men, the best argument with which he was met in the Senate was, that legislation at that point would be utterly superfluous, that the negro was rapidly dying out, and must inevitably and speedily disappear and become extinct.

"Inhuman and shocking as was this consignment of millions of human beings to extinction, the extremity of the negro at that date did not contradict, but favored, the prophecy. The policy of the old master-class, dictated by passion, pride and revenge, was to make the freedom of the negro a greater calamity to him, if possible, than had been his slavery. But happily, both for the old master-class and for the recently emancipated, there came then, as there will come now, the sober second thought. The old master-class then found it had made a great mistake. It had driven away the means of its own support. It had destroyed the hands, and left the mouths. It had starved the negro and starved itself. Not even to gratify its own anger and resentment could it afford to allow its fields to go uncultivated and its tables unsupplied with food. Hence the freedman, less from humanity than cupidity, less from choice than necessity, was speedily called back to labor and life.

"But now, after fourteen years of service and fourteen years of separation from the visible presence of slavery, during which he has shown both disposition and ability to supply the labor-market of the South, and that he could do so far better as a freedman than he ever did as a slave, that more cotton and sugar can be raised by the same hands under the inspiration of liberty and hope than can be raised under the influence of bondage and the whip, he is again, alas! in the deepest trouble, again without a home, out under the open sky with his wife and little ones. He lines the sunny banks of the Mississippi, fluttering in rags and wretchedness, mournfully imploring hard-hearted steamboat captains to take him on board, while the friends of the emigration movement are diligently soliciting funds all over the North to help him away from his old home to the new Canaan of Kansas."

I am sorry to be obliged to omit the statement which here follows, of the reasons given for the Exodus movement, and my explanation of them, but from want of space I can present only such portions of the paper as express most vividly and in fewest words my position in regard to the question. I go on to say:

"Bad as is the condition of the negro to-day at the South, there was a time when it was flagrantly and incomparably worse. A few years ago he had nothing—he had not even himself. He belonged to somebody else, who could dispose of his person and his labor as he pleased. Now he has himself, his labor, and his right to dispose of one and the other as shall best suit his own happiness. He has more. He has a standing in the supreme law of the land—in the Constitution of the United States—not to be changed or affected by any conjunction of circumstances likely to occur in the immediate or remote future. The Fourteenth Amendment makes him a citizen, and the Fifteenth makes him a voter. With power behind him, at work for him, and which cannot be taken from him, the negro of the South may wisely bide his time. The situation at the moment is exceptional and transient. The permanent powers of the government are all on his side. What though for the moment the hand of violence strikes down the negro's rights in the South, those rights will revive, survive, and flourish again. They are not the only people who have been, in a moment of popular passion, maltreated and driven from the polls. The Irish and Dutch have frequently been so treated. Boston, Baltimore, and New York have been the scenes of lawless violence; but those scenes have now disappeared. . . . Without abating one jot of our horror and indignation at the outrages committed in some parts of the Southern States against the negro, we cannot but regard the present agitation of an African exodus from the South as ill-timed and, in some respects, hurtful. We stand to-day at the beginning of a grand and beneficent reaction. There is a growing recognition of the duty and obligation of the American people to guard, protect, and defend the personal and political rights of all the people of all the States, and to uphold the principles upon which rebellion was suppressed, slavery abolished, and the country saved from dismemberment and ruin.

"We see and feel to-day, as we have not seen and felt before, that the time for conciliation and trusting to the honor of the late rebels and slaveholders has passed. The President of the United States himself, while still liberal, just, and generous toward the South, has yet sounded a halt in that direction, and has bravely, firmly, and ably asserted the constitutional authority to maintain the public peace in every State in the Union and upon every day in the year, and has maintained this ground against all the powers of House and Senate.

"We stand at the gateway of a marked and decided change in the statesmanship of our rulers. Every day brings fresh and increasing evidence that we are, and of right ought to be, a nation, that Confederate notions of the nature and powers of our government ought to have perished in the rebellion which they supported, that they are anachronisms and superstitions, and no longer fit to be above ground. . . .

"At a time like this, so full of hope and courage, it is unfortunate that a cry of despair should be raised in behalf of the colored people of the South, unfortunate that men are going over the country begging in the name of the poor colored man of the South, and telling the people that the government has no power to enforce the Constitution and laws in that section, and that there is no hope for the poor negro but to plant him in the new soil of Kansas or Nebraska.

"These men do the colored people of the South a real damage. They give their enemies an advantage in the argument for their manhood and freedom. They assume their inability to take care of themselves. The country will be told of the hundreds who go to Kansas, but not of the thousands who stay in Mississippi and Louisiana.

"It will be told of the destitute who require material aid, but not of the multitude who are bravely sustaining themselves where they are.

"In Georgia the negroes are paying taxes upon six millions of dollars, in Louisiana upon forty or fifty millions, and upon unascertained sums elsewhere in the Southern States.

"Why should people who have made such progress in the course of a few years be humiliated and scandalized by exodus agents, begging money to remove them from their homes, especially at a time when every indication favors the position that the wrongs and hardships which they suffer are soon to be redressed?

"Besides the objection thus stated, it is manifest that the public and noisy advocacy of a general stampede of the colored people from the South to the North is necessarily an abandonment of the great and paramount principle of protection to person and property in every State in the Union. It is an evasion of a solemn obligation and duty. The business of this nation is to protect its citizens *where they are*, not to transport them where they will not need protection. The best that can be said of this exodus in this respect is, that it is an attempt to climb up some other way—it is an expedient, a half-way measure, and tends to weaken in the public mind a sense of the absolute right, power and duty of the government, inasmuch as it concedes, by implication at least, that on the soil of the South the law of the land cannot command obedience, the ballot-box cannot be kept pure, peaceable elections cannot be held, the Constitution cannot be enforced, and the lives and liberties of loyal and peaceable citizens cannot be protected. It is a surrender, a premature disheartening surrender, since it would secure freedom and free institutions by migration rather than by protection, by flight rather than by right, by going into a strange land rather than by staying in one's own. It leaves the whole question of equal rights on the soil of the South open and still to be settled, with the moral influence of the exodus against us, since it is a confession of the utter impracticability of equal rights and equal protection in any State where those rights may be struck down by violence.

"It does not appear that the friends of freedom should spend either time or talent in furtherance of this exodus as a desirable measure, either for the North or the South. If the people of this country cannot be protected in every State of the Union, the government of the United States is shorn of its rightful dignity and power, the late rebellion has triumphed, the sovereignty of the nation is an empty name, and the power and authority in individual States is greater than the power and authority of the United States. . . .

"The colored people of the South, just beginning to accumulate a little property, and to lay the foundation of family, should not be in haste to sell that little and be off to the banks of the Mississippi. The habit of roaming from place to place in pursuit of better conditions of existence is never a good one. A man should never leave his home for a new one till he has earnestly endeavored to make his immediate surroundings accord with his wishes. The time and energy expended in wandering from place to place, if employed in making him a comfortable home where he is, will, in nine cases out of ten, prove the best investment. No people ever did much for themselves or for the world without the sense and inspiration of native land, of a fixed home, of familiar neighborhood, and common associations. The fact of being to the manor born has an elevating power upon the mind and heart of a man. It is a more cheerful thing to be able to say, I was born here and know all the people, than to say, I am a stranger here and know none of the people.

"It cannot be doubted that, in so far as this exodus tends to promote restlessness in the colored people of the South, to unsettle their feeling of home, and to sacrifice positive advantages where they are for fancied ones in Kansas or elsewhere, it is an evil. Some have sold their little homes, their chickens, mules, and pigs, at a sacrifice, to follow the exodus. Let it be understood that you are going, and you advertise the fact that your mule has lost half its value, for your staying with him makes half his value. Let the colored people of Georgia offer their six millions' worth of property for sale, with the purpose to leave Georgia, and they will not realize half its value. Land is not worth much where there are no people to occupy it, and a mule is not worth much where there is no one to drive him.

"It may be safely asserted that, whether advocated and commended to favor on the ground that it will increase the political power of the Republican party, and thus help to make a solid North against a solid South, or upon the ground that it will increase the power and influence of the colored people as a political element, and enable them the better to protect their rights, and insure their moral and social elevation, the exodus will prove a disappointment, a mistake, and a failure; because, as to strengthening the Republican party, the emigrants will go only to those States where the Republican party is strong and solid enough already with their votes; and in respect to the other part of the argument, it will fail because it takes colored voters from a section of the country where they are sufficiently numerous to elect some of their number to places of honor and profit, and places them in a country where their proportion to other classes will be so small as not to be recognized as a political element or entitled to be represented by one of themselves. And further, because go where they will, they must for a time inevitably carry with them poverty, ignorance, and other repulsive incidents inherited from their former condition of slaves—a circumstance which is about as likely to make votes for Democrats as for Republicans, and as likely to raise up bitter prejudice against them as to raise up friends for them. . . .

"Plainly enough, the exodus is less harmful as a measure than are the arguments by which it is supported. The one is the result of a feeling of outrage and despair, but the other comes of cool, selfish calculation. One is the result of honest despair, and appeals powerfully to the sympathies of men; the other is an appeal to our selfishness, which shrinks from doing right because the way is difficult.

"Not only is the South the best locality for the Negro, on the ground of his political powers and possibilities, but it is best for him as a field of labor. He is there, as he is nowhere else, an absolute necessity. He has a monopoly of the labor market. His labor is the only labor which can successfully offer itself for sale in that market. This fact, with a little wisdom and firmness, will enable him to sell his labor there on terms more favorable to himself than he can elsewhere. As there are no competitors or substitutes, he can demand living prices with the certainty that the demand will be complied with. Exodus would deprive him of this advantage. . . .

"The Negro, as already intimated, is preëminently a Southern man. He is so both in constitution and habits, in body as well as mind. He will not only take with him to the North southern modes of labor, but southern modes of life. The careless and improvident habits of the South cannot be set aside in a generation. If they are adhered to in the North, in the fierce winds and snows of Kansas and Nebraska, the emigration must be large to keep up their numbers. . . .

"As an assertion of power by a people hitherto held in bitter contempt, as an emphatic and stinging protest against high-handed, greedy, and shameless injustice to the weak and defenseless, as a means of opening the blind eyes of oppressors to their folly and peril, the exodus has done valuable service. Whether it has accomplished all of which for the present it is capable in this direction is a question which may well be considered. With a moderate degree of intelligent leadership among the laboring class of the South properly handling the justice of its cause and wisely using the exodus example, it can easily exact better terms for its labor than ever before. Exodus is a medicine, not food; it is for disease, not health; it is not to be taken from choice, but from necessity. In anything like a normal condition of things the South is the best place for the Negro. Nowhere else is there for him a promise of a happier future. Let him stay there if he can, and save both the South and himself to civilization. While, however, it may be the highest wisdom in the circumstances for the freedmen to stay where they are, no encouragement should be given to any measures of coercion to keep them there. The American people are bound, if they are or can be bound to anything, to keep the north gate of the South open to black and white and to all the people. The time to assert a right, Webster says, is when it is called in question. If it is attempted by force or fraud to compel the colored people to stay there, they should by all means go—go quickly and die, if need be, in the attempt.". . .

CHAPTER XVI

"Time Makes All Things Even"

The leading incidents to which it is my purpose to call attention and make prominent in the present chapter will, I think, address the imagination of the reader with peculiar and poetic force, and might well enough be dramatized for the stage. They certainly afford another striking illustration of the trite saying that "truth is stranger than fiction."

The first of these events occurred four years ago, when, after a period of more than forty years, I visited and had an interview with Captain Thomas Auld at St. Michaels, Talbot County, Maryland. It will be remembered by those who have followed the thread of my story that St. Michaels was at one time the place of my home and the scene of some of my saddest experiences of slave life, and that I left there, or rather was compelled to leave there, because it was believed that I had written passes for several slaves to enable them to escape from slavery, and that prominent slaveholders in that neighborhood had, for this alleged offense, threatened to shoot me on sight, and to prevent the execution of this threat my master had sent me to Baltimore.

My return, therefore, in peace, to this place and among the same people, was strange enough in itself; but that I should, when there, be formally invited by Captain Thomas Auld, then over eighty years old, to come to the side of his dying bed, evidently with a view to a friendly talk over our past relations, was a fact still more strange, and one which, until its occurrence, I could never have thought possible. To me Captain Auld had sustained the relation of master—a relation which I had held in extremest abhorrence, and which for forty years I had denounced in all bitterness of spirit and fierceness of speech. He had struck down my personality, had subjected me to his will, made property of my body and soul, reduced me to a chattel, hired me out to a noted slave breaker to be worked like a beast and flogged into submission, taken my hard earnings, sent me to prison, offered me for sale, broken up my Sunday-school, forbidden me to teach my fellow-slaves to read on pain of nine and thirty lashes on my bare back and had, without any apparent disturbance of his conscience, sold my body to his brother Hugh and pocketed the price of my flesh and blood. I, on my part, had traveled through the length and breadth of this country and of England, holding up this conduct of his, in common with that of other slaveholders, to the reprobation of all men who would listen to my words. I had by my writings made his name and his deeds familiar to the world in four different languages, yet here we were, after four decades, once more face to face—he on his bed, aged and tremulous, drawing near the sunset of life, and I, his former slave, United States Marshal of the District of Columbia, holding his hand and in friendly conversation with him in a sort of final settlement of past differences preparatory to his stepping into his grave, where all distinctions are at an end, and where the great and the small, the slave and his master, are reduced to the same level. Had I been asked in the days of slavery to visit this man I should have regarded the invitation as one to put fetters on my ankles and handcuffs on my wrists. It would have been an invitation to the auction-block and the slave-whip. I had no business with this man under the old regime but to keep out of his way. But now that slavery was destroyed, and the slave and the master stood upon equal ground, I was not only willing to meet him, but was very glad to do so. The conditions were favorable for remembrance of all his good deeds, and generous extenuation of all his evil ones. He was to me no longer a slaveholder either in fact or in spirit, and I regarded him as I did myself, a victim of the circumstances of birth, education, law, and custom.

Our courses had been determined for us, not by us. We had both been flung, by powers that did not ask our consent, upon a mighty current of life, which we could neither resist nor control. By this current he was a master, and I a slave; but now our lives were verging towards a point where differences disappear, where even the constancy of hate breaks down and where the clouds of pride, passion and selfishness vanish before the brightness of infinite light. At such time, and in such a place, when a man is about closing his eyes on this world and ready to step into the eternal unknown, no word of reproach or bitterness should reach him or fall from his lips; and on this occasion there was to this rule no transgression on either side.

As this visit to Capt. Auld has been made the subject of mirth by heartless triflers, and by serious-minded men regretted as a weakening of my life-long testimony against slavery, and as the report of it, published in the papers immediately after it occurred, was in some respects defective and colored, it may be proper to state exactly what was said and done at this interview.

It should in the first place be understood that I did not go to St. Michaels upon Capt. Auld's invitation, but upon that of my colored friend, Charles Caldwell; but when once there, Capt. Auld sent Mr. Green, a man in constant attendance upon him during his sickness, to tell me he would be very glad to see me, and wished me to accompany Green to his house, with which request I complied. On reaching the house I was met by Mr. Wm. H. Bruff, a son-in-law of Capt. Auld, and Mrs. Louisa Bruff, his daughter, and was conducted by them immediately to the bed-room of Capt. Auld. We addressed each other simultaneously, he calling me "Marshal Douglass," and I, as I had always called him, "Captain Auld." Hearing myself called by him "Marshal Douglass," I instantly broke up the formal nature of the meeting by saying, "not *Marshal*, but Frederick to you as formerly." We shook hands cordially, and in the act of doing so, he, having been long stricken with palsy, shed tears as men thus afflicted will do when excited by any deep emotion. The sight of him, the changes which time had wrought in him, his tremulous hands constantly in motion, and all the circumstances of his condition affected me deeply, and for a time choked my voice and made me speechless. We both, however, got the better of our feelings, and conversed freely about the past.

Though broken by age and palsy, the mind of Capt. Auld was remarkably clear and strong. After he had become composed I asked him what he thought of my conduct in running away and going to the north. He hesitated a moment as if to properly formulate his reply, and said: "Frederick, I always knew you were too smart to be a slave, and had I been in your place, I should have done as you did." I said, "Capt. Auld, I am glad to hear you say this. I did not run away from *you*, but from *slavery*; it was not that I loved Caesar less, but Rome more." I told him that I had made a mistake in my narrative, a copy of which I had sent him, in attributing to him ungrateful and cruel treatment of my grandmother; that I had done so on the supposition that in the division of the property of my old master, Mr. Aaron Anthony, my grandmother had fallen to him, and that he had left her in her old age, when she could be no longer of service to him, to pick up her living in solitude with none to help her, or, in other words, had turned her out to die like an old horse. "Ah!" he said, "that was a mistake, I never owned your grandmother; she in the division of the slaves was awarded to my brother-in-law, Andrew Anthony; but," he added quickly, "I brought her down here and took care of her as long as she lived." The fact is, that, after writing my narrative describing the condition of my grandmother, Capt. Auld's attention being thus called to it, he rescued her from her destitution. I told him that this mistake of mine was corrected as soon as I discovered it, and that I had at no time any wish to do him injustice; that I regarded both of us as victims of a system. "Oh, I never liked slavery," he said, "and I meant to emancipate all of my slaves when they reached the age of twenty-five years." I told him I had always been curious to know how old I was and that it had been a serious trouble to me, not to know when was my birthday. He said he could not tell me that, but he thought I was born in February, 1818. This date made me one year younger than I had supposed myself from what was told me by Mistress Lucretia, Captain Auld's former wife, when I left Lloyd's for Baltimore in the Spring of 1825; she having then said that I was eight, going on nine. I know that it was in the year 1825 that I went to Baltimore, because it was in that year that Mr. James Beacham built a large frigate at the foot of Alliceana street, for one of the South American Governments. Judging from this, and from certain events which transpired at Col. Lloyd's such as a boy under eight years old, without any knowledge of books, would hardly take cognizance of, I am led to believe that Mrs. Lucretia was nearer right as to my age than her husband.

Before I left his bedside Captain Auld spoke with a cheerful confidence of the great change that awaited him, and felt himself about to depart in peace. Seeing his extreme weakness I did not protract my visit. The whole interview did not last more than twenty minutes, and we parted to meet no more. His death was soon after announced in the papers, and the fact that he had once owned me as a slave was cited as rendering that event noteworthy.

It may not, perhaps, be quite artistic to speak in this connection of another incident of something of the same nature as that which I have just narrated, and yet it quite naturally finds place here; and that is, my visit to the town of Easton, county seat of Talbot County, two years later, to deliver an address in the Court House, for the benefit of some association in that place. The visit was made interesting to me, by the fact that forty-five years before I had, in company with Henry and John Harris, been dragged behind horses to Easton, with my hands tied, put in jail and offered for sale, for the offense of intending to run away from slavery.

It may easily be seen that this visit, after this lapse of time, brought with it feelings and reflections such as only unusual circumstances can awaken. There stood the old jail, with its white-washed walls and iron gratings, as when in my youth I heard its heavy locks and bolts clank behind me.

Strange too, Mr. Joseph Graham, who was then sheriff of the County, and who locked me in this gloomy place, was still living, though verging towards eighty, and was one of the gentlemen who now gave me a warm and friendly welcome, and was among my hearers when I delivered my address at the Court House. There too in the same old place stood Sol. Law's Tavern, where once the slave traders were wont to congregate, and where I now took up my abode and was treated with a hospitality and consideration undreamed of by me in the olden time as possible.

When one has advanced far in the journey of life, when he has seen and traveled over much of this great world, and has had many and strange experiences of shadow and sunshine, when long distances of time and space have come between him and his point of departure, it is natural that his thoughts should return to the place of his beginning, and that he should be seized with a strong desire to revisit the scenes of his early recollection, and live over in memory the incidents of his childhood. At least such for several years had been my thoughts and feeling in respect of Col. Lloyd's plantation on Wye River, Talbot County, Maryland; for I had never been there since I left it, when eight years old, in 1825.

While slavery continued, of course this very natural desire could not be safely gratified; for my presence among slaves was dangerous to the public peace, and could no more be tolerated than could a wolf among sheep, or fire in a magazine. But now that the results of the war had changed all this, I had for several years determined to return, upon the first opportunity, to my old home. Speaking of this desire of mine last winter, to Hon. John L. Thomas, the efficient collector at the port of Baltimore, and a leading republican of the State of Maryland, he urged me very much to go, and added that he often took a trip to the eastern shore in his revenue cutter Guthrie, (otherwise known in time of war as the Ewing,) and would be much pleased to have me accompany him on one of these trips. I expressed some doubt as to how such a visit would be received by the present Col. Edward Lloyd, now proprietor of the old place, and grandson of Governor Ed. Lloyd, whom I remembered. Mr. Thomas promptly assured me that from his own knowledge I need have no trouble on that score. Mr. Lloyd was a liberal-minded gentleman, and he had no doubt would take a visit from me very kindly. I was very glad to accept the offer. The opportunity for the trip however did not occur till the 12th of June, and on that day, in company with Messrs. Thomas, Thompson, and Chamberlain, on board the cutter, we started for the contemplated visit. In four hours after leaving Baltimore we were anchored in the river off the Lloyd estate, and from the deck of our vessel I saw once more the stately chimneys of the grand old mansion which I had last seen from the deck of the Sallie Lloyd when a boy. I left there as a slave, and returned as a freeman; I left there unknown to the outside world, and returned well known; I left there on a freight boat, and returned on a revenue cutter; I left on a vessel belonging to Col. Edward Lloyd, and returned on one belonging to the United States.

As soon as we had come to anchor, Mr. Thomas dispatched a note to Col. Edward Lloyd, announcing my presence on board his cutter, and inviting him to meet me, informing him it was my desire, if agreeable to him, to revisit my old home. In response to this note, Mr. Howard Lloyd, a son of Col. Lloyd, a young gentleman of very pleasant address, came on board the cutter, and was introduced to the several gentlemen and myself.

He told us that his father had gone to Easton on business, expressed his regret at his absence, hoped he would return before we should leave, and in the meantime received us cordially, and invited us ashore, escorted us over the grounds, and gave us as hearty a welcome as we could have wished. I hope I shall be pardoned for speaking with much complacency of this incident. It was one which could happen to but few men, and only once in the life time of any. The span of human life is too short for the repetition of events which occur at the distance of fifty years. That I was deeply moved and greatly affected by it can be easily imagined. Here I was, being welcomed and escorted by the great grandson of Colonel Edward Lloyd—a gentleman I had known well fifty-six years before, and whose form and features were as vividly depicted on my memory as if I had seen him but yesterday. He was a gentleman of the olden time, elegant in his apparel, dignified in his deportment, a man of few words and of weighty presence; and I can easily conceive that no Governor of the State of Maryland ever commanded a larger measure of respect than did this great-grandfather of the young gentleman now before me. In company with Mr. Howard was his little brother Decosa, a bright boy of eight or nine years, disclosing his aristocratic descent in the lineaments of his face, and in all his modest and graceful movements. As I looked at him I could not help the reflections naturally arising from having seen so many generations of the same family on the same estate. I had seen the elder Lloyd, and was now walking around with the youngest member of that name. In respect to the place itself, I was most agreeably surprised to find that time had dealt so gently with it, and that in all its appointments it was so little changed from what it was when I left it, and from what I have elsewhere described it. Very little was missing except the squads of little black children which were once seen in all directions, and the great number of slaves in its fields. Col. Lloyd's estate comprised twenty-seven thousand acres, and the home-farm seven thousand. In my boyhood sixty men were employed in cultivating the home farm alone. Now, by the aid of machinery, the work is accomplished by ten men. I found the buildings, which gave it the appearance of a village, nearly all standing, and I was astonished to find that I had carried their appearance and location so accurately in my mind during so many years. There was the long quarter, the quarter on the hill, the dwelling-house of my old master Aaron Anthony, and the overseer's house, once occupied by William Sevier, Austin Gore, James Hopkins, and other overseers. In connection with my old master's house was the kitchen where Aunt Katy presided, and where my head had received many a thump from her unfriendly hand. I looked into this kitchen with peculiar interest, and remembered that it was there I last saw my mother. I went round to the window at which Miss Lucretia used to sit with her sewing, and at which I used to sing when hungry, a signal which she well understood, and to which she readily responded with bread. The little closet in which I slept in a bag had been taken into the room; the dirt floor, too, had disappeared under plank. But upon the whole the house is very much as it was in the old time. Not far from it was the stable formerly in charge of old Barney. The storehouse at the end of it, of which my master carried the keys, had been removed. The large carriage house, too, which in my boyhood days contained two or three fine coaches, several phaetons, gigs, and a large sleigh, (for the latter there was seldom any use) was gone. This carriage house was of much interest to me, because Col. Lloyd sometimes allowed his servants to use of it for festal occasions, and in it there was at such times music and dancing. With these two exceptions the houses of the estate remained. There was the shoemaker's shop, where Uncle Abe made the mended shoes; and there the blacksmith's shop, where Uncle Tony hammered iron, and the weekly closing of which first taught me to distinguish Sundays from other days. The old barn, too, was there—time-worn, to be sure, but still in good condition—a place of wonderful interest to me in my childhood, for there I often repaired to listen to the chatter and watch the flight of swallows among its lofty beams, and under its ample roof. Time had wrought some changes in the trees and foliage. The Lombardy poplars, in the branches of which the red-winged black birds used to congregate and sing, and whose music awakened in my young heart sensations and aspirations deep and undefinable, were gone; but the oaks and elms, where young Daniel (the uncle of the present Edward Lloyd) used to divide with me his cakes and biscuits, were there as umbrageous and beautiful as ever. I expressed a wish to Mr. Howard to be shown into the family burial ground, and thither we made our way. It is a remarkable spot—the resting place for all the deceased Lloyds for two hundred years, for the family have been in possession of the estate since the settlement of the Maryland colony.

The tombs there remind one of what may be seen in the grounds of moss-covered churches in England. The very names of those who sleep within the oldest of them are crumbled away and become undecipherable. Everything about it is impressive, and suggestive of the transient character of human life and glory. No one could stand under its weeping willows, amidst its creeping ivy and myrtle, and look through its somber shadows, without a feeling of unusual solemnity. The first interment I ever witnessed was in this place. It was the great-great-grandmother, brought from Annapolis in a mahogany coffin, and quietly, without ceremony, deposited in this ground.

While here Mr. Howard gathered for me a bouquet of flowers and evergreens from the different graves around us, and which I carefully brought to my home for preservation.

Notable among the tombs were those of Admiral Buchanan, who commanded the Merrimac in the action at Hampton Roads with the Monitor, March 8, 1862, and that of General Winder of the Confederate army, both sons-in-law of the elder Lloyd. There was also pointed out to me the grave of a Massachusetts man, a Mr. Page, a teacher in the family, whom I had often seen and wondered what he could be thinking about as he silently paced up and down the garden walks, always alone, for he associated neither with Captain Anthony, Mr. McDermot, nor the overseers. He seemed to be one by himself. I believe he originated somewhere near Greenfield, Massachusetts, and members of his family will perhaps learn for the first time, from these lines, the place of his burial; for I have had intimation that they knew little about him after he once left home.

We then visited the garden, still kept in fine condition, but not as in the days of the elder Lloyd, for then it was tended constantly by Mr. McDermot, a scientific gardener, and four experienced hands, and formed, perhaps, the most beautiful feature of the place. From this we were invited to what was called by the slaves the Great House—the mansion of the Lloyds, and were helped to chairs upon its stately veranda, where we could have full view of its garden, with its broad walks, hedged with box and adorned with fruit trees and flowers of almost every variety. A more tranquil and tranquilizing scene I have seldom met in this or any other country.

We were soon invited from this delightful outlook into the large dining-room, with its old-fashioned furniture, its mahogany sideboard, its cut-glass chandeliers, decanters, tumblers, and wine-glasses, and cordially invited to refresh ourselves with wine of most excellent quality.

To say that our reception was every way gratifying is but a feeble expression of the feeling of each and all of us.

Leaving the Great House, my presence became known to the colored people, some of whom were children of those I had known when a boy. They all seemed delighted to see me, and were pleased when I called over the names of many of the old servants, and pointed out the cabin where Dr. Cooper, an old slave, used, with a hickory stick in hand, to teach us to say the "Lord's Prayer." After spending a little time with these, we bade good-bye to Mr. Howard Lloyd, with many thanks for his kind attentions, and steamed away to St. Michaels, a place of which I have already spoken.

The next part of this memorable trip took us to the home of Mrs. Buchanan, the widow of Admiral Buchanan, one of the two only living daughters of old Governor Lloyd, and here my reception was as kindly as that received at the Great House, where I had often seen her when a slender young lady of eighteen. She is now about seventy-four years of age but marvelously well preserved. She invited me to a seat by her side, introduced me to her grandchildren and conversed with me as freely and with as little embarrassment as if I had been an old acquaintance and occupied an equal station with the most aristocratic of the Caucasian race. I saw in her much of the quiet dignity as well as the features of her father. I spent an hour or so in conversation with Mrs. Buchanan, and when I left a beautiful little grand-daughter of hers, with a pleasant smile on her face, handed me a bouquet of many-colored flowers. I never accepted such a gift with a sweeter sentiment of gratitude than from the hand of this lovely child. It told me many things, and among them that a new dispensation of justice, kindness, and human brotherhood was dawning not only in the North, but in the South; that the war and the slavery that caused the war were things of the past, and that the rising generation are turning their eyes from the sunset of decayed institutions to the grand possibilities of a glorious future.

The next, and last noteworthy incident in my experience, and one which further and strikingly illustrates the idea with which this chapter sets out, is my visit to Harper's Ferry on the 30th of May, of this year, and my address on John Brown, delivered in that place before Storer College, an Institution established for the education of the children of those whom John Brown endeavored to liberate. It is only a little more than twenty years ago when the subject of my discourse (as will be seen elsewhere in this volume) made a raid upon Harper's Ferry; when its people, and we may say the whole nation were filled with astonishment, horror, and indignation at the mention of his name; when the government of the United States coöperated with the State of Virginia in efforts to arrest and bring to capital punishment all persons in any way connected with John Brown and his enterprise; when United States marshals visited Rochester and elsewhere in search of me, with a view to my apprehension and execution, for my supposed complicity with Brown; when many prominent citizens of the North were compelled to leave the country to avoid arrest, and men were mobbed, even in Boston, for daring to speak a word in vindication or extenuation of what was considered Brown's stupendous crime; and yet here, upon the very soil he had stained with blood and among the very people he had startled and outraged and who a few years ago would have hanged me in open daylight to the first tree, I was, after two decades, allowed to deliver an address, not merely defending John Brown, but extolling him as a hero and martyr to the cause of liberty, and doing it with scarcely a murmur of disapprobation. I confess that as I looked out upon the scene before me and the towering heights around me, and remembered the bloody drama there enacted; as I saw the loghouse in the distance where John Brown collected his men and saw the little engine-house where the brave old Puritan fortified himself against a dozen companies of Virginia Militia, and the place where he was finally captured by the United States troops under Col. Robert E. Lee, I was a little shocked at my own boldness in attempting to deliver in such presence an address of the character advertised in advance of my coming. But there was no cause of apprehension. The people of Harper's Ferry have made wondrous progress in their ideas of freedom, of thought and speech. The abolition of slavery has not merely emancipated the negro, but liberated the whites. It has taken the lock from their tongues and the fetters from their press. On the platform from which I spoke, sat Hon. Andrew J. Hunter, the prosecuting attorney for the State of Virginia, who conducted against John Brown, the cause of the State that consigned him to the gallows. This man, now well stricken in years, greeted me cordially and in conversation with me after the address, bore testimony to the manliness and courage of John Brown, and though he still disapproved of the raid made by him upon Harper's Ferry, commended me for my address and gave me a pressing invitation to visit Charlestown, where he lives, and offered to give me some facts which might prove interesting to me, as to the sayings and conduct of Captain Brown while in prison and on trial, up to the time of his execution. I regret that my engagements and duties were such that I could not then and there accept his invitation, for I could not doubt the sincerity with which it was given, or fail to see the value of compliance. Mr. Hunter not only congratulated me upon my speech, but at parting, gave me a friendly grip, and added that if Robert E. Lee were alive and present, he knew he would give me his hand also.

This man, by his frequent interruptions, added much to the interest of the occasion, approving and condemning my sentiments as they were uttered. I only regret that he did not undertake a formal reply to my speech, but this, though invited, he declined to do. It would have given me an opportunity of fortifying certain positions in my address which were perhaps insufficiently defended. Upon the whole, taking the visit to Capt. Auld, to Easton with its old jail, to the home of my old master at Col. Lloyd's, and this visit to Harper's Ferry, with all their associations, they fulfill the expectation created at the beginning of this chapter.

CONCLUSION

As far as this volume can reach that point I have now brought my readers to the end of my story. What may remain of life to me, through what experiences I may pass, what heights I may attain, into what depths I may fall, what good or ill may come to me, or proceed from me in this breathing world where all is change and uncertainty and largely at the mercy of powers over which the individual man has no absolute control; all this, if thought worthy and useful, will probably be told by others when I have passed from the busy stage of life. I am not looking for any great changes in my fortunes or achievements in the future. The most of the space of life is behind me and the sun of my day is nearing the horizon. Notwithstanding all that is contained in this book my day has been a pleasant one. My joys have far exceeded my sorrows and my friends have brought me far more than my enemies have taken from me. I have written out my experience here, not in order to exhibit my wounds and bruises and to awaken and attract sympathy to myself personally, but as a part of the history of a profoundly interesting period in American life and progress. I have meant it to be a small individual contribution to the sum of knowledge of this special period, to be handed down to after-coming generations which may want to know what things were allowed and what prohibited; what moral, social and political relations subsisted between the different varieties of the American people down to the last quarter of the nineteenth century and by what means they were modified and changed. The time is at hand when the last American slave and the last American slaveholder will disappear and when neither master nor slave will be left to tell the story of their respective relations or what happened to either in those relations. My part has been to tell the story of the slave. The story of the master never wanted for narrators. The masters, to tell their story, had at call all the talent and genius that wealth and influence could command. They have had their full day in court. Literature, theology, philosophy, law and learning have come willingly to their service, and, if condemned, they have not been condemned unheard.

It will be seen in these pages that I have lived several lives in one: first, the life of slavery; secondly, the life of a fugitive from slavery; thirdly, the life of comparative freedom; fourthly, the life of conflict and battle; and, fifthly, the life of victory, if not complete, at least assured. To those who have suffered in slavery I can say, I, too, have suffered. To those who have taken some risks and encountered hardships in the flight from bondage I can say, I, too, have endured and risked. To those who have battled for liberty, brotherhood, and citizenship I can say, I, too, have battled. And to those who have lived to enjoy the fruits of victory I can say, I, too, live and rejoice. If I have pushed my example too prominently for the good taste of my Caucasian readers, I beg them to remember that I have written in part for the encouragement of a class whose aspirations need the stimulus of success.

I have aimed to assure them that knowledge can be obtained under difficulties; that poverty may give place to competency; that obscurity is not an absolute bar to distinction, and that a way is open to welfare and happiness to all who will resolutely and wisely pursue that way; that neither slavery, stripes, imprisonment nor proscription need extinguish self-respect, crush manly ambition, or paralyze effort; that no power outside of himself can prevent a man from sustaining an honorable character and a useful relation to his day and generation; that neither institutions nor friends can make a race to stand unless it has strength in its own legs; that there is no power in the world which can be relied upon to help the weak against the strong or the simple against the wise; that races, like individuals, must stand or fall by their own merits; that all the prayers of Christendom cannot stop the force of a single bullet, divest arsenic of poison, or suspend any law of nature. In my communication with the colored people I have endeavored to deliver them from the power of superstition, bigotry, and priestcraft. In theology I have found them strutting about in the old clothes of the masters, just as the masters strut about in the old clothes of the past. The falling power remains among them long since it has ceased to be the religious fashion in our refined and elegant white churches. I have taught that the "fault is not in our stars, but in ourselves, that we are underlings," that "who would be free, themselves must strike the blow." I have urged upon them self-reliance, self-respect, industry, perseverance, and economy, to make the best of both worlds, but to make the best of this world first because it comes first, and that he who does not improve himself by the motives and opportunities afforded by this world gives the best evidence that he would not improve in any other world. Schooled as I have been among the abolitionists of New England, I recognize that the universe is governed by laws which are unchangeable and eternal, that what men sow they will reap, and that there is no way to dodge or circumvent the consequences of any act or deed. My views at this point receive but limited endorsement among my people. They, for the most part, think they have means of procuring special favor and help from the Almighty; and, as their "faith is the substance of things hoped for and the evidence of things not seen," they find much in this expression which is true to faith, but utterly false to fact. But I meant here only to say a word in conclusion. Forty years of my life have been given to the cause of my people, and if I had forty years more they should all be sacredly given to the same great cause. If I have done something for that cause, I am, after all, more a debtor to it than it is debtor to me.

CHAPTER 9

Douglass to Theophilus Gould Steward, July 27, 1886 (1921)

I n his autobiography, *Fifty Years in the Gospel Ministry* (1921), Rev. Theophilus Gould Steward, pastor of the Metropolitan A.M.E. church in Washington, D.C. from 1886 to 1888, records the following letter* from his parishioner Frederick Douglass. Noting that "I had heard that he was not a believer in Christianity," Steward sent Douglass a pastoral inquiry. In his response Douglass outlined his liberal religious views, studiedly avoiding a clear yes or no on the question of his belief in Christianity, the better to highlight his support of a practical social gospel capable of advancing the moral and cultural interests of African Americans.

❖ ❖ ❖

Anacostia, D.C., July 27, 1886.

Rev. T. G. Steward.

Dear Sir: In response to your respected letter of yesterday, I have to say, without circumlocution or concealment, that I care less for names, hard or soft than for things; less for forms than for substance; less for professions than for practice; less for sectarian creeds than for manly character. I have frequently heard myself called, in anything but an amiable spirit, infidel, atheist, and disorganizer, by ignorant men, inside and outside the pulpit, who really did not know the significance of the epithets they applied to me, and yet I have never heard such men quote one sentence or syllable from any writings in proof of the justice of charges so noisily made.

I do not wonder, therefore, in view of the frequency of such utterances, you should be surprised to find me a regular reader of your

---

*T. G. Steward, *Fifty Years in the Gospel Ministry* (Philadelphia: A. M. E. Book Concern, 1921), pp. 232–36.

church organ, a supporter of your church over which you preside. My line of conduct in this matter is not determined by my approval of the theological dogmas often promulgated from the pulpit. In respect to many of those dogmas I should, perhaps, differ very widely from yourself and others, while I yet find ground entirely satisfactory to my judgment and conscience for contributing my mite to the treasury of your church, and that of others.

You, yourself, in asking for contributions last Sunday stated in theological form the philosophical ground upon which, in this respect, I justify my conduct. You called upon us to give for the glory of God and for the good of man: and in giving, I did both. As to my infidelity, so-called, it has never denied any attribute of the Deity. To me, God is good! God is light! God is truth! God is love! and to glorify God is to lead a life in harmony with these attributes. In this respect man is related to his Creator as the watch to its maker. A watch glorifies its maker when it answers the end of its manufacture, which is to keep good time—always to be true, and never to be false in its measurement of time. As God is true, I would have man true! As God is holy, I would have man holy! As God is pure, I would have man pure. An unclean man in body or mind does not glorify his Maker. He may sing praises to the Lord and call himself a Christian, but he brings no glory to the Lord, no good to his fellow man. Christianity is nothing to me, except as it stands as the representative of the sigh of the soul for a noble life; for herein is the true glory of God.

Now looking at the church, apart from what is purely theological and abstract, I see it in means of promoting honorable character and conduct; and, as I have said, for this reason, I contribute my mite towards its support.

I have still another reason for this action, though not one of equal weight with that already given. It is because I would have colored people enjoy advantages for assembling themselves together, for moral and spiritual improvement, equal to those enjoyed by others.

A large, commodious and well-appointed church, in pulpit, choir and architecture, is attractive to the people who assemble, and commands respect from the outside world. The African Methodist Episcopal Church (the name by the way is altogether too long and stilted for my taste) is such a church, and therefore, I want to see it flourish.

I notice what you say of the Bible, but I have neither time nor inclination to go into questions in respect of its plenary or other inspiration; for if it contains the will of God to man, it is vastly more important to know what that will is, than to know precisely how that will has been communicated—whether by man or by angels, by voices in the air, or by the out breathings and higher aspirations of the human soul. For, if the Bible contains the will of God to man, it contains it in that sense in which God meant it to be understood, and in no other; for it would be absurd and monstrous to suppose an all-wise God to reveal His will and His law in a sense in which He did not mean to be understood. Hence, as a practical man, I hold it to be much more important to know what the Bible really means, than to know how it was composed, and what degree of inspiration we shall accord to it. And here we are met by a confusion of tongues, and by endless contradictions, each man and sect drawing from it that meaning which commends itself to his or her judgment, and a purely human judgment withal. Whether this interpretation be for peace or for war, for love or for hate, for charity or for bigotry, for men of all races and colors at the same communion table, or whether it excludes a part and sends it off to a little kind of kitchen communion table by itself, like your church— whether the Christian religion is for one race, or for all races; whether free salvation or predestination, is the true meaning of the Bible; whether the Roman Catholic Church is the true Church, or the innumerable Protestant sects, constitute the true Church. About these and other endless contradictions I might write interminably, but I lay them aside in that spirit of charity which leaves each to stand or fall to his own master, and justify myself in contributing my mite to the support of your church and the other individual churches, because, upon the whole, I think they contribute to the improvement and moral elevation of those who come within the reach of their influence; because I hold that the pulpit is capable of being a powerful agent in the dissemination of truth, and I hold that truth is the power of God for the salvation of the world, and I do not limit truth to mere spiritual matters, but to man in all his relations in the family, in the church, in the government, in the world.

Very truly yours,
FREDERICK DOUGLASS

CHAPTER 10

From *Life and Times of Frederick Douglass* (1892)

W hen the last copies of Douglass's third autobiography sold out, he prepared the final version of his *Life and Times,* which was published in December 1892 by De Wolfe, Fiske, and Company of Boston. The new Third Part of the autobiography added thirteen more chapters to the 1882 edition, which was itself revised stylistically before republication in 1892. These efforts to improve and update the *Life and Times* made little difference to American bookbuyers, however. The final version of Douglass's autobiography sold only 399 copies in the first two years of its existence. A friendly word in a journal of public affairs like *The Independent* could not counter suggestions from other critics that Douglass's story was a bit passé. Translated into Swedish in 1895, the 1892 edition of the *Life and Times,* although never a popular book, has always held a position of honor in African American literature and culture, if only because it constitutes Douglass's final statement on both his own history and that of his era. In 1940, when the Douglass League set about the task of "revitalizing Negro life today through the revival and rediscovery of its heroic past," it was not the *Narrative* but the 1892 *Life and Times* that was commissioned to be reprinted with a Foreword by the noted African American intellectual, Alain Locke.

The following chapters reprinted from the 1892 *Life and Times* illustrate Douglass's return in his final autobiography to the ideals and themes that had made him become a writer in the first place. His personal successes notwithstanding, the overriding concern in 1892 is the necessity of preserving African American civil and human rights in the face of "the reactionary tendencies of public opinion against the black man and of the increasing decline, since the war for the Union, in the power of resistance to the onward march of the rebel states to their former control and ascendency in the councils of the nation."

❖ ❖ ❖

THIRD PART

CHAPTER 1

Later Life

Ten years ago when the preceding chapters of this book were written, having then reached in the journey of life the middle of the decade beginning at sixty and ending at seventy, and naturally reminded that I was no longer young, I laid aside my pen with some such sense of relief as might be felt by a weary and over-burdened traveler when arrived at the desired end of a long journey, or as an honest debtor wishing to be square with all the world might feel when the last dollar of an old debt was paid off. Not that I wished to be discharged from labor and service in the cause to which I have devoted my life, but from this peculiar kind of labor and service. I hardly need say to those who know me, that writing for the public eye never came quite as easily to me as speaking to the public ear. It is a marvel to me that under the circumstances I learned to write at all. It has been a still greater marvel that in the brief working period in which they lived and wrought, such men as Dickens, Dumas, Carlyle and Sir Walter Scott could have produced the works ascribed to them. But many have been the impediments with which I have had to struggle. I have, too, been embarrassed by the thought of writing so much about myself when there was so much else of which to write. It is far easier to write about others than about one's self. I write freely of myself, not from choice, but because I have, by my cause, been morally forced into thus writing. Time and events have summoned me to stand forth both as a witness and an advocate for a people long dumb, not allowed to speak for themselves, yet much misunderstood and deeply wronged. In the earlier days of my freedom, I was called upon to expose the direful nature of the slave system, by telling my own experience while a slave, and to do what I could thereby to make slavery odious and thus to hasten the day of emancipation. It was no time to mince matters or to stand upon a delicate sense of propriety, in the presence of a crime so gigantic as our slavery was, and the duty to oppose it so imperative. I was called upon to expose even my stripes, and with many misgivings obeyed the summons and tried thus to do my whole duty in this my first public work and what I may say proved to be the best work of my life.

Fifty years have passed since I entered upon that work, and now that it is ended, I find myself summoned again by the popular voice and by what is called the negro problem, to come a second time upon the witness stand and give evidence upon disputed points concerning myself and my emancipated brothers and sisters who, though free, are yet oppressed and are in as much need of an advocate as before they were set free. Though this is not altogether as agreeable to me as was my first mission, it is one that comes with such commanding authority as to compel me to accept it as a present duty. In it I am pelted with all sorts of knotty questions, some of which might be difficult even for Humboldt, Cuvier or Darwin, were they alive, to answer. They are questions which range over the whole field of science, learning and philosophy, and some descend to the depths of impertinent, unmannerly and vulgar curiosity. To be able to answer the higher range of these questions I should be profoundly versed in psychology, anthropology, ethnology, sociology, theology, biology, and all the other ologies, philosophies and sciences. There is no disguising the fact that the American people are much interested and mystified about the mere matter of color as connected with manhood. It seems to them that color has some moral or immoral qualities and especially the latter. They do not feel quite reconciled to the idea that a man of different color from themselves should have all the human rights claimed by themselves. When an unknown man is spoken of in their presence, the first question that arises in the average American mind concerning him and which must be answered is, Of what color is he? and he rises or falls in estimation by the answer given. It is not whether he is a good man or a bad man. That does not seem of primary importance. Hence I have often been bluntly and sometimes very rudely asked, of what color my mother was, and of what color was my father? In what proportion does the blood of the various races mingle in my veins, especially how much white blood and how much black blood entered into my composition? Whether I was not part Indian as well as African and Caucasian? Whether I considered myself more African than Caucasian, or the reverse? Whether I derived my intelligence from my father, or from my mother, from my white, or from my black blood? Whether persons of mixed blood are as strong and healthy as persons of either of the races whose blood they inherit? Whether persons of mixed blood do permanently remain of the mixed complexion or finally take on the complexion of one or the other of the two or more races of which they may be composed? Whether they live as long and raise as large families as other people? Whether they inherit only evil from both parents and good from neither? Whether evil dispositions are more transmissible than good? Why did I marry a person of my father's complexion instead of marrying one of my mother's complexion? How is the race problem to be solved in this country? Will the negro go back to Africa or remain here? Under this shower of purely American questions, more or less personal, I have endeavored to possess my soul in patience and get as much good out of life as was possible with so much to occupy my time; and, though often perplexed, seldom losing my temper, or abating heart or hope for the future of my people. Though I cannot say I have satisfied the curiosity of my countrymen on all the questions raised by them, I have, like all honest men on the witness stand, answered to the best of my knowledge and belief, and I hope I have never answered in such wise as to increase the hardships of any human being of whatever race or color.

When the first part of this book was written, I was, as before intimated, already looking toward the sunset of human life and thinking that my children would probably finish the recital of my life, or that possibly some other persons outside of family ties to whom I am known might think it worth while to tell what he or she might know of the remainder of my story. I considered, as I have said, that my work was done. But friends and publishers concur in the opinion that the unity and completeness of the work require that it shall be finished by the hand by which it was begun.

Many things touched me and employed my thoughts and activities between the years 1881 and 1891. I am willing to speak of them. Like most men who give the world their autobiographies I wish my story to be told as favorably towards myself as it can be with a due regard to truth. I do not wish it to be imagined by any that I am insensible to the singularity of my career, or to the peculiar relation I sustain to the history of my time and country. I know and feel that it is something to have lived at all in this Republic during the latter part of this eventful century, but I know it is more to have had some small share in the great events which have distinguished it from the experience of all other centuries. No man liveth unto himself, or ought to live unto himself. My life has conformed to this Bible saying, for, more than most men, I have been the thin edge of the wedge to open for my people a way in many directions and places never before occupied by them. It has been mine, in some degree, to stand as their defense in moral battle against the shafts of detraction, calumny and persecution, and to labor in removing and overcoming those obstacles which, in the shape of erroneous ideas and customs, have blocked the way to their progress. I have found this to be no hardship, but the natural and congenial vocation of my life. I had hardly become a thinking being when I first learned to hate slavery, and hence I was no sooner free than I joined the noble band of Abolitionists in Massachusetts, headed by William Lloyd Garrison and Wendell Phillips. Afterward, by voice and pen, in season and out of season, it was mine to stand for the freedom of people of all colors, until in our land the last yoke was broken and the last bondsman was set free. In the war for the Union I persuaded the colored man to become a soldier. In the peace that followed, I asked the Government to make him a citizen. In the construction of the rebellious States I urged his enfranchisement.

Much has been written and published during the last ten years purporting to be a history of the anti-slavery movement and of the part taken by the men and women engaged in it, myself among the number. In some of these narrations I have received more consideration and higher estimation than I perhaps deserved. In others I have not escaped undeserved disparagement, which I may leave to the reader and to the judgment of those who shall come after me to reply to and to set right.

The anti-slavery movement, that truly great moral conflict which rocked the land during thirty years, and the part taken by the men and women engaged in it, are not quite far enough removed from us in point of time to admit at present of an impartial history. Some of the sects and parties that took part in it still linger with us and are zealous for distinction, for priority and superiority. There is also the disposition to unduly magnify the importance of some men and to diminish the importance of others. While over all this I spread the mantle of charity, it may in a measure explain whatever may seem like prejudice, bigotry and partiality in some attempts already made at the history of the anti-slavery movement. As in a great war, amid the roar of cannon, the smoke of powder, the rising dust and the blinding blaze of fire and counterfire of battle, no one participant may be blamed for not being able to see and correctly to measure and report the efficiency of the different forces engaged, and to render honor where honor is due; so we may say of the late historians who have essayed to write the history of the anti-slavery movement. It is not strange that those who write in New England from the stand occupied by William Lloyd Garrison and his friends, should fail to appreciate the services of the political abolitionists and of the Free Soil and Republican parties. Perhaps a political abolitionist would equally misjudge and underrate the value of the non-voting and moral-suasion party, of which Mr. Garrison was the admitted leader; while in fact the two were the halves necessary to make the whole. Without Adams, Giddings, Hale, Chase, Wade, Seward, Wilson and Sumner to plead our cause in the councils of the nation, the taskmasters would have remained the contented and undisturbed rulers of the Union, and no condition of things would have been brought about authorizing the Federal Government to abolish slavery in the country's defense. As one of those whose bonds have been broken, I cannot see without pain any attempt to disparage and undervalue any man's work in this cause.

Hereafter, when we get a little farther away from the conflict, some brave and truth-loving man, with all the facts before him, uninfluenced by filial love and veneration for man, or party associations, or pride of name, will gather from here and there the scattered fragments, my small contribution perhaps among the number, and give to those who shall come after us an impartial history of this the grandest moral conflict of the century. Truth is patient and time is just. With these and like reflections, which have often brought consolation to better men than myself, when upon them has fallen the keen edge of censure, and with the scrupulous justice done me in the biography of myself lately written by Mr. Frederick May Holland of Concord, Massachusetts, I can easily rest contented.

CHAPTER IV

Recorder of Deeds

Although I was not reappointed to the office of Marshal of the District of Columbia as I had reason to expect and to believe that I should be, not only because under me the office had been conducted blamelessly, but because President Garfield had solemnly promised Senator Conkling that I should be so appointed, I was given the office of Recorder of Deeds for the District of Columbia. This office was, in many respects, more congenial to my feelings than was that of United States Marshal of the District which made me the daily witness in the criminal court of a side of the District life to me most painful and repulsive. Happily, I was never required personally to superintend or witness an execution or to take any part in one. That sad and solemn business had, prior to my appointment, been committed to the warden of the jail, but the contact with the criminal class and the responsibility of watching and taking care of criminals were in every way distasteful to me, and hence I would, under any circumstances, have preferred the office of Recorder of Deeds to that of Marshal. The duties of Recorder, though specific, exacting, and imperative, are easily performed. The office is one that imposes no social duties whatever, and therefore neither fettered my pen nor silenced my voice in the cause of my people. I wrote much and spoke often, and perhaps because of this activity gave to envious tongues a pretext against me. I think that I was not, while in this office or in that of Marshal, less outspoken against what I considered the errors of rulers, than while outside of the office. My cause first, midst, last, and always, whether in office or out of office, was and is that of the black man; not because he is black, but because he is a man, and a man subjected in this country to peculiar wrongs and hardships.

As in the case of United States Marshal, so in that of Recorder of Deeds, I was the first colored man who held the office, and like all innovations on established usage, my appointment did not meet with the approval of the conservatives and old-time rulers of the country, but, on the contrary, met with resistance from both these and the press as well as from the street corners. Happily for me the American people possess in large measure a proneness to acquiescence. They readily submit to the "powers that be" and to the rule of the majority. This sheet anchor of our national stability, prosperity and peace served me in good stead in this crisis in my career, as indeed it had done in many others.

I held the office of Recorder of Deeds of the District of Columbia for nearly five years. Having, so to speak, broken the ice by giving to the country the example of a colored man at the head of that office, it has become the one special office to which, since that time, colored men have aspired. Much that is sheep-like is illustrated in the colored race, and perhaps the same is true in all races. Where one goes the others are apt to follow. The office has, ever since I left it, been sought for and occupied by colored men. In this, if not in anything else, I have opened the gate and led the way upward for the people with whom I am identified. The office of Recorder was far less remunerative when I held it than it has since become. With the almost wonderful increase of population, after long years of stationary condition due to the existence of slavery, and with the vast improvements in its sanitary conditions, there has come to Washington a surprising activity in the real estate business. As the office of Recorder is supported by fees, and every transfer of property and every deed of trust and every mortgage executed must be recorded, the income of this office has risen to a larger sum than that of any office of the National Government except that of the President of the United States.

In my experience in public life I have learned that there are many ways by which confidence in public men may be undermined and destroyed, and against which they are comparatively helpless. One of the most successful methods is to start the rumor that a man has made a large fortune out of the Government and is rich. This method of political warfare, I will hardly say assassination, has not escaped the vigilant eye of the Afro-American press or of the aspirant and office-seeker, who, when he has found a public man supposed to be in the way of his ambition, has resorted to this device. In my case this method has not only been well studied but diligently and vigorously employed. The surprising feature is that at this point no amount of testimony and denial has any effect. It is only necessary to get the rumor well started to have it roll on and increase like a ball in adhesive snow. I have, for instance, seen myself described, in some of our Afro-American newspapers, as a man of large fortune, worth half a million of dollars, and the impression was given by the writer that I had made this large fortune out of the Government. The absurdity of all this would readily assert itself to the thoughtful readers of these papers, if they would only stop to think; but, unfortunately, all the readers of Afro-American or other newspapers are not very thoughtful or painstaking in such investigations, but usually accept a "rumor" or an "It is said" as law and gospel. The rumors of my wealth are not only not true, but in the nature of my work and history could not be true. A half a million indeed! The fact is, I never was worth one-fifth of that sum and never expect to be. The offices held by me during the eleven years of my official life never brought me over three thousand dollars a year above the current expenses of living, and during some of the years my income was much less than this sum.

While I hold it to be no sin to be rich, but, on the contrary, wish there were many rich men among American citizens of color, the notoriety foolishly or maliciously given me has, in some measure, placed me unfavorably before the people I have most endeavored to serve, and has naturally enough subjected me to some annoyances which I might otherwise have escaped. Aside from the envy and prejudice excited by seeing one man in better circumstances than another, it has overwhelmed me with applications to travel and lecture at my own expense for this and that good object. It has also brought me much correspondence to occupy and consume the time and attention which perhaps might be more usefully employed in other directions. Numerous pressing and pathetic appeals for assistance, written under the delusion of my great wealth, have come to me from colored people from all parts of the country, with heart-rending tales of destitution and misery, such as I would gladly relieve did my circumstances admit of it. This confidence in my benevolent disposition has been flattering enough and gratefully appreciated by me, but I have found it difficult to make the applicants believe that I have no power to justify it. While some of these applications for aid have been distressing, others have been simply amusing in their absurdity. One person wholly unknown to me besought me for the modest sum of four thousand dollars. She had seen a house that would exactly suit herself and daughter for a home. It could be purchased for that amount, and she implored me to send her the money. Another wrote me setting forth the goodness of divine providence in blessing me with great riches, and beseeching me to forward to her the price of a piano, assuring me that she had never before troubled me for money. She knew that her daughter was remarkably gifted in music, and could make her way in the world if to start with she could only have a piano. These were no doubt honest people, and applied to me confidently expecting to get the money for which they asked. They were not of that class of professional beggars who hide away in garrets, cellars, and other out-of-the-way places, and load the mails with ingeniously framed begging letters to persons known to have means and supposed to be benevolent, and upon whom they think they can impose. They are, however, of that large class of persons who are perfectly willing to subsist at other people's expense. Happily, the speculators in human credulity generally reveal the presence of fraud by their elaborate and overdrawn tales of woe and suffering, and thus defeat themselves. The witness who gives evidence merely from memory, and not from the knowledge of the case then present to his mind, may tell a straight story, but one not so straight will often better secure belief. The skilful lawyer can generally detect in the perfection of the story the vice of the evidence.

Among the numerous and persistent beggars whom I have to encounter in this class are those who come in the character of creditors to demand from me the payment of a debt which I especially owe them for the great services which they or their fathers or grandfathers have rendered to the cause of emancipation. "They have assisted slaves in their flight from bondage." "They have traveled miles to hear me lecture." "They remember some things which they heard me say." "They read everything that I ever wrote." "Their fathers kept stations on the underground railroad." "They voted the Liberty party ticket many years ago, when no one else did." And much else of the same sort, but always concluding with a solid demand for money or for my influence to get positions under the Government for themselves or for their friends. Though I could not exactly see how or why I should be called upon to pay the debt of emancipation for the whole four millions of liberated people, I have always tried to do my part as opportunity has offered. At the same time it has seemed to me incomprehensible that they did not see that the real debtors in this woeful account are themselves, and that the absurdity of their posing as creditors did not occur to them.

CHAPTER V

President Cleveland's Administration

The last year of my service in the comfortable office of Recorder of Deeds for the District of Columbia, to which aspirants have never been few in number or wanting in zeal, was under the early part of the remarkable administration of President Grover Cleveland. It was thought by some of my friends, and especially by my Afro-American critics, that I ought instantly to have resigned this office upon the incoming of the new administration. I do not know how much the desirableness of the office influenced my opinion in an opposite direction, for the human heart is very deceitful, but I took a different view in this respect from my colored critics. The office of Recorder, like that of the Register of Wills, is a purely local office, though held at the pleasure of the President, and it is in no sense a federal or political office. The Federal Government provides no salary for it. It is supported solely by fees paid for work actually done by its employees for the citizens of the District of Columbia. While these citizens, outside the eager applicants for the place, made no complaint of my continuance in the office, I saw no reason to retire from it. Then, too, President Cleveland did not appear to be in haste or to desire my resignation half as much as some of my Afro-American brethren desired me to make room for them. Besides, he owed his election to a peculiar combination of circumstances favorable to my remaining where I was. He had been supported by Republican votes as well as by Democratic votes. He had been the candidate of civil-service reformers, the fundamental idea of whom is that there should be no removal from an office the duties of which have been fully and faithfully performed by the incumbent. Being elected by the votes of civil-service reformers, there was an implied political obligation imposed upon Mr. Cleveland to respect the idea represented by the votes of these reformers. During the first part of his administration, the time in which I held office under him, the disposition on the part of the President to fulfil that obligation was quite manifest, and the feeling at the time was that we were entering upon a new era of American politics, in which there would be no removals from office on the ground of party politics. It seemed that for better or for worse we had reversed the practice of both parties in our political history, and that the old formula, "To the victor belong the spoils," was no longer to be the approved rule in politics. Then again I saw that there was less reason for resigning because of the election of a President of a different party from my own, when the political status of the people of the District of Columbia was considered. These people are outside of the United States. They occupy neutral ground and have no political existence. They have neither voice nor vote in all the practical politics of the United States. They are hardly to be called citizens of the United States. Practically they are aliens; not citizens, but subjects. The District of Columbia is the one spot where there is no government for the people, of the people, and by the people. Its citizens submit to rulers whom they have had no choice in selecting. They obey laws which they had no voice in making. They have a plenty of taxation, but no representation. In the great questions of politics in the country they can march with neither army, but are relegated to the position of neuters.

I have nothing to say in favor of this anomalous condition of the people of the District of Columbia, and hardly think that it ought to be or will be much longer endured; but while it exists it does not appear that the election of a President of the United States should make it the duty of a purely local officer, holding an office supported, not by the United States, but by the disfranchised people of the District of Columbia, to resign such office. For these reasons I rested securely in the Recorder's office until the President, whether intentionally or not, had excited the admiration of the civil-service reformers by whom he was elected, after which he vigorously endeavored to conform his policy to the opposing ideas of the Democratic party. Having received all possible applause from the reformers, and thus made it difficult for them to contradict their approval and return to the Republican party, he went to work in earnest at the removal from office of all those whom he regarded as offensive partisans, myself among the number. Seldom has a political device worked better. In face of all the facts, the civil-service reformers adhered to their President. He had not done all they had hoped for, but he had done what they insisted was the best that he could do under the circumstances.

In parting with President Grover Cleveland, it is due to state that, personally, I have no cause of complaint against him. On the contrary, there is much for which I have reason to commend him. I found him a robust, manly man, one having the courage to act upon his convictions, and to bear with equanimity the reproaches of those who differed from him. When President Cleveland came to Washington, I was under a considerable cloud not altogether free from angry lightning. False friends of both colors were loading me with reproaches. No man, perhaps, had ever more offended popular prejudice than I had then lately done. I had married a wife. People who had remained silent over the unlawful relations of the white slave masters with their colored slave women loudly condemned me for marrying a wife a few shades lighter than myself. They would have had no objection to my marrying a person much darker in complexion than myself, but to marry one much lighter, and of the complexion of my father rather than of that of my mother, was, in the popular eye, a shocking offense, and one for which I was to be ostracized by white and black alike. Mr. Cleveland found me covered with these unjust, inconsistent, and foolish reproaches, and instead of joining in with them or acting in accordance with them, or in anywise giving them countenance as a cowardly and political trickster might and probably would have done, he, in the face of all vulgar criticism, paid me all the social consideration due to the office of Recorder of Deeds of the District of Columbia. He never failed, while I held office under him, to invite myself and wife to his grand receptions, and we never failed to attend them. Surrounded by distinguished men and women from all parts of the country and by diplomatic representatives from all parts of the world, and under the gaze of the late slaveholders, there was nothing in the bearing of Mr. and Mrs. Cleveland toward Mrs. Douglass and myself less cordial and courteous than that extended to the other ladies and gentlemen present. This manly defiance, by a Democratic President, of a malignant and time-honored prejudice, won my respect for the courage of Mr. Cleveland. We were in politics separated from each other by a space ocean wide. I had done all that I could to defeat his election and to elect Mr. James G. Blaine, but this made no apparent difference with Mr. Cleveland. He found me in office when he came into the Presidency, and he was too noble to refuse me the recognition and hospitalities that my official position gave me the right to claim. Though this conduct drew upon him fierce and bitter reproaches from members of his own party in the South, he never faltered or flinched, and continued to invite Mrs. Douglass and myself to his receptions during all the time that I was in office under his administration, and often wrote the invitations with his own hand. Among my friends in Europe, a fact like this will excite no comment. There, color does not decide the civil and social position of a man. Here, a white scoundrel, because he is white, is preferred to an honest and educated black man. A white man of the baser sort can ride in first-class carriages on railroads, attend the theaters and enter the hotels and restaurants of our cities, and be accommodated, while a man with a the least drop of African blood in his veins would be refused and insulted. Nowhere in the world are the worth and dignity of manhood more exalted in speech and press than they are here, and nowhere is manhood pure and simple more despised than here. We affect contempt for the castes and aristocracies of the old world and laugh at their assumptions, but at home foster pretensions far less rational and much more ridiculous.

I have spoken freely of the sensible and manly course of Mr. Cleveland, and shall perhaps, for this reason, be thought and described as having a leaning towards the Democratic party. No greater mistake could be made. No such inference should be drawn from anything that I have said. I am a Republican and am likely to remain a Republican, but I was never such a partisan that I could not commend a noble action performed by any man of whatever party or sect.

During the administration of Chester A. Arthur, as also during that of Rutherford B. Hayes, the spirit of slavery and rebellion increased in power and advanced towards ascendency. At the same time, the spirit which had abolished slavery and saved the Union steadily and proportionately declined, and with it the strength and unity of the Republican party also declined. The dawn of this deplorable action became visible when the Republican Speaker of the House of Representatives defeated the bill to protect colored citizens of the South from rapine and murder. Under President Hayes it took organic, chronic form, and rapidly grew in bulk and force. This well-meaning President turned his back upon the loyal state governments of the South, gave the powerful Post-Office Department into the hands of a Southern Democrat, filled the Southern States with rebel postmasters, went South, praised the honesty and bravery of the rebels, preached pacification, and persuaded himself and others to believe that this conciliation policy would arrest the hand of violence, put a stop to outrage and murder, and restore peace and prosperity to the rebel States. The results of this policy were no less ruinous and damning because of the good intention of President Hayes. Its effect upon the Republican spirit of the country was like the withering blast of the sirocco upon all vegetation within its reach. The sentiment that gave us a reconstructed Union on a basis of liberty for all people was blasted as a flower is blasted by a killing frost. The whole four years of this administration were, to the loyal colored citizen, full of darkness and dismal terror. The only gleam of hope afforded him was that the empty form, at least, of the Republican party was still in power, and that it would yet regain something of the strength and vitality that characterized it in the days of Grant, Sumner, and Conkling and the period of reconstruction. How vain was this hope I need not here stop to describe. Fate was against us. The death of Mr. Garfield placed in the Presidential chair Chester A. Arthur, who did nothing to correct the errors of President Hayes, or to arrest the decline and fall of the Republican party, but, on the contrary, by his self-indulgence, indifference and neglect of opportunity, allowed the country to drift (like an oarless boat in the rapids) towards the howling chasm of the slaveholding Democracy.

It was not "Rum, Romanism, and Rebellion" that defeated Mr. James G. Blaine, but it was Mr. Blaine who defeated himself. The foundation of his defeat was laid by his own hand in the defeat of the bill to protect the lives and political rights of Southern Republicans. Up to that hour the Republican party was courageous, confident and strong, and able to elect any candidate it might deem it wise to put in nomination for the Presidency; but from that hour it was smitten with moral decay; its courage quailed, its confidence vanished, and it has since hardly lived at all, but has been suspended, and has, comparatively, only lingered between life and death. The lesson taught by its example and its warning is, that political parties, like individual men, are only strong while they are consistent and honest, and that treachery and deception are only the sand on which political fools vainly endeavor to build. When the Republican party ceased to care for and protect its Southern allies, and sought the smiles of the Southern negro murderers, it shocked, disgusted, and drove away its best friends. The scepter of power could no longer be held by it, and it opened the way for the defeat of Mr. Blaine and the election of Mr. Cleveland.

Clinging in hope to the Republican party, thinking it would cease its backsliding and resume its old character as the party of progress, justice and freedom, I regretted its defeat and shared in some measure the painful apprehension and distress felt by my people at the South from the return to power of the old Democratic and slavery party. To many of them it seemed that they were left naked to their enemies; in fact, lost; that Mr. Cleveland's election meant the revival of the slave power, and that they would now be again reduced to slavery and the lash. The misery brought to the South by this widespread alarm can hardly be described or measured. The wail of despair from the late bondsmen was for a time deep, bitter and heart rending. Illiterate and unable to learn to read or to learn of any limit to the power of the party now in the ascendant, their fears were unmitigated and intolerable, and their outcry of alarm was like the cry of dismay uttered by an army when its champion has fallen and no one appears to take his place. It was well for the poor people in this condition that Mr. Cleveland himself kindly sent word South to allay their fears and to remove their agony. In this trepidation of the unlettered negro something is apparent aside from his ignorance. If he knew nothing of letters, he knew something of events and of the history of parties to them. He knew that the Republican party was the party hated by the old master class, and that the Democratic party was the party beloved of the old master class.

CHAPTER VI

The Supreme Court Decision

In further illustration of the reactionary tendencies of public opinion against the black man and of the increasing decline, since the war for the Union, in the power of resistance to the onward march of the rebel States to their former control and ascendency in the councils of the nation, the decision of the United States Supreme Court, declaring the Civil Rights law of 1875 unconstitutional, is striking and convincing. The strength and activities of the malign elements of the country against equal rights and equality before the law seem to increase in proportion to the increasing distance between that time and the time of the war. When the black man's arm was needed to defend the country; when the North and the South were in arms against each other and the country was in danger of dismemberment, his rights were well considered. That the reverse is now true, is a proof of the fading and defacing effect of time and the transient character of Republican gratitude. From the hour that the loyal North began to fraternize with the disloyal and slaveholding South; from the hour that they began to "shake hands over the bloody chasm;" from that hour the cause of justice to the black man began to decline and lose its hold upon the public mind, and it has lost ground ever since.

The future historian will turn to the year 1883 to find the most flagrant example of this national deterioration. Here he will find the Supreme Court of the nation reversing the action of the Government, defeating the manifest purpose of the Constitution, nullifying the Fourteenth Amendment, and placing itself on the side of prejudice, proscription, and persecution.

Whatever this Supreme Court may have been in the past, or may by the Constitution have been intended to be, it has, since the days of the Dred Scott decision, been wholly under the influence of the slave power, and its decisions have been dictated by that power rather than by what seemed to be sound and established rules of legal interpretation.

Although we had, in other days, seen this court bend and twist the law to the will and interest of the slave power, it was supposed that by the late war and the great fact that slavery was abolished, and the further fact that the members of the bench were now appointed by a Republican administration, the spirit as well as the body had been exorcised. Hence the decision in question came to the black man as a painful and bewildering surprise. It was a blow from an unsuspected quarter. The surrender of the national capital to Jefferson Davis in time of the war could hardly have caused a greater shock. For the moment the colored citizen felt as if the earth was opened beneath him. He was wounded in the house of his friends. He felt that this decision drove him from the doors of the great temple of American justice. The nation that he had served against its enemies had thus turned him over naked to those enemies. His trouble was without any immediate remedy. The decision must stand until the gates of death could prevail against it.

The colored men in the capital of the nation where the deed was done were quick to perceive its disastrous significance, and in the helpless horror of the moment they called upon myself and others to express their grief and indignation. In obedience to that call a meeting was assembled in Lincoln Hall, the largest hall in the city, which was packed by an audience of all colors, to hear what might be said to this new and startling event. Though we were powerless to arrest the wrong or modify the consequences of this extraordinary decision, we could, at least, cry out against its absurdity and injustice.

On that occasion our cause was ably and eloquently presented by that distinguished lawyer and eminent philanthropist, Robert G. Ingersoll. For my own part I felt it to be a serious thing to contradict the judgment of the highest court in the land, especially in view of the danger of being betrayed into unwise and extravagant language by the wild excitement of the moment. As the first speaker on that memorable occasion, I present here as a part of my "Life and Times" what I there said.

I have only a few words to say to you this evening. . . . It may be, after all, that the hour calls more loudly for silence than for speech. Later on in this discussion, when we shall have before us the full text of the Supreme Court and the dissenting opinion of Judge Harlan, who must have weighty reasons for separating from his associates and incurring thereby, as he must, an amount of criticism from which even the bravest man might shrink, we may be in a better frame of mind, better supplied with facts, and better prepared to speak calmly, correctly and wisely than now. The temptation at this time is to speak more from feeling than reason, more from impulse than reflection.

We have been, as a class, grievously wounded, wounded in the house of our friends, and this wound is too deep and too painful for ordinary and measured speech.

"When a deed is done for freedom,
    Through the broad earth's aching breast
Runs a thrill of joy prophetic,
    Trembling on from east to west."

But when a deed is done for slavery, caste and oppression, and a blow is struck at human progress, whether so intended or not, the heart of humanity sickens in sorrow and writhes in pain. It makes us feel as if some one were stamping upon the graves of our mothers, or desecrating our sacred temples. Only base men and oppressors can rejoice in a triumph of injustice over the weak and defenseless; for weakness ought itself to protect from assaults of pride, prejudice and power.

The cause which has brought us here to-night is neither common nor trivial. Few events in our national history have surpassed it in magnitude, importance and significance. It has swept over the land like a cyclone, leaving moral desolation in its track. This decision belongs with a class of judicial and legislative wrongs by which we have been oppressed.

We feel it as we felt years ago the furious attempt to force the accursed system of slavery upon the soil of Kansas; as we felt the enactment of the Fugitive Slave Bill, the repeal of the Missouri Compromise, and the Dred Scott decision. I look upon it as one more shocking development of that moral weakness in high places which has attended the conflict between the spirit of liberty and the spirit of slavery, and I venture to predict that it will be so regarded by aftercoming generations. Far down the ages, when men shall wish to inform themselves as to the real state of liberty, law, religion, and civilization in the United States at this juncture of our history, they will overhaul the proceedings of the Supreme Court, and read this strange decision declaring the Civil Rights Bill unconstitutional and void.

From this more than from many volumes they will learn how far we had advanced, in this year of grace, from the barbarism of slavery toward civilization and the rights of man.

Fellow-citizens! Among the great evils which now stalk abroad in our land, the one, I think, which most threatens to undermine and destroy the foundations of our free institutions in this country is the great and apparently increasing want of respect entertained for those to whom are committed the responsibility and the duty of administering our government. On this point I think all good men must agree, and against the evil I trust you feel the deepest repugnance, and that we will, neither here nor elsewhere, give it the least breath of sympathy or encouragement. We shall never forget, whatever may be the incidental mistakes or misconduct of rulers, that government is better than anarchy, and that patient reform is better than violent revolution.

But while I would increase this feeling and give it the emphasis of a voice from heaven, it must not be allowed to interfere with free speech, honest expression of opinion, and fair criticism. To give up this would be to give up progress, and to consign the nation to moral stagnation, putrefaction and death.

In the matter of respect for dignitaries, it should, however, never be forgotten that duties are reciprocal, and that while the people should frown down every manifestation of levity and contempt for those in power, it is the duty of the possessors of power so to use it as to deserve and insure respect and reverence.

To come a little nearer to the case now before us. The Supreme Court of the United States, in the exercise of its high and vast constitutional power, has suddenly and unexpectedly decided that the law intended to secure to colored people the civil rights guaranteed to them by the following provision of the Constitution of the United States, is unconstitutional and void. Here it is:—

"No state," says the Fourteenth Amendment, "shall make or enforce any law which shall abridge the privileges or immunities of citizens of the United States; nor shall any state deprive any person of life, liberty, or property, without due process of the law; or deny any person within its jurisdiction the equal protection of the laws."

Now, when a bill has been discussed for weeks and months and even years, in the press and on the platform, in Congress and out of Congress; when it has been calmly debated by the clearest heads and the most skillful and learned lawyers in the land; when every argument against it has been over and over again carefully considered and fairly answered; when its constitutionality has been especially discussed, *pro* and *con;* when it has passed the United States House of Representatives and has been solemnly enacted by the United States Senate (perhaps the most imposing legislative body in the world); when such a bill has been submitted to the cabinet of the nation, composed of the ablest men in the land; when it has passed under the scrutinizing eye of the Attorney-General of the United States; when the Executive of the nation has given to it his name and formal approval; when it has taken its place upon the statute-book and has remained there for nearly a decade, and the country has largely assented to it, you will agree with me that the reasons for declaring such a law unconstitutional and void should be strong, irresistible, and absolutely conclusive.

Inasmuch as the law in question is a law in favor of liberty and justice, it ought to have had the benefit of any doubt which could arise as to its strict constitutionality. This, I believe, will be the view taken of it, not only by laymen like myself, but by eminent lawyers as well.

All men who have given any thought to the machinery, structure, and practical operation of our government, must have recognized the importance of absolute harmony between its various departments and their respective powers and duties. They must have seen clearly the mischievous tendency and danger to the body politic of any antagonisms between any of its various branches. To feel the force of this thought, we have only to remember the history of the administration of President Johnson, and the conflict which took place between the national Executive and the national Congress, when the will of the people was again and again met by the Executive veto, and when the country seemed upon the verge of another revolution. No patriot, however bold, can wish for his country a repetition of those gloomy days.

Now let me say here, before I go on a step or two further in this discussion, that if any man has come here to-night with his breast heaving with passion, his heart flooded with acrimony, and wishing and expecting to hear violent denunciation of the Supreme Court on account of this decision, he has mistaken the object of this meeting and the character of the men by whom it is called.

We neither come to bury Cæsar nor to praise him. The Supreme Court is the autocratic point of our government. No monarch in Europe has a power more absolute over the laws, lives, and liberties of his people than that court has over our laws, lives and liberties. Its judges live, and ought to live, an eagle's flight beyond the reach of fear or favor, praise or blame, profit or loss. No vulgar prejudice should touch the members of that court anywhere. Their decisions should come down to us like the calm, clear light of infinite justice. We should be able to think of them and to speak of them with profoundest respect for their wisdom and deepest reverence for their virtue; for what his Holiness the Pope is to the Roman Catholic Church, the Supreme Court is to the American state. Its members are men, to be sure, and may not, like the Pope, claim infallibility, and they are not infallible, but they are the supreme law-giving power of the nation, and their decisions are law until changed by that court.

What will be said here to-night will be spoken, I trust, more in sorrow than in anger; more in a tone of regret than in bitterness and reproach, and more to promote sound views than to find bad motives for unsound views.

We cannot, however, overlook the fact that though not so intended, this decision has inflicted a heavy calamity upon seven millions of the people of this country, and left them naked and defenseless against the action of a malignant, vulgar and pitiless prejudice from which the Constitution plainly intended to shield them.

It presents the United States before the world as a nation utterly destitute of power to protect the constitutional rights of its own citizens upon its own soil.

It can claim service and allegiance, loyalty and life from them, but it cannot protect them against the most palpable violation of the rights of human nature; rights to secure which governments are established. It can tax their bread and tax their blood, but it has no protecting power for their persons. Its national power extends only to the District of Columbia and the Territories—to where the people have no votes, and to where the land has no people. All else is subject to the States. In the name of common sense, I ask what right have we to call ourselves a nation, in view of this decision and of this utter destitution of power?

In humiliating the colored people of this country, this decision has humbled the nation. It gives to the railroad conductor in South Carolina or Mississippi more power than it gives to the National Government. He may order the wife of the Chief Justice of the United States into a smoking-car full of hirsute men, and compel her to go and to listen to the coarse jests and inhale the foul smoke of a vulgar crowd. It gives to hotel-keepers who may, from a prejudice born of the Rebellion, wish to turn her out at midnight into the storm and darkness, power to compel her to go. In such a case, according to this decision of the Supreme Court, the National Government has no right to interfere. She must take her claim for protection and redress, not to the nation, but to the State; and when the State, as I understand it, declares that there is upon its statute-book no law for her protection, and that the State has made no law against her, the function and power of the National Government are exhausted and she is utterly without any redress.

Bad, therefore, as our case is, under this decision, the evil principle affirmed by the court is not wholly confined to or spent upon persons of color. The wife of Chief-Justice Waite—I speak it respectfully—is protected to-day, not by the law, but solely by the accident of her color. So far as the law of the land is concerned, she is in the same condition as that of the humblest colored women in the Republic. The difference between colored and white here is that the one, by reason of color, does not need protection. It is nevertheless true that manhood is insulted in both cases. "No man can put a chain about the ankle of his fellow-man, without at last finding the other end of its about his own neck."

The lesson of all the ages upon this point is, that a wrong done to one man is a wrong done to all men. It may not be felt at the moment, and the evil may be long delayed, but so sure as there is a moral government of the universe, so sure as there is a God of the universe, so sure will the harvest of evil come.

Color prejudice is not the only prejudice against which a Republic like ours should guard. The spirit of caste is malignant and dangerous everywhere. There is the prejudice of the rich against the poor, the pride and prejudice of the idle dandy against the hard-handed workingman. There is, worst of all, religious prejudice, a prejudice which has stained whole continents with blood. It is, in fact, a spirit infernal, against which every enlightened man should wage perpetual war. Perhaps no class of our fellow-citizens has carried this prejudice against color to a point more extreme and dangerous than have our Catholic Irish fellow-citizens, and yet no people on the face of the earth have been more relentlessly persecuted and oppressed on account of race and religion than have this same Irish people.

But in Ireland persecution has at last reached a point where it reacts terribly upon her persecutors. England is to-day reaping the bitter consequences of her own injustice and oppression. Ask any man of intelligence, "What is the chief source of England's weakness? What has reduced her to the rank of a second-class power?" and if truly answered, the answer will be "Ireland!" But poor, ragged, hungry, starving, and oppressed as Ireland is, she is strong enough to be a standing menace to the power and glory of England.

Fellow-citizens! We want no black Ireland in America. We want no aggrieved class in America. Strong as we are without the negro, we are stronger with him than without him. The power and friendship of seven millions of people, however humble and scattered all over the country, are not to be despised.

To-day our Republic sits as a queen among the nations of the earth. Peace is within her walls and plenteousness within her palaces, but he is bolder and a far more hopeful man than I am who will affirm that this peace and prosperity will always last. History repeats itself. What has happened once may happen again.

The negro, in the Revolution, fought for us and with us. In the war of 1812 General Jackson, at New Orleans, found it necessary to call upon the colored people to assist in its defense against England. Abraham Lincoln found it necessary to call upon the negro to defend the Union against rebellion. In all cases the negro responded gallantly.

Our legislators, our Presidents, and our judges should have a care, lest, by forcing these people outside of law, they destroy that love of country which in the day of trouble is needful to the nation's defense.

I am not here in this presence to discuss the constitutionality or the unconstitutionality of this decision of the Supreme Court. The decision may or may not be constitutional. That is a question for lawyers and not for laymen; and there are lawyers on this platform as learned, able and eloquent as any who have appeared in this case before the Supreme Court, or as any in the land. To these I leave the exposition of the Constitution; but I claim the right to remark upon a strange and glaring inconsistency of this decision with former decisions, where the rules of law apply. It is a new departure, entirely out of the line of precedents and decisions of the Supreme Court at other times and in other directions where the rights of colored men were concerned. It has utterly ignored and rejected the force and application of the object and intention of the adoption of the Fourteenth Amendment. It has made no account whatever of the intention and purpose of Congress and the President in putting the Civil Rights Bill upon the statute book of the nation. It has seen fit in this case affecting a weak and much persecuted people, to be guided by the narrowest and most restricted rules of legal interpretation. It has viewed both the Constitution and the law with a strict regard to their letter, but without any generous recognition and application of their broad and liberal spirit. Upon those narrow principles the decision is logical and legal of course. But what I complain of, and what every lover of liberty in the United States has a right to complain of, is this sudden and causeless reversal of all the great rules of legal interpretation by which this court was once governed in the construction of the Constitution and of laws respecting colored people.

In the dark days of slavery this court on all occasions gave the greatest importance to intention as a guide to interpretation. The object and intention of the law, it was said, must prevail. Everything in favor of slavery and against the negro was settled by this object and intention rule. We were over and over again referred to what the framers meant, and plain language itself was sacrificed and perverted from its natural and obvious meaning that the so affirmed intention of these framers might be positively asserted and given the force of law. When we said in behalf of the negro that the Constitution of the United States was intended to establish justice and to secure the blessings of liberty to ourselves and our posterity, we were told that the words said so, but that that was obviously not its intention; that it was intended to apply only to white people, and that the intention must govern.

When we came to the clause of the Constitution which declares that the immigration or importation of such persons as any of the States may see fit to admit shall not be prohibited, and the friends of liberty declared that this provision of the Constitution did not describe the slave-trade, they were told that while its language applied not to the slaves but to persons, still the object and intention of that clause of the Constitution was plainly to protect the slave-trade, and that that intention was the law and must prevail. When we came to the clause of the Constitution which declares the "No person held to labor or service in one State under the laws thereof, escaping into another, shall in consequence of any law or regulation therein be discharged from such labor or service, but shall be delivered up on claim of the party to whom such labor or service may be due," we insisted that it neither described nor applied to slaves; that it applied only to persons owing service and labor; that slaves did not and could not owe service and labor; that this clause of the Constitution said nothing of slaves or of the masters of slaves; that it was silent as to slave States or free States; that it was simply a provision to enforce a contract and not to force any man into slavery, for the slave could not owe service or make a contract.

We affirmed that it gave no warrant for what was called "The Fugitive Slave Bill," and we contended that the bill was therefore unconstitutional; but our arguments were laughed to scorn by that court and by all the courts of the country. We were told that the intention of the Constitution was to enable masters to recapture slaves, and that the law of '93 and the Fugitive Slave Law of 1850 were constitutional, binding not only on the State but upon each citizen of a State.

Fellow-citizens! While slavery was the base line of American society, while it ruled the church and state; while it was the interpreter of our law and the exponent of our religion, it admitted no quibbling, no narrow rules of legal or scriptural interpretations of the Bible or of the Constitution. It sternly demanded its pound of flesh, no matter how the scale turned or how much blood was shed in the taking of it. It was enough for it to be able to show the intention to get all it asked in the courts or out of the courts. But now slavery is abolished. Its reign was long, dark and bloody. Liberty is now the base line of the Republic. Liberty has supplanted slavery, but I fear it has not supplanted the spirit or power of slavery. Where slavery was strong, liberty is now weak.

Oh, for a Supreme Court of the United States which shall be as true to the claims of humanity as the Supreme Court formerly was to the demands of slavery! When that day comes, as come it will, a Civil Rights Bill will not be declared unconstitutional and void, in utter and flagrant disregard of the objects and intentions of the national legislature by which it was enacted and of the rights plainly secured by the Constitution.

This decision of the Supreme Court admits that the Fourteenth Amendment is a prohibition on the States. It admits that a State shall not abridge the privileges or immunities of citizens of the United States, but commits the seeming absurdity of allowing the people of a State to do what it prohibits the State itself from doing.

It used to be thought that the whole was more than a part; that the greater included the less, and that what was unconstitutional for a State to do was equally unconstitutional for an individual member of a State to do. What is a State, in the absence of the people who compose it? Land, air and water. That is all. Land and water do not discriminate. All are equal before them. This law was made for people. As individuals, the people of the State of South Carolina may stamp out the rights of the negro wherever they please, so long as they do not do so as a State, and this absurd conclusion is to be called a law. All the parts can violate the Constitution, but the whole cannot. It is not the act itself, according to this decision, that is unconstitutional. The unconstitutionality of the case depends wholly upon the party committing the act. If the State commits it, the act is wrong; if the citizen of the State commits it, the act is right.

O consistency, thou art indeed a jewel! What does it matter to a colored citizen that a State may not insult and outrage him, if the citizen of the State may? The effect upon him is the same, and it was just this effect that the framers of the Fourteenth Amendment plainly intended by that article to prevent.

It was the act, not the instrument; it was the murder, not the pistol or dagger, which was prohibited. It meant to protect the newly enfranchised citizen from injustice and wrong, not merely from a State, but from the individual members of a State. It meant to give the protection to which his citizenship, his loyalty, his allegiance, and his services entitled him; and this meaning and this purpose and this intention are now declared by the Supreme Court of the United States to be unconstitutional and void.

I say again, fellow-citizens, Oh, for a Supreme Court which shall be as true, as vigilant, as active and exacting in maintaining laws enacted for the protection of human rights, as in other days was that court for the destruction of human rights!

It is said that this decision will make no difference in the treatment of colored people; that the Civil Rights Bill was a dead letter and could not be enforced. There may be some truth in all this, but it is not the whole truth. That bill, like all advance legislation, was a banner on the outer wall of American liberty; a noble moral standard uplifted for the education of the American people. There are tongues in trees, sermons in stones, and books in the running brooks. This law, though dead, did speak. It expressed the sentiment of justice and fair play common to every honest heart. Its voice was against popular prejudice and meanness. It appealed to all the noble and patriotic instincts of the American people. It told the American people that they were all equal before the law; that they belonged to a common country and were equal citizens. The Supreme Court has hauled down this broad and glorious flag of liberty in open day and before all the people, and has thereby given joy to the heart of every man in the land who wishes to deny to others the rights he claims for himself. It is a concession to race pride, selfishness, and meanness, and will be received with joy by every upholder of caste in the land, and for this I deplore and denounce this decision.

It is a frequent and favorite device of an indefensible cause to misstate and pervert the views of those who advocate a good cause, and I have never seen this device more generally resorted to than in the case of the late decision on the Civil Rights Bill. When we dissent from the opinion of the Supreme Court and give the reasons why we think the opinion unsound, we are straightway charged in the papers with denouncing the court itself, and thus put in the attitude of bad citizens. Now, I utterly deny that there has ever been any denunciation of the Supreme Court by the speakers on this platform, and I defy any man to point out one sentence or one syllable of any speech of mine in denunciation of that court.

Another illustration of this tendency to put opponents in a false position, is seen in the persistent effort to stigmatize the Civil Rights Bill as a Social Rights Bill. Now, where under the whole heavens, outside of the United States, could any such perversion of truth have any chance of success? No man in Europe would ever dream that because he has a right to ride on a railway, or stop at a hotel, he therefore has the right to enter into social relations with anybody. No one has a right to speak to another without that other's permission. Social equality and civil equality rest upon an entirely different basis, and well enough the American people know it; yet, in order to inflame a popular prejudice, respectable papers like the New York *Times* and the Chicago *Tribune* persist in describing the Civil Rights Bill as a Social Rights Bill.

When a colored man is in the same room or in the same carriage with white people, as a servant, there is no talk of social equality, but if he is there as a man and a gentleman, he is an offense. What makes the difference? It is not color, for his color is unchanged. The whole essence of the thing is in its purpose to degrade and stamp out the liberties of the race. It is the old spirit of slavery and nothing else. To say that because a man rides in the same car with another, he is therefore socially equal, is one of the wildest absurdities.

When I was in England, some years ago, I rode upon highways, byways, steamboats, stage-coaches and omnibuses. I was in the House of Commons, in the House of Lords, in the British Museum, in the Coliseum, in the National Gallery, everywhere; sleeping in rooms where lords and dukes had slept; sitting at tables where lords and dukes were sitting; but I never thought that *those* circumstances made me socially the equal of these lords and dukes. I hardly think that some of our Democratic friends would be regarded among those lords as their equals. If riding in the same car makes one equal, I think that the little poodle dog I saw one day sitting in the lap of a lady was made equal by riding in the same car with her. Equality, social equality, is a matter between individuals. It is a reciprocal understanding. I do not think that when I ride with an educated, polished rascal he is thereby made my equal, or that when I ride with a numskull it makes him my equal. Social equality does not necessarily follow from civil equality, and yet for the purpose of a hell-black and damning prejudice, our papers still insist that the Civil Rights Bill is a bill to establish social equality.

If it is a bill for social equality, so is the Declaration of Independence, which declares that all men have equal rights; so is the Sermon on the Mount; so is the golden rule that commands us to do to others as we would that others should do to us; so is the teaching of the Apostle that of one blood God has made all nations to dwell on the face of the earth; so is the Constitution of the United States, and so are the laws and customs of every civilized country in the world; for nowhere, outside of the United States, is any man denied civil rights on account of his color.

CHAPTER 11

The Lessons of the Hour (1894)

B efore the 1890s, lynching was almost entirely confined to the American West, where it was used by whites to administer instant punishment to other white law-breakers. But in the 1890s lynching became a predominantly southern phenomenon exploited by whites to intimidate blacks. Between 1889 and 1899 the United States witnessed the lynching of someone every other day; two-thirds of the victims were African Americans. The unprecedented racial violence reached its apex in 1892, when 156 African Americans were executed by lynch mobs, often in a manner characterized by an appalling sadism. Before the end of the century, more than 2500 lynchings had taken place in the United States, with the Deep South bearing the brunt of responsibility for this unprecedented racist lawlessness.

Southern defenders of lynchings explained away and often justified mob violence by claiming it was the only way to punish and prevent the rape of white women by "black brutes" who, in the absence of the restraints of slavery, had supposedly reverted to sexual savagery. More impartial studies later revealed that only about one-third of the lynchings in the South proceeded from even the accusation of a rape. Ida B. Wells, whose pioneering antilynching journalism led to threats on her life in the South, was among the first African American writers to argue publicly that lynching was actually a terror campaign unleashed to threaten any black man whose pride or achievement might challenge the racial status quo. An early admirer of Wells, Douglass in 1892 went on the offensive not only against lynching but against those, North and South, who palliated it. His article "Lynch Law in the South" appeared in the July 1892 issue of the *North American Review*. Thousands heard or read his speech, "The Lessons of the Hour," which he delivered in several prominent venues in 1892 and 1893 before publishing it as a pamphlet under the title, *Address by Hon. Frederick Douglass, Delivered in the Metropolitan A.M.E. Church, Washington, D.C., Tuesday, January 9th, 1894, on The Lessons of the Hour* (Baltimore: Thomas & Evans, 1894).

❖ ❖ ❖

FRIENDS AND FELLOW CITIZENS:—No man should come before an audience like the one by whose presence I am now honored, without a noble object and a fixed and earnest purpose. I think that, in whatever else I may be deficient, I have the qualifications indicated, to speak to you this evening. I am here to speak for, and to defend, so far as I can do so within the bounds of truth, a long-suffering people, and one just now subject to much misrepresentation and persecution. Charges are at this time preferred against them, more damaging and distressing than any which they have been called upon to meet since their emancipation.

I propose to give you a colored man's view of the unhappy relations at present existing between the white and colored people of the Southern States of our union. We have had the Southern white man's view of the subject. It has been presented with abundant repetition and with startling emphasis, colored by his peculiar environments. We have also had the Northern white man's view tempered by time, distance from the scene, and his higher civilization.

This kind of evidence may be considered by some as all-sufficient upon which to found an intelligent judgment of the whole matter in controversy, and that therefore my testimony is not needed. But experience has taught us that it is sometimes wise and necessary to have more than the testimony of two witnesses to bring out the whole truth, especially is this the case where one of the witnesses has a powerful motive for concealing or distorting the facts in any given case. You must not, therefore, be surprised if my version of the Southern question shall widely differ from both the North and the South, and yet I shall fearlessly submit my testimony to the candid judgment of all who hear me. I shall do so in the firm belief that my testimony is true.

There is one thing, however, in which I think we shall all agree at the start. It is that the so-called, but mis-called, negro problem is one of the most important and urgent subjects that can now engage public attention. It is worthy of the most earnest consideration of every patriotic American citizen. Its solution involves the honor or dishonor, glory or shame, happiness or misery of the whole American people. It involves more. It touches deeply not only the good name and fame of the Republic, but its highest moral welfare and its permanent safety. Plainly enough the peril it involves is great, obvious and increasing, and should be removed without delay.

The presence of eight millions of people in any section of this country constituting an aggrieved class, smarting under terrible wrongs, denied the exercise of the commonest rights of humanity, and regarded by the ruling class in that section, as outside of the government, outside of the law, and outside of society; having nothing in common with the people with whom they live, the sport of mob violence and murder is not only a disgrace and scandal to that particular section but a menace to the peace and security of the people of the whole country.

I have waited patiently but anxiously to see the end of the epidemic of mob law and persecution now prevailing at the South. But the indications are not hopeful, great and terrible as have been its ravages in the past, it now seems to be increasing not only in the number of its victims, but in its frantic rage and savage extravagance. Lawless vengeance is beginning to be visited upon white men as well as black. Our newspapers are daily disfigured by its ghastly horrors. It is no longer local, but national; no longer confined to the South, but has invaded the North. The contagion is spreading, extending and over-leaping geographical lines and state boundaries, and if permitted to go on it threatens to destroy all respect for law and order not only in the South, but in all parts of our country—North as well as South. For certain it is, that crime allowed to go on unresisted and unarrested will breed crime. When the poison of anarchy is once in the air, like the pestilence that walketh in the darkness, the winds of heaven will take it up and favor its diffusion. Though it may strike down the weak to-day, it will strike down the strong to-morrow.

Not a breeze comes to us now from the late rebellious States that is not tainted and freighted with negro blood. In its thirst for blood and its rage for vengeance, the mob has blindly, boldly and defiantly supplanted sheriffs, constables and police. It has assumed all the functions of civil authority. It laughs at legal processes, courts and juries, and its red-handed murderers range abroad unchecked and unchallenged by law or by public opinion. Prison walls and iron bars are no protection to the innocent or guilty, if the mob is in pursuit of negroes accused of crime. Jail doors are battered down in the presence of unresisting jailors, and the accused, awaiting trial in the courts of law are dragged out and hanged, shot, stabbed or burned to death as the blind and irresponsible mob may elect.

We claim to be a Christian country and a highly civilized nation, yet, I fearlessly affirm that there is nothing in the history of savages to surpass the blood chilling horrors and fiendish excesses perpetrated against the colored people by the so-called enlightened and Christian people of the South. It is commonly thought that only the lowest and most disgusting birds and beasts, such as buzzards, vultures and hyenas, will gloat over and prey upon dead bodies, but the Southern mob in its rage feeds its vengeance by shooting, stabbing and burning when their victims are dead.

Now the special charge against the negro by which this ferocity is justified, and by which mob law is defended by good men North and South, is alleged to be assaults by negroes upon white women. This charge once fairly started, no matter by whom or in what manner, whether well or ill-founded, whether true or false, is certain to subject the accused to immediate death. It is nothing, that in the case there may be a mistake as to identity. It is nothing that the victim pleads "not guilty." It is nothing that he only asks for time to establish his innocence. It is nothing that the accused is of fair reputation and his accuser is of an abandoned character. It is nothing that the majesty of the law is defied and insulted; no time is allowed for defence or explanation; he is bound with cords, hurried off amid the frantic yells and cursing of the mob to the scaffold and under its shadow he is tortured till by pain or promises, he is made to think he can possibly gain time or save his life by confession, and then whether innocent or guilty, he is shot, hanged, stabbed or burned to death amid the wild shouts of the mob. When the will of the mob has been accomplished, when its thirst for blood has been quenched, when its victim is speechless, silent and dead, his mobocratic accusers and murderers of course have the ear of the world all to themselves, and the world generally approves their verdict.

Such then is the state of Southern civilization in its relation to the colored citizens of that section and though the picture is dark and terrible I venture to affirm that no man North or South can deny the essential truth of the picture.

Now it is important to know how this state of affairs is viewed by the better classes of the Southern States. I will tell you, and I venture to say if our hearts were not already hardened by familiarity with such crimes against the negro, we should be shocked and astonished by the attitude of these so-called better classes of the Southern people and their lawmakers. With a few noble exceptions the upper classes of the South are in full sympathy with the mob and its deeds. There are few earnest words uttered against the mob or its deeds. Press, platform and pulpit are either generally silent or they openly apologize for the mob. The mobocratic murderers are not only permitted to go free, untried and unpunished, but are lauded and applauded as honorable men and good citizens, the guardians of Southern women. If lynch law is in any case condemned, it is only condemned in one breath, and excused in another.

The great trouble with the negro in the South is, that all presumptions are against him. A white man has but to blacken his face and commit a crime, to have some negro lynched in his stead. An abandoned woman has only to start the cry that she has been insulted by a black man, to have him arrested and summarily murdered by the mob. Frightened and tortured by his captors, confused into telling crooked stories about his whereabouts at the time when the alleged crime was committed and the death penalty is at once inflicted, though his story may be but the incoherency of ignorance or distraction caused by terror.

Now in confirmation of what I have said of the better classes of the South, I have before me the utterances of some of the best people of that section, and also the testimony of one from the North, a lady, from whom, considering her antecedents, we should have expected a more considerate, just and humane utterance.

In a late number of the "Forum" Bishop Haygood, author of the "Brother in Black," says that "The most alarming fact is, that execution by lynching has ceased to surprise us. The burning of a human being for any crime, it is thought, is a horror that does not occur outside of the Southern States of the American Union, yet unless assaults by negroes come to an end, there will most probably be still further display of vengeance that will shock the world, and men who are just will consider the provocation."

In an open letter addressed to me by ex-Governor Chamberlain, of South Carolina, and published in the "Charleston News and Courier," a letter which I have but lately seen, in reply to an article of mine on the subject published in the "North American Review," the ex-Governor says: "Your denunciation of the South on this point is directed exclusively, or nearly so, against the application of lynch law for the punishment of one crime, or one sort of crime, the existence, I suppose, I might say the prevalence of this crime at the South is undeniable. But I read your (my) article in vain for any special denunciation of the crime itself. As you say your people are lynched, tortured and burned for assault on white women. As you value your own good fame and safety as a race, stamp out the infamous crime." He further says, the way to stop lynching is to stamp out the crime.

And now comes the sweet voice of a Northern woman, of Southern principles, in the same tone and the same accusation, the good Miss Frances Willard, of the W. C. T. U. She says in a letter now before me, "I pity the Southerner. The problem on their hands is immeasurable. The colored race," she says, "multiplies like the locusts of Egypt. The safety of woman, of childhood, of the home, is menaced in a thousand localities at this moment, so that men dare not go beyond the sight of their own roof tree." Such then is the crushing indictment drawn up against the Southern negroes, drawn up, too, by persons who are perhaps the fairest and most humane of the negro's accusers. But even they paint him as a moral monster ferociously invading the sacred rights of women and endangering the homes of the whites.

The crime they allege against the negro, is the most revolting which men can commit. It is a crime that awakens the intensest abhorrence and invites mankind to kill the criminal on sight. This charge thus brought against the negro, and as constantly reiterated by his enemies, is not merely against the individual culprit, as would be in the case with an individual culprit of any other race, but it is in a large measure a charge against the colored race as such. It throws over every colored man a mantle of odium and sets upon him a mark for popular hate, more distressing than the mark set upon the first murderer. It points him out as an object of suspicion and avoidance. Now it is in this form that you and I, and all of us, are required to meet it and refute it, if that can be done. In the opinion of some of us, it is thought that it were well to say nothing about it, that the least said about it the better. In this opinion I do not concur. Taking this charge in its broad and comprehensive sense in which it is presented, and as now stated, I feel that it ought to be met, and as a colored man, I am grateful for the opportunity now afforded me to meet it. For I believe it can be met and successfully met. I am of opinion that a people too spiritless to defend themselves are not worth defending.

Without boasting, on this broad issue as now presented, I am ready to confront ex-Governor Chamberlain, Bishop Fitzgerald, Bishop Haygood, and Miss Frances Willard and all others, singly or altogether, without any doubt of the result.

But I want to be understood at the outset. I do not pretend that negroes are saints or angels. I do not deny that they are capable of committing the crime imputed to them, but I utterly deny that they are any more addicted to the commission of that crime than is true of any other variety of the human family. In entering upon my argument, I may be allowed to say, that I appear here this evening not as the de-fender of any man guilty of this atrocious crime, but as the defender of the colored people as a class.

In answer to the terrible indictment, thus read, and speaking for the colored people as a class, I, in their stead, here and now plead not guilty and shall submit my case with confidence of acquittal by good men and women North and South.

It is the misfortune of the colored people in this country that the sins of the few are visited upon the many, and I am here to speak for the many whose reputation is put in peril by the sweeping charge in question. With General Grant and every other honest man, my motto is, "Let no guilty man escape." But while I am here to say this, I am here also to say, let no innocent man be condemned and killed by the mob, or crushed under the weight of a charge of which he is not guilty.

You will readily see that the cause I have undertaken to support, is not to be maintained by any mere confident assertions or general denials. If I had no better ground to stand upon than this I would leave the field of controversy and give up the colored man's cause at once to his able accusers. I am aware, however, that I am here to do in some measure what the masters of logic say cannot be done,—prove a neg-ative.

Of course, I shall not be able to succeed in doing the impossible, but this one thing I can and will do. I can and will show that there are sound reasons for doubting and denying this horrible and hell-black charge of rape as the peculiar crime of the colored people of the South. My doubt and denial are based upon two fundamental and invincible grounds.

The first is, the well established and well tested character of the negro on the very point upon which he is now violently and persistently accused. The second ground for my doubt and denial is based upon what I know of the character and antecedents of the men and women who bring this charge against him. I undertake to say that the strength of this position will become more manifest as I proceed with my argument.

At the outset I deny that a fierce and frenzied mob is or ought to be deemed a competent witness against any man accused of any crime whatever. The ease with which a mob can be collected and the slight causes by which it may be set in motion, and the elements of which it is composed, deprives its testimony of the qualities that should inspire confidence and command belief. It is moved by impulses utterly unfavorable to an impartial statement of the truth. At the outset, therefore, I challenge the credibility of the mob, and as the mob is the main witness in the case against the negro, I appeal to the common sense of mankind in support of my challenge. It is the mob that brings this charge, and it is the mob that arraigns, condemns and executes, and it is the mob that the country has accepted as its witness.

Again, I impeach and discredit the veracity of southern men generally, whether mobocrats or otherwise, who now openly and deliberately nullify and violate the provisions of the constitution of their country, a constitution, which they have solemnly sworn to support and execute. I apply to them the legal maxim, "False in one, false in all."

Again I arraign the negro's accuser on another ground, I have no confidence in the truthfulness of men who justify themselves in cheating the negro out of his constitutional right to vote. The men, who either by false returns, or by taking advantage of his illiteracy or surrounding the ballot-box with obstacles and sinuosities intended to bewilder him and defeat his rightful exercise of the elective franchise, are men who are not to be believed on oath. That this is done in the Southern States is not only admitted, but openly defended and justified by so-called honorable men inside and outside of Congress.

Just this kind of fraud in the South is notorious. I have met it face to face. It was boldly defended and advocated a few weeks ago in a solemn paper by Prof. Weeks, a learned North Carolinian, in my hearing. His paper was one of the able papers read before one of the World's Auxiliary Congresses at Chicago.

Now men who openly defraud the negro by all manner of artifice and boast of it in the face of the world's civilization, as was done at Chicago, I affirm that they are not to be depended upon for truth in any case whatever, where the rights of the negro are involved. Their testimony in the case of any other people than the negro, against whom they should thus commit fraud would be instantly and utterly discredited, and why not the same in this case? Every honest man will see that this point is well taken, and I defy any argument that would drive me from this just contention. It has for its support common sense, common justice, common honesty, and the best sentiment of mankind, and has nothing to oppose it but a vulgar popular prejudice against the colored people of our country, which prejudice strikes men with moral blindness and renders them incapable of seeing any distinction between right and wrong.

But I come to a stronger position. I rest my conclusion not merely upon general principles, but upon well known facts. I reject the charge brought against the negro as a class, but all through the late war, while the slave masters of the South were absent from their homes in the field of rebellion, with bullets in their pockets, treason in their hearts, broad blades in their blood stained hands, seeking the life of the nation, with the vile purpose of perpetuating the enslavement of the negro, their wives, their daughters, their sisters and their mothers were left in the absolute custody of these same negroes, and during all those long four years of terrible conflict, when the negro had every opportunity to commit the abominable crime now alleged against him, there was never a single instance of such crime reported or charged against him. He was never accused of assault, insult, or an attempt to commit an assault upon any white woman in the whole South. A fact like this, although negative, speaks volumes and ought to have some weight with the American people.

Then, again on general principles, I do not believe the charge because it implies an improbable, if not impossible, change in the mental and moral character and composition of the negro. It implies a change wholly inconsistent with well known facts of human nature. It is a contradiction to well known human experience. History does not present an example of such a transformation in the character of any class of men so extreme, so unnatural and so complete as is implied in this charge. The change is too great and the period too brief. Instances may be cited where men fall like stars from heaven, but such is not the usual experience. Decline in the moral character of a people is not sudden, but gradual. The downward steps are marked at first by degrees and by increasing momentum from bad to worse. Time is an element in such changes, and I contend that the negroes of the South have not had time to experience this great change and reach this lower depth of infamy. On the contrary, in point of fact, they have been and still are, improving and ascending to higher levels of moral and social worth.

Again, I do not believe it and utterly deny it, because those who bring the charge do not and dare not, give the negro a chance to be heard in his own defence. He is not allowed to explain any part of his alleged offense. He is not allowed to vindicate his own character or to criminate the character and motives of his accusers. Even the mobocrats themselves admit that it would be fatal to their purpose to have the character of his accusers brought into court. They pretend to a delicate regard for the feelings of the parties assaulted, and therefore object to giving a fair trial to the accused. The excuse in this case is contemptible. It is not only mock modesty but mob modesty. Men who can collect hundreds and thousands, if we may believe them, and can spread before them in the tempest and whirlwind of vulgar passion, the most disgusting details of crime with the names of women, with the alleged offense, should not be allowed to shelter themselves under any pretense of modesty. Such a pretense is absurd and shameless. Who does not know that the modesty of womanhood is always an object for protection in a court of law? Who does not know that a lawless mob composed in part of the basest of men can have no such respect for the modesty of women as a court of law. No woman need be ashamed to confront one who has insulted or assaulted her in a court of law. Besides innocence does not hesitate to come to the rescue of justice.

Again, I do not believe it, and deny it because if the evidence were deemed sufficient to bring the accused to the scaffold, through the action of an impartial jury, there could be, and would be, no objection to having the alleged offender tried in conformity to due process of law.

Any pretense that a guilty negro, especially one guilty of the crime now charged, would in any case be permitted to escape condign punishment, is an insult to common sense. Nobody believes or can believe such a thing as escape possible, in a country like the South, where public opinion, the laws, the courts, the juries, and the advocates are all known to be against him, he could hardly escape if innocent. I repeat, therefore, I do not believe it, because I know, and you know, that a passionate and violent mob bent upon taking life, from the nature of the case, is not a more competent and trustworthy body to determine the guilt or innocence of a negro accused in such a case, than is a court of law. I would not, and you would not, convict a dog on such testimony.

But I come to another fact, and an all-important fact, bearing upon this case. You will remember that during all the first years of reconstruction and long after the war when the Southern press and people found it necessary to invent, adopt, and propagate almost every species of falsehood to create sympathy for themselves and to formulate an excuse for gratifying their brutal instincts, there was never a charge then made against a negro involving an assault upon any white woman or upon any little white child. During all this time the white women and children were absolutely safe. During all this time there was no call for Miss Willard's pity, or Bishop Haygood's defense of burning negroes to death.

You will remember also that during this time the justification for the murder of negroes was said to be negro conspiracies, insurrections, schemes to murder all the white people, to burn the town, and commit violence generally. These were the excuses then depended upon, but never a word was then said or whispered about negro outrages upon white women and children. So far as the history of that time is concerned, white women and children were absolutely safe, and husbands and fathers could leave home without the slightest anxiety on account of their families.

But when events proved that no such conspiracies; no such insurrections as were then pretended to exist and were paraded before the world in glaring head-lines, had ever existed or were even meditated; when these excuses had run their course and served their wicked purpose; when the huts of negroes had been searched, and searched in vain, for guns and ammunition to prove these charges, and no evidence was found, when there was no way open thereafter to prove these charges against the negro and no way to make the North believe in these excuses for murder, they did not even then bring forward the present allegation against the negro. They, however, went on harassing and killing just the same. But this time they based the right thus to kill on the ground that it was necessary to check the domination and supremacy of the negro and to secure the absolute rule of the Anglo-Saxon race.

It is important to notice that there has been three distinct periods of persecution of negroes in the South, and three distinct sets of excuses for persecution. They have come along precisely in the order in which they were most needed. First you remember it was insurrection. When that was worn out, negro supremacy became the excuse. When that is worn out, now it is assault upon defenseless women. I undertake to say, that this order and periodicity is significant and means something and should not be overlooked. And now that negro supremacy and negro domination are no longer defensible as an excuse for negro persecutions, there has come in due course, this heartrending cry about the white women and little white children of the South.

Now, my friends, I ask what is the rational explanation of this singular omission of this charge in the two periods preceding the present? Why was not the charge made at that time as now? The negro was the same then as to-day. White women and children were the same then as to-day. Temptations to wrong doing were the same then as to-day. Why then was not this dreadful charge brought forward against the negro in war times and why was it not brought forward in reconstruction times?

I will tell you; or you, yourselves, have already answered the question. The only rational answer is that there was no foundation for such a charge or that the charge itself was either not thought of or was not deemed necessary to excuse the lawless violence with which the negro was then pursued and killed. The old charges already enumerated were deemed all sufficient. This new charge has now swallowed up all the old ones and the reason is obvious.

Things have changed since then, old excuses were not available and the negro's accusers have found it necessary to change with them. The old charges are no longer valid. Upon them the good opinion of the North and of mankind cannot be secured. Honest men no longer believe in the worn-out stories of insurrection. They no longer believe that there is just ground to apprehend negro supremacy. Time and events have swept away these old refuges of lies. They did their work in their day, and did it with terrible energy and effect, but they are now cast aside as useless. The altered times and circumstances have made necessary a sterner, stronger, and more effective justification of Southern barbarism, and hence, according to my theory, we now have to look into the face of a more shocking and blasting charge than either negro supremacy or insurrection or that of murder itself.

This new charge has come at the call of new conditions, and nothing could have been hit upon better calculated to accomplish its purpose. It clouds the character of the negro with a crime the most revolting, and is fitted to drive from him all sympathy and all fair play and all mercy. It is a crime that places him outside of the pale of the law, and settles upon his shoulders a mantle of wrath and fire that blisters and burns into his very soul.

It is for this purpose, as I believe, that this new charge unthought of in the times to which I have referred, has been largely invited, if not entirely trumped up. It is for this purpose that it has been constantly reiterated and adopted. It was to blast and ruin the negro's character as a man and a citizen.

I need not tell you how thoroughly it has already done its wonted work. You may feel its malign influence in the very air. You may read it in the faces of men. It has cooled our friends. It has heated our enemies, and arrested in some measure the efforts that good men were wont to make for the colored man's improvement and elevation. It has deceived our friends at the North and many good friends at the South, for nearly all have in some measure accepted the charge as true. Its perpetual reiteration in our newspapers and magazines has led men and women to regard us with averted eyes, increasing hate and dark suspicion.

Some of the Southern papers have denounced me for my unbelief, in their new departure, but I repeat I do not believe it and firmly deny it. I reject it because I see in it, evidence of an invention, called into being by a well defined motive, a motive sufficient to stamp it as a gross expedient to justify murderous assault upon a long enslaved and hence a hated people.

I do not believe it because it bears on its face, the marks of being a makeshift for a malignant purpose. I reject it not only because it was sprung upon the country simultaneously with well-known efforts now being industriously made to degrade the negro by legislative enactments, and by repealing all laws for the protection of the ballot, and by drawing the color line in all railroad cars and stations and in all other public places in the South; but because I see in it a means of paving the way for our entire disfranchisement.

Again, I do not believe it, and deny it, because the charge is not so much against the crime itself, as against the color of the man alleged to be guilty of it. Slavery itself, you will remember, was a system of legalized outrage upon the black women of the North, and no white man was ever shot, burned, or hanged for availing himself of all the power that slavery gave him at this point.

Upon these grounds then,—grounds which I believe to be solid and immovable—I dare here and now in the capital of the nation and in the presence of Congress to reject it, and ask you and all just men to reject this horrible charge so frequently made and construed against the negro as a class.

To sum up my argument on this lynching business. It remains to be said that I have shown that the negro's accusers in this case have violated their oaths an have cheated the negro out of his vote; that they have robbed and defrauded the negro systematically and persistently, and have boasted of it. I have shown that when the negro had every opportunity to commit the crime now charged against him he was never accused of it by his bitterest enemies. I have shown that during all the years of reconstruction, when he was being murdered at Hamburg, Yazoo, New Orleans, Copiah and elsewhere, he was never accused of the crime now charged against him. I have shown that in the nature of things no such change in the character and composition of a people as this charge implies could have taken place in the limited period allowed for it. I have shown that those who accuse him dare not confront him in a court of law and have their witnesses subjected to proper legal inquiry. And in showing all this, and more, I have shown that they who charge him with this foul crime may be justly doubted and deemed unworthy of belief.

But I shall be told by many of my Northern friends that my argument, though plausible, is not conclusive. It will be said that the charges against the negro are specific and positive, and that there must be some foundation for them, because as they allege men in their normal condition do not shoot and hang their fellowmen who are guiltless of crime. Well! This assumption is very just, very charitable. I only ask something like the same justice and charity could be shown to the negro as well as to the mob. It is creditable to the justice and humanity of the good people of the North by whom it is entertained. They rightly assume that men do not shoot and hang their fellowmen without just cause. But the vice of their argument is in their assumption that the lynchers are like other men. The answer to that argument is what may be truly predicated of human nature under one condition is not what may be true of human nature under another. Uncorrupted human nature may shudder at the commission of such crimes as those of which the Southern mob is guilty.

But human nature uncorrupted is one thing and human nature corrupted and perverted by long abuse of irresponsible power, is quite another and different thing. No man can reason correctly on this question who reasons on the assumption that the lynchers are like ordinary men.

We are not, in this case, dealing with men in their natural condition, but with men brought up in the exercise of arbitrary power. We are dealing with men whose ideas, habits and customs are entirely different from those of ordinary men. It is, therefore, quite gratuitous to assume that the principles that apply to other men apply to the Southern murderers of the negro, and just here is the mistake of the Northern people. They do not see that the rules resting upon the justice and benevolence of human nature do not apply to the mobocrats, or to those who were educated in the habits and customs of a slave-holding community. What these habits are I have a right to know, both in theory and in practice.

I repeat: The mistake made by those who on this ground object to my theory of the charge against the negro, is that they overlook the natural effect and influence of the life, education and habits of the lynchers. We must remember that these people have not now and have never had any such respect for human life as is common to other men. They have had among them for centuries a peculiar institution, and that peculiar institution has stamped them as a peculiar people. They were not before the war, they were not during the war and have not been since the war in their spirit or in their civilization, a people in common with the people of the North. I will not here harrow up your feelings by detailing their treatment of Northern prisoners during the war. Their institutions have taught them no respect for human life and especially the life of the negro. It has in fact taught them absolute contempt for his life. The sacredness of life which ordinary men feel does not touch them anywhere. A dead negro is with them a common jest.

They care no more for a negro's right to live than they care for his rights to liberty, or his rights to the ballot. Chief Justice Taney told the exact truth about these people when he said: "They did not consider that the black man had any rights which the white men were bound to respect." No man of the South ever called in question that statement and they never will. They could always shoot, stab and burn the negro without any such remorse or shame as other men would feel after committing such a crime. Any Southern man who is honest and is frank enough to talk on the subject, will tell you that he has no such ideas as we have of the sacredness of human life and especially, as I have said, of the life of the negro. Hence it is absurd to meet my arguments with the facts predicated on our common human nature.

I know I shall be charged with apologizing for criminals. Ex-Governor Chamberlain has already virtually done as much. But there is no foundation for any such charge. I affirm that neither I nor any other colored man of like standing with myself, has ever raised a finger or uttered a word in defense of any one really guilty of the dreadful crime now in question.

But, what I contend for, and what every honest man, black or white should contend for, is that when any man is accused of this or any other crime, of whatever name, nature, or extent, he shall have the benefit of a legal investigation; that he shall be confronted by his accusers; and that he shall through proper counsel, be able to question his accusers in open court and in open day-light so that his guilt or his innocence may be duly proved and established.

If this is to make be liable to the charge of apologizing for crime, I am not ashamed to be so charged. I dare to contend for the colored people of the United States that they are a law-abiding people, and I dare to insist upon it that they or any man, black or white, accused of crime, shall have a fair trial before he is punished.

Again, I cannot dwell too much upon the fact that colored people are much damaged by this charge. As an injured class we have a right to appeal from the judgment of the mob to the judgment of the law and the American people. Our enemies have known well where to strike and how to stab us most fatally. Owing to popular prejudice it has become the misfortune of the colored people of the South and of the North as well, to have as I have said, the sins of the few visited upon the many. When a white man steals, robs or murders, his crime is visited upon his own head alone. but not so with the black man. When he commits a crime the whole race is made to suffer. The cause before us is an example. This unfairness confronts us not only here, but it confronts us everywhere else.

Even when American art undertakes to picture the types of the two races it invariably places in comparison not the best of both races as common fairness would dictate, but it puts side by side in glaring contrast the lowest type of the negro with the highest type of the white man and calls upon you to "look upon this picture then upon that."

When a black man's language is quoted, in order to belittle and degrade him, his ideas are put into the most grotesque and unreadable English, while the utterances of negro scholars and authors are ignored. A hundred white men will attend a concert of white negro minstrels with faces blackened with burnt cork, to one who will attend a lecture by an intelligent negro.

On this ground I have a criticism to make, even of the late World's Columbian Exposition. While I join with all other men in pronouncing the Exposition itself one of the grandest demonstrations of civilization that the world has ever seen, yet great and glorious as it was, it was made to show just this kind of unfairness and discrimination against the negro.

As nowhere else in the world it was hoped that here the idea of human brotherhood would have been fully recognized and most gloriously illustrated. It should have been, and would have been, had it been what it professed to be, a World's Exposition. It was, however, in a marked degree an American Exposition. The spirit of American caste made itself conspicuously felt against the educated American negro, and to this extent, the Exposition was made simply an American Exposition and that in one of America's most illiberal features.

Since the day of Pentecost, there has never assembled in any one place or on any one occasion, a larger variety of peoples of all forms, features and colors, and all degrees of civilization, than was assembled at this World's Exposition. It was a grand ethnological lesson, a chance to study all likenesses and differences. Here were Japanese, Soudanese, Chinese, Cingalese, Syrians, Persians, Tunisians, Algerians, Egyptians, East Indians, Laplanders, Esquimaux, and as if to shame the educated negro of America, the Dahomeyans were there to exhibit their barbarism, and increase American contempt for the negro intellect. All classes and conditions were there save the educated American negro. He ought to have been there if only to show what American slavery and freedom have done for him. The fact that all other nations were there and there at their best, made his exclusion the more marked, and the more significant. People from abroad noticed the fact that while we have eight millions of colored people in the United States, many of them gentlemen and scholars, not one of them was deemed worthy to be appointed a Commissioner, or a member of an important committee, or a guide, or a guard on the Exposition grounds. What a commentary is this upon our boasted American liberty and American equality! It is a silence to be sure, but it is a silence that speaks louder than words. It says to the world that the colored people of America are deemed by Americans not within the compass of American law and of American civilization. It says to the lynchers and mobocrats of the South, go on in your hellish work of negro persecution. What you do to their bodies, we do to their souls.

I come now to the question of negro suffrage. It has come to be fashionable of late to ascribe much of the trouble at the South to ignorant negro suffrage. The great measure according suffrage to the negro recommended by General Grant and adopted by the loyal nation is now denounced as a blunder and a failure. They would, therefore, in some way abridge and limit this right by imposing upon it an educational or some other qualification. Among those who take this view are Mr. John J. Ingalls, and Mr. John M. Langston. They are both eloquent, both able, and both wrong. Though they are both Johns neither of them is to my mind a "St. John" and not even a "John the Baptist."

They have taken up an idea which they seem to think quite new, but which in reality is as old as despotism and about as narrow and selfish. It has been heard and answered a thousand times over. It is the argument of the crowned heads and privileged classes of the world. It is as good against our Republican form of government as it is against the negro. The wonder is that its votaries do not see its consequences. It does away with that noble and just idea of Abraham Lincoln, that our government should be a government of the people, by the people, and for the people, and for *all* the people.

These gentlemen are very learned, very eloquent and very able, but I cannot follow them. Much learning has made them mad. Education is great, but manhood is greater. The one is the principle, the other is the accident. Man was not made as an attribute to education, but education is an attribute to man. I say to these gentlemen, first protect the man and you will thereby protect education. I would not make illiteracy a bar to the ballot, but would make the ballot a bar to illiteracy. Take the ballot from the negro and you take from him the means and motives that make for education. Those who are already educated and are vested with political power and have thereby an advantage, will have a strong motive for refusing to divide that advantage with others, and least of all will they divide it with the negro to whom they would deny all right to participate in the government.

I, therefore, cannot follow these gentlemen in their proposition to limit suffrage to the educated alone. I would not make suffrage more exclusive, but more inclusive. I would not have it embrace merely the elite, but would include the lowly. I would not only include the men, I would gladly include the women, and make our government in reality as in name a government of the people and of the whole people.

But manifestly suffrage to the colored people is not the cause of the failure of good government, or the cause of trouble in the Southern States, but it is the lawless limitations of suffrage that makes the trouble.

Much thoughtless speech is heard about the ignorance of the negro in the South. But plainly enough it is not the ignorance of the negro, but the malevolence of his accusers, which is the real cause of Southern disorder. The illiteracy of the negro has no part or lot in the disturbances there. They who contend for disfranchisement on this ground know, and know very well, that there is no truth whatever in their contention. To make out their case they must show that some oppressive and hurtful measure has been imposed upon the country by negro voters. But they cannot show any such thing.

The negro has never set up a separate party, never adopted a negro platform, never proclaimed or adopted a separate policy for himself or for the country. His assailants know that he has never acted apart from the whole American people. They know that he has never sought to lead, but has always been content to follow. They know that he has not made his ignorance the rule of his political conduct, but the intelligence of white people has always been his guide. They know that he has simply kept pace with the average intelligence of his age and country. They know that he has gone steadily along in the line of his politics with the most enlightened citizens of the country. They know that he has always voted with one or the other of the two great political parties. They know that if the votes of these parties have been guided by intelligence and patriotism, the same may be said for the vote of the negro. They ought to know, therefore, that it is a shame and an outrage upon common sense and common fairness to make the negro responsible, or his ignorance responsible, for any disorder and confusion that may reign in the Southern States. Yet, while any lie may be safely told against the negro and be credited, this lie will find eloquent mouths bold enough to tell it, and pride themselves upon their superior wisdom in denouncing the ignorant negro voter.

It is true that the negro once voted solidly for the candidates of the Republican party, but what if he did? He then only voted with John Mercer Langston, John J. Ingalls, John Sherman, General Harrison, Senator Hoar, Henry Cabot Lodge, and Governor McKinley, and many of the most intelligent statesmen and patriots of whom this country can boast. The charge against him at this point is, therefore, utterly groundless. It is a mere pretense, a sham, an excuse for fraud and violence, for persecution and a cloak for popular prejudice.

The proposition to disfranchise the colored voter of the South in order to solve the race problem I hereby denounce as a mean and cowardly proposition, utterly unworthy of an honest, truthful and grateful nation. It is a proposition to sacrifice friends in order to conciliate enemies; to surrender the constitution to the late rebels for the lack of moral courage to execute its provisions. It says to the negro citizens, "The Southern nullifiers have robbed you of a part of your rights, and as we are powerless and cannot help you, and wish to live on good terms with our Southern brethren, we propose to join your oppressors so that our practice shall be consistent with their theories. Your suffrage has been practically rendered a failure by violence, we now propose to make it a failure by law. Instead of conforming our practice to the theory of our government and the genius of our institutions, we now propose, as means of conciliation, to conform our practice to the theory of your oppressors."

Than this, was there ever a surrender more complete, more cowardly or more base? Upon the statesmen, black or white, who could dare to hint such a scheme of national debasement as a means of settling the race problem, I should inflict no punishment more severe than to keep him at home, and deprived of all legislative trusts forever.

Do not ask me what will be the final result of the so-called negro problem. I cannot tell you. I have sometimes thought that the American people are too great to be small, too just and magnanimous to

355

oppress the weak, too brave to yield up the right to the strong, and too grateful for public services ever to forget them or fail to reward them. I have fondly hoped that this estimate of American character would soon cease to be contradicted or put in doubt. But the favor with which this cowardly proposition of disfranchisement has been received by public men, white and black, by Republicans as well as Democrats, has shaken my faith in the nobility of the nation. I hope and trust all will come out right in the end, but the immediate future looks dark and troubled. I cannot shut my eyes to the ugly facts before me.

Strange things have happened of late and are still happening. Some of these tend to dim the lustre of the American name, and chill the hopes once entertained for the cause of American liberty. He is a wiser man than I am, who can tell how low the moral sentiment of this republic may yet fall. When the moral sense of a nation begins to decline and the wheel of progress to roll backward, there is no telling how low the one will fall or where the other may stop. The downward tendency already manifest has swept away some of the most important safeguards. The Supreme Court has surrendered. State sovereignty is restored. It has destroyed the [C]ivil [R]ights Bill, and converted the Republican party into a party of money rather than a party of morals, a party of things rather than a party of humanity and justice. We may well ask what next?

The pit of hell is said to be bottomless. Principles which we all thought to have been firmly and permanently settled by the late war, have been boldly assaulted and overthrown by the defeated party. Rebel rule is now nearly complete in many States and it is gradually capturing the nation's Congress. The cause lost in the war, is the cause regained in peace, and the cause gained in war, is the cause lost in peace.

There was a threat made long ago by an American statesman, that the whole body of legislation enacted for the protection of American liberty and to secure the results of the war for the Union, should be blotted from the national statute book. The threat is now being sternly pursued, and may yet be fully realized. The repeal of the laws intended to protect the elective franchise has heightened the suspicion that Southern rule may yet become complete, though I trust, not permanent. There is no denying that the trend is in the wrong way at present. The late election, however, gives us hope that the loyal Republican party may return to its first born.

But I come now to another proposition held up just now as a solution of the race problem, and this I consider equally unworthy with the one just disposed of. The two belong to the same low-bred family of ideas.

This proposition is to colonize the colored people of America in Africa, or somewhere else. Happily this scheme will be defeated, both by its impolicy and its impracticability. It is all nonsense to talk about the removal of eight millions of the American people from their homes in America to Africa. The expense and hardships, to say nothing of the cruelty of such a measure, would make success to such a measure impossible. The American people are wicked, but they are not fools, they will hardly be disposed to incur the expense, to say nothing of the injustice which this measure demands. Nevertheless, this colonizing scheme, unworthy as it is, of American statesmanship and American honor, and though full of mischief to the colored people, seems to have a strong hold on the public mind and at times has shown much life and vigor.

The bad thing about it is that it has now begun to be advocated by colored men of acknowledged ability and learning, and every little while some white statesman becomes its advocate. Those gentlemen will doubtless have their opinion of me; I certainly have mine of them. My opinion of them is that if they are sensible, they are insincere, and if they are sincere they are not sensible. They know, or they ought to know, that it would take more money than the cost of the late war, to transport even one-half of the colored people of the United States to Africa. Whether intentionally or not they are, as I think, simply trifling with an afflicted people. They urge them to look for relief, where they ought to know that relief is impossible. The only excuse they can make is that there is no hope for the negro here and that the colored people in America owe something to Africa.

This last sentimental idea makes colonization very fascinating to dreamers of both colors. But there is really for it no foundation.

They tell us that we owe something to our native land. But when the fact is brought to view, which should never be forgotten, that a man can only have one native land, and that is the land in which he was born, the bottom falls entirely out of this sentimental argument.

Africa, according to her advocates, is by no means modest in her demand upon us. She calls upon us to send her only our best men. She does not want our riff raff, but our best men. But these are just the men we want at home. It is true we have a few preachers and laymen with a missionary turn of mind who might be easily spared. Some who would possibly do as much good by going there as by staying here. But this is not the only colonization idea. Its advocates want not only the best, but millions of the best. They want the money to be voted by the United States Government to send them there.

Now I hold that the American negro owes no more to the negroes in Africa than he owes to the negroes in America. There are millions of needy people over there, but there are also millions of needy people over here as well, and the millions here need intelligent men of their numbers to help them, as much as intelligent men are needed in Africa. We have a fight on our hands right here, a fight for the whole race, and a blow struck for the negro in America is a blow struck for the negro in Africa. For until the negro is respected in America, he need not expect consideration elsewhere. All this native land talk is nonsense. The native land of the American negro is America. His bones, his muscles, his sinews, are all American. His ancestors for two hundred and seventy years have lived, and labored, and died on American soil, and millions of his posterity have inherited Caucasian blood.

It is competent, therefore, to ask, in view of this admixture, as well as in view of other facts, where the people of this mixed race are to go, for their ancestors are white and black, and it will be difficult to find their native land anywhere outside of the United States.

But the worse thing, perhaps, about this colonization nonsense is, that it tends to throw over the negro a mantle of despair. It leads him to doubt the possibility of his progress as an American citizen. It also encourages popular prejudice with the hope that by persecution or persuasion the negro can finally be driven from his natural home, while in the nature of the case, he must stay here, and will stay here and cannot well get away.

It tends to weaken his hold on one country while it can give him no rational hope of another. Its tendency is to make him dispondent and doubtful, where he should be made to feel assured and confident. It forces upon him the idea that he is forever doomed to be a stranger and sojourner in the land of his birth, and that he has no permanent abiding place here.

All this is hurtful, with such ideas constantly flaunted before him he cannot easily set himself to work to better his condition in such ways as are open to him here. It sets him to groping everlastingly after the impossible.

Every man who thinks at all must know that home is the fountain head, the inspiration, the foundation and main support not only of all social virtue, but of all motives to human progress and that no people can prosper or amount to much without a home. To have a home, the negro must have a country, and he is an enemy to the moral progress of the negro, whether he knows it or not, who calls upon him to break up his home in this country for an uncertain home in Africa.

But the agitation of this subject has a darker side still. It has already been given out that we may be forced to go at the point of the bayonet. I cannot say we shall not, but badly as I think of the tendency of our times, I do not think that American sentiment will ever reach a condition which will make the expulsion of the negro from the United States by such means possible.

Colonization is no solution of the race problem. It is an evasion. It is not repenting of wrong but putting out of sight the people upon whom wrong has been inflicted. Its reiteration and agitation only serve to fan the flame of popular prejudice and encourage the hope that in some way or other, in time or in eternity, those who hate the negro will get rid of him.

If the American people could endure the negro's presence while a slave, they certainly can and ought to endure his presence as a freeman. If they could tolerate him when he was a heathen, they might bear with him when he is a Christian, a gentleman and a scholar.

But woe to the South when it no longer has the strong arm of the negro to till its soil! And woe to the nation if it shall ever employ the sword to drive the negro from his native land!

Such a crime against justice, such a crime against gratitude, should it ever be attempted, would certainly bring a national punishment which would cause the earth to shudder. It would bring a stain upon the nation's honor, like the blood on Lady Macbeth's hand. The waters of all the oceans would not suffice to wash out the infamy that such an act of ingratitude and cruelty would leave on the character of the American people.

Another mode of impeaching the wisdom of emancipation, and one that seems to give pleasure to our enemies, is, as they say, that the condition of the colored people of the South has been made worse; that freedom has made their condition worse.

The champions of this idea are the men who glory in the good old times when the slaves were under the lash and were bought and sold in the market with horses, sheep and swine. It is another way of saying that slavery is better than freedom; that darkness is better than light and that wrong is better than right. It is the American method of reasoning in all matters concerning the negro. It inverts everything; turns truth upside down and puts the case of the unfortunate negro wrong end foremost every time. There is, however, always some truth on their side.

When these false reasoners assert that the condition of the emancipated is wretched and deplorable, they tell in part the truth, and I agree with them. I even concur with them that the negro is in some respects, and in some localities, in a worse condition to-day than in the time of slavery, but I part with these gentlemen when they ascribe this condition to emancipation.

To my mind, the blame for this condition does not rest upon emancipation, but upon slavery. It is not the work of the spirit of liberty, but the work of the spirit of bondage, and of the determination of slavery to perpetuate itself, if not under one form, then under another. It is due to the folly of endeavoring to retain the new wine of liberty in the old bottles of slavery. I concede the evil but deny the alleged cause.

The land owners of the South want the labor of the negro on the hardest possible terms. They once had it for nothing. They now want it for next to nothing and they have contrived three ways of thus obtaining it. The first is to rent their land to the negro at an exorbitant price per annum, and compel him to mortgage his crop in advance. The laws under which this is done are entirely in the interest of the landlord. He has a first claim upon everything produced on the land.

The negro can have nothing, can keep nothing, can sell nothing, without the consent of the landlord. As the negro is at the start poor and empty handed, he has to draw on the landlord for meat and bread to feed himself and family while his crop is growing. The landlord keeps books; the negro does not; hence, no matter how hard he may work or how saving he may be, he is, in most cases, brought in debt at the end of the year, and once in debt, he is fastened to the land as by hooks of steel. If he attempts to leave he may be arrested under the law.

Another way, which is still more effective, is the payment of the labor with orders on stores instead of in lawful money. By this means money is kept entirely out of the hands of the negro. He cannot save money because he has no money to save. He cannot seek a better market for his labor because he has no money with which to pay his fare and because he is, by that vicious order system, already in debt, and therefore already in bondage. Thus he is riveted to one place and is, in some sense, a slave; for a man to whom it can be said, "You shall work for me for what I shall choose to pay you and how I shall choose to pay you," is in fact a slave though he may be called a free man.

We denounce the landlord and tenant system of England, but it can be said of England as cannot be said of our free country, that by law no laborer can be paid for labor in any other than lawful money. England holds any other payment to be a penal offense and punishment by fine and imprisonments. The same should be the case in every State in the Union.

Under the mortgage system, no matter how industrious or economical the negro may be, he finds himself at the end of the year in debt to the landlord, and from year to year he toils on and is tempted to try again and again, seldom with any better result.

With this power over the negro, this possession of his labor, you may easily see why the South sometimes brags that it does not want slavery back. It had the negro's labor heretofore for nothing, and now it has it for next to nothing, and at the same time is freed from the obligation to take care of the young and the aged, the sick and decrepit.

I now come to the so-called, but mis-called "Negro Problem," as a characterization of the relations existing in the Southern States.

I say at once, I do not like or admit the justice or propriety of this formula. Words are things. They certainly are such in this case, and I may say they are a very bad thing in this case, since they give us a misnomer and one that is misleading. It is a formula of Southern origin, and has a strong bias against him. It has been accepted by the good people of the North, as I think, without investigation. It is a crafty invention and is in every way, worthy of its inventors.

The natural effect and purpose on its face of this formula is to divert attention from the true issue now before the American people. It does this by holding up and preoccupying the public mind with an issue entirely different from the real one in question. That which really is a great national problem and which ought to be so considered, dwarfs into a "negro problem."

The device is not new. It is an old trick. It has been oft repeated, and with a similar purpose and effect. For truth, it gives us falsehood. For innocence, it gives us guilt. It removes the burden of proof from the old master class, and imposes it upon the negro. It puts upon a race a work which belongs to the nation. It belongs to that craftiness often displayed by disputants, who aim to make the worse appear the better reason. It gives bad names to good things, and good names to bad things.

The negro has often been the victim of this kind of low cunning. You may remember that during the late war, when the South fought for the perpetuity of slavery, it called the slaves "domestic servants," and slavery "a domestic institution." Harmless names, indeed, but the things they stood for were far from harmless.

The South has always known how to have a dog hanged by giving him a bad name. When it prefixed "negro" to the national problem, it knew that the device would awaken and increase a deep-seated prejudice at once, and that it would repel fair and candid investigation. As it stands, it implies that the negro is the cause of whatever trouble there is in the South. In old slave times, when a little white child lost his temper, he was given a little whip and told to go and whip "Jim" or "Sal" and thus regained his temper. The same is true, to-day on a larger scale.

I repeat, and my contention is, that this negro problem formula lays the fault at the door of the negro, and removes it from the door of the white man, shields the guilty, and blames the innocent. Makes the negro responsible and not the nation.

Now the real problem is, and ought to be regarded by the American people, a great national problem. It involves the question, whether, after all, with our Declaration of Independence, with our glorious free constitution, whether with our sublime Christianity, there is enough of national virtue in this great nation to solve this problem, in accordance with wisdom and justice.

The marvel is that this old trick of misnaming things, so often played by Southern politicians, should have worked so well for the bad cause in which it is now employed,—for the Northern people have fallen in with it. It is still more surprising that the colored press of the country, and some of the colored orators of the country, insist upon calling it a "negro problem," or a Race problem, for by it they mean the negro Race. Now—there is nothing the matter with the negro. He is all right. Learned or ignorant, he is all right. He is neither a Lyncher, a Mobocrat, or an Anarchist. He is now, what he has ever been, a loyal, law-abiding, hard working, and peaceable man; so much so, that men have thought him cowardly and spiritless. They say that any other people would have found some violent way in which to resent their wrongs. If this problem depended upon *his* character and conduct, there would be no problem to solve; there would be no menace to the peace and good order of Southern society. He makes no unlawful fight between labor and capital. That problem which often makes the American people thoughtful, is not of his bringing—though he may some day be compelled to talk, and on this tremendous problem.

He has as little to do with the cause of Southern trouble as he has with its cure. There is no reason, therefore, in the world, why he should give a name to this problem, and this lie, like all other lies, must eventually come to naught. A lie is worth nothing when it has lost its ability to deceive, and if it is at all in my power, this lie shall lose its power to deceive.

I well remember that this same old falsehood was employed and used against the negro, during the late war. He was then charged and stigmatized with being the cause of the war, on the principle that there would be no highway robbers if there were nobody on the road to be robbed. But as absurd as this pretense was, the color prejudice of the country was stimulated by it and joined in the accusation, and the negro has to bear the brunt of it.

Even at the North, he was hated and hunted on account of it. In the great city of New York, his houses were burned, his children were hunted down like wild beasts, and his people were murdered in the streets, because "they were the cause of the war." Even the noble and good Mr. Lincoln, one of the best men that ever lived, told a committee of negroes who waited upon him at Washington, that "they were the cause of the war." Many were the men who accepted this theory, and wished the negro in Africa, or in a hotter climate, as some do now.

There is nothing to which prejudice is not equal in the way of perverting the truth and inflaming the passions of men.

But call this problem what you may, or will, the all important question is: How can it be solved? How can the peace and tranquility of the South, and of the country, be secured and established?

There is nothing occult or mysterious about the answer to this question. Some things are to be kept in mind when dealing with this subject and never be forgotten. It should be remembered that in the order of Divine Providence the man who puts one end of a chain around the ankle of his fellow man will find the other end around his own neck. And it is the same with a nation. Confirmation of this truth is as strong as thunder. "As we sow, we shall reap," is a lesson to be learned here as elsewhere. We tolerated slavery, and it cost us a million graves, and it may be that lawless murder, if permitted to go on, may yet bring vengeance, not only on the reverend head of age and upon the heads of helpless women, but upon the innocent babe in the cradle.

But how can this problem be solved? I will tell you how it can *not* be solved. It cannot be solved by keeping the negro poor, degraded, ignorant and half-starved, as I have shown is now being done in the Southern States.

It cannot be solved by keeping the wages of the laborer back by fraud, as is now being done by the landlords of the South.

It cannot be done by ballot-box stuffing, by falsifying election returns, or by confusing the negro voter by cunning devices.

It cannot be done by repealing all federal laws enacted to secure honest elections.

It can, however, be done, and very easily done, for where there's a will, there's a way!

Let the white people of the North and South conquer their prejudices.

Let the great Northern press and pulpit proclaim the gospel of truth and justice against war now being made upon the negro.

Let the American people cultivate kindness and humanity.

Let the South abandon the system of "mortgage" labor, and cease to make the negro a pauper, by paying him scrip for his labor.

Let them give up the idea that they can be free, while making the negro a slave. Let them give up the idea that to degrade the colored man, is to elevate the white man.

Let them cease putting new wine into old bottles, and mending old garments with new cloth.

They are not required to do much. They are only required to undo the evil that they have done, in order to solve this problem.

In old times when it was asked, "How can we abolish slavery?" the answer was "Quit stealing."

The same is the solution of the Race problem to-day. The whole thing can be done by simply no longer violating the amendments of the Constitution of the United States, and no longer evading the claims of justice. If this were done, there would be no negro problem to vex the South, or to vex the nation.

Let the organic law of the land be honestly sustained and obeyed.

Let the political parties cease to palter in a double sense and live up to the noble declarations we find in their platforms.

Let the statesmen of the country live up to their convictions.

In the language of Senator Ingalls: "Let the nation try justice and the problem will be solved."

Two hundred and twenty years ago, the negro was made the subject of a religious problem, one which gave our white forefathers much perplexity and annoyance. At that time the problem was in respect of what relation a negro would sustain to the Christian Church, whether he was a fit subject for baptism, and Dr. Godwin, a celebrated divine of his time, and one far in advance of his brethren, was at the pains of writing a book of two hundred pages, or more, containing an elaborate argument to prove that it was not a sin in the sight of God to baptize a negro.

His argument was very able, very learned, very long. Plain as the truth may now seem, there were at that time very strong arguments against the position of the learned divine.

As usual, it was not merely the baptism of the negro that gave trouble, but it was what might follow his baptism. The sprinkling him with water was a very simple thing, but the slave holders of that day saw in the innovation something more dangerous than water. They said that to baptize the negro and make him a member of the Church of Christ, was to make him an important person—in fact, to make him an heir of God and a joint heir of Jesus Christ. It was to give him a place at the Lord's supper. It was to take him out [of] the category of heathenism, and make it inconsistent to hold him as a slave; for the Bible made only the heathen a proper subject for slavery.

These were formidable consequences, certainly, and it is not strange that the Christian slave holders of that day viewed these consequences with immeasurable horror. It was something more terrible and dangerous than the fourteenth and fifteenth amendments to our Constitution. It was a difficult thing, therefore, at that day to get the negro in the water.

Nevertheless, our learned Doctor of Divinity, like many of the same class in our day, was quite equal to the emergency. He was able to satisfy all the important parties to the problem, except the negro, and him it did not seem necessary to satisfy.

The Doctor was [a] skilled dialectician. He did not only divide the word with skill, but he could divide the negro in two parts. He argued that the negro had a soul as well as a body, and insisted that while his body rightfully belonged to his master on earth, his soul belonged to his Master in heaven. By this convenient arrangement, somewhat metaphysical, to be sure, but entirely evangelical and logical, the problem of negro baptism was solved.

But with the negro in the case, as I have said, the argument was not entirely satisfactory. The operation was much like that by which the white man got the turkey and the Indian got the crow. When the negro looked around for his body, that belonged to his earthly master. When he looked around for his soul, that had been appropriated by his Heavenly Master. And when he looked around for something that really belonged to himself, he found nothing but his shadow, and that vanished in the shade.

One thing, however, is to be noticed with satisfaction, it is this: Something was gained to the cause of righteousness by this argument. It was a contribution to the cause of liberty. It was largely in favor of the negro. It was recognition of his manhood, and was calculated to set men to thinking that the negro might have some other important rights, no less than the religious right to baptism.

Thus with all its faults, we are compelled to give the pulpit the credit of furnishing the first important argument in favor of the religious character and manhood rights of the negro. Dr. Godwin was undoubtedly a good man. He wrote at a time of much moral darkness, and property in man was nearly everywhere recognized as a rightful institution. He saw only a part of the truth. He saw that the negro had a right to be baptized, but he could not all at once see that he had a paramount right to himself.

But this was not the only problem slavery had in store for the negro. Time and events brought another and it was this very important one:

Can the negro sustain the legal relation of a husband to a wife? Can he make a valid marriage contract in this Christian country.

This problem was solved by the same slave holding authority, entirely against the negro. Such a contact, it was argued, could only be binding upon men providentially enjoying the right to life, liberty, and the pursuit of happiness, and, since the negro is a slave, and slavery a divine institution, legal marriage was wholly inconsistent with the institution of slavery.

When some of us at the North questioned the ethics of this conclusion, we were told to mind our business, and our Southern brethren asserted, as they assert now, that they alone are competent to manage this, and all other questions relating to the negro.

In fact, there has been no end to the problems of some sort or other, involving the negro in difficulty.

Can the negro be a citizen? was the question of the Dred Scott decision.

Can the negro be educated? Can the negro be induced to work for himself, without a master? Can the negro be a soldier? Time and events have answered these and all other like questions. We have amongst us, those who have taken the first prizes as scholars; those who have won distinction for courage and skill on the battlefield; those who have taken rank as lawyers, doctors and ministers of the gospel; those who shine among men in every useful calling; and yet we are called "a problem;" "a tremendous problem;" a mountain of difficulty; a constant source of apprehension; a disturbing force, threatening destruction to the holiest and best interests of society. I declare this statement concerning the negro, whether by Miss Willard, Bishop Haygood, Bishop Fitzgerald, ex-Governor Chamberlain or by any and all others as false and deeply injurious to the colored citizen of the United States.

But, my friends, I must stop. Time and strength are not equal to the task before me. But could I be heard by this great nation, I would call to mind the sublime and glorious truths with which, at its birth, it saluted a listening world. Its voice then, was as the trump of an archangel, summoning hoary forms of oppression and time honored tyranny, to judgment. Crowned heads heard it and shrieked. Toiling millions heard it and clapped their hands for joy. It announced the advent of a nation, based upon human brotherhood and the self-evident truths of liberty and equality. Its mission was the redemption of the world from the bondage of ages. Apply these sublime and glorious truths to the situation now before you. Put away your race prejudice. Banish the idea that one class must rule over another. Recognize the fact that the rights of the humblest citizen are as worthy of protection as are those of the highest, and your problem will be solved; and, whatever may be in store for it in the future, whether prosperity, or adversity; whether it shall have foes without, or foes within, whether there shall be peace, or war; based upon the eternal principles of truth, justice and humanity, and with no class having any cause of complaint or grievance, your Republic will stand and flourish forever.

Suggested Reading

❖

Andrews, William L., ed. *Critical Essays on Frederick Douglass*. Boston: G. K. Hall, 1991.

———. *To Tell a Free Story: The First Century of Afro-American Autobiography, 1760–1865*. Urbana: U of Illinois P, 1986.

Baker, Houston A., Jr. *Blues, Ideology, and Afro-American Literature*. Chicago: U of Chicago P, 1984.

———. *The Journey Back*. Chicago: U of Chicago P, 1980.

Blassingame, John W. *The Slave Community*. 2nd ed. New York: Oxford U P, 1979.

———, ed. *Slave Testimony*. Baton Rouge: Louisiana State U P, 1977.

Blight, David W. *Frederick Douglass' Civil War*. Baton Rouge: Louisiana State U P, 1989.

Butterfield, Stephen. *Black Autobiography in America*. Amherst: U of Massachusetts P, 1974.

Davis, Charles T., and Henry Louis Gates, Jr., eds. *The Slave's Narrative*. New York: Oxford U P, 1985.

Douglass, Frederick. *Autobiographies*. New York: Library of America, 1994.

———. *Frederick Douglass on Women's Rights*. Ed. Philip S. Foner. Westport, Conn.: Greenwood, 1976.

———. *The Frederick Douglass Papers*. Ed. John W. Blassingame. 5 vols. New Haven: Yale U P, 1979– .

———. *Life and Times of Frederick Douglass*. Ed. Rayford W. Logan. New York: Crowell-Collier, 1962.

———. *Life and Writings of Frederick Douglass*. Ed. Philip S. Foner. 5 vols. New York: International, 1950–1975.

———. *My Bondage and My Freedom*. Ed. William L. Andrews. Urbana: U of Illinois P, 1987.

———. *Narrative of the Life of Frederick Douglass*. Ed. Houston A. Baker, Jr. New York: Viking Penguin, 1982.

———. *Narrative of the Life of Frederick Douglass*. Ed. David W. Blight. New York: St. Martin's, 1993.

Dudley, David L. *My Father's Shadow: Intergenerational Conflict in African American Men's Autobiography*. Philadelphia: U of Pennsylvania P, 1991.

Foster, Frances Smith. *Witnessing Slavery*. 2nd ed. Madison: U of Wisconsin P, 1993.

Fredrickson, George M. *The Black Image in the White Mind*. New York: Harper & Row, 1971.

Gates, Henry Louis, Jr. *Figures in Black*. New York: Oxford U P, 1987.

———. *The Signifying Monkey*. New York: Oxford U P, 1988.

Holland, Frederic May. *Frederick Douglass, the Colored Orator*. New York: Funk & Wagnalls, 1891.

Huggins, Nathan Irvin. *Slave and Citizen: The Life of Frederick Douglass*. Boston: Little, Brown, 1980.

Martin, Waldo E. *The Mind of Frederick Douglass*. Chapel Hill: U of North Carolina P, 1982.

McDowell, Deborah E., and Arnold Rampersad, eds. *Slavery and the Literary Imagination*. Baltimore: Johns Hopkins U P, 1989.

McFeely, William S. *Frederick Douglass*. New York: W. W. Norton, 1991.

Meier, August. *Negro Thought in America, 1880–1915*. Ann Arbor: U of Michigan P, 1966.

Patterson, Orlando. *Slavery and Social Death*. Cambridge: Harvard U P, 1982.

Preston, Dickson J. *Young Frederick Douglass: The Maryland Years*. Baltimore: Johns Hopkins U P, 1980.

Quarles, Benjamin. *Frederick Douglass*. Washington, D.C.: Associated Publishers, 1948.

Sekora, John, and Darwin T. Turner, eds. *The Art of Slave Narrative*. Macomb: Western Illinois University, 1982.

Smith, Valerie. *Self-Discovery and Authority in Afro-American Narrative*. Cambridge: Harvard U P, 1987.

Stepto, Robert B. *From Behind the Veil: A Study of Afro-American Narrative*. Urbana: U of Illinois P, 1979.

Sundquist, Eric J., ed. *Frederick Douglass: New Literary and Historical Essays*. Cambridge: Cambridge U P, 1990.

———. *To Wake the Nations: Race in the Making of American Literature*. Cambridge: Harvard U P, 1993.

Walker, Peter F. *Moral Choices: Memory, Desire, and Imagination in Nineteenth Century American Abolition*. Baton Rouge: Louisiana State U P, 1978.

42 314WW1 7610
FM
5/97 72136-45 NULD